DEVELOPMENT MENT FIELD WORK

DEVELOPMENT MENT FIELD WORK

A PRACTICAL GUIDE

EDITED BY

REGINA SCHEYVENS

Los Angeles | London | New Delhi
Singapore | Washington DC

Los Angeles | London | New Delhi
Singapore | Washington DC

SAGE Publications Ltd
1 Oliver's Yard
55 City Road
London EC1Y 1SP

SAGE Publications Inc.
2455 Teller Road
Thousand Oaks, California 91320

SAGE Publications India Pvt Ltd
B 1/I 1 Mohan Cooperative Industrial Area
Mathura Road
New Delhi 110 044

SAGE Publications Asia-Pacific Pte Ltd
3 Church Street
#10-04 Samsung Hub
Singapore 049483

Editor: Natalie Aguilera
Assistant editor: James Piper
Production editor: Katie Forsythe
Copyeditor: Solveig Gardner Servian
Proofreader: Clare Weaver
Marketing manager: Sally Ransom
Cover design: Francis Kenney
Typeset by: C&M Digitals (P) Ltd, Chennai, India

First edition published 2003. Reprinted 2008, 2009 and 2010.
This edition first published 2014

Library of Congress Control Number: 2013940295

British Library Cataloguing in Publication data

A catalogue record for this book is available from the British Library

ISBN 978-1-4462-5476-9
ISBN 978-1-4462-5477-6 (pbk)

This book is dedicated to the diverse group of people who seek to conduct development research in order to address inequalities or contribute to 'good change' around the world.

CONTENTS

List of Figures and Tables	xii
List of Boxes	xiii
Notes on Contributors	xv
Preface and Acknowledgements	xix

1 Introduction — 1
Regina Scheyvens and Sharon McLennan

Purpose	1
'The field'	3
Concerns over appropriateness of doing development fieldwork	4
Responses to the crisis of legitimacy facing researchers	6
The potential value of research with 'others'	10
Scope and limitations	12
Format and contents	13
Questions for reflection	15
Recommended readings	15
Notes	16

PART I: METHODOLOGY — 17

2 Designing Development Research — 19
Warwick E. Murray and John Overton

Design: the ideal field research project	21
Which methods should I use?	30
Logistics – proposing and planning	31
Conclusion – expect the unexpected	36
Questions for reflection	37
Recommended readings	37
Note	38

3 Quantitative Research — 39
John Overton and Peter van Diermen

What is quantitative data?	40
What techniques should be used?	41

Sampling   44
How can data be analysed?   46
Limitations and pitfalls   51
Conclusions   55
Questions for reflection   56
Recommended readings   57
Notes   58

4   **Qualitative Research**   59
    Rochelle Stewart-Withers, Glenn Banks, Andrew McGregor
    and Litea Meo-Sewabu

    When should we use qualitative research?   60
    Qualitative research attributes   60
    Data collection methods   63
    Mixed methods   66
    Examples of qualitative approaches to research in Development Studies   67
    Analysing qualitative data   75
    Addressing the pitfalls of qualitative research   76
    Conclusion   78
    Questions for reflection   79
    Recommended readings   79
    Note   80

5   **Something Old, Something New: Research Using Archives,**
    Texts and Virtual Data   81
    Sharon McLennan and Gerard Prinsen

    Textual data and non-academic written sources   82
    Managed written sources: archives and websites   86
    Unmanaged written sources: old boxes and new social media   90
    Correspondence and private messages   94
    Interactive online data collection   97
    Conclusion   98
    Questions for reflection   99
    Recommended readings   100

PART II: PREPARATION FOR THE FIELD   101

6   **Practical Issues**   103
    Maria Borovnik, Helen Leslie and Donovan Storey

    Research resources   103
    Establishing contacts   105
    Research permission   107
    Health and safety   109

Places to stay, or not to stay   114
Where to go and when to go   116
Packing   117
Conclusion   122
Questions for reflection   123
Recommended readings   124
Notes   124

7   **Personal Issues**   **125**
    Henry Scheyvens, Regina Scheyvens and Barbara Nowak

    Creating a good impression   126
    Desirable personal traits   128
    Preparing for discomfort and depression   132
    Families and partners in the field   133
    Conclusion   139
    Questions for reflection   140
    Recommended readings   140

PART III: IN THE FIELD   **141**

8   **Entering the Field**   **143**
    Sharon McLennan, Donovan Storey and Helen Leslie

    Entering the field   143
    Culture shock   146
    Behaviour during fieldwork   149
    Working with research assistants   152
    Language issues   156
    Conclusions   157
    Questions for reflection   158
    Recommended readings   159
    Notes   159

9   **Ethical Issues**   **160**
    Glenn Banks and Regina Scheyvens

    Ethics in research   161
    Official ethics procedures   163
    Gatekeepers   172
    Reciprocity   174
    Feeding back research findings   178
    Truth and deception   179
    Sex and sexuality   182
    Conclusions   185
    Questions for reflection   186

Recommended readings   186
Notes   187

10 **Working with Marginalised, Vulnerable or Privileged Groups**   188
    Regina Scheyvens, Henry Scheyvens and Warwick E. Murray

    Research with children and youths   190
    Research with women   193
    Research with minority ethnic groups and indigenous people   195
    Researching the poor   198
    Research with the elite and powerful   201
    Advocacy and activism   207
    Conclusion   211
    Questions for reflection   213
    Recommended readings   213
    Notes   214

PART IV: LEAVING THE FIELD   215

11 **Anything to Declare? The Politics and Practicalities of Leaving the Field** 217
    Sara Kindon and Julie Cupples

    Reasons for leaving   219
    Factors influencing experiences of leaving   220
    Feelings/emotions associated with leaving   221
    Ethical considerations and exit strategies   226
    Practical concerns   231
    Concluding remarks   233
    Questions for reflection   234
    Recommended readings   235

12 **Returning to University and Writing the Field**   236
    Julie Cupples and Sara Kindon

    Getting started   237
    The politics of representation   239
    Using theory and style of writing   241
    Reflexivity and positionality   244
    Emotional issues   245
    Becoming a writer   246
    Managing post-fieldwork relationships   247
    Publishing from research   249
    Conclusions   250
    Questions for reflection   251
    Recommended readings   251

13 Ways Forward   **253**
Regina Scheyvens

Reflections on the value of fieldwork   253
How can we as development researchers work in a more just, ethical
and effective manner?   253

References   258
Index   284

LIST OF FIGURES AND TABLES

FIGURES

3.1   Frequency distribution of country mean income per capita, 2010   48
3.2   Female life expectancy and mean income per capita, 2010   50
3.3   Female life expectancy and the fertility rate, 2010   53

11.1 Leaving strategies   233

TABLES

4.1   Characteristics of qualitative research   61
4.2   Qualitative data collection techniques   63
4.3   Data analysis stages   76
4.4   Criteria for judging rigour in qualitative research   77

5.1   Textual data and non-academic written sources   83

LIST OF BOXES

1.1 A lesson about obsessive researchers   2
1.2 Kapoor's suggestions for practice and representation in
     development research   8
1.3 The value of anthropological fieldwork   11

2.1 Different types of science   23
2.2 Research types   25
2.3 Suggestions for thinking of a research topic   26
2.4 Successful and unsuccessful research   28
2.5 How to devise clear research questions   29
2.6 Essential components of a good research proposal   32
2.7 Rigid methodology melting in the Chilean sun   34

3.1 Simple descriptive statistics for a single variable: measurements
     of average income, 2010   47
3.2 Measures of relationships between variables: average incomes
     and female life expectancy, 2010   50
3.3 Relationships between variables: life expectancy and fertility, 2010   53

4.1 A mix of interviews and story-telling through *talanoa*
     research in the Pacific   65
4.2 Mixing methods around mine sites in Papua New Guinea   67
4.3 Examples of participatory methods   70
4.4 Ethical issues and collective responsibility of an indigenous researcher   73

5.1 Research permission in online networks   84
5.2 The Anglophone's blind spot – and blinded eye   86
5.3 Photocopying and scanning   88
5.4 Searching the Internet   89
5.5 Digital data storage and security   90

6.1 Perspiration and persistence: how to gain research permission   108
6.2 First aid materials   111
6.3 Going to the field with security considerations in mind   113
6.4 Breaking down barriers between researcher and community   116
6.5 Electronic devices in the field   119
6.6 Using visual tools ethically   121

7.1 Thugs, drugs and other challenges of doing research in
     a Bangladeshi slum   125
7.2 An overriding feeling of bothering people   130
7.3 The problem of over-researched projects or communities   131
7.4 The pros and cons of having family in the field in Fiji   138

8.1 The value of a preliminary visit to the field   144
8.2 Culture shock and cultural identity in returning researchers   146
8.3 Diaries and journals   148
8.4 Social technology in the field: some guidelines   150
8.5 Finding a suitable cultural advisor   154
8.6 Recruitment of research assistants: dilemmas facing
     a Namibian researcher   155

9.1 Ethics from the bottom up   161
9.2 RMIT's Timor-Leste Research Program: ethical objectives   163
9.3 What is best for cross-cultural research: an 'informed consent
     form' or a 'letter of commitment'?   166
9.4 Financing fieldwork: managing a conflict of interest   170
9.5 How gatekeepers can attempt to manage the researcher
     and the research process   173
9.6 The therapeutic value of interviews for women in El Salvador   175
9.7 'Reciprocity' during research with an NGO in Nicaragua   177
9.8 Feeding back findings: the possibility of causing offence   179
9.9 What to do with 'privileged information' from fieldwork 'friends' 181

10.1 Guidelines for research involving children and youths   190
10.2 The challenge of accessing adolescent slum-dwelling women
      in Bangladesh to talk about their reproductive health   194
10.3 Indigenous principles to guide researcher conduct   198
10.4 Twenty-five times the price for two eggs   199
10.5 Principles regarding research with marginalised groups   201
10.6 Elites questioning the legitimacy and accuracy of academic research 205

11.1 Knowing when it is time to leave   219
11.2 Factors influencing experiences of leaving   221
11.3 The difficulties of leaving: Binh and Mizna's experiences   223
11.4 Wrapping-up research and giving thanks: Lauren's experience   227
11.5 Negotiating responsibilities to research participants by
      sharing our work: Monica's experience   228
11.6 A quick and formal exit strategy: an example from Costa Rica 230
11.7 Practical questions to ask when leaving   232

12.1 Weaving together indigenous Latin American and English
      language literature   241
12.2 Alternative forms of writing: Jamie's story   243
12.3 Strategies for adjusting to being back at university and writing 247
12.4 Giving back to indigenous communities: Simon's story   248

NOTES ON CONTRIBUTORS

Glenn Banks is a development geographer who has worked on issues connected to the Papua New Guinea mining industry since the late 1980s. He is a graduate of the University of Canterbury (BScHons, MSc) and Australian National University (PhD), and is currently Associate Professor in Development Studies at Massey University. His work is concerned with issues of sustainable development, resource conflicts, impact assessment and the global wine industry. Theoretically he seeks to foreground community perspectives, agency, politics and practices in development. In his occasional spare time he rides a bike, travels a bit, shares a wine with his wife, and reads a book, until his two daughters want to play or need a lift somewhere.

Maria Borovnik is a lecturer in the School of People, Environment and Planning at Massey University, New Zealand. Her research is at the intersection of development, social geography and mobilities. She has mainly focused on social strategies and experiences of seafarers and their families from Kiribati and Tuvalu. More recent research engages with development of Pacific youth. Fieldwork practices include participatory and mobile methods, such as conducting interactive focus groups with Kiribati youth, or spending a month with a group of multinational seafarers on a containership. She has published in *Asia Pacific Viewpoint,* the *Asian Pacific Migration Journal* and *Sites.*

Julie Cupples lectures in Human Geography at the University of Edinburgh. She has been engaged in development fieldwork, primarily in Nicaragua, since the 1990s and has published on gender and development, disasters, municipal governance, environmental risk, elections and indigenous media. Her work has appeared in the *Annals of the Association of American Geographers, Transactions of the Institute of British Geographers, Antipode, Latin American Perspectives* and *Television and New Media.* She is the author of *Latin American Development*, published by Routledge in 2013.

Sara Kindon is a social geographer at Victoria University of Wellington, Aotearoa New Zealand. Since 2005, she has been working with postgraduate students and refugee-background young people to carry out participatory and visual research into resettlement experiences to inform better service provision and youth wellbeing. She also publishes on participatory video for research from her work with members of Te Iwi o Ngaati Hauiti in the central north island. Sara teaches in Geography and Development Studies and supervises postgraduate students researching in Central and South America, Sub-Saharan Africa, the Middle East, Southeast Asia and the Pacific.

Helen Leslie is a diplomat at the New Zealand High Commission in Suva. She manages NZ's Regional Development Programmes including engagement with Pacific Regional Agencies and United Nations Organisations working in the Pacific. Since her first contribution to the development fieldwork book, Helen has lived and worked in various parts of the Pacific and has been able to continue her interest in research/fieldwork that makes a positive contribution to the lives of people.

Andrew McGregor graduated from the University of Sydney in 2000 before taking up a Project Officer role with UNICEF Australia where he was responsible for projects in Myanmar, South Sudan, Bangladesh, Bhutan, and Indonesia. Since 2002 he has been teaching and researching human geography and development studies at the University of Otago, Victoria University of Wellington and in his current role at Macquarie University. He is author of *Southeast Asian Development* (2008: Routledge) and is Editor-in-Chief of *Asia Pacific Viewpoint*. Andrew's research interests focus on foreign aid, political ecology and post-development theory in Indonesia, Timor-Leste and Myanmar. He's also the proud father of a brand new little fella called Finley.

Sharon McLennan is a post-doctoral fellow and lecturer in Development Studies at Massey University. Working with a team of researchers, her post-doctoral research investigates corporate community development initiatives in the Pacific. This is somewhat of a change from her PhD research, completed in 2012, which looked at the networking of small, volunteer organisations in Honduras. Fieldwork for this research involved online methods as well as more traditional qualitative fieldwork in the often chaotic environment of post-coup Honduras. Linking her PhD and post-PhD research together is an interest in new actors in development, and in contemporary development processes and globalisation.

Litea Meo-Sewabu is lectures in the College of Health at Massey University, and was recently appointed as the Coordinator of the university's new Pacific Research and Policy Centre. Litea is towards the end of her PhD. Her research looks at the lay understanding of health and wellbeing amongst indigenous Fijian women in Fiji and New Zealand. Her research interests include the praxis of ethics processes within indigenous populations, community development in Pacific communities and notions of empowerment within Indigenous population groups.

Warwick Murray is Professor of Human Geography and Development Studies at Victoria University of Wellington. Warwick's research delves into the fields of development and economic geography, focusing especially on Chile and Latin America, as well as the Pacific Islands. His guitar, banjo or ukulele tend to accompany him on field research trips. He is the author of the textbook *Geographies of Globalization*, and from 2002 to 2010, he was the main editor of *Asia Pacific Viewpoint*. In addition to his penchant for keeping a tidy office, he is also known for singing and playing original songs in class about academic material, allegedly including, "I can't believe it's not on Wikipedia".

Barbara Nowak is an anthropologist who has done extensive research among Hma' Btsisi' in Malaysia since 1980. She was trained at the State University of New York at Buffalo, and later became a lecturer at Grinnell College, USA and at Massey University, New Zealand. She was also based at National University of Singapore for two years, working as a Senior Research Fellow in the Asia Research Institute. As a consequence of her research with Btsisi', she has became involved in a cross-national study examining the local socio-economic and environmental impact of the oil palm industry, at both the small holder as well as multi-national producer level. Research on this topic has taken her to Southeast Asia and Central America.

John Overton is a geographer who teaches Development Studies at Victoria University of Wellington in New Zealand. Over the years he has conducted research in Kenya, the Pacific Islands, Southeast Asia and Latin America. His main research interests have been in the area of rural change, specifically aspects such as land tenure, agricultural change and rural development projects. More recently, he has engaged in a major project of aid and sovereignty in the Pacific Islands and he has also maintained an interest in the global wine industry and the issue of geographical indications in commodity chains.

Gerard Prinsen currently works as a lecturer at Massey University, New Zealand, after an earlier career in development work in several African countries; often as a manager, sometimes as a trainer or evaluator, and mostly around education and health services. His on-going research and consultancy work concentrates on the sovereignty of sub-national or small polities in Africa and the Pacific, and he explores the upscaling and quantification of participatory methods for policy-making and research.

Henry Scheyvens currently serves as the Area Leader of the Natural Resources and Ecosystems Services Area at the Japan-based Institute for Global Environmental Strategies. His research covers a broad range of sustainable development issues, from the role of micro-finance in building climate change resilience to incentive mechanisms for combating illegal logging. Poverty and rights are key themes that run through all his work. These days, on the weekends you will find him living on the edge, either searching for big sea waves in his kayak or cycling the fast and furious roads of Japan, though sometimes he has a still moment meditating at a temple near Tokyo.

Regina Scheyvens heads Development Studies at Massey University. Here she combines a passion for teaching about international development with research on tourism and development. Two books have emerged from this research, *Tourism for Development: Empowering Communities* (Pearson, 2002), and *Tourism and Poverty* (Routledge, 2011), along with articles on themes such as backpacker tourism, ecotourism, and sustainable tourism. She has conducted qualitative field research in a number of countries in southern Africa, the Pacific Islands and Southeast Asia. While family life now keeps her feet firmly planted in New Zealand soil most of the time, she takes great pleasure in sending her Master's and PhD students off to embark on their own research journeys.

Rochelle Stewart-Withers is an academic with the Institute of Development Studies at Massey University, New Zealand. She originally comes from a healthcare background. Rochelle maintains a passion for research and fieldwork by teaching a postgraduate methodology course, supervising Masters and Doctoral students, and by getting out into the field. Most of Rochelle's research is Pacific-based and her current focus is to investigate the ways that sport can be utilised to address social and economic development goals, and related complexities. On a personal note, she enjoys the distractions of her five favourite children: Indiya, Finn, Samara, Cassius and India.

Donovan Storey is currently Chief of the Sustainable Urban Development Section, Environment and Development Division of the United Nations Economic and Social Commission for Asia and the Pacific (ESCAP). Prior to joining the United Nations he was a researcher and academic at several universities specializing in development studies, social development, environmental management and urban planning/governance. His career has been inspired by PhD research in Development Studies which involved living with Filipino families in urban poor communities in Metro Manila, with whom he still keeps contact. He has authored or co-authored over 30 journal articles, book chapters and books on his areas of specialization.

Peter van Diermen is currently Chief Technical Adviser for Indonesia's National Team for the Acceleration of Poverty Reduction which is attached to the Office of the Vice President of Indonesia. Previously he worked as an academic in several New Zealand and Australian Universities and has worked in the Asia and the Pacific region for ADB, the World Bank Group and others. His publications have focused on economic development in South East Asia. He also served as AusAID's Senior Economic Adviser and was managing director for a small international development consulting company specialising in economic research, program and project design and M&E.

PREFACE AND ACKNOWLEDGEMENTS

In 2002 I had the pleasure of working on the first edition of *Development Fieldwork* with Donovan Storey, who was at that time my colleague at Massey University. Many of our friends and acquaintances contributed to chapters in that book. Fast forward 10 years and Donovan had moved on from academia and was residing in Bangkok thanks to a position with UN-ESCAP. While we were both delighted when Sage approached us to edit a second edition of *Development Fieldwork*, Donovan acknowledged that he didn't have the time to do this justice so he reluctantly withdrew from the project. His name, however, remains on two chapters to which he made significant contributions in the first edition.

In essence, the book is structured in the same manner as the first edition – the sections are Methodology, Preparation for the Field, In the Field, and Leaving the Field – with the addition of one new chapter on 'Something old, something new: research using archives, texts and virtual data' (Chapter 5). Those familiar with the first edition will recognise many of the contributing authors as almost all of them were keen to update their work for this edition. You might also notice a few new authors, including those who have completely rewritten Chapter 4 on 'Qualitative research', and others who have contributed to changes in Chapters 1, 6, 7 and 9.

Updating of this book was a really enjoyable experience due to two main factors: first, the fantastic job that Sharon McLennan did in providing chapter authors with up-to-date references which were relevant to specific sections of the book; and second, the great material we were working with on intrinsically fascinating topics such as ethics, avoiding danger, reciprocity, negotiating with gatekeepers, and developing mutually beneficial research relationships. Thank you to all the authors, including postgraduate students, whose work is cited in this book or which is the focus of one of the text-box examples.

I would like to take this opportunity to thank a range of other people without whom this book would not have come to fruition. Before Sage's approach, John Overton and Warwick Murray from Victoria University urged me to consider updating the first edition as they were still finding *Development Fieldwork* to be of immense value for their postgraduate Development Studies students. They then joined me and Glenn Banks for a workshop at the Paekakariki Institute of Social Sciences where we spent an enjoyable day brainstorming what changes and additions were needed in the second edition. We finished the day by sharing pizza and wine: all good development research is, after all, based on cultivating good relationships! Thanks guys for your good company and humour as well as your insights. Our discussions that day were guided by reviews of the first edition and recent field research experiences of our students. We also reflected on the ways in which new development challenges had emerged in the past decade, and how technologies were changing the ways in which people were doing development research as well as analysing and communicating their results. Readers will thus see much more on issues such as social media, digital data and the ethics of online research in this edition. The usual caveat applies: technologies are constantly evolving and thus some of our discussions of these technologies may soon be out of date.

I would also like to thank all of the chapter authors for the care and time they put into their writing: the second edition has really been enriched by your efforts, and it has been a pleasure working with you. Massey University supported this book directly by providing a MURF award which funded Sharon to assist me with searching out new material, as noted above, as well as proofreading and formatting: thanks so much Sharon for your professionalism and willingness to work some long hours in the final stages! On the same note, Natalie Aguilera from Sage was very supportive during those rather stressful last weeks in which the book was brought together.

Finally, thanks so much to my lovely family – you are at the heart of everything I do. Craig, your faith in my work is much appreciated. Harry, Jessie and Sophie – as you get a little older I hope you might be inspired to learn more about our diverse world and its peoples from reading some of the works herein.

1

INTRODUCTION

REGINA SCHEYVENS AND SHARON MCLENNAN

PURPOSE

The purpose of this book is to assist researchers, especially postgraduate students, to prepare for development-related fieldwork. A broad approach is taken to allow ample attention to be paid to practical, methodological, and ethical issues. We endeavour to show that where researchers are well-prepared for 'the field' and sensitive to the local context and culture, development fieldwork can be a valuable experience for both the researcher and their participants.

We also assert that development research can be carried out in the North, the South, the East and the West. Given global interconnectedness, the economic successes of some countries formerly considered to be 'third world',[1] the effects of financial crises on wealthier countries, and, most importantly, the pervasive inequality and poverty in almost every country in the world (Sumner and Tiwari, 2011), there are new 'fields' for development research. Obviously to be 'development research' the issues examined will have a development focus: that is, they will be associated with positive social change and enhanced well-being, particularly for those who are poor, oppressed or marginalised. For example, the research may investigate the effectiveness of intentional development initiatives or explore the impacts of immanent development processes on vulnerable communities (see Cowen and Shenton, 1996), or it might examine the values of development actors or probe the workings of people's movements for change. This book could thus have general relevance to researchers working in any cross-cultural context in which there are critical social and economic development issues, from the hill tribes of Thailand to the reclaimed tribal lands of Maori in New Zealand, from the rural poverty of Burkino-Faso to the urban decay of Brixton. We assume that most development researchers will be working cross-culturally, and/or across significant lines of socio-economic difference.

The contributors to this book are well aware of the mixture of excitement, apprehension and even self-doubt which commonly faces researchers who are preparing for fieldwork. To prepare well for their field experience the advice they need extends beyond practical tips to guidance on ethical issues and personal/psychological preparation for the difficulties they may encounter in the field. Often it is these issues that determine the success or otherwise of fieldwork – at least as much as methodological challenges. As Devereux and Hoddinott concur, 'Anyone who has done research outside his or her home community knows that questions relating to lifestyle and personal relationships loom as large as narrowly defined technical issues' (1992: 2). We have therefore aimed to provide a text which:

- first, provides practical information for researchers entering 'the field' and wishing to effectively explore questions about development with their respondents;
- second, prepares researchers for some of the ethical issues and personal challenges they may face, and also makes supervisors aware of these issues; and
- third, overviews issues of research design and the selection of appropriate research methods.

This allows the book to cover a wide range of critical issues facing researchers in the field, from managing relationships with the 'host' community and avoiding cross-cultural misunderstanding, to negotiating with 'gatekeepers', practising reciprocity, and keeping up morale while facing unanticipated obstacles.

This book is primarily aimed at both qualitative and quantitative researchers and postgraduate research students based in universities who are planning to do development fieldwork. Their work is often interdisciplinary, drawing from disciplines including politics, human geography, sociology, economics, international relations and social anthropology, as well as development studies.

We take it as given that most readers of this book will be convinced that there is value in conducting development research, even after reading the entertaining view of researchers that a research participant put to an Indian anthropologist (see Box 1.1). Although there are valid criticisms of fieldwork, which will be raised in this chapter, we hope that overall readers of this book will gain insights into how valuable development field research can be when conducted in an ethical and appropriate manner.

Box 1.1   A lesson about obsessive researchers

'Suppose you and I are walking on road', said Swamiji. 'You've gone to University. I haven't studied anything. We're walking. Some child has shit on the road. We both step in it. "That's shit!" I say. I scrape my foot; it's gone. But educated people have doubts about everything. You say, "What's this?!" and you rub your foot against the other.' Swamiji shot up from his prone position in the deckchair, and placing his feet on the linoleum, stared at them with intensity. He rubbed the right sole against the left ankle. 'Then you reach down to feel what

> it could be,' his fingers now explored the ankle. A grin was breaking over his face. '"Something sticky!" You lift some up and sniff it. Then you say, "Oh! This is shit:"' [...]
>
> 'Educated people always doubt everything. They lie awake at night thinking, "What was that? Why did it happen? What is the meaning and the cause of it?" Uneducated people pass judgment and walk on. They get a good night's sleep.'
>
> Source: Narayan (1998: 178)

'THE FIELD'

So, what is 'the field', this locus of development-related 'fieldwork'? Spatial differences are inherent in dominant conceptualisations of 'the field': 'When one speaks of working in the field, or going into the field, one draws on mental images of a distinct place with an inside and outside, reached by practices of physical movement' (Clifford, 1997: 54). In addition, 'the field' encapsulates cultural difference in that traditionally, fieldwork was about a search for the 'exotic other'. Such differences added to the mystique of fieldwork and also made adjustment difficult for first time fieldworkers:

> 'being there' demands at the minimum hardly more than a travel booking and permission to land; a willingness to endure a certain amount of loneliness, invasion of privacy, and physical discomfort; a relaxed way with odd growths and unexplained fevers; a capacity to stand still for artistic insults, and the sort of patience that can support an endless search for invisible needles in infinite haystacks. (Geertz, 1988: 23–24)

Academics have queried the binary oppositions suggested by conventional understandings of 'the field', including 'home' versus 'away' or 'here' versus 'there', and 'staying' or 'moving', 'insider' and 'outsider' (Clifford, 1997: 84), terms which are embedded with the notion of spatiality. But, as Coleman and Collins note, 'in a world of interconnections, we never leave the field' (2006: 5). Their book on *Locating the Field* asserts that spatial considerations are 'significant but not absolutely primary dimensions of ethnographic practice' (2006: 17). Meanwhile, Hannerz (2012) suggests that if our primary interest is in social relationships, 'place' is not necessarily central to fieldwork. Such thinking aligns with Gupta and Ferguson,[2] who posit that we should conceptualise field sites as 'political locations' rather than 'spatial sites':

> Ethnography's great strength has always been in its explicit and well-developed sense of location, of being set here-and-not-elsewhere. This strength becomes a liability when notions of 'here' and 'elsewhere' are assumed to be features of geography, rather than sites constructed in fields of unequal power relations. (1997: 35)

Their views are supported by contributors to a special edition of the *Professional Geographer* devoted to 'Women in the field', which supports the idea of the 'field' being a 'social terrain' where there is considerable overlap between the realms of the personal and the political (Nast, 1994: 57). Hall (2011a: 12–16) adds a layer of complexity to the definitional debates by agreeing that we can see 'the field' as a political and a social space, but also suggesting it can be a temporal space, a physical space, an ethical space, and a theoretical/methodological space.

Clearly many social scientists agree that 'the field' is not simply a distant, geographical space. It is useful to move beyond a spatialised sense of the field, as this 'uphold[s] an evaluative hierarchy regarding the kinds of fieldwork and subjects of research that are deemed "appropriate"' (Caputo, 2000: 19). It used to be considered that the more exotic and distant the site, the more difficult or dangerous the experience (Passaro, 1997), and the longer it was endured, the more valuable it was.

When compared to the diverse experiences of fieldwork practice today, such traditional conceptions of fieldwork can seem limited, inaccurate, romanticised, or largely fictional (Amit, 2000: 2). Much valuable research is being conducted in cosmopolitan, urban centres rather than in remote villages, there has been a growth of research on transnationalism, and work among the powerful is being seen as increasingly important (see Chapter 10 on elite research). For example, examining the experience of Western mining company employees working as expatriates in developing countries (Cannon, 2002) can be just as valuable as intensive research at grassroots level among the supposed 'victims' of mining activity. There is also a good deal of multi-sited ethnography that is conducted including Teaiwa's research across Fiji, Kiribati and Australia (Hannerz, 2012; Teaiwa, 2004): as posited above, fieldwork can be a legitimate practice in any country experiencing poverty and inequality. Meanwhile, other researchers have reflected on the value of development fieldwork which uses the Internet/cyberspace (Burrell, 2009; see also Chapter 5; Hall, 2011b; Mawdsley, 2006; Muir, 2004).

For the purposes of this book on development fieldwork then, 'the field' is understood to be a socio-political and/or geographical site where a researcher spends time collecting data to gain a deeper understanding of development issues such as poverty and inequality.

As an aside, we are not particularly supportive of the traditional anthropological practice of preserving the mystique of fieldwork (Gupta and Ferguson, 1997: 2), and throwing unprepared students into unknown field situations to see if they will sink or swim. Rather, we feel they should carefully choose their field sites and examine their motivations for doing so (see Chapters 6 and 7), be meticulous when selecting an appropriate methodology (Chapters 2, 3 and 4), and conscientiously consider relevant ethical issues (Chapters 9 and 10). Under such circumstances fieldwork is more likely to be less of a 'baptism of fire' and more of a mutually beneficial experience.

CONCERNS OVER APPROPRIATENESS OF DOING DEVELOPMENT FIELDWORK

An important concern about fieldwork needs to be raised at the outset. Before discussing *how* to do fieldwork, there is the ethical dilemma of *whether* to do development fieldwork. This is an issue which has stimulated much debate in recent years, primarily from those concerned about the power gradients inherent in events such as a relatively privileged researcher travelling from a Western university to a developing country to study people living in poverty. Some have referred to such research as 'academic tourism' (Epprecht, 2004: 695; Mowforth and Munt, 2008: 98).

Twenty years ago, Madge argued that academics had 'not yet adequately explored the power relations, inequalities and injustices' upon which differences between ourselves and those we research are based (Madge, 1993: 297). Challenging questions have since been directed at geographers, social anthropologists, sociologists and others who carry out social research in developing countries, and a great deal of soul-searching by both academics and students has occurred (see, e.g., Hales, 2008; Kapoor, 2004; Simpson, 2007).

One concern is that fieldwork can be intrusive and expose those we are studying to considerable risk, with England (1994: 85) even suggesting that 'exploitation and possibly betrayal are endemic to fieldwork'. Too often in the past, development research has been of no benefit at all for the country or communities concerned, bringing into question its relevance (Edwards, 1989). According to Lather (1988: 570), in the worst cases 'rape research' has occurred whereby exploitative methods of inquiry have been used exclusively in the interests of the researcher's own career.

A further, major criticism is that much development discourse has been constructed so as to legitimate the voices of Western 'experts' while undermining those of local people (Escobar, 2012). A number of post-colonial scholars have made a contribution to such critiques. Nagar and Geiger, for example, assert that 'scholars based in resource-rich institutions of the north continue to dominate the international context in which knowledge about southern peoples and places is produced, circulated and discussed' (2007: 2 – footnote). Similarly, Abbott titled her (2006) article 'Disrupting the "whiteness" of fieldwork in geography', while Epprecht suggests that field trips taking Western students to developing countries might 'contribute to the very kinds of underdevelopment and colonial-style North–South relations that they are intended to critically address' (2004: 693). Missbach (2011) provides a pertinent example of concerns about the domination of research in Aceh, Indonesia, by foreigners. Aceh has become something of a 'social laboratory' in the aftermath of the 2004 Asian tsunami and the end of armed conflict in the following year. While this research has accelerated the academic careers of the foreigners, local researchers who lack funding, have poor access to international literature and struggle with language barriers, have to make do with playing a data collection role, rather than contributing to analysis and the production of academic outputs.

In association with the domination of foreign researchers in designing development research, collecting and analysing data, concerns have arisen about how we represent 'others' in our writing (Kapoor, 2004; Raghuram and Madge, 2006; Sumner and Tribe, 2008a). For example, post-colonial feminist writers including Mohanty (1988) and Spivak (1988a, 1988b) were particularly vigilant in drawing attention to issues concerning the politics of representation of women of the 'third world' in texts produced by Western researchers. England asks, 'can we incorporate the voices of "others" without colonizing them in a manner that reinforces patterns of domination?' (1994: 81). Unease about this issue continues to occupy Linda Tuhiwai Smith also, as seen in the second edition of her ground-breaking book on indigenous research (Smith, 2012).

While there are no simple solutions to such concerns, they have forced Western researchers to be more accountable and to engage in some serious self-reflection. There have been calls for 'greater consideration of the role of the (multiple) "self", showing how a researcher's positionality (in terms of race, nationality, age, gender, social and economic status, sexuality) may influence the "data"' (Madge, 1993: 294). We now see many researchers demonstrating an acute awareness of their positionality in relation to those they are researching, thus problematising their own histories and identities, and reflecting upon how these things influence the research process and relationships that are formed (Abbott, 2006; Chacko, 2004; Henry et al., 2009; see also Chapter 4, section on 'Positionality and reflexivity'). Such critical self-reflection by researchers quashes the notion of fieldwork as being 'no more than the application of relevant techniques to problems' (Clarke, 1975: 96).

The various critiques above have caused a great deal of 'discomfort' among some researchers, both during fieldwork and in the post-fieldwork context (Wolf, 1996: 32). This is demonstrated by Katz's (1994: 70) use of the term 'the arrogance of research' when reflecting on her own early motivation for fieldwork and behaviour in the field. Critical self-reflection has consequently also 'dislodged the smugness of much feminist and anti-racist scholarship' (Kobayashi, 1994: 74). The critiques continue to unsettle those of us engaging in field research, creating something of a crisis of legitimacy affecting researchers based at Western universities (this includes many graduate students planning to go 'home' to do research) who have been urged to reconsider their roles in development research.

RESPONSES TO THE CRISIS OF LEGITIMACY FACING RESEARCHERS

Perhaps the most dramatic way in which researchers have chosen to respond to the crisis of legitimacy is simply to abandon development research altogether, or 'stay home' as Robbins (2006: 315) puts it. As noted by Kobayashi, debates over who has the right to research whom, and therefore who has the right to speak for whom, have 'led some academic women – and men – to withdraw completely from research that might place them in territory to which they have no social claim, or that might put in question their credentials for social representation' (1994: 74).

A second response, often associated with the first, has been to privilege the knowledge and understanding of the 'others' we are researching. This sometimes involves the sorts of claims identified by Wolf, for example, that 'only those who are of a particular race or ethnic group can study or understand others in a similar situation, or that only those who are women of colour or lesbian can generate antiracist or anti-homophobic insights' (1996: 13). Kobayashi resists such notions:

the question of 'who speaks for whom?' cannot be answered upon the slippery slope of what personal attributes – what colour, what gender, what sexuality – legitimize our existence, but on the basis of our history of involvement, and on the basis of understanding how difference is constructed and used as a political tool. (1994: 78)

Social scientists now tend to agree that it is simplistic to posit that only indigenous people are competent to speak on the social issues affecting their communities, or that only a woman, a person of colour or a homosexual can carry out justice-inspiring research on, respectively, other women, people of colour or homosexuals (Briggs and Sharp, 2004; Goodman, 1985; Taggart and Sandstrom, 2011): 'To assume that "insiders" automatically have a more sophisticated and appropriate approach to understanding social reality in "their" society is to fall into the fallacy of Third Worldism, and a potentially reactionary relativism' (Sidaway, 1992: 406). This also assumes that there is 'truth out there' waiting to be discovered by those with the most appropriate culture and identity, and that representations of certain voices are closer to 'reality'.

In fact, we all sit on a continuum between the 'insider' and 'outsider' extremes and shift endlessly as the contexts and individuals are reconstituted along this sliding scale. For example, the 'native' researcher may not feel like they are an 'insider': 'They are very often both insider/outsider and subject/object. Their positions are fluid, and often embody multiple identities' (Ng, 2011: 446). It should not then be assumed that developing country scholars based in Western universities will be able to return 'home' to do research immune to issues of power relations and ethics (Chacko, 2004; Oriola and Haggerty, 2012; Subedi, 2006). It is likely that even if they speak the same language as their research participants they are separated from them by way of class and ethnic differences. Both Back (1993) and Amadiume (1993) have noted that when studying their cultures of origin, their supposed shared backgrounds with their participants did not prevent them from often feeling emotionally and politically set apart from the people they studied.

Romanticising or privileging 'local' knowledge does not solve the ethical problems of cross-cultural research because it allows the Western researcher to ignore their own responsibilities. As Radcliffe explains, 'disclaiming the right to speak about/with Third World women [and men] acts ... to justify an abdication of responsibility with regard to global relations of privilege and authority which are granted, whether we like it or not, to First World women [and men]' (1994: 28).

Another response to the crisis of legitimacy has been for researchers to continue with development fieldwork while adopting new approaches to research design, implementation, analysis and writing. Some, for example, have adopted non-traditional research methodologies such as participatory learning and action (PLA), which potentially allow participants more power in the research process: 'Participatory methods are a step towards ... creating meaningful connections with researchers in the South, ensuring that fieldwork is collaborative and engaging with local researchers at each stage of the research process, from project formulation and design to publication' (McEwan, 2011: 24; see also Chapter 4, section on 'Participatory approaches'; Sumner and Tribe, 2008a: 142–149). Similarly, Nast suggests using methodologies 'that promote mutual respect and identification of commonalities and differences between researcher and researched in non-authoritative ways [that] allow for "others" to be heard and empowered' (1994: 58). Some researchers have attempted (not always successfully) to redress inequities via various forms of collaboration (e.g., Fisher, 2011; Sharp, 2005). Researchers can also actively promote opportunities for the less privileged to undertake research with the privileged. Sidaway (1992: 407), for example, argues that the vitality of geography as a discipline would be 'enhanced in a world where Third World geographers came in large numbers to conduct research of "exotic" and "different" European and North American societies'.

In the post-fieldwork stage, a number of researchers have shared authorship with local people or given them editorial power over final works (Staeheli and Lawson, 1994; Wolf, 1996). Others have assisted marginalised individuals and groups by offering research training and mentoring to emerging researchers, or have assisted them to obtain research funding.[3]

Kapoor (2004) draws on the deconstructionist writing of Gayatri Spivak to make a number of other suggestions that could help development researchers to show awareness of development issues while moving forward with their work in an ethical manner (see Box 1.2).

Box 1.2   Kapoor's suggestions for practice and representation in development research

'Intimately inhabiting' and 'negotiating' discourse

It is possible to work within the belly of the beast and still engage in persistent critique of hegemonic representations. Development may indeed have become a shady business, but this does not mean one cannot retrieve from within it an ethico-political orientation to the Third World and the subaltern.

Acknowledging complicity

We need, then, to be unscrupulously vigilant (i.e. hyper-self-reflexive) about our complicities. Acknowledging one's contamination, for Spivak, helps temper and contextualise one's claims, reduces the risk of personal arrogance or geoinstitutional imperialism, and moves one toward a non-hierarchical encounter with the Third World/subaltern.

Unlearning one's privilege as loss

What this means, in effect, is casting a keen eye on the familiar and the taken-for-granted … the idea is to retrace the history and itinerary of one's prejudices and learned habits (from racism, sexism and classism to academic elitism and ethnocentrism), stop thinking of oneself as better or fitter, and unlearn dominant systems of knowledge and representation.

Learning to learn from below

Being open to the subaltern … implies, specifically, a reversal of information and knowledge production so that they flow from South to North, and not always in the other direction. One of Spivak's suggestions to this end is that we 'learn well one of the languages of the rural poor of the South' (2004: 550). By so doing, we begin the process of not defining them, but listening to them name and define themselves.

Working 'without guarantees'

Working without guarantees is … becoming aware of the vulnerabilities and blind spots of one's power and representational systems. It is accepting failure, or put positively, seeing failure as success. The implication for development is that we need to learn to be open, not just, in the short-term, to the limits of our knowledge systems, but also to the long-term logic of our profession: enabling the subaltern while working ourselves out of our jobs.

Source: Kapoor (2004: 640–644)

Before we move on to discuss the potential value of such research, it is important to remind ourselves that those we seek to do research with are not, as is sometimes suggested, powerless. They can exert a great deal of influence over the research process, and this in itself might temper some of the concerns which were raised earlier about foreign dominance of research agendas and practices in developing countries.

THE POWER OF THOSE WE RESEARCH

The suggestion that development research is always exploitative is based on the assumption that people in developing countries have no power. Power, though, is rarely a zero-sum phenomenon. The reality is that researchers seldom hold all of the control in the research process and that individuals and communities may well be very effective in forms of 'research resistance' (see Ballamingie and Johnson, 2011; Fisher, 2011). Respondents can, for example, exercise control by withholding information from the researcher, failing to co-operate, or refusing to answer questions (Cotterill, 1992). They may also intentionally provide sanitised, or erroneous, information.

Many researchers now recognise problems with the simplistic binaries typically used to show difference in their field research situations, particularly that 'researcher' equals 'powerful outsider', and 'the researched' equals 'powerless or impoverished locals' (Lammers, 2007; Ballamingie and Johnson, 2011 – whose piece is entitled 'The Vulnerable Researcher'). Nencel, for example, notes a fundamental flaw in the belief of the researcher that their participants lack power: 'because the research group is envisioned as vulnerable, it is often assumed they find it difficult to protect themselves, overlooking the fact that most vulnerable people are continuously protecting themselves and usually more experienced in this area than the anthropologist' (2001: 112).

In addition, the reality is that much development research will not only involve collecting data from marginalised communities or impoverished individuals: rather, as the discussion of elite research in Chapter 10 shows, we will be working with other development actors such as donors, managers of NGO programmes, corporate heads and so forth. This has central implications for the ways in which power relations play out in the field. As Sultana found when conducting research at 'home' in Bangladesh, for example:

> I was also 'othered' by those who were observing and studying me in the field. This was perhaps particularly true of the men I interviewed, especially in educated and policy circles. The reverse power relations were obvious in the many rejections of meetings, disregarding appointments granted, guarded responses and rushed interviews, and condescending attitude towards me and my work. (2007: 379)

THE POTENTIAL VALUE OF RESEARCH WITH 'OTHERS'

Most responses to the crisis of legitimacy facing researchers from Western institutions fail to consider the potential *value* of cross-cultural research, instead focusing on possible harmful aspects of such research. Nagar and Geiger warn that 'there is much to be lost by abandoning this face-to-face and necessarily problematic interactive research practice called 'fieldwork' (2007: 3). It is important that social science students and academics conducting development research realise there can be considerable merit in research which crosses the bounds of one's own culture, sex, class, age and other categories of social positioning (Brodsky and Faryal, 2006). Sluka and Robben (2012a: 24) thus refer to the 'compassionate turn' in social anthropology, which is based on recognition of the benefits of engaging compassionately with the subjects of our research, rather than turning away.

Sumner notes that 'Many people are attracted to DS [Development Studies] by some sense of concern and commitment about social justice and the prevailing levels of global poverty and inequality' (2008: 7). When well thought out, research on these issues can be very valuable. Many researchers, despite agreeing with the concerns raised earlier, still see the need for development research (Simpson, 2007; M. Smith and Humble, 2007). At the 40th anniversary of the Institute of Development Studies at Sussex, a number of roundtables were held in different parts of the world to discuss development research, and there was broad consensus on how development research could be made more relevant. The key points were that Development Studies should:

• Provide citizens with evidence that enables them to hold policymakers, governments and institutions to account.

- Contribute more effectively to social transformation, improve people's lives and expand choices available to the poor and marginalised.
- Increase capacities in developing countries and enable the poor to carry out research based on their priorities. (Trivedy, 2007: 100)

Gupta and Ferguson's (1997) ideas on the value of anthropological fieldwork are cited in Box 1.3, while more general reasons as to why fieldwork is likely to remain a central feature of thesis-related degrees and development work are considered below. Narayan also seems to value what an outside researcher can offer:

> [W]hat about non-"native" anthropologists who have dedicated themselves to long-term fieldwork, returning years after years to sustain ties to a particular community? Should we not grant them some recognition for the different texture this brings to their work? (1997: 30)

Sidaway claims that 'Research in/of "other" cultures and societies ... offers a counter to universalistic and ethnocentric views. It is the enemy of parochialism [and it] may pose challenges to frameworks and assumptions developed in the core' (1992: 406–407). Similarly, Heggenhougen refers to the value of being 'touched by a different reality' (2000: 269). One reason for this, as noted by Shaw, is that 'there is much to be gained through cross-cultural exchange, in that structural problems between North and South cannot be solved by the South alone' (1995: 96). Potter takes this point further: 'The value of Third World research should be clear for all to see in an interdependent world in which rich and poor, rural and urban, formal and informal are the opposite sides of the same coin ... there is vast potential for enlightened outsider research' (1993: 294). Binns also asserts a strong personal belief that 'a detailed understanding of people and environment in different parts of the Third World is essential to the development of global understanding, empathy and action' (2006: 14).

Box 1.3   The value of anthropological fieldwork

1. The fieldwork tradition counters Western ethnocentrism and values detailed and intimate knowledge of economically and politically marginalized places, peoples, histories, and social locations.
2. Fieldwork's stress on taken-for-granted social routines, informal knowledge, and embodied practices can yield understanding that cannot be obtained either through standardized social science research methods (e.g. surveys) or through decontextualized reading of cultural products (e.g. text-based criticism).
3. Fieldwork reveals that a self-conscious shifting of social and geographical location can be an extraordinarily valuable methodology for understanding social and cultural life, both through the discovery of phenomena that would otherwise remain invisible and through the acquisition of new perspectives on things we thought we already understood.

Source: Gupta and Ferguson (1997: 36–37)

Much, however, will depend on *how* we do our research. Scheyvens and Leslie posit that it can be very valuable to do cross-cultural research, but this depends on 'how well informed, how politically aware, and how sensitive the researcher is, to the topic in question and to the local context' (2000: 126). Meanwhile, Nagar suggests that 'field-work can be productive and liberating, as long as researchers keep in mind the critiques and undertake research that is more politically engaged, materially grounded, and institutionally sensitive' (2002). This may also require that new approaches to reflexiv-ity and positionality are applied (Nagar and Geiger, 2007: 3), as suggested in Box 1.2. Briggs and Sharp assert that, 'rather than abandon fieldwork, it is perhaps now more than ever necessary to decentralise Western centrism' (2004: 673). In other words, development fieldwork can play an important role in 'unsettling the idea that Western cultural practices and whiteness are normal and that everything else is "other". In order to do fieldwork ethically, therefore, it is important for Northern researchers to decentre themselves: geographically, linguistically and culturally' (McEwan, 2011: 24).

The criticisms of fieldwork outlined above have contributed to healthy debate and reflection on fieldwork which have helped us to move beyond positivist assumptions about the neutral role of the researcher to more nuanced understandings of ways in which one's positionality, relationships and personality affect the research process. This book then represents an effort to contribute to raising awareness of such issues, as well as offering some strategies to deal with them, and should be considered alongside other texts which focus on primarily methodological concerns.

SCOPE AND LIMITATIONS

This book is not intended to be a manual which addresses or answers all problems encountered in the field. Indeed, as Burgess (1982: 9) noted several decades ago, there is not one successful formula for doing effective fieldwork. Rather, it adheres to the conviction that much can be learned from reading others' experiences and problems and how they were dealt with. We also support Moser's (2008) notion that success in the field depends at least partly on the personality, or emotional intelligence, of the researcher.

This book is primarily intended for students undertaking a Master's or PhD thesis with a development focus. Those conducting 'home-based' research will find regular mention of specific issues they may face, and a number of boxed examples derive from the experiences of African, Pacific Island, Latin American and Asian students. We hope that development practitioners, who are increasingly expected to con-duct on-going research as part of their work and who are engaging in constructive research partnerships, will find this a useful and accessible reference book. Similarly, while we focus on social science research, this book may also be of interest to those from more technical or scientific backgrounds (e.g. geologists or botanists) who are planning fieldwork in developing countries or marginalised areas and want to be cognisant of relevant issues surrounding ethics, cross-cultural interaction and the logistics of working in foreign settings.

This is not a book of methods, but it does have chapters that document a range of qualitative and quantitative methods used in the social sciences and shows how they might be applied to different research topics and settings. Students and others planning their research will find it useful to consult other sources on fieldwork methods and techniques, including those listed at the end of Chapters 2, 3, 4 and 5.

FORMAT AND CONTENTS

The tone of this book is intentionally informal, sometimes even irreverent. While we are dealing with some serious issues such as ethics and relationships between researchers and the researched, we also know from first-hand experience that things can and do go wrong during fieldwork, and the best way to deal with these matters is to have an open mind and a sense of humour. This is confirmed by the following email which was received from a Master's student who was two weeks into a 10-week field visit to a Polynesian island:

> My participants are proving hard to find, or get to. ... I had a really good contact arranged to take me to a rural area. Today I rang him to reconfirm our meeting and trip to the village this week, to find he was in Japan – he went last night. So what the heck I think I will go to McDonald's today instead. My computer also won't work; it has worked twice since being here. So as you can see all is going just as I hoped. (Personal communication, December 2001)

We have ensured that such anecdotal accounts of the experiences of chapter authors and other researchers are included in text boxes throughout the book. These boxed examples demonstrate both positive and negative fieldwork experiences, showing how fieldwork rarely goes as smoothly as we may anticipate. Van Maanen (2011) refers to these as 'confessional tales'.

At the end of each chapter, the authors provide convenient summary points, along with questions for reflection which indicate things that researchers might like to ponder with respect to their own planned field research. Readers will also find an annotated list of recommended readings at the end of each chapter, so they can delve more deeply into specific ideas or issues.

The chapters draw on the rich and diverse experiences of a range of researchers. Most of us are academic staff or recent PhD graduates, but we also have four authors who work directly in the development field, working for a donor, a UN agency, an environmental think tank, and as a consultant (see 'Notes on contributors'). We have conducted fieldwork on topics ranging from the effectiveness of NGOs in aid delivery to the corporate responsibilities of transnational mining companies, from women's mental health in a post-conflict zone to ecotourism as a livelihood option for rural communities, and from local forms of governance in Africa through to the efforts of a virtual social network to build connections between small charitable organisations. We have worked in both urban and rural settings in geographical regions around the globe. Frequently the ideas we present in individual chapters are complemented by issues raised in other chapters of this book, so readers will find regular cross-references to follow up on. Particularly pertinent themes such as ethics, positionality, representation and reciprocity are threaded throughout the chapters of the book, rather than being confined to a discrete section: the Index should be helpful with navigation in such cases.

Twelve chapters follow this introductory piece. Part I: 'Methodology' provides material to assist students in planning for field research and has chapters on 'Designing development research' (Chapter 2), 'Quantitative research' (Chapter 3), 'Qualitative research' (Chapter 4), and a new (since the first edition) Chapter 5 on 'Something old, something new: research using archival, textual and digital data'.

Part II: 'Preparation for the Field' includes Chapter 6 on 'Practical issues', which considers matters such as funding, research permission, health preparations and what to pack. This is followed by Chapter 7 on 'Personal issues', which examines what motivates people to do research and how this influences attitudes and behaviour in the field, and also considers relative merits of taking family or a partner to the field.

Part III: 'In the Field' launches the reader into fieldwork proper, with three chapters examining entering the field (Chapter 8), 'Ethical issues' (Chapter 9) and 'Working with marginalised, vulnerable or privileged groups' (Chapter 10). The first of these chapters contemplates issues such as culture shock (including reverse culture shock for researchers going 'home') and hiring research assistants, while the two following chapters address a number of 'big questions': who should sanction fieldwork, how to manage power relations between researchers and the researched, negotiating access to the field via gatekeepers, and the need for reciprocity in research relationships. Chapter 10 also includes a discussion on how development research can go hand-in-hand with advocacy and activism regarding the rights of the poor and oppressed.

Part IV: 'Leaving the Field' begins with Chapter 11 which reflects on the experience of leaving, from saying farewell to new friends and colleagues, to what one 'owes' the research participants. This is followed by Chapter 12 on returning to university and 'writing the field'. Finally, Chapter 13, 'Ways forward', examines how we can do development research in even more ethical and just ways in the future.

Summary

- Where researchers are well-prepared for 'the field' and sensitive to the local context and culture, development fieldwork can be a valuable experience for both the researcher and their research participants.
- To prepare well for development fieldwork the researcher must give due consideration to practical, methodological and ethical issues.
- 'The field' is a socio-political and/or geographical site where a researcher spends time collecting data to gain a deeper understanding of development issues. These sites can be in the North, South, East and West.

- Serious questions have been directed at those undertaking development research in recent years based, for example, on concerns about uneven power relations between the researcher and the researched, the appropriation of knowledge by outsiders, and ways in which research subjects have been represented.
- Many researchers now demonstrate an acute awareness of their positionality in relation to those they are researching, and actively reflect about how this influences the research process and relationships that are formed.
- We have moved beyond the crisis of legitimacy in development fieldwork. This is both due to recognition that there can be considerable merit in research which crosses the bounds of one's own culture, sex, class, age and other categories of social positioning, and due to the need to work across the North, South, East and West to find solutions to pervasive issues of poverty and inequality.
- Some researchers are often now choosing to 'do' fieldwork differently, to work more in collaboration with partners and to ensure that their research is ethical and 'gives back' to research participants.

Questions for reflection

- What does 'the field' mean to you? Is it more of a social, political or geographical location?
- Which of the criticisms directed at field researchers do you think are most pertinent? What implications do you think these criticisms should have for the practice of development fieldwork?
- How will you address such criticisms in your own research?
- What do you see as the main points in favour of continued development fieldwork?
- What are some ways we can attempt to work ethically and effectively in practising development fieldwork?

RECOMMENDED READINGS

Appadurai, A. (2006). The right to research. *Globalisation, Societies and Education*, 4(2), 167–177.

Article exploring the right of those in poorer countries to do research, and the nexus between research and action, particularly in the context of a rapidly changing world where knowledge is increasingly accessible.

Corbridge, S., and Mawdsley, E. (2003). Special issue: Fieldwork in the 'tropics': Power, knowledge and practice. *Singapore Journal of Tropical Geography*, 24(2).

This special issue provides a stimulating range of papers dealing with practical issues that arise when carrying out fieldwork in 'the tropics' as well as addressing concerns associated with power and positionality.

McEwan, C. (2011). Development and fieldwork. *Geography*, *96*(1), 22–26.

Article outlining ethical issues in development fieldwork for researchers and students, particularly in relation to power and privilege.

Sluka, J. A., and Robben, A. C. G. M. (eds) (2012b). *Ethnographic Fieldwork: An Anthropological Reader*. Malden, MA: Wiley-Blackwell.

Particularly useful for those coming from an anthropological tradition, this book provides a comprehensive overview of the role of fieldwork in anthropology, and covers issues including relationships, positionality, reflexivity and power.

Sumner, A., and Tribe, M. (2008b). What could Development Studies be? *Development in Practice*, *18*(6), 755–766.

Article outlining the history and future of development studies and development research.

NOTES

1. Readers of the first edition of this book might notice a change in our use of terminology. In 2003, we used 'Third World' based on the meaning accorded to it by Alfred Sauvy, a French economist and demographer who coined the term in 1952. He was referring to the one-third of the world that was 'excluded from its proper role in the world by two other worlds' (Hadjor, 1992: 11). This 'Third World' was never meant to be associated with inferior status, rather, to denote countries left out from the realms of political and economic power. This term seems less appropriate today, however, given that the 'Second World' has been transformed since the 1990s with the fall of Communism in Europe, while some 'Third World' countries have achieved staggering rates of economic growth and are no longer official development assistance (ODA) recipients. The authors of this text therefore had a discussion about which terms we would be most comfortable using, all of us cognizant of the contested nature of the language of development. The terms 'developing countries' and 'marginalised areas' gained the most support and are used throughout, except for Chapters 11 and 12 where the authors prefer to use their own descriptors. 'Western' is still used to refer to those societies exhibiting the economic systems, consumer culture and individualism characteristic of North American, Australasian and European countries.
2. This book chapter has recently been republished in Robben and Sluka's 2012 edited book *Ethnographic Fieldwork: An Anthropological Reader*.
3. Chapter 10 provides further ideas as to how researchers can acknowledge the input of research participants and ensure that they give something back which is valuable to the community they have worked with.

PART I
METHODOLOGY

2

DESIGNING DEVELOPMENT RESEARCH

WARWICK E. MURRAY AND JOHN OVERTON

Good research requires good design, yet the process of research design can be fraught with difficulties and frustration. Fortunately, there is a wide literature on the principles of research design in social and economic studies that offers both theoretical and practical guidance (Blaxter et al., 2006; Denscombe, 2010; Kitchin and Tate, 2000; O'Leary, 2010; Robinson, 1998). For research design advice specific to development research, see Desai and Potter (2006) or Sumner and Tribe (2008a). Research design is an enormous theme. It covers three broad overlapping areas that are crucial to the genesis and initiation of a viable and relevant research topic. First, research *philosophy* covers issues of ontology (theories of what the world is) and epistemology (theories of what it is possible to know about the world and how we might come to know it). Second, research philosophy flows into *methodologies* (theories of how the world can be interpreted) and methods (sets of techniques for interpreting the world). Third, and crucially, 'design' also incorporates issues of research *logistics and practice* which include site selection, proposal writing, research timing, budgetary issues, and planning for ethical research.

For new researchers the design phase is often daunting, coming at the beginning of the investigation period with the expectation that it should be made watertight, within a neat timeframe, before flying off to 'do' the real research. This conception of the process can be unhelpful. Design is a fundamental and integral part of actually *doing* research, and in most social research at least, design is likely to evolve as the subsequent phases of the project unfold and the perspectives of the researcher almost invariably shift. This does not imply that design should not be thoroughly worked-out before 'fieldwork' begins – it should. Using a 'building' analogy, Kitchin and Tate echo this point:

> We are moving from the choice of what type of building we want to construct to decisions regarding the process of construction. To take the analogy further, if we miss out this stage and

progress straight to constructing the building without adequate planning then there is a good chance we will run into problems at a later date. (2000: 34)

It is important to reiterate, however, that design should be seen as an essential part of the *on-going* research process requiring, as does every other component of research activity, flexibility and reflexivity. To extend the analogy, this means that you may have to be prepared for some walls to falter and buckle as the ground shifts during construction. Ultimately, it is the balance between rigidity and flexibility that is likely to determine the success or otherwise of the project. Those who live in earthquake zones know well that architecture that is too rigid can be disastrous.

Given the wide literature that already exists, why include a chapter on design in a book such as this? We argue that a range of issues particular to development research design often sets it apart from design in other areas of social science. Although all research is built from fundamentally similar (albeit highly contested) foundations, it is important to understand something of the *difference* of development field research.

WHAT MAKES DEVELOPMENT RESEARCH DIFFERENT?

A number of points can be offered in order to support our claim that development research is somehow different (Laws, 2003; Sumner and Tribe, 2008a). First, research often takes place in localities and cultures that are relatively unfamiliar to the researcher. This is not always the case, of course, and 'foreignness' lies on a continuum which is influenced by cultural, life-cycle, gender and geographical factors. Consider a female Londoner from high-income Hampstead Heath conducting research into male rural labour markets in low-income Herefordshire in the United Kingdom – is this any less 'foreign' than an urban New Zealander doing urban research in the Philippines? In practical terms, however, it is often the case that both the territorial geographies and cultural traits of the research 'site' are relatively unknown to the development researcher. Related to the first point is a second, which concerns language. Despite the rapid globalisation of English, it is likely that the researcher will undertake his or her work in a foreign or second language. Particularly if the research is socio-cultural in nature, it can be argued that without a high level of proficiency, or excellent assistance, whole worlds will remain unexplored, misinterpreted and, ultimately, poorly conveyed. Third, development research by researchers from Western institutions often necessarily involves a discrete period of research activity in the field with little chance of returning to 'fill the gaps'. Fourth, as Sidaway (1992) and Abbott (2006) remind us, development researchers from the 'first world' will often enter local society further up the hierarchy than their respective position at 'home' – it has been increasingly argued that the consideration of this should not only influence the practice of doing research, but should also be explicitly fed into design (see Chapter 9 and 10).

In the increasingly common case of foreign students from developing countries doing home-based development research (see, e.g., Chacko, 2004; Mandiyanike, 2009; Ng, 2011; Subedi, 2006; Sultana, 2007), some of the above discussion remains pertinent.

Doing development research away from home is distinct to doing research on one's own society and culture while based there indefinitely. For example, the researcher is likely to have a discrete fieldwork period available and will thus face all the same problems of limited piloting, distance from supervisors whilst in the field, and the perils of the return phase. Also, if the student is working in a Western university, this implies that they are relatively privileged. Even if this is not the case, it is likely to be perceived as such during fieldwork and will undoubtedly influence data collection and the outcome of research. Finally, the foreign student doing home-based research is likely – or may be bound – to take something of the philosophical and methodological baggage picked up from the foreign institutions and supervisors with whom they are working. Just as the distinction between 'foreign' and 'home-based' research is far from watertight, research can never be free of 'external' influences however 'local' it may appear.

This chapter makes the case that successful development research, whilst not inherently different from social research in general, does require a special set of skills and sensitivities. The development researcher needs to be more eclectic than is the case with research in more familiar terrains, more sensitive to cultural and ethical issues, and more willing to re-design research strategy as the research project evolves. Nevertheless, there are a range of generic issues in social science research design, which we deal with first.

DESIGN: THE IDEAL FIELD RESEARCH PROJECT

The business of research design is about putting philosophy into practice and operationalising ways of exploring theoretical ideas. As the 'bridge' between the conceptual and the logistical, it involves both abstract and practical issues and the lines between them are not always clearly demarcated. The following section touches on both of these areas, moving in general from philosophy to practice. We are mindful that the reader may well be embarking on his or her first research project, and thus we have attempted to keep the following as jargon-free as possible. For those who wish to pursue these generic themes in greater depth, please refer to the reading list at the end of the chapter and follow up the references used in the text.

IS PHILOSOPHY IMPORTANT TO RESEARCH?

Before beginning your design it is worth considering the philosophy and nature of research in general and the various types of research that can be undertaken. You may wonder, understandably, what on earth philosophy has to do with the practical business of undertaking a sound field research project. Indeed some people do ignore such questions – but always at their peril. There is a common misconception outside of academia that research is a value-free, objective process, often undertaken by men and women with white coats, thick-rimmed glasses and untidy hair. Whilst this may be true of some types of research, and perhaps some researchers, such generalisations are less relevant in the postmodern world. In the social sciences and Development Studies in particular, there has been a flowering in the range of alternative philosophies and methodologies resulting partly from the 'cultural turn' of the 1980s (see Harriss, 2005; Sumner and Tribe, 2008b). Lamentably, research and the term 'science' have long been colonised by one approach which has assumed the mantle of 'scientific-method': the empirical-analytical perspective. This approach, generally built on positivistic epistemological assumptions, is more often associated with the natural sciences. However, an on-going debate concerning whether or not social science can be approached using similar philosophies and methods (the naturalist/anti-naturalist debate) continues to rage. As with all examples of contesting paradigms (Kuhn, 1970; Lakatos and Musgrave, 1970), proponents of opposing factions are active in research in Development Studies, often in the same departments! It has to be said that there is now widespread recognition that social science is somehow different and requires differentiated foundations and tools from the natural sciences (see Sayer, 1988 for the classic argument in this regard).

In fact, there are a number of different types of science. It is important to have a basic grasp of these essentially different 'worldviews' as no research can take place in a philosophical vacuum. It is important to know something about where you fit in as this makes design, practice and the defence of your arguments far easier. In this context Graham argues:

> Philosophy is to research as grammar is to language, whether we immediately recognise it or not. Just as we cannot speak a language successfully without following certain grammatical rules, so we cannot conduct a successful piece of research without making certain philosophical choices. (2005: 10)

DIFFERENT TYPES OF SCIENCE AND DEVELOPMENT STUDIES

Habermas (1978) divides science into three types; *empirical-analytical*, *historical-hermeneutic* and *critical* (see Box 2.1). Each of these branches is host to a range of approaches, and it is perhaps best to see the three as lying on a continuum, given the considerable overlap that exists. The first is composed of approaches where it is largely believed that facts speak for themselves, that science should concern itself with observable entities and that there is no room for 'normative' or value judgement based research.[1] The most influential branch of this approach is 'positivism', which seeks to verify or falsify propositions though the collection of empirical data and argues for the construction of laws based on its findings. It is this branch of science that has come to dominate the public imagination and, to some erroneously, define intellectual endeavour or progress.

Historical-hermeneutic science lies at the other end of the spectrum and rejects the empirical view of the world. Facts do not exist independently of experience and individual perception is paramount. As such, outcomes are not predictable, laws are not derivable and the objective becomes the *interpretation* of patterns and processes. Examples of such approaches include humanism, phenomenology and, arguably, postmodernism and post-structuralism (see Kitchin and Tate, 2000 for a useful summary of these approaches).

In between these two views lie critical sciences, of which Marxism, realism and (some types of) feminism are three very different examples (see Johnston and Sidaway, 2010). What these approaches have in common – although some would argue that the differences are greater than the similarities – is that they have a moral dimension. The purpose of critical research is to uncover non-explicit processes and relations (including the nature of previous research findings) and communicate these to people so that they may act upon them in order to improve society, a process referred to as 'emancipation'.

Box 2.1   Different types of science

Empirical-analytical

Essential elements: Facts speak for themselves; science should seek facts about observable objects; normative and moral questions are avoided as they cannot be measured scientifically; proposes that processes and patterns can be predicted.

Most common methods: Surveys, closed questionnaires, some cartographic analysis, and secondary data can be important, although primary data is central also.

Development Studies example: The availability of public services and the types of building materials used in urban squatter settlements in Fiji.

Historical-hermeneutic

Essential elements: Rejects the empirical view of the world; facts do not exist independently of experience; interpretation of process and pattern rather than prediction.

Common methods: Interviews, open questionnaires, visual texts, participatory methods including participant observation and ethnography; primary data generally more important.

Development Studies example: Perception of land tenure security by residents of squatter settlements in Fiji.

Critical

Essential elements: The uncovering of non-explicit processes and relations; the communication of these findings to promote progressive social change; the explicit incorporation of moral questions.

Main approaches: A broad range of methods are used depending on the nature of the critical science being employed. Mixed methods are often appropriate for such studies.

Development Studies example: Civil society advocacy of the legal rights of the residents of squatter settlements in Fiji.

Changes in Development Studies over the 50 or so years of its disciplinary history illustrate the shifts and tides of changing paradigms in the social sciences in general. Initially, Development Studies was generally more empirical-analytical, especially given its preoccupation with economic growth and modernisation which it was felt could be 'measured' in objective ways (Lewis, 1954; McClelland, 1970; Rostow, 1960; Soja, 1968). The 1960s, and in particular the rise of dependency analysis, saw a flourishing of critical approaches in Development Studies – some of which were explicitly action-oriented and policy based (dos Santos, 1970; Frank, 1967; Prebisch, 1962). More recently, development has been contested by more reflexive, explicitly subjective philosophies. The postmodern and post-colonial critiques have been particularly influential in academic (if not policy) circles as totalising strategies and the research used to generate them has been heavily criticised. In particular the 'value-free' nature of modernisation research was labelled a façade (Brohman, 1995; Chambers, 1983; Esteva, 1992; Rahnema and Bawtree, 1997). There are, of course, major exceptions to the neat chronology described above: modernisation was often researched from a hermeneutic viewpoint (as in some forms of Anthropology and Sociology); some of the dependency theory of the 1960s and 1970s was based on an empirical-analytical worldview (especially structuralist influenced versions); some of the more recent post-turns are heavily critical, while others are highly conservative given their almost complete relativism (see Corbridge, 2000 for an introductory critique). This illustrates the danger of stereotyping different types of research and different worldviews.

What should you do about all the above philosophical debates? Is it essential that you have your theoretical colours nailed on to the mast before you begin? We would sound a note of warning here. It is possible to get too deeply, sometimes painfully, involved in such considerations. Unless your project is specifically about the application of philosophy, try not to become too tied up in it. The nature of your training to date and your intellectual character will partly pre-determine which of the 'worldviews' you most closely identify with. While in the field it will quickly become quite apparent where you best 'fit'. It is quite possible that you may hold two worldviews at the same time (especially if you believe that opposing worldviews are incommensurable as some postmodernists do), or you may find that the research process changes how you feel about competing philosophies. Very few academics have fully resolved where they sit in this respect and are constantly evolving their theoretical lenses to interpret and understand what they observe. If you think you know the answer in its entirety, then clearly you do not fully understand the question!

CONSIDERING YOUR POSITION – WHAT KIND OF RESEARCH?

Flowing from the idea of different types of science comes the recognition that there are therefore many different 'types' of research in which one can become engaged. There are a number of continuums which are likely to apply to all projects, shown in Box 2.2.

Box 2.2   Research types

Applied	–	Pure
Descriptive	–	Explanatory
Market	–	Academic
Exploratory	–	Problem-solving
Covert	–	Collaborative
Value-free	–	Action-based
Subjective	–	Objective

Source: Blaxter et al. (1996)

Every individual project will be located somewhere along each of these continuums, making each unique. You may decide that you wish to locate yourself at specific points along these planes. In this case it will be fruitful to consider *positionality* early on. Where are you coming from? Whose side are you on? Are you a pragmatist or an idealist? It is impossible not to have a position and for your individuality to not influence the research process in some way. How does the avowed 'positivist' who undertakes a regression analysis of causal variables in economic growth decide which variables to include, and how does he or she arrive at this research topic in the first place? All research, however positivist in appearance, has value-judgements at its root. Edward Soja (1979), for example, has written a stinging self-critique on the application of positivism in his research on modernisation in Kenya.

Considerable academic debate surrounds the issue of positionality and other linked themes, and this has been greatly amplified since it was first considered by feminist researchers in the late 1970s and 1980s (Dear, 1988; Moser, 2008; Nagar and Geiger, 2007; Shope, 2006). Your position, however, may 'fall-out' naturally as the research project and the questions you will address become clearer. Despite the myriad possibilities, based to a large extent on the differential philosophical foundations,

the basic characteristics shared by all of these different kinds or views of research is that they are, or aim to be, planned, cautious, systematic and reliable ways of finding out or deepening understanding. (Blaxter et al., 2006)

It should be made very clear that non empirical-analytical science is equally as rigorous as its counterparts. Indeed, it could be argued that in order to convince, other types of science have to be even more rigorous in their analysis as they swim against the popular tide of what is considered really 'scientific'. This has certainly been the case in Development Studies where modernisation approaches continue to dominate in the policy sphere. Those who adopt 'alternative' approaches, beware, as in some ways you have an extra responsibility to be diligent and systematic. There are some excellent examples of research in this vein to which you can turn for guidance, however; consult your colleagues or supervisor on which examples would be relevant to your particular topic.

HOW CAN I THINK OF A PROJECT OR TOPIC?

Robson (2011) likens research design to crossing a river, whereby with each step you move between the stones which represent focus, questions, strategy, methods. Before questions or hypotheses can be set up, it is necessary then to cross the first stone and come up with a focus for the study. This period can be both stressful and enjoyable, involving a fair bit of dreaming and drifting through the literature. Some may already have the general area of their project decided for them if they choose to study with a supervisor that only offers postgraduate study in areas of his or her expertise. Although this might seem like an easy option at the time and the student may be flattered that the academic wants to have him or her working on a pet theory or topic, in the long run (and the research period feels like a *very* long run at times) it is not always the best idea. The student should choose a topic that rings bells and sets off fireworks in the mind. Being *very* interested in the matter you are going to invest a significant part of your life in is a bare minimum. How then do you decide on a topic that has these qualities? The suggestions in Box 2.3 may be useful (see also Barrett and Cason, 2010; Desai et al., 2008).

Box 2.3   Suggestions for thinking of a research topic

- Pick up some of the current development journals such as *Third World Quarterly, Development and Change* or *World Development* and see what published researchers are doing. You will be amazed how much of the material that is published comes from postgraduate or post-doctoral work.
- Think of a country you are interested in, and have perhaps studied or travelled in to some extent before. Find a journal for that country or the region in which it is located, like *The Contemporary Pacific, Asia Pacific Viewpoint, Journal of Modern African Studies* or *Bulletin of Latin American Studies*. Consider what is being studied in the region of your choice and whether it would excite you to do more, or take another angle.
- Talk to people about development issues in the department where you are working or plan to work. Find out what the strengths of the department are if you don't already know them. Talk to both staff and previous students. Try also to talk to people outside the department about what are perceived as the strengths from their vantage point.
- Look at previous postgraduate work that has been deposited in the library. Most departments will store their theses in some form. Build from these ideas, while taking care to distinguish the better quality theses.
- You could consider developing some of your previous research. You may have done an undergraduate research essay or an honours dissertation on a development topic of interest to you.

- You might like to relate it to other interests you have. You may have done charity work, advocacy, or you may have travelled. If you are from a developing country you may have worked for a government department focused on a particular aspect of development.
- Drawing a diagram may also be useful. Place the very general area of interest to you in the centre (e.g. urbanisation) and draw linking topics from it, creating a spider-like effect.
- Consider what puzzles and/or 'bugs' you in terms of development issues. Is there anything that you feel very strongly about? You may take every opportunity to educate friends and family about the moral outrage associated with impacts of European and US protectionism on agricultural trade from developing countries – do a project on some aspect of it then!
- Enjoy the freedom of not knowing exactly what you are doing at this point. This won't always be the case. Don't be scared to follow wild ideas – your supervisor will help you make them manageable. Just dream a little bit.

Source: Adapted from Blaxter et al. (2006)

Don't be scared about being confused at the early stages of research: it can even be useful. Reading and thinking widely helps push out our intellectual boundaries and, though it might threaten to confuse and overwhelm you at first, out of that broadness of view, with all its contradictions, blind alleys and unresolved issues, comes a good appreciation of the breadth of your topic and its possibilities.

When deciding what to focus upon, a number of things should be borne in mind. As previously mentioned, your motivation is very important. The project will have to sustain your interest for one or two and possibly many more years, so you need something you are passionate about. It is not hard to find such issues in Development Studies – although we would like to point out that the most unlikely of topics (such as the social and economic impacts of pumpkin exports from Tonga) will often turn out to be fascinating. Simultaneously, there are some development-related topics which become popularised and therefore get a lot of research attention for a time, for example, climate change, ecotourism or micro-finance. Be wary about jumping onto a 'research bandwagon'.

You will also need to consider the regulations of the department you are working in; the size and manageability of the project in the time period that you have to complete it; the cost and any sources of funding you may need to find; the resources available in and around the department; and your project's demand for support. Finally, and this may be especially relevant for development research, you will need to consider access issues – it may not be automatic that research permits are granted (see Chapter 6). This may be the case if the research is around sensitive issues (see Chapter 10). This is not to say that such issues should be avoided, however, as with all aspects of research a fine balance between pragmatism and idealism needs to be struck.

Robson (2011) offers a useful categorisation of the roots of successful and unsuccessful research – although these ideas will not apply in every case (see Box 2.4). Arguably, research does not have to have 'real world value' to be successful. How is real world value measured? What of pure research which pushes back academic and theoretical boundaries? Look particularly at the roots of unsuccessful research. You should avoid taking the 'easy options' – such as relying on secondary data – as they often involve hidden pitfalls. Resist attempting to build a research project around a method you believe you are particularly adept at; methods are means, not ends.

Box 2.4   Successful and unsuccessful research

Successful research begins from:

a) **Activity and involvement** – good and frequent contacts in the field and with colleagues.
b) **Convergence** – coming together of two or more activities or interest.
c) **Intuition** – feeling the work is important, timely, right.
d) **Theory** – concern for theoretical understanding.
e) **Real world value** – work leading to tangible and useful ideas.

Unsuccessful research begins from:

a) **Expedience** – undertaken because it is easy, cheap, quick or convenient.
b) **Method or technique** – using it to try out a specific method or technique.
c) **Motivation by publication, money or funding** – research done for publication interest rather than interest in the issue.
d) **Lack of theory** – without this research is easier, but will be of less value.

Source: Robson (2011)

HOW CAN I NARROW IT DOWN?

Thinking widely helps to inspire, extend and contextualise your research topic, but it can also overwhelm you and distract you from conducting well-focused fieldwork. In any research, there comes a time when the exploring of the boundaries has to finish and commitment must be made to a specific topic and design. Such a process is also mirrored in the structure of many research reports.

We can think of a piece of research (and a thesis or academic paper) as being shaped like an hour glass. It starts wide at the top. Here we have a broad scope to explore and encompass existing knowledge: knowledge about the philosophy and methodology of study, the themes for the study, and the region being studied. Out of this, as the hour glass begins to narrow, we should identify gaps or debates in existing knowledge or aspects that you think are inadequate or wrong. These define our key general research questions, which we then refine to develop specific questions that we seek to answer in our research. This takes us to the start of the narrow section of the hour glass, analogous to the focused fieldwork we undertake. This done, and our data collected, we then begin our analysis, at first narrow and specific but gradually widening out to re-address more general issues and debates as we see our contribution to knowledge across a broad base.

There are some ways in which we can try to narrow our ideas down from the general to the specific:

- *Talk*: Talking to others (rather than being buried in our own thoughts) helps to articulate ideas more clearly. Issues that seemed muddy in your mind often become clearer when you have to express them to others.
- *The auntie/uncle sentence*: This is a refinement of the talking strategy. Imagine you are at home with your relatives on holiday and you are asked by Auntie Flo or Uncle Fred 'What are you studying at university?'. You have one sentence to offer a reply about your research topic. Because Flo/Fred are not academics, you must not use any jargon or language that cannot be understood by a non-expert ('It is an examination of the socio-psychological parameters underpinning the construction of meta-narratives relating to the incremental impoverishment of a selected sub-section of a marginalised population') but, because you don't want to patronise them by offering a glib response ('I'm going to free the world from poverty'), you must give a sense of what the research is about. It is a tough exercise but well worth doing. If you can construct such a sentence that you are happy with, write it down in large letters, pin it to your wall, show others and keep it in mind throughout your work.
- *Draw a picture*: Just as we suggested above using a diagram to begin to explore a possible project, a drawing can help you identify the key elements of a research project and their linkages. See what the central issue is, what the main components are to support this central issue, and identify linkages amongst them. Your drawing could be a neat box-and-line type or a more free-form doodle that evolves as you add or emphasise different components. Again, if you are happy with the end result, store it away, discuss it and keep it in mind. Such a drawing might even pass as a 'conceptual framework' for your project and it can help later to inform the structure of what you write.
- *Ask questions*: Research usually involves finding answers to a series of questions. Sometimes these are big, earth-shattering questions ('What are the causes of poverty?'); other times they are more simple and specific ('Why do children in this region suffer from malnutrition more than nearby?'). Think of research as having one central focusing question (the question you really want to answer and the one that will define your contribution to knowledge – this is rather like your auntie/uncle sentence) and a series of secondary questions that you need to answer first if you are to address the main one. See Box 2.5 for some advice in this regard.

Box 2.5   How to devise clear research questions

1   Once you have a broad idea for a research topic you need to clearly define it. O'Leary provides some useful questions that can help you work out what aspect of your research topic interests you.

- What is your topic?
- What is the context (e.g. geographical location, institution)?
- What do you want to achieve (to explore, to change, to discover, to understand)?

(Continued)

(Continued)

- Are there relationships you want to explore (impacts, increases, decreases, relationships, correlations, causes)?
- What is the nature of your question (what, why, when, where, how or who)?

2 When you have answers to some or all of these questions, experiment with putting them together in various configurations. This will give you draft questions to consider.

3 As you come up with research questions, try to answer the 'so what' question: 'Why might your question interest others?' Try using the phrase: *'I am studying ___ because ___ in order to help people understand ___.'* This helps you to see beyond your own interests and to clarify the potential contribution your research could make.

4 You may find that as you work through this process your question becomes increasingly complex. If this happens, break the question into parts. Try to identify a key or main question and list sub-questions.

5 Once you have a research question (or questions) you are happy with, discuss it with peers or a supervisor/mentor and ensure that it:

- is clear and intelligible;
- is researchable – overly abstract topics are difficult to turn into research terms;
- has connections to existing theory and literature; and
- is not too broad to be practicably researchable, nor too narrow to be significant.

Sources: Booth et al., 2009: 47; O'Leary, 2010: 53; Walliman, 2006: 90

WHICH METHODS SHOULD I USE?

Having defined your question and the approach you wish to take you will have a range of methods at your disposal (see Chapters 3 and 4, as well as Mayoux, 2006; Moses and Knutsen, 2007 for examples). You need to decide on methods for generating data and methods for analysing the data you produce. Certain methods are often associated with particular approaches; however, there is greater flexibility than some may think. Crang and Cook (2007) argue for a more realistic exploration of these links and question whether particular philosophies necessitate certain methods. It is true that some methods are better suited to some approaches (e.g. textual analysis in hermeneutic research or chi-squared analysis in empirical-analytical studies). This need not be the case at all times, however. In this context Giddens' argues:

> However statistical a given study might be, however abstract and remote it is, it presumes some kind of ethnography of individuals involved in the context of what is being described. (1984, quoted in Wolfe, 1989: 71)

There is something of an artificial distinction which has evolved concerning the use of qualitative and quantitative methods – the former for hermeneutic and the latter for empirical-analytical science. There is no reason why methods cannot be mixed; one shouldn't fall into the trap of being qualitative or quantitative and thinking that they are mutually exclusive. This idea of the applicability of mixed methods is taken up in greater detail in Chapter 4.

Chapters 3, 4 and 5 review some of the methods open to researchers, but before making a choice about methods, it is important to remember the place of methods in research design. Methods are a means to an end, not an end in themselves. Your methods must be appropriate to what you seek to discover or answer and they must be appropriate to you as an individual: your abilities, values and preferences. Again, it is important to be flexible in research design. We suggest moving from philosophy to positionality to choice of topic, and then to method. However, in practice, this may be more reflexive. If you are an expert in multi-variate statistical analysis, there may be no point in locking yourself into a path that takes you only to qualitative participant observation as a method. Draw on your strengths, but do not be a prisoner to them.

In considering which methods to adopt, think of research as being like preparing a meal. You may start with an idea, you then explore the cookbooks to see if others have done this before, you eventually settle on a menu and, later, specific recipes. Your menu is like your research design and your recipes are like your methods (bearing in mind that you might favour recipes you have used before but which suit the overall menu). Your recipes then should specify a list of ingredients (your data needs). This shopping list is important: remember that you have defined what you need to get the job done and you do not need to buy up the whole market or cook the same dish six different ways. Yet, when you go to the market, you might find that not all the ingredients are available. This requires some quick thinking: you either have to find acceptable substitutes or, in the worst case, you have to revise your menu.

The market might also reveal some exciting ingredients that you had not thought of but which you can acquire and accommodate within your menu. In cooking and serving your meal, be prepared to make changes: some seasoning added near the end can make a big difference to the taste and good presentation of the meal will make its consumption more pleasurable! In the above, we have outlined in a roughly chronological way the first steps of the research process, flowing from general philosophy to particular methods. In reality, research very rarely follows a linear path and is usually circular, if not spaghetti-like.

LOGISTICS – PROPOSING AND PLANNING

We have considered overall research design but this broad planning process is not sufficient. There are some critical practical issues that flow from the general design and these, again, require both careful planning as well as a flexible attitude that allows modification (see O'Leary, 2010 Ch. 5; Rossman and Rallis, 2012: 118–128).

One of the most critical aspects of research design is the research proposal. Proposals may be drawn up at different stages and for different purposes (e.g., requesting funds, immigration clearance, ethics approval, PhD programme application or confirmation), and the purpose and timing of the proposal affects the particular shape and length of what is written. Nonetheless, a good proposal must have certain elements (see Box 2.6).

Box 2.6   Essential components of a good research proposal

- A research title or statement of intent: this should be concise and jargon-free (the auntie/uncle sentence helps here).
- Key research question(s) – see Box 2.5.
- An acknowledgement of the wider literature and issues as they pertain to the topic: what do we know or not know already? Only the key references should be listed.
- The context of the research: the particular region or locality for the research and the way this shapes the topic.
- The methods to be used, including data needs, location, methods of collection and analysis.
- A discussion of ethical issues, and ethics procedures/permissions which may need to be obtained.
- A timetable: when will the main phases of the work be conducted?
- A budget: what are the anticipated costs and sources of income?

Keep the proposal as concise as possible: you are writing a statement of intent, not draft chapters. Unless you are required to produce something more substantial, a proposal should be able to cover the above aspects in 3,000 words or less. However, more specific proposals, for example for an ethical approval process, may require a longer paper or a more specific format. In line with our overall theme about flexibility, treat the research proposal as a working document. It may meet a particular need and summarise your intent at one point in time but it should not put your project in a straightjacket. Review and, if necessary, revise your proposal as you go.

Within the proposal, several logistical issues may need to be covered. Furthermore, such issues may take on particular importance or shape in a piece of Development Studies research. Examples of such issues include:

- *Site selection*: What is the intended location for field research? Choose a site or sites that, from what you can find out, are likely to give you appropriate data. This can be difficult if you do not have first-hand knowledge of the place and you may have to modify your selection once in the field. Bear in mind practical issues of accessibility, health, safety and sustenance (can I find a place to stay?) as well as suitability for the topic of study. Do try to find out as much as possible about health and safety hazards beforehand and either avoid overly hazardous places or take reasonable steps to mitigate the hazards (such as anti-malarial measures or personal safety plans). Always have an emergency plan so you can get help and get to safety from the places you are in.

- *Pre-testing*: Ideally, it is desirable to test and refine your methods in the field before embarking on the full field project. Given the difficulties and expense of travelling overseas to a field site, this is not always possible. In some circumstances, some sort of virtual pre-testing might be tried, for example using friends or, if possible, expatriates from your intended country/region.
- *Language and cultural issues*: Are you going to be able to communicate effectively in the field and behave appropriately? If you have doubts, language courses should be looked at and/or enquiries made to arrange a field assistant and translator. A 'cultural mentor' – someone from the cultural group you intend to work in – can also help pave the way and educate you both before you enter the field and during your work. In addition, prior contact with key informants and gatekeepers (if possible) should be considered to ease the path to the field. See Chapter 8 for more on language and field assistance.
- *Ethics and immigration clearance*: Most research activity requires some form of official clearance to proceed. Many universities now have human ethics approval procedures that require prior application before a project can be approved. You need to find out about such principles and procedures at an early stage and plan for this in your timetable (see Chapter 9). Similarly, if you are working in a country that you are not a citizen of, you will almost always need a special research visa. Investigate this early, for some countries have a very lengthy and difficult application process (see Chapter 6).
- *Budget*: Estimating the costs of research is not straightforward, especially if it is an unfamiliar location. Apart from the obvious costs of international travel and field equipment (voice recorders, etc.), you may need to add items such as visa and insurance costs, photocopying of documents, local travel, pay for translator/research assistant, gifts (if appropriate), and personal accommodation and sustenance. One of the best ways to estimate these latter costs is to consult an up-to-date backpacker guide (such as the *Lonely Planet* series) or online forums and blogs which cover cheaper accommodation and travel better than official tourist guides. You often succeed in finding accommodation with local households but do not underestimate the costs of this, and you should never exploit local hospitality. Be prepared to contribute to household expenses and give gifts above what may be asked for as 'rent'. See Chapter 6 for more information on funding and budgeting.
- *Timetable*: A good timetable is critical for guiding not just your time in the field but also your whole research project. It is often best to start at the end! Set a completion date for your work (this may be determined by funding, etc.) and keep to it. To assist you in this, making a completion date public to friends, family and supervisors creates a disincentive to drag your research on too long. Within this outer timeframe, set intermediate signposts: for example, finish literature review, leave for the field, finish fieldwork, complete data analysis, submit first draft and so on. You may have to revise these as you go and, of course, disasters or mishaps may justify extensions, but try to keep to your end date. Meeting intermediate targets might create pressures and panics along the way but they are better than leaving them all to the end. Also, when you meet those targets, reward yourself – have a (short) break – so you can maintain your energy and enthusiasm throughout the process. Some people, in preparing a timetable, also draw up a 'Plan B timetable': if things don't go according to Plan A, have a fall-back option that you can manage. Although you need to remain flexible, you can always find a reason to stay longer in the field. Use your data 'shopping list' to define the priorities of the data you see as essential (as opposed to that which is in the 'might be useful or interesting' category) and use the completion date to sharpen your decision when to stop.

Thus, research design is a critical process. You can plan what you have to do, you can anticipate what lies ahead and you can develop contingencies if things don't go quite as intended. Some degree of rigidity is necessary: keep a focus on your topic and don't be distracted by too many interesting cul-de-sacs; develop a budget and keep to it as much as possible; and set a timetable that allows for some latitude and down-time but sets an achievable end-date. But balance this rigidity with flexibility: be prepared to modify the plan as you go, for no piece of research ever goes exactly as anticipated. Expect shocks and disappointments. Be prepared to accommodate exciting and serendipitous opportunities. And always review throughout your research what you want to achieve, how you are going to achieve it and when you will have it done by. This is reflected upon in the boxed case study 2.7 below (see also Drybread, 2006; Gros, 2010; Haer and Becher, 2012).

Box 2.7   Rigid methodology melting in the Chilean sun

In April 1994, feeling scared and elated at the same time, I (Warwick) arrived in Chile to begin a year's PhD fieldwork. My only real comfort on arrival was the knowledge that my research objectives were clearly laid out with a neat methodology to suit. A lot of hard work had gone into developing the topic. By June of the same year, I had the feeling that these efforts had been of little worth as the rigid methodology had all but melted in the Chilean sun. In truth, this was far from the case. The research methodology and the nature of the project had 'evolved' considerably but, in retrospect, this was not only inevitable – it was desirable.

The main aim of my research was to assess the implications of neo-liberalism for small-scale fruit growers, and the relationship existing between such growers and multinational export companies. This would require a lot of qualitative and quantitative primary and secondary material, for which a detailed and timetabled plan had been devised. In the case of the small-scale growers, a questionnaire/semi-structured interview schedule had been developed which would be used with at least one hundred growers in two localities. Two sites were pre-selected for study, El Palqui (in the 'Norte Chico' region) and West Curicó (Maule region). Both localities (reputedly) had large populations of small-scale growers, and were important fruit export sources. In order to investigate the multinational exporters a postal questionnaire had been written. Further to this it was intended that a range of other informants – including agronomists, packing-house managers, local agricultural input suppliers, labour agencies etc. – would be interviewed. I planned to spend at least two months engaged in intensive research in each locality and return to Santiago to pick-up secondary data at the conclusion of the project. I even knew what bus company I was going to use to get about!

Hopes of sticking to this methodology soon evaporated. The first major problem lay in the selection of the study localities. In the case of West Curicó, the secondary information I used was unexpectedly outdated and the census from Santiago was wrong – virtually no apple growers existed in the area! Those that did were invariably of a different size to that quoted. Eventually, a suitable area – East Curicó – was identified for study with the help of the local agricultural extension agency and a pilot study organised. By the time a specific focus area had been identified, two weeks had passed.

I also encountered considerable problems getting to as many small-scale growers as I had hoped and getting the type of information anticipated. A major shortcoming was linguistic. A three-month, once-a-week, course in Spanish was not sufficient preparation for the nuances of countryside Chilean. It was necessary to take an intensive course back in the capital and hang around a lot of cafés and bars talking, but mainly listening, to people. It is extremely educational to just 'hang-out' at times.

There were further logistical impediments. First, there were problems with obtaining a 'random' sample. A number of 'gatekeepers' (see Chapter 9) had to be relied on and this led to a bias, as the individuals would select those who they felt would be 'most interested' and 'interesting'. Second, the postal questionnaire was a failure (three responses from thirty, two of which were to inform me that they couldn't help!). Personal, pre-appointed visits were the only way that the export companies could be successfully approached. Third, it was time consuming to track down individuals. The growers' work took place from sun-up until sun-down. More often than not I would attempt to locate them at their plots (parcelas) often located very far apart. This was particularly the case in Curicó. Riding up to 50 km in the Chilean sun on mainly rough stone surface roads and with pockets full of stones to scare off mad dogs, was not envisaged during the research design phase.

A number of positive 'chance' discoveries also partly altered the direction of research. Whilst in a legal office in Ovalle near El Palqui for another purpose, a large set of fruit sale contracts drawn up between export firms and farmers was stumbled upon. The analysis of these contracts formed a major section in the final thesis.

Surprise meetings also became increasingly important. In a restaurant I ended up chatting with one of Ovalle's lawyers; somebody who had worked in the defence of small farmers in disputes concerning the re-possession of their property by companies. You should not become excessively concerned if the research timetable is altered.

The first few months in the field led to a large re-definition of the aims and methods of my project. Crucially, not as much time as originally hoped for could be spent in the field. I really wished to avoid the worst excesses of researching as a 'visiting outsider' (Chambers, 1983) but spending more time outside probably helped create a 'bigger picture'. Ambitions as to the number of farmers to be interviewed were cut and language difficulties meant that the information was not always as rich as hoped for. This, however, forced me to think about and focus on the really important issues. Chance findings convinced me that there was a much greater role for qualitative elements in the research. Overall, it became obvious that it was important to be flexible and eclectic. Designing by doing often leads to development research projects that better capture the essential elements of locality.

Source: Murray (1997)

CONCLUSION – EXPECT THE UNEXPECTED

Each field experience, like the places in which they unfold, will be totally different. However, a number of broad points can be offered, some of which may be of use to those about to start their fieldwork period. The study in Box 2.7 seems to suggest that a fine balance between rigidity and flexibility is required in fieldwork. It is important that the researcher has a clear idea of the purpose of his or her research aims and objectives. It is also advisable to have a clear idea of what methods will be employed in order to achieve these things. One must also be prepared to refine and, in some cases, let go of these plans once in the field – often at very short notice. In the same context, it may also be important to be prepared to think on one's feet. But the most important thing, perhaps, is not to give up: the authors know of very few researchers who have not experienced the above types of problems – almost invariably they have managed to sort them out.

Research is not easy, but it is remarkably rewarding. Expecting the unexpected and undertaking contingency planning can help researchers cope with unforeseen outcomes, raising the quality of the final output and the undoubted joys associated with arriving at that point. Good researchers are those who can design their work well and organise their time and resources accordingly. But there are also those who can react, adapt and revise their plans so that they can retain an eye on their objectives yet, if necessary, re-draw the map in order to get there.

Summary

- Philosophical issues are important in research design, particularly matters relating to world-views and epistemology. Interrogate your own starting points and reflect on these issues throughout your research.
- Deciding on a research topic involves weighing up matters of inspiration, passion and practicalities. Choose a topic that will sustain your interest throughout the process but also consider its relevance, its feasibility and links to existing knowledge and theory.
- The choice of methods for a piece of research should flow logically from the methodology of the researcher and the key research questions. Methods are a means to an end.
- A good research proposal is a critical element in designing research. It should spell out key elements of the proposed research, but remember that is a statement of intent rather than a straightjacket for the research that follows.
- Good research design helps put in place important fixed elements for research, mainly a clear focus, direction and research question. However, in practice this clear vision and rigid framework need to be balanced by flexibility during the research process to respond to unforeseen obstacles and new opportunities.

Questions for reflection

- What is your starting point in doing development research (insider/outsider, language proficiency, social status, etc.?)
- What are your views on epistemology (how knowledge is created and reproduced), and how does this help shape the approach to your research?
- Can you articulate your research topic in a single jargon-free sentence (or some other device to simplify and clarify what you intend to do)?
- Can you identify a clear central research question and a small number of secondary questions that allow you to answer the central one?
- What data will you require to address these questions and what methods are most appropriate to gather such data?
- To what extent can you foresee and plan for important practical issues such as logistics, ethics, finances and milestones?

RECOMMENDED READINGS

Crang, M., and Cook, I. (2007). *Doing Ethnographies*. Los Angeles, CA: Sage.

For those engaged in intensive primary fieldwork this is an excellent, relatively jargon-free introduction covering theoretical and practical issues.

Creswell, J. W. (2008). *Research Design: Qualitative, Quantitative, and Mixed Methods Approaches*. London: Sage.

This book provides a broad-ranging introduction aimed at postgraduates and covering both qualitative and quantitative research design. In particular it deals with the possibility of combining approaches.

Desai, V., Elmhirst, B., Lemanski, C., Mawdsley, E., Meth, P., Oldfield, J., Page, B., Souch, C., Williams, G., and Willis, K. (2008). *Doing Development/Global South Dissertations: A Guide for Undergraduates*. Retrieved 14 July 2013 from www.gg.rhul.ac.uk/DARG/DARG%20dissertation%20booklet.pdf.

An e-book covering practical, ethical and research considerations of development research, written for undergraduates (but also useful as a basic guide for postgraduates).

Graham, E. (2005). Philosophies underlying human geography research. In R. Flowerdew and D. J. Martin (eds), *Methods in Human Geography: A Guide for Students Doing a Research Project* (2nd edn, pp. 8–34). Harlow: Pearson Education.

This is a comprehensive and jargon-free introduction to the philosophies underlying human geography research and is applicable across the social sciences.

Robson, C. (2011). *Real World Research: A Resource for Social Scientists and Practitioner-Researchers* (3rd edn). Chichester: Wiley.

Robson provides a non-specialist introduction to the practical and philosophical issues surrounding research in what he terms the 'real world'. Excellent for those who are doing 'applied' research.

Sumner, A., and Tribe, M. (2008a). What can we 'know' in development studies? (pp. 53–80). *International Development Studies: Theories and Methods in Research and Practice.* London: Sage.

This chapter from a useful development studies text examines matters of ontology and epistemology: that is, what we can know and how we can know it in development studies.

NOTE

1. Kitchen and Tate (2000: 7) remind us that the term 'empirical' should not be confused with the term 'empiricism'. The latter refers to the research philosophy described in this chapter, whilst the former refers to the collection of data for testing, which can take place within many different philosophical frameworks.

3

QUANTITATIVE RESEARCH

JOHN OVERTON AND PETER VAN DIERMEN

Quantitative techniques in the past have dominated most social science research. Such techniques can be a powerful aid to Development Studies research for they can give us precise and accurate results, they can allow us to gain a picture of broad patterns and phenomena, and they can provide us with evidence to inform policy formulation. They have particular utility when firm answers are required. How many people do not have access to clean water? What is the likely monetary impact of a scheme to convert from subsistence to cash crops? How much income and employment are generated by street traders? The Gapminder website for example, makes very effective use of statistics to challenge our views of development and inequality globally (see www.gapminder.org). Yet the use of quantitative techniques in developing countries, whilst essential in many aspects of research, does raise some particular problems and limitations.

The use of quantitative techniques tends to polarise researchers. Some, without sufficient training in statistics, go weak at the sight of a formula or spreadsheet or talk of 'margins of error' or 'statistical significance'. Others have a deep suspicion of quantitative methods from a more philosophical postmodernist perspective: empiricism is seen as flawed because it seeks truth and objectivity from a research process, so it is suggested, that will always be subjective and contested. However, there are many researchers who rely on quantitative techniques because they believe that only these techniques allow us to uncover verifiable and meaningful 'facts' that have scientific validity. We suggest here that a common-sense view of research will place us somewhere in between: quantitative techniques can be very useful, and are often essential, but they must be treated with caution and often supplemented by other techniques.[1]

In this chapter we explore some potential benefits and pitfalls in the use of quantitative techniques. We do not aim to present a detailed guide to the range or use of such techniques (see Recommended Readings at the end of the chapter to follow-up further). We start by discussing why we use these techniques before suggesting some basic approaches. We finish by stressing some problems commonly encountered and suggesting simple strategies for avoiding them.

WHAT IS QUANTITATIVE DATA?

Almost all fieldwork generates quantitative data. In many cases this is done intentionally as either the main methodology or as a secondary technique to supplement and support other research strategies. The intentional collection of data by the fieldworker occurs through methods such as questionnaires, observations, structured interviews and the use of published data. The collection of data may also be incidental to the main fieldwork strategy. Where the researcher uses case studies or ethnographic fieldwork, informal quantitative data collection often occurs in the footsteps of the main methodology: in interviews we discuss how many people might live in a household, what rice prices are at present, or how much land a household can access. Regardless of the reasons or methods for quantitative data collection, the discussion here is useful for those considering using quantitative analysis. The focus in this section is first on identifying the main characteristics of quantitative data before we move to discussing the techniques for collecting and analysing such data.

Quantitative data is characterised by many of its proponents as objective, representative and, most important, it is specified in numbers (Fotheringham, 2006; Lewin, 2011). In contrast, qualitative data is often said to be subjective, not representative and prescribed in text. It is assumed that quantitative data are objective because they are collected as independent 'facts' in studies that can be replicated by other researchers. Further, with careful sampling, it can be argued that the findings generated from such data can be representative of a larger population from which the sample was drawn or for other populations with the same characteristics. For example, if a sample survey in a village in Java, Indonesia, showed 20 per cent of women in the village received some income from informal sector work, it can be assumed, with a certain degree of error, this is the same for the entire village and other similar villages in Java.

The representation of information by numbers is an important characteristic of quantitative data. The use of numbered data can be characterised into two types: discrete and continuous. *Discrete* data does not contain fractions and is usually associated with a count within a category. For example, counting family size provides discrete data – you cannot have 2.5 children! *Continuous* data, in contrast, comes mostly from measuring a variable. For example, age can be measured in years and fractions of a year – you *can* be 2.5 years old.

Quantitative data has a particular strength because it can be verified and replicated. Because it is 'objective' and scientific – collected using specified (and putatively neutral) assumptions and techniques – other researchers can examine what one piece of research has done, repeat the methods and, hopefully, acquire the same results. In doing so, they replicate and verify the original work or, if they fail to replicate the results, they may begin to question the original work and its conclusions. Thus the objectiveness of quantitative data analysis allows for confidence in predictions and policy recommendations. For example, from survey data it is often possible to predict quite accurately the changes in population and its requirements in terms of schools, hospitals and transport and telecommunication networks. Furthermore, it has been argued that quantitative approaches to field research are possible even in difficult, dangerous and politically sensitive sites (Haer and Becher, 2012; Tsai, 2010).

WHAT TECHNIQUES SHOULD BE USED?

Thus far we have considered important issues relating to the nature of quantitative data. The next step is to think about how to collect the data. In doing fieldwork the four primary means for collecting quantitative data are through observations, questionnaires, structured interviews and the use of secondary data.

OBSERVATIONS

Observations are used for both quantitative and qualitative data collection and provide a straightforward and seemingly accurate means of collecting data. Observations are one of the most crucial tools for researchers, whether they result in the generation of 'hard data' or merely impressions and surprises which help the way we shape and interpret our research. Observation may involve relatively simple techniques, such as counting the number of cars passing a certain point, or measuring the area of land under a certain crop. These result in, usually, precise measurements that are amenable to quantitative data analysis (see below). However, observations might also involve measurements and analysis of human behaviour, and this may require more subjective assessments of what is actually happening and being measured, hence the need for qualitative methods such as participant observation (see Chapter 4).

QUESTIONNAIRES

Questionnaires are the most common means for collecting quantitative data. They are widely used by a range of agents, including NGOs, government authorities, multilateral donors and academic researchers. The design of questions and the questionnaire is a well-developed science, with most books on social science research methods dedicating one or two chapters to this alone (Babbie, 2010;

Barker, 2006; David and Sutton, 2011; de Vaus, 2002; Denscombe, 2010; Iarossi, 2006). Therefore, since most of the technical information is readily available, what we do here is touch on some general points, particularly as they relate to doing fieldwork in developing countries. In general, questionnaires should begin with the basic and least intrusive questions and progress to the more complex and sensitive questions. All questions should be simple to understand and unambiguous. This is particularly important when your questionnaire will need to be translated into a local language. It is important to avoid reference to concepts that are not common in the population to whom you will administer the questionnaire. Piloting the questionnaire and afterwards asking the respondents to comment on the questionnaire can quickly identify such problems.[2]

How to deliver the questionnaire is also an important issue. In developing countries a mail-out or telephone interview is unlikely to be successful. Even in the West, returns on postal questionnaires are usually low. An alternative is to administer the questionnaire directly by yourself or with the help of a local research assistant. If you conduct the questionnaire yourself you will need to be sufficiently fluent in the local language (see Chapter 8, section on 'Language issues'). If you use research assistants such as graduate students from a local university, you will need to brief them thoroughly and have a means to check quality (Gleisberg, 2008).

A number of online survey tools are also available (such as Zoomerang, SurveyMonkey, FluidSurveys and MySurveyLab) that allow the construction and application of online surveys. For fieldwork in developing countries they still have limited application, as it requires respondents to have access to the Internet, although this is changing rapidly as Internet and mobile technologies spread. They also require that participants are literate. Online survey tools may thus be particularly useful for research with development professionals and volunteers, NGOs, government and private entities (see Chapter 5 for further discussion of online research).

Several other points can also be made when constructing and implementing questionnaires in developing countries or marginalised areas:

- Present questions in an unbiased way as respondents will often look for prompts as to what kind of answer you want. Finishing a sentence with 'don't you agree?' is an obvious cue as to the kind of response you are seeking.
- Conduct the questionnaire away from others, so the person being interviewed does not feel pressured by their peers in giving a particular response. Note that this is not always possible and it may be particularly difficult to speak with women or children without someone else such as a parent or husband overseeing the process (see Chapter 10). You must also maintain confidentiality and not divulge to other respondents what someone has said.
- Don't make the questionnaire too long. An hour is about the maximum time you can ask from someone for an open-ended questionnaire before it becomes an imposition. Try to make closed-answer surveys even shorter. Include only questions that are essential rather than everything you would like to get information on. Remember that respondents are doing you a favour by giving freely of their time and, in a developing country context, will sometimes see outside researchers as someone to defer to and please with their answers regardless of how busy they are. Do not abuse their goodwill.

- Allow for notes to be made in the margin of the questionnaire, as these can help later in writing up the research. Note, for example, other comments that are made beyond what was asked in the questionnaire as well as things such as body language (e.g., did the respondent look uncomfortable when asked a particular question, were they joking?) and others present. It is also important to put a date and location on each questionnaire. These notes are best made soon after the interview while these observations are still fresh in your mind.
- Obtain their informed consent. Make sure you explain to the respondent who you are and what the research is for. A covering letter from your institution usually helps (see Chapter 9).
- Construct the questionnaire in such a way that it is easy later to enter the quantitative data into a computer. This means that questions are often better framed as 'closed questions' (e.g., a 'yes/no' answer or one that asks for a particular fact or figure) or prescribed by a range of options ('tick the appropriate box'). However, note that such questions might not always be appropriate given either the objectives of your study or the possibility that yes/no answers do not always capture the subtlety of what a person might wish to express. Inclusion of more qualitative open-ended questions as part of the questionnaire can help deal with such problems.

STRUCTURED INTERVIEWS

Structured interviews are less rigidly constructed than questionnaires, but nevertheless follow a set pattern in asking questions or bringing topics up for discussion. Much of the discussion on questionnaires above can also be applied to structured interviews. Structured interviews may be of the 'closed question' type but often they will involve more open-ended questions (e.g., 'What is your view on …?') and they are sometimes designed to elicit data on opinions and behaviour as much as they are to get hard facts. Therefore they tend to cross the boundary between quantitative and qualitative techniques.

In conducting research for his PhD in squatter settlements in Fiji, Luke Kiddle used structured interviews to obtain data on basic information about households and employment. He also asked each interviewee how long they had lived in their present dwelling. This elicited standard quantitative data to allow him to analyse length of residence, but it also opened up wider and very useful open-ended discussion about how they obtained and maintained their access to land and their relationships with landowners (Kiddle, 2011). Although the quantitative material was important, and revealed some interesting patterns about the age of settlements and turnover of tenants, it was open-ended questions used most commonly in qualitative research that were of more value because they illuminated more about the issues of perceived security of tenure in Fiji.

In designing an interview schedule, it is important to balance the need to ask the same questions of each respondent (so that you have some standard frame for comparison and analysis) with the need to allow respondents to roam more freely with their answers (which can open up new possibilities for data but make analysis more difficult). In recording the data, you may need to consider taping the conversations (if appropriate and if you obtain consent) rather than relying on a tightly formatted questionnaire form.

USE OF SECONDARY DATA

Collecting secondary data is standard practice for doing fieldwork in developing countries, whether the researcher undertakes primarily quantitative or qualitative data collection (see Chapter 5, especially regarding collection of archival data). The range of secondary data is enormous, including published government statistics, local or regional government reports, local newspaper and magazine archives, universities, NGO and other organisations' reports and data, local government maps and company reports, to name just a few sources (Findlay, 2006). Even when the published data is not directly applicable, it is often useful for understanding the context of the more narrowly defined research topic.

Such data can be critical not just to analyse in its own right but also to supplement or triangulate your own primary research data. For example, it is common practice to compare the characteristics of a sample population (age and sex distribution, income, religion, etc.) with census data to see if the profile of your sample matches that of a wider population.

Be aware, however: just because data is published or official, it may not necessarily be truthful or valid. There are many examples of the way governments and other agencies publish data that are deliberately false, selective or distorted in order to support a particular policy or point of view (Bulmer, 1993: 4–5; Da Corta and Venkateshwarlu, 1992: 104). Pages of official and important-looking statistics can often disguise suspect data collection techniques and ill-informed analysis or deliberate tampering.

SAMPLING

Research is always constrained by a lack of time or resources. Whilst we would usually like to cast our net as widely as possible and gather as much data as we can to increase the confidence we have in our results, in nearly all cases it is simply not possible to gather data from a whole population (a national population census is a rare exception). Therefore we need to sample: to select a small group which is representative of the wider population (Bryman and Cramer, 1995: 99–114; David and Sutton, 2011; Denscombe, 2010). If we can be confident that our sample is reasonably representative of the population, then we can extrapolate the results from our sample to the population. A polling survey of voter preferences prior to an election is a common example of sampling.

In order to make generalisations from the sample to the population, a sample needs to conform to certain rules. First, it needs to be chosen in a representative way. It is possible to collect a non-representative (non-probability) sample that provides valuable information but cannot be used to generalise with any confidence about the entire population. While it is preferable to collect a representative sample (also referred to as 'probability sampling'), this is not always possible. The most common reason for a non-representative sample is when you don't know who is included in the entire population. The entire population refers to all those with the same characteristic and with some natural boundary. For example, the population for a study of school children's access to vaccines could be all school children in the district or village you are concerned with, or if it were a national study it would be all school children in the country. In the developing world there is often a lack of recorded information or poor access to information, which means it is difficult to know the precise population. When this is the case, it is possible to use one of four types of non-representative sampling:

- *Convenience sample:* Occurs when people are chosen because they are conveniently available. For example, interviewing circular migrants while back home in their village may be convenient but cannot be used to represent the entire population of circular migrants from the village.
- *Snowball (or chain) sample:* This can be a useful technique for selecting respondents with particular characteristics where information on people with those characteristics is lacking. It involves finding and selecting one person and then asking if he or she knows others that suit your criteria (e.g., farmers who have experimented with a new seed variety or women who attended a particular meeting). You can then find this next list of people and ask them for others, so your sample should keep expanding. It runs the risk of being very selective – some of your respondents may not know, or want to exclude, others – but it can be the most practical means of selection in some circumstances.
- *Purposeful sample:* Occurs when the researcher makes a judgement on whom to include in the sample. It requires a prior assessment of the typical characteristics of a target population. An example would be the selection of one or two villages with 'typical' health problems (Nichols, 1991: 68). How representative the sample is depends largely on the judgement of the researcher, but it cannot be said to be a probability sample because the choice of sample units is determined by subjective judgement.
- *Quota sample:* Occurs when people are chosen with characteristics representative of the total population. For example, a researcher interested in gender issues would select a sample that had the same proportion of males and females as the total population. This method requires good information on the characteristics of the total population but, if it is at hand, it can help ensure that the sample has a good fit – and is therefore more representative – of the total population.

When we know the total membership of a population, usually from published data, or if the population is small enough, from our own numeration of the population, it becomes possible to select a representative sample. For the sample to be representative, each member of the population must be chosen at random and have the same probability of being selected. This process can be further refined by stratified sampling. This is done in order to capture certain sub-groups within the population. Using the previous example of the school children and vaccination, the school population could be stratified by parents' income. It is then possible to select a proportionately random number from each income group. That is, if 50 per cent of school children's families were low income, then 50 per cent of the entire sample should come from this group. Another strategy for selecting a probability sample is the cluster or area sample (Frankfort-Nachmias and Nachmias, 2008: 173). The advantage of cluster sampling is that it reduces the overall workload, especially in large studies. Clustering is done by dividing the population into large groupings and selecting probability samples from the groupings. Again, using the school children and vaccination example, if this was a national study, clustering could be used to divide the country into major provinces or states and from each state a school is randomly chosen for use in the sample. This technique would reduce the sample size but still provide the researcher with a probability sample.

In selecting a representative sample, the researcher will be confronted with the problem of how many sampling units (or cases) are enough. This is an important consideration, as too few would undermine the validity of any generalisation the researcher makes from the sample. Equally, each interview/questionnaire 'not needed' is extra time in the field and creates additional costs. Therefore, it is important to know how many is enough. Where the population is small, it is not unreasonable to 'sample' the entire population, providing high level of accuracy and good data for later analysis. A rule of thumb is that usually 30 cases is the minimum required for any useful statistical analysis. However, statisticians often prefer 100 or more cases before doing any analysis. You should also consider the need for more cases if you intend to divide your sample into sub-populations. For example, if you divide the school children from the previous example into girls and boys to see if there are gender differences, then you will need a larger number of cases. Further, you should be aware that you might reject certain cases later for various reasons and therefore you should make allowance for this when determining the sample size.

In any sample size there will be a sampling error or standard error. That is, the probability that the characteristics of your random sample does not reflect the characteristics of the total population. The smaller the sample and the more heterogeneous the population, the larger this standard error will be. Conversely, the larger the sample and the more homogeneous the population, the smaller the standard error. Moreover, the total population has little bearing on the accuracy of your sample. You should also keep in mind that in a small sample a small increase in sample size reduces substantially the standard error. While the sample size you collect is partly determined by the statistical use you want to make of the data and the standard error you are willing to accept, in reality it is often determined by access to people and available time and money for fieldwork.

HOW CAN DATA BE ANALYSED?

Once the data has been collected there are several techniques for analysing and representing it. Using such techniques in conjunction with appropriate charts provides a powerful means for representing information. From the raw data collected the first step is to create a data set. Such a data set is normally entered into a software package. With today's large range of sophisticated but simple-to-use software packages (such as Excel or SPSS), once the data has been entered it is relatively straightforward for the computer to calculate the statistics and generate the graphs or tables (Barnes and Lewin, 2011; David and Sutton, 2011: Ch. 23–27;

Denscombe, 2010). Such relative simplicity in generating statistical results and graphs has highlighted the importance for the researcher to understand how and why the data should be represented by particular statistical measures on graphs and tables. While the computer can generate endless statistical measures from data, the researcher must explain and justify them to the reader. Briefly, then, the following are some of the main statistical measurements for representing quantitative data:

- *Central tendency:* The three measures of central tendency are mean, mode and median. The *mean* is the arithmetic average, *mode* the most frequently occurring value and *median* the middle-ranked observation. While central tendency analyses are very simple, they offer a powerful tool for representing data. Data such as average age, income, weight or height for any given population provide an immediate image to the reader (see Box 3.1). These statistical measures are often used for introducing a population to the reader.
- *Frequency distribution:* Used to illustrate the distribution of a single variable across categories and allows us to appreciate diversity alongside the above measures of central tendency. It can be used for both discrete and continuous data. The number of times the variable occurs in each category is recorded (Nichols, 1991: 84–86). Frequently that data is represented by graphs, including histograms and pie charts (see Box 3.1). Frequency distributions are also an excellent and simple way of introducing data. For example, to give an overview of an urban informal settlement, before entering into more specific issues, frequency distributions for income, age and education provide a 'snapshot' of the settlement and its diversity.
- *Dispersion:* Measurements of dispersion provide a picture of how the data is distributed around the central tendency – another important measure of diversity within a sample. For example, average income may be exactly the same for two villages closely located. However, one village may have a few very wealthy people with the rest being relatively poor, while the second village has everyone on roughly the same income. Such differences would not be revealed by the average income figure but would be by measurements of dispersion. It is possible to calculate the dispersion of data around the central tendency in several ways; however, the two most common are the use of the *range,* which measures the difference between the highest and lowest values in the distribution, and the *standard deviation*, which calculates the difference in a population between every observation and the mean (see Box 3.1). The deviations are represented by one standardised figure that allows comparison to be made with standard deviations of other populations.

Box 3.1 Simple descriptive statistics for a single variable: measurements of average income, 2010

There are different ways we can depict data statistically. The following examples use World Bank data for mean income by country. A total of 182 countries for which data was available are analysed for the year 2010 (http://devdata.worldbank.org/data-query/). Income data is given is current US dollars.

(Continued)

(Continued)

Central tendency

Mean income $11,821   The numerical average (total
                               Gross National Income divided
                               by total population for the 183
                               countries)

Mode $2,730   The most frequently occurring
                               value (this is the mean income
                               for three countries)

Median income: $4,260   The middle value (91 values are
                               greater and 91 are smaller)

Consider the worth of these three measurements. Which gives the best single picture of average incomes on a global scale and why?

Frequency distribution

The following diagram (Figure 3.1) presents a frequency histogram for different categories of income for the 182 countries. Note that the categories are not uniform (some cover a range of

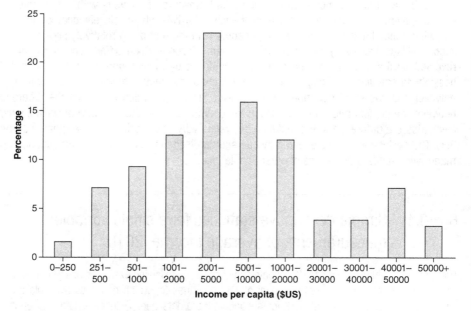

Figure 3.1   Frequency distribution of country mean income per capita, 2010

only $250, whilst others span $10,000 and one is open). Why might we use such uneven categories? What conclusions might we draw about world income distribution from this figure?

Dispersion

Range:	$180–$86,390	The lowest and highest values
Standard deviation:	$16,926	A statistical measurement to show average variation around the mean

Note that whilst the range gives a simple picture of variation, the standard deviation cannot be easily interpreted. Where we would see its use would be if we compared the standard deviation of two similar data sets (e.g., the variation of income in countries of Asia compared with those in Africa and Europe).

- *Cross-tabulation:* A simple means of examining the relationship between two variables, and is a continuation of the use of a frequency distribution. For each observation two variables are measured and set out in a table. A variation of the cross-tabulation is the use of a *scattergram*, which plots the two variables on a graph. However, the scattergram should only be used for representing variables that have a natural order.
- *Correlation coefficient:* Another means of measuring the relationship between two variables. In effect, the measurement of the correlation coefficient (using the Pearson r measurement) is the statistical equivalent of drawing a scattergram. The correlation coefficient is a single number in the range of -1 to 1 indicating the strength and direction of the relationship between two variables. When r = -1 there is a perfect negative relationship (as one variable increases, the other declines), when r = 1 there is a perfect positive relationship (as one increases, so does the other), while 0 indicates no relationship at all. An example of a positive relationship is between income and education, while there is usually a negative relationship between income size and infant mortality. The correlation coefficient can be illustrated and explained by drawing on its relationship with the scattergram. A scattergram could be constructed for a given population by graphing every observation as a dot on a scattergram for the variables income along the horizontal axis and education on the vertical axis (see Box 3.2). It is then possible to draw a line of best fit (the regression line). If there was a perfect positive relationship between income and education, all observations (points) would fall on the straight line moving upwards to the right and the correlation coefficient would be 1. The more the points are scattered away from the regression line, the weaker the relationship and the closer the number will tend to zero. At zero the points are perfectly scattered across the graph and there is no relationship between the two variables. In more sophisticated analyses, multiple regression can be used to test the relative strength of different variables.

Box 3.2   Measures of relationships between variables: average incomes and female life expectancy, 2010

Beyond simple description of data sets, we can also begin to analyse relationships. Here we consider the same data set for average income as in Box 3.1, but also consider its relationship with data for average female life expectancy at birth for the year 2010 (http://devdata.worldbank.org/data-query/).

Cross-tabulation

A scattergram (Figure 3.2) plots the data for each of 175 countries with income on the horizontal axis and life expectancy on the vertical. We imply that income (GNI per capita) is an 'independent' variable and that life expectancy is to some extent 'dependent' on this: that is, as income changes, there may be changes in life expectancy. The graph gives an interesting result from which we can infer some aspects of the relationship between income and life expectancy. We might expect that in wealthier countries people live longer, and this seems to be the case. However, this is not a simple linear relation: there seems to be a marked improvement in life expectancy as income increases at the lower end (up to about $5,000 per capita). Thereafter we seem to reach a threshold over about 70 years of age, and furthermore wealth is not as strongly translated into longer life spans.

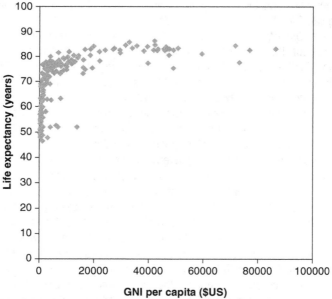

Figure 3.2   Female life expectancy and mean income per capita, 2010

Correlation coefficient

We can gain a better statistical measurement of the above data by employing the correlation coefficient. Applied to our data set, we get a correlation coefficient of 0.56. This indicates a positive and moderately strong relationship: as income increases so too does life expectancy. However, we have noted that the relationship changes around a per capita income of $5,000. If we calculate two correlation coefficients, one for the 95 countries with average incomes of $5,000 per capita and below and one for the 80 countries above that mark, we get coefficients of 0.67 and 0.46 respectively. In other words, up to $5,000 income per capita, there is a stronger relationship between income and life expectancy and this becomes weaker after the $5,000 threshold.

If we were to draw a best fit (regression) line on the above scattergram, we could find a weak straight line slope upwards from the left but a more accurate fit would come from a curved line moving upwards sharply from the left and then levelling out to the right.

- *Randomised control trials:* The international development community is increasingly focused on evaluating impacts of interventions, whether the interventions are by governments, NGOs, bilateral or multilateral organisations. Researchers and practitioners alike often use quantitative methods to measure the impact of interventions that range from immunisation, clean water supply, and housing improvement to micro-finance programmes. One technique centres on measuring the before-and-after impact of an intervention: that is, comparing the impact with and without the intervention. Economists tend to refer to the actual and the counterfactual: a comparison between what actually happened and what would have happened if the intervention had not occurred. A method to measure this borrows from the field of science, specifically, the experimental design of randomised control trials (RCT). The defining characteristic of a RCT is the random allocation of the intervention to only part of a group of subjects that have the same characteristics. The other part of the group becomes the control group. For example, from a large number of similar small businesses, half can be given micro-finance support while the other half receives no support. From this the researcher can measure what the impact of the micro-finance has been compared to those that did not receive any support. Such a study and other RCTs have been pioneered by the Poverty Action Lab (J-PAL) (Banerjee and Duflo, 2011). Other academic institutions using such techniques are the Innovations for Poverty Action (IPA) network. While RCTs are usually large, expensive and long-term experiments involving quite a number of researchers, a growing number of Masters and PhD students are also applying this method.

The above list is not exhaustive and there are a range of other statistical tests that are possible. Texts such as Babbie (2010), Barnes and Lewin (2011), Bryman and Cramer (1995) and de Vaus (2002) give more detail on these techniques and their application.

From the above discussion and examples it is clear that quantitative data collection offers several advantages in doing research in developing countries. If precise, objective and replicable answers are needed, then quantitative data collection and research offers an appropriate methodology.

LIMITATIONS AND PITFALLS

We have seen that quantitative techniques can have much value in research in development contexts. Used well, they can become a powerful set of tools in describing conditions, analysing problems and informing policy. However, it is easy to use them badly or inappropriately. The following issues are some of the most commonly encountered problems (see also Moses and Knutsen, 2007).

REPRESENTATION

One of the most frequent criticisms of quantitative methods – and one of the greatest dangers in their use – is the issue of representation. We have seen above that some quantitative methods allow us to make conclusions about a large population based on our analysis of a smaller sample. Yet, unless we are scrupulous about the selection of our sample, we soon run into problems over the nature of that representation. Can men speak for women (or vice-versa)? Can the rich speak for the poor? And who speaks for children, or the disabled or the elderly? Chambers (1983: 13–25) reminds us that much research done in rural areas of developing countries is subject to a range of biases that mean many people are excluded from the researcher's work, typically women, those in remote areas, the poor, the elderly, the young and the disabled.[3] Similarly, feminist researchers (e.g. Falconer Al-Hindi, 2001) have criticised the way much research has for long been sexist because it has excluded or marginalised women in the selection of respondents, the formulation of questions asked, the interviewing practices and even the research design. If we do not ask the right people the right sort of questions in the right sort of way, we will not be able to draw general conclusions no matter how good our data looks.

INFERRING PROCESS

The collection and analysis of numbers is a powerful research tool and can allow us to draw conclusions and inferences from our data. This is particularly the case when we see strong relationships between data sets – correlation and regression analyses give us an indication of the nature and strength of such relationships. It is then tempting to suggest what the underlying processes might be. For example, it is common to see a close and negative relationship between rate of population growth and income: as income increases, population growth rates fall. So we might reasonably conclude that a good way of lowering the birth rate is to encourage economic growth. However, we could also see it the other way around (as many have done): a good way of encouraging economic growth is to limit population growth. Whatever the answer might be, it should be apparent that our quantitative data do not give us a clear scientific indication of process, even though the evidence of a strong relationship is compelling. The leap from correlation to causation should be made with great caution (see Box 3.3).

Box 3.3   Relationships between variables: life expectancy and fertility, 2010

In our examples earlier with scattergrams, we saw how we might be able to infer relationships between income levels and life expectancy. We saw a reasonable positive correlation between the two and had cause to suggest that increased incomes could be associated with – maybe help contribute to – longer life spans.

Here we consider two similar data sets for the year 2010: first, the same data for female life expectancy; and second, data for fertility (the measurement of the average number of live births per woman in a country) (http://devdata.worldbank.org/data-query/). These yield the scattergram shown in Figure 3.3 and a correlation coefficient of –0.83.

First indications from the scattergram and correlation coefficient suggest to us that there is a strong negative relationship between the two: as the fertility rate increases, life expectancy falls. Note that the correlation coefficient of –0.84 is stronger than that relating female life expectancy to income (0.56). We might be tempted to conclude that fertility (how many children women have) has a stronger impact on life expectancy than income. Yet this makes no intuitive sense and we are wrong to infer such causation from this relationship. In fact, both life expectancy and fertility rate are related to income: that is, both perhaps have a similar underlying cause that is not apparent from our statistical analysis.

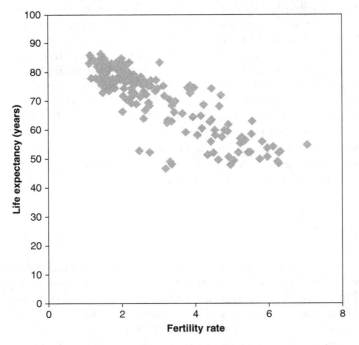

Figure 3.3   Female life expectancy and the fertility rate, 2010

THE MEANING OF DATA

Quantitative methods are attractive because there is an air of precision about the numbers we collect and analyse. We can say with an impression of authority that 34.7 per cent of respondents shared a particular characteristic – much more authoritative than a vague statement about the diversity in the life histories of ten people interviewed at length!

Other difficulties arise when we ask people to give numbers for things they have little concept of in a numerical sense. In the West we are used to dealing with personal and household incomes: we know what our salaries are and we are used to making tax returns. Therefore, we seek and expect to find the same information from rural people in developing countries: we ask them their annual income. Faced with incomprehension – for regular salaries and wages could be rare for those we interview – we might resort to building up a picture of income sources over time ('How much do you usually get for selling your vegetables at the market?' followed by 'How many times a year do you sell your vegetables at the market?'). However, these are similarly problematic – people see money as something that comes and goes and the very idea of an annual (or weekly) income may be completely foreign. So our analyses of such data need to be treated with a great deal of caution.

Even fairly obvious quantitative data might not be all it seems in a different cultural context (Bradburd, 1998: 6–11). Researcher Margaret Chung recounts the story of her PhD research on women's fertility in Fiji (Chung, 1991: 105), when asking a simple question to women ('How many children have you given birth to?') surprisingly led to different responses from the same person at different times. She soon found that this was not so odd: a woman may have given birth to ten children, two of which may have died in infancy – are they still counted? Are stillbirths counted? Are children who are 'given' to close relatives to raise as their own counted? What about children born out of wedlock who may have been raised by others since they were very young? Demography is as much an art as a science!

Given these problems with collecting and analysing much of the research data we use when investigating development issues, it is worth remembering Lockwood's view that all data obtained by asking questions are 'qualitative' (1992: 176).

TOO MUCH DATA

It is easy to be seduced by the attraction of quantitative data, especially when it appears easy to collect. It is tempting to add 'just another question' to a questionnaire survey, and in the field it is common to adopt the vacuum-cleaner method: gather every bit of data that is available and sort it out later. This can have advantages – it may allow you to collect data that originally you did not think were critical but which later turned out to have value – but it can easily lead to problems. Time in the field and in data analysis can extend beyond practical limits; questionnaires explode into large unwieldy exercises that alienate respondents; much data ends up being unused; and, critically, the focus of research can become lost under the weight of data. In data collection it is always wise to keep in mind the central research question(s). If the data being sought does not contribute to answering that question, it should not be collected. Simply collecting more data does not mean a better research outcome: it may mean the opposite.[4]

GARBAGE-IN-GARBAGE-OUT

An old computer adage is 'garbage-in-garbage-out'. No matter how sophisticated one's methods of analysis or how complex one's statistical techniques, the results will be worthless if the raw data is flawed. Furthermore, sophisticated techniques are sometimes used to hide questionable data.

Therefore, researchers need to be wary of their data: a first priority is to ensure that the data to be collected will be authentic, valid and appropriate. It should have meaning – for those from whom it is collected as much as for the researcher. It should be inclusive – it should include all sectors of the target population, even those who appear less visible or 'important' than others. It should be truthful – fictions and half-facts as well as incomplete or incorrect observations easily creep in when working in different cultural contexts. And it should be accurate. Only when there is confidence in the quality of the data can attention turn to refining the methods of analysis.

CONCLUSIONS

In doing social science research in developing countries, quantitative data analysis is usually best used in conjunction with other qualitative techniques. Quantitative data analysis is strong at describing the 'what' but weak at explaining the 'why'. It is good at predicting what will happen, the magnitude of changes and the relationship between variables, but not why things occur. Therefore, when doing research in developing countries, quantitative methods are best used when integrated into a more holistic research design. Nevertheless, the degree to which quantitative data collection and analysis is used depends to a great extent on the nature of the research question and the preference of the researcher.

To conclude, several points should be borne in mind when using quantitative methods in a developing country context:

- *Don't be intimidated:* Statistics and statistical analysis, not to mention the particular problems faced in the collection and use of these in developing countries, may seem daunting especially to those without specialist training in statistics. Yet quantitative techniques need not be complex and they remain amongst the most important tools for researchers in Development Studies.
- *Don't get too complicated:* Often the most valuable and insightful use of quantitative data comes from fairly basic descriptive statistics.

- *Let the questions determine the methods:* Quantitative techniques, like any other, are merely means to conduct our research. Methods must be driven by the questions we wish to answer and the information we need to answer those questions (see Chapter 2). Avoid the temptation to apply a newly-learned and fashionable technique merely because you know it, rather than because it will enhance significantly what you are trying to find out.
- *Don't out-run your competence:* Quantitative techniques run the full gamut of tools from some of the simple descriptive methods described earlier to very sophisticated multi-factor analytical tools. As researchers we have to weigh up the costs and time of mastering such techniques against the benefit of what they bring to our work. Too often we can spend too long learning methods that will be of marginal use to our overall research task.
- *Suspect the data:* Especially in a developing country context, we have seen how the data we collect and analyse may be seriously flawed. Bad data, no matter how complex our methods of analysis, will produce bad results. Common sense and healthy cynicism are good allies when questioning the data you collect (or the data collected by others) and their value for analysis.

Summary

- The suitability of quantitative techniques depends on the nature of the research questions we wish to answer and the information we need to answer those questions.
- If precise, objective and replicable answers are needed, then quantitative data collection and research offers an appropriate methodology.
- Quantitative data analysis is strong at describing the 'what' but weak at explaining the 'why'.
- In doing social science research in developing countries, quantitative data analysis is usually best used in conjunction with some qualitative techniques.
- No matter how sophisticated one's methods of analysis or how complex one's statistical techniques, the results will be worthless if the raw data is flawed.

Questions for reflection

- What data do you need to answer the research question or test your hypothesis?
- What are you hoping that the data will show and are you asking the right questions to find this information?
- Has the data you want already been collected by others?
- How will the quantitative data you collect be complemented with qualitative and other secondary data?
- What type of instrument and techniques will you use to collect the data?
- Who will collect the data and what training will they need?
- Have you piloted/tested the data collection instrument (e.g., survey) to see if it 'works'?

- What type of analysis do you want to use on the data and will you be able to do this on the data you're collecting?
- If you find relationships in the data how will you explain causality and what information would you need for that?
- In the end, you have to ask yourself: have I collected and arranged my data and material in such a way that it tells a valid and verifiable 'story' to the reader?

RECOMMENDED READINGS

Babbie, E. R. (2010). *The Practice of Social Research* (12th edn). Belmont, CA: Wadsworth Cengage.

A comprehensive general text with detailed chapters on a range of quantitative techniques and issues in quantitative research. An excellent guide.

Barker, D. (2006). Field surveys and inventories. In V. Desai and R. Potter (eds), *Doing Development Research* (pp. 130–143). London: Sage.

This book chapter outlines the basic issues in completing field surveys and inventories, and gives some examples from three research contexts.

David, M., and Sutton, C. D. (2011). *Social Research: An Introduction* (2nd edn). London: Sage.

Comprehensive introduction to social research methods, including ethnography, quantitative data collection and quantitative data analysis.

de Vaus, D. A. (2002). *Surveys in Social Research* (5th edn). St. Leonards: Allen and Unwin.

A general text with helpful chapters on surveys and questionnaires.

Denscombe, M. (2010). *The Good Research Guide: For Small-Scale Social Research Projects* (4th edn). Maidenhead: McGraw-Hill/Open University Press.

An introductory book on the basics of social research, covering research strategies, methods and analysis.

Findlay, A. M. (2006). The importance of census and other secondary data in development studies. In V. Desai and R. Potter (eds), *Doing Development Research* (pp. 262–272). London: Sage.

This book chapter discusses why secondary data is important in development research, and the problems, strengths and weaknesses of working with this type of data.

Holland, J., and Campbell, J. (2005). *Methods in Development Research: Combining Qualitative and Quantitative Approaches*. Cambridge: ITDG.

Written for development academics, practitioners and policy makers, this book discusses best practice mixed methods research.

NOTES

1. For an excellent critical essay on the use of quantitative techniques, see Caws (1989). See also Holland and Campbell (2005) for a development practitioner's view of combining qualitative and quantitative techniques in development research.
2. See Adams and Megaw (1997: 222–224) for tips on questionnaire design and administration.
3. See Chapter 10 for a discussion on appropriate ways of conducting research with marginalised groups.
4. See the discussion on leaving the field in Chapter 11.

4

QUALITATIVE RESEARCH

ROCHELLE STEWART-WITHERS, GLENN BANKS,
ANDREW MCGREGOR AND LITEA MEO-SEWABU

Qualitative research has grown out of a plethora of 'intellectual and disciplinary traditions' (Mason, 2002: 2). Qualitative research should be viewed as both art and science, thereby ensuring that there is a balance between rigour and creativity (Patton, 2002). The term 'qualitative research' broadly encapsulates approaches to research which focus on the human experience and seek to understand the social world, recognising this world for its richness in context, detail and experience (Mason, 2002; also see Bailey, 2007; Denzin and Lincoln, 2011).

As a method of inquiry, qualitative research seeks to collect or generate data in natural settings. That is, qualitative researchers generally go to particular locations or sites ('the field') to study the people, communities and societies that reside there. Hence qualitative research can take place in rural villages or in corporate offices, in slums or new housing settlements, in health centres or schools, with NGOs, businesses or government organisations, or in a range of other locations: anywhere where people live, work or visit. These investigations in naturalistic settings result in rich, in-depth information which provides the potential for understanding the complexities of social life (Patton, 2002).

The nature of this understanding means qualitative research typically seeks to produce theory rather than test it (Bryman and Burgess, 1999). 'Where quantitative researchers seek causal determination, prediction, and generalization of findings, qualitative researchers seek instead illumination, understanding, and extrapolation to similar situations' (Hoepfl, 1997: 13). Because qualitative research is about generating and building up theory as opposed to being hypothesis-driven, it works in an inductive manner (from the specific to the general) rather than deductive (moving down from the general to the particular).

While this chapter cannot do full justice to the diversity, depth and breadth of qualitative research, the purpose is to introduce the reader to the art of qualitative investigation, show its relevance to development research, and unpack some of the ways qualitative research differs from quantitative approaches. Not only does a qualitative mode of inquiry lend itself to particular methods of data collection, such as observation, interviews ('conversations with purpose') or focus groups, it also requires acknowledgement of, and commitment to, specific ways of understanding the nature of the social world and the ways in which this can be observed and understood (Hesse-Biber and Leavy, 2010: 5; Mason, 2002).

WHEN SHOULD WE USE QUALITATIVE RESEARCH?

We should use a qualitative approach when we are looking to describe, explore or explain social phenomena. Qualitative research typically seeks understanding of complex social phenomena that takes place in a naturalistic setting, where the goal is to both understand and find meaning, and perhaps bring about change. It asks 'what is this?' and 'what is happening here?' (Hesse-Biber and Leavy, 2010: 39). In asking these questions it seeks to better understand an issue, or gain new insights into an already well-known problem. Qualitative research can help us explore people's attitudes, interpretations, behaviours, value systems, concerns, motivations, aspirations, culture or lifestyle (Marshall and Rossman, 2006).

There are common characteristics belonging to the different forms of qualitative inquiry (see Table 4.1). As can be seen in Table 4.1, the role of the researcher is paramount, especially as the researcher is the key 'instrument' in the research process.

QUALITATIVE RESEARCH ATTRIBUTES

Associated with the characteristics of qualitative research are a number of specific attributes. We examine three such attributes: the researcher as the prime 'instrument' of data collection and analysis, the positionality of the researcher, and issues of power differentials between the researcher and the researched.

RESEARCHER AS INSTRUMENT

In qualitative research the researcher is the central instrument in the research process:

[T]he human element of qualitative inquiry is both its strength and weakness – its strength in allowing human insight and experience to blossom into new understandings and ways of seeing the world, its potential weakness in being so heavily dependent on the inquirer's skill, training, intellect, discipline, and creativity. Because the researcher is the instrument of qualitative inquiry, the quality of the result depends heavily on the qualities of that human being. (Patton, 2002: 513)

Table 4.1 Characteristics of qualitative research

Characteristic	Examples/Explanation
Seeks to explore phenomena.	Social change in a rural or urban setting; attitudes and behaviours in institutional settings; understanding local processes.
Takes place in a naturalistic environment.	Villages, cities, organisations, institutions.
The goal is to understand the 'how', 'what' and 'why', finding meaning.	Getting to the meaning behind figures, behaviours, processes.
Is emergent and flexible in design.	Might start with key questions to explore rather than being tied to a fixed hypothesis.
Subscribes to inductive analysis, which is done by the researcher.	Begins with researcher's experience and observations.
Is interpretive, so the researcher seeks to elucidate.	Not simply about description (of people, places or processes).
Views the social world and phenomena holistically.	Seeks understanding of the interrelationships between peoples, contexts and processes.
The researcher is engaged in the research, values are present and made explicit.	Researcher is typically aware of and reflects on own positionality.
Often focussed on specific groups or communities rather than larger populations.	Lends itself to purposive and snowball sampling, rather than random sampling of a population; generally works from the specific up to the broader questions.
Generates rich, thick description.	Social detail and context is seen as critical to understanding.
Findings tend to be unique and context/case specific; to generalise the findings is not the goal.	Mostly theory generating, not theory testing.

Researchers thus need to understand and clearly acknowledge their role in the co-construction of knowledge. Emphasis should be placed on 'the researcher being an *active learner* who can tell the story from the participants' view rather than as an "expert" who passes judgment on participants' (Creswell, 1998: 18). Active learning involves being attentive to people's local realities, and genuinely hearing the voices of those telling the story. This requires awareness of our own personal subjectivities and the ways in which our actions may impact the research process and knowledge production. Hence an understanding of one's positionality and any personal values and biases you may bring to the research is fundamental.

POSITIONALITY AND REFLEXIVITY

Positionality is acknowledgement by the researcher that her or his own position in relation to the research 'may influence aspects of the study, such as the types of information collected, or the way in which it is interpreted' (Sultana, 2007: 376). When considering positionality we need to consider our own gender, religion, class, sexual orientation, race or ethnicity, or other more personal attributes such as age, life experiences or history. These may influence who we can talk to (in some cultures male researchers may find it difficult to speak directly to younger women: in others, younger female researchers may find males resistant to being included), or the type of material collected (young outsiders may not be trusted with sensitive cultural material), and hence the research will only ever provide a partial picture of the social world being interrogated. This need not be a weakness of the research, so long as we acknowledge it.

Reflexivity is the process of reflecting on 'self, process, and representation, and critically examining power relations and politics in the research process, and researcher accountability in data collection and interpretation' (Sultana, 2007: 376). To be a good qualitative researcher involves being aware of your positionality in relation to the research context and relationships, and requires continuous 'critical self-scrutiny by the researcher' (Mason, 2002: 7). Reflective diaries or fieldwork journals can be a good means for regularly practising reflexivity in the field (see also Chapter 7), considering the meaning behind unexpected encounters in your day, and the development of relationships with your research participants.

POWER IN RESEARCH RELATIONSHIPS

One of the main features of qualitative research is that it can involve close, dynamic and often complex relationships between the researcher and the research participants. This is different from quantitative research, where there may be little direct contact between the researcher and participants (e.g., with an online survey). Development Studies research, with its bias towards deeper understandings and emancipatory practices, requires more direct human interaction and therefore the researcher needs to place importance on the building of relationships. This is especially the case where the data collection involves undertaking in-depth face-to-face interviews and requires responses to often quite personal questions. While research participants are often viewed as having the knowledge that the researcher is seeking, due to their lived experience of an event (e.g., having survived a disaster or living next to an industrial plant) or being part of a social/cultural/political context (e.g., being part of a community organisation), the process of conducting enquiry based on relationships also introduces issues of power.

The widely held assumption of these relationships is that the researcher holds power over the researched (Fontes, 1998). For a range of reasons this issue is often more complex. Hence participants can find many ways to control participation (by simply not showing up for agreed interviews), or by providing partial or misleading (sometimes deliberately so) information (see Chapter 9 and 10; Stewart-Withers, 2007: 110). However, we also need to be aware of the fact that the researcher–researched relationship is situated within broader social structures (Gottfried, 1996). Relational research brings forth potential power biases not only in terms of who the gatekeepers of knowledge are (Grant et al., 1987) but in terms of what facts are selected and which ones are excluded.

DATA COLLECTION METHODS

When thinking about data collection it is helpful to ask some key questions. First, what information do I have already and what other information will I need? Second, how will I collect this data, from whom, and what other data sources will I use? These can include material from or on people, places, events, groups, time periods, organisations, encounters, and interactions. Third, you might wonder how many people you should speak to, and how to judge when you have enough data. *Qualitative* researchers do not usually begin with a fixed number of participants in mind. Instead they typically continue to collect data until saturation, which means that repetition is occurring in terms of the data being collected, and no new findings are emerging (O'Leary, 2010). Fourth, qualitative researchers need to consider how they will record, store and organise this data (see Chapter 5).

There are a wide range of methods or techniques that are common in qualitative research (see Table 4.2). The most common of these can be grouped in the following ways: interviews, including semi-structured interviews, focus groups or life histories; observations, such as undertaking participant observation or keeping a fieldwork journal; and review of materials and documents such as policy documents or audio-visual materials (Locke et al., 2010; Marshall and Rossman, 2006).

Table 4.2 Qualitative data collection techniques

Technique	Description	Potential problems
Interviewing	Interviews can take a range of forms, from open conversations, to semi-structured discussions around particular topics, to highly structured questionnaires (although it is hard for the latter to elicit good qualitative data). Interviews do not have to be face to face as researchers are now maximising technology and using Skype, email, Facebook or instant messaging (see Chapter 5).	Recording the data is the difficulty here. Remember that not everyone will allow their interview to be audio-recorded, particularly if the topic is sensitive. In these instances one may have to take notes. However, writing while people are speaking is off-putting, and it can be challenging for the writer to keep up. Thus straight after the interview the researcher may need to find a private space and make as many notes as possible while the memory is fresh. Recording then transcribing or summarising also takes time.
Focus groups	A group discussion of a particular issue where it is instructive to learn from the group dynamics and the way people discuss things as much as what they say.	Setting up a focus group, time, place, date which suits people can be complex due to people's busy lives; it is better to see if the group can be run as part of an existing group. Best undertaken when the researcher knows the people or situations well enough to interpret the group dynamics. Group facilitation is harder than it looks.

(Continued)

Table 4.2 *(Continued)*

Technique	Description	Potential problems
Conversation and discourse analysis	Intimate and detailed recording of conversation and talk where personal expressions, pauses and delivery are recorded and analysed.	A research tool which requires much effort. Conversation analysis is part of discourse analysis, a diffuse term which covers several disciplines (Bauer and Gaskell, 2000; Gee and Handford, 2011; Gill, 2000). The researcher must ensure that the techniques of discourse analysis to be used are appropriate for the type of questions to be asked.
Fieldwork diaries	A day-to-day record of events, experiences, work or observations kept by the researcher or an informant.	Being a good diarist is not easy. Read published diaries to see what makes for good reading and consider whether they would also make good fieldwork notes. Have a look at Malinowski's (1967) private diary of fieldwork from Papua New Guinea in the 1920s, for example, or Rabinow's (2007) fieldwork notes from Morocco. Practice also before going into the field (Emerson et al., 1995; see also the seminal text by Briggs, 1986).
Life histories and oral histories	Audio-recorded histories of people, places and events. A detailed literature exists giving advice about how to undertake this (Miles & Crush, 1993; Perks & Thomson, 1988; Slim & Thompson, 1993). This technique provides unique insights into unrecorded situations and alternative views on written histories (see Cross & Barker, 1991; Kothari & Hulme, 2004).	Be prepared to transcribe the recordings so that other people can have access to the raw data. These data should be treated as any other – sceptically, looking for corroboration.
Photograph, film and video and documents	Texts such as letters, archives and diaries make useful primary and secondary sources. So too are photographs, film and video (which are different sorts of text). Using templates can also be helpful when undertaking a document review so one knows what to look for as opposed to just aimlessly reviewing.	Detailed cataloguing of notes is required if the images and documents are voluminous, otherwise it will be hard to trace which document provided what information.
Participant observation	This requires the researcher to immerse themselves in the place/societies they are studying. By living closely with the people being studied, it is possible to empathise with their way of looking at and interpreting the world. The note-taking involved is rigorous and one is required constantly to test impressions and ideas.	Some people's worlds are hard and unpleasant to experience. It requires great effort and determination to learn the language and understand what people mean. All the techniques mentioned above can be used in participant observation. The skill is combining structured data collection with relaxing and letting things happen.
Structured observation	More purposeful form of observation. Involves determining in advance the phenomena to be observed (e.g. how different sectors of a community participate in a community meeting) and the various categories of activity or behaviour that the researcher is seeking to observe.	One must know beforehand the context and forms of behaviours that the observation will focus on – can be less flexible and focus can mean other significant elements can be missed. Might be seen as more extractive.

Source: Adapted from Brockington and Sullivan (2003: 58–9)

We can think of different methods in relation to different sorts of inquiry:

- To find out what people do in public: *observation.*
- To find out what people do in private: *interviews or questionnaires/surveys.*
- To find out what people think, feel or believe: *interviews, questionnaires/surveys or document analysis.*

While Table 4.2 provides a good overview of the most common qualitative data collection techniques, you might like to consider if there are associated culturally specific techniques that would work in your particular research context. Box 4.1 provides an example of *talanoa* research, which is gaining popularity due to its cultural relevance to research in parts of the Pacific.

Box 4.1 A mix of interviews and story-telling through *talanoa* research in the Pacific

Talanoa can be defined in Fijian, Tongan and Samoan as sharing a conversation and knowledge (Nabobo-Baba, 2006; Otsuka, 2005; Vaioleti, 2006). It is also a specific indigenous approach to data gathering used in parts of the Pacific, but bears similarities with other indigenous cultures in which there are culturally defined forums for informal gathering and discussion.

Nabobo-Baba defines talanoa 'as a process in which two or more peoples talk together or in which one person tells a story to an audience of peoples who are largely listeners' (2006: 27). Otsuka states that 'talanoa asks researchers to establish a good interpersonal relationship and rapport with ethnic Fijian participants', adding that 'talanoa research expects researchers and participants to share not only their time and interests but also emotions' (2005: 2). The relationships established must be trustful if such emotions are to be shared.

Talanoa can take place in both formal and informal settings. Talanoa in the formal setting within the context of my research took place when adhering to the cultural protocols associated with entry into the land. Most of the time, however, when conducting research on the cultural constructs around women's health and well-being in Fiji, I (Litea) took part in talanoa in an informal setting with my participants. This meant that all social status within Fijian society, including age differences, were put aside and participants were made to feel at ease and candidly discuss experiences. These talanoa included stories, metaphors, jokes and explanations that allowed other participants to agree, disagree or tell their own stories in relation to what was being discussed.

My role as the facilitator of the talanoa was to guide the conversations according to the open-ended questions I had prepared. Rather than reciting the questions, I had a fair idea of what information I wanted to gather and as stories were being told I would look for cues, asking participants to elaborate or adding to their stories or sharing jokes with a purpose in mind. As mentioned, talanoa can be carried out formally and informally, with the formal process being more time-specific, so it may continue for 30 minutes to an hour or more, depending on the topic of the talanoa. An informal talanoa on the other hand could be compared to an on-going conversation, whereby from the time I arrived at the research site to the time I left, the conversation helped with the knowledge production or helped me to make sense of daily

(Continued)

(Continued)

realities. At the end of the talanoa, it often felt like we were all just relating stories back and forth, but in reality the purpose of the study had been achieved.

These conversations are often filled with laughter, but there were instances where stories were relayed to me in confidence and, once the issues were discussed thoroughly, the laughter would begin once again. I felt that in all of my talanoa sessions, a sense of trust had developed and women were able to share openly.

Source: Meo-Sewabu (2014)

MIXED METHODS

As stated above, qualitative research is most appropriate when looking to explain, explore or find meaning, and we have also outlined various research methods which lend themselves to qualitative methodologies. However, qualitative and quantitative methods should not be seen as mutually exclusive approaches to learning as each can complement the other, depending on the research questions that are being asked (Brockington and Sullivan, 2003: 72). Hence appreciating the potential value and insights of both qualitative and quantitative research is important (see also Brannen, 2005; Creswell, 2011; Elwood, 2010; Mason, 2006; Onwuegbuzie and Leech, 2005). We also advocate that despite often differing epistemological assumptions being attributed to quantitative and qualitative approaches, there is space for the intersection and utilisation of a mixed methods approach that recognises the value of working with different types of data.

Using a mix of complementary methods from both paradigms can make for an approach to research which enriches understanding and adds rigour: 'Different techniques are appropriate to different settings ... combining both quantitative and qualitative work can strengthen both' (White, 2002: 512). As each approach comes with its own inherent strengths and weaknesses, using a mixed methods approach can provide the researcher with space to capitalise on the strengths of each while also mitigating the other's weak points.

It is also important to note that simply labelling a combination of approaches 'mixed methods' does not by itself make for 'better' research: a lot of attention needs to be paid to the rationale for why and how a mix of methods can provide a fuller understanding or more reliable findings (see Box 4.2). While some researchers will always ascribe to epistemological purity, we need to choose the types of methods that are appropriate for collecting data on the research questions we might be interested in and to know how to combine different types of data into powerful and relevant analyses (Creswell, 2011). Regardless of the type of approach adopted, we should also critically reflect on the data generated: does it make sense and do we as researchers think it is valid, have we in fact answered our research questions or achieved the aim of our research?

Box 4.2 Mixing methods around mine sites in Papua New Guinea

As part of a team of researchers, I (Glenn) was involved in a number of household surveys around large-scale mine sites in Papua New Guinea, and Papua Province in Indonesia (see Banks, 2000: 13). Part of the rationale for this work was that little was known regarding the nature, scale and extent of social and economic transformation in the communities affected by mining, and so some basic descriptive material on the socio-economic status of households was an important prerequisite before deeper forms of analysis could be carried out. As a result, the household survey instrument I designed consisted of a mix of structured questions (around household size and composition, access to different benefit streams and gardening sites, house size, materials and condition, water supply etc.) and semi-structured, open questions on the experience of different aspects of the changes that the households had been through.

The mix of questions generated both quantitative material suitable for basic forms of comparative analysis and graphic presentation, and qualitative data that reflected, in narrative forms, the felt experience of living through the transformations that the large-scale mines had wrought. This combination of question types then allowed me to describe and analyse broad patterns of change (through the quantitative material) and also provide, in the words of the affected community, much deeper and richer descriptions of these changes from the people who had experienced them.

EXAMPLES OF QUALITATIVE APPROACHES TO RESEARCH IN DEVELOPMENT STUDIES

The term 'qualitative research' covers a diverse range of approaches, including some that specifically seek to cede control over the research process to the subjects of the research, and others that target the broader empowerment of the participants. This section will focus specifically on participatory research, ethnographic research and an indigenous approach to research.

PARTICIPATORY APPROACHES

Participatory approaches are popular within development fieldwork. Encompassing a wide range of strategies and techniques, active stakeholder participation within research processes is now an expectation rather than an exception. This means that everyone from the World Bank and NGOs through to university researchers purport to 'do' participatory research.

Participatory research is strongly influenced by Friere's (1972) work on conscientisation, which saw research as a way of generating knowledge *with* communities that would ultimately lead to their empowerment through informed political action and social transformation. These ideas, along with grassroots development theories and participatory methods more generally, have led to communities being seen as subjects rather than objects of research. Unlike many other forms of research, the success of participatory approaches is often assessed in terms of community empowerment rather than the information gathered (Cornwall, 2008).

Within development, participatory approaches are strongly associated with the work of Robert Chambers, who has spent his career devising ways of resisting extractive top-down research methods in order to put 'the last first' (Chambers, 1983) and 'the first last' (Lareau, 1996). Chambers was one of the people behind the emergence of rapid rural appraisal (RRA) in the 1970s. This was as a mixed methods response to the large-scale, time-consuming quantitative surveys that had dominated development fieldwork. RRA techniques created a space where innovative research techniques such as focus groups, transect walks, mapping, ranking and community biographies were seen as acceptable. However, RRA was primarily driven by concerns about the time demands of large-scale surveys rather than concerns about power relations, and as a result was still fundamentally extractive in nature.

Participatory rural appraisal (PRA) differs, at least in theory, by prioritising community learning and subsequent empowerment and action as key research outcomes (Chambers, 1994a). A core idea of PRA is to 'hand over the stick' to rural populations, and increasingly urban populations as well, to pursue their own futures. Rather than extracting data for expert analysis, PRA sees outsiders as 'conveners and facilitators, the insiders actors and analysts' (Chambers, 1994b: 1263).

PRA has been particularly popular amongst non-governmental organisations (NGOs) within development, and many of the techniques have evolved through experimentation and South–South collaboration. As a consequence there are a wide range of innovative practices associated with participatory research, a sample of which is listed in Box 4.3. It is beyond the scope of this chapter to explain these techniques in any detail: interested readers are encouraged to follow up with PRA manuals (e.g. Kanwat and Kumar, 2011; Kumar, 2002). The techniques are diverse but share some commonalities. These include:

- a commitment to empower local actors within development;
- respect for local knowledge, worldviews and the ability of local communities to analyse their own realities;
- self-reflectivity and equality between researchers and participants;
- researchers as convenors, catalysts and facilitators for mutual learning;
- an inclusive rather than exclusive environment that involves marginalised groups; and
- low-technology visualisation tools and techniques that are open-ended, experiential, creative and enjoyable (Chambers, 1994a, 1994b; Kanwat and Kumar, 2011; Kumar, 2002).

Researchers are encouraged to live with the communities while PRA activities take place and collaboratively plan and initiate activities that the community can use long after the research process is complete.

Recent innovations in PRA have combined modern technologies with the accessible low-tech methodologies described in Box 4.3. Computers and geographic information system (GIS) hardware often accompany PRA activities with a focus on a quick electronic recording of the material generated. This reflects the commitment of practitioners to share the materials generated by PRA with the communities who participated – rather than leaving communities with little more than memories as is all too common in extractive development research. Participatory GIS mapping of customary land use and the production of electronic maps, for example, can be an important resource for communities seeking to protect their village boundaries (see, e.g., McKinnon, 2010).

It is not surprising given the widespread popularity of PRA that it has attracted considerable critique and lively debate (see Cooke and Kothari, 2001; Lee, 1995). Some critics focus on the short timeframe of PRA, contrasting it negatively to more in-depth large-scale survey techniques or long-term anthropological ethnographic work (Richards, 1995). Others, including PRA practitioners, are concerned about maintaining quality as the methods have disseminated around the world and through unlikely institutions (e.g. Cornwall and Pratt, 2011; Lareau, 1996: 8). Others have cautioned against romanticising the community focus within PRA. Most PRA techniques work at the community scale through public meetings and group activities, valorising local knowledge over that produced by outsiders. However, with an emphasis on consensus there is a risk that such approaches may replicate or hide local power relations and associated inequalities (Francis, 2001). Rather than challenging local power structures, PRA can reinforce and normalise these (see Kothari, 2001).

Other constraints such as time, language, distance and inexperience may also work against research achieving its empowering goals. PRA can place extra burdens on marginal groups who already have busy lives. In a study of PRA practitioners, Cornwall and Pratt (2011) identify a range of strategies communities have developed to avoid PRA, including one case of a community so frustrated with regularly having to be involved in PRA mapping exercises that they simply started presenting the same weather-proof social map to each new PRA team!

Such criticisms are not intended to turn researchers away from PRA. Instead they are mentioned in the spirit of constructive critique. PRA, like any other methodology, has its strengths and weaknesses and these should be carefully considered when designing and conducting research. Newer approaches (and acronyms) including participatory action research (PAR) and participatory learning and action (PLA) have continued to develop and expand the range and depth of participatory methodologies. Both have similar goals of seeking to empower participants to pursue social transformation through participatory methodologies. A key difference, however, is that while PLA places more emphasis on community learning and empowerment aspects of the process (Brockington and Sullivan, 2003), PAR more directly engages politics and social theory, with a focus on how the research will inspire change (Kindon et al., 2007).

PRA, PAR and PLA often share the same methods, a number of which are summarised in Box 4.3.

Box 4.3   Examples of participatory methods

In Kumar's (2002) comprehensive manual, 28 PRA methods are grouped according to whether they focus on space, time or relations. Some techniques are summarised here.

Space-related PRA methods

Social map: This activity can be carried out on large sheets of paper or on the ground. Social mapping brings people together to map the social dimensions of their locality from a bird's eye view. The focus is on houses and infrastructure; other things like income, food security, children at school, single-parent households and so on can also be mapped. Large groups of people, including children, can participate with facilitation oriented towards reflection on social issues within the community.

Transect walk: Transect walks provide a cross-sectional view of different agro-ecological zones. Vegetation and land types, community uses, ownership, key management issues, water sources and so forth can all be discussed as the researcher walks with two or three local participants along a path across the land. The team collaboratively draws the different zones informing the researcher about agro-ecological issues.

Time-related PRA methods

Daily activity schedule: In this activity different social groups (separated by gender, age, wealth, ethnicity, etc.) map out their usual day. Using cards, pen and paper or chalk on a floor, the facilitator asks small groups to draw their normal activities and arrange in a timeline from morning till night. The task is useful in generating discussions about gender roles and workloads and the burdens (and solutions) some social groups have.

Dream map: In this activity participants are asked to draw a diagram of their current situation and then produce a dream map of the future. Sometimes participants are also asked to devise pathways to this desired goal. Dream maps can be done as a group or by sub-groups within the locality to heighten awareness about difference and direction.

PRA relation methods

Venn diagrams: This method builds awareness about the importance of different institutions, their influence and power, or can alternatively be applied to concerns about various social phenomena such as disease. Participants identify institutions that are relevant in a particular subject area (e.g. education) before rating their importance by allocating them differently sized pre-prepared paper circles (or other material such as *chapati*). These are then laid out on a flat surface and positioned according to their accessibility, with the most accessible in the centre and the least accessible towards the fringe.

Force-fields: This technique seeks to generate discussion about the positive and negative forces affecting particular situations. Using cards, participants identify the driving forces for positive change and the forces restraining that change. The cards are lined up on either side or a centre line and rated in terms of importance. This can be done via distance from centre line or by weighting using local materials to indicate strength. Increased knowledge is expected to generate impetus for change.

A more theoretically informed approach to participation influences much development fieldwork today. This is particularly the case for research informed by post-development theory, such as work on diverse economies (see Cameron and Gibson, 2005; Gibson-Graham, 2005; Raybeck, 1996).[1] This research seeks to unpack the multiple economies that exist beside or in combination with the dominant capitalist economies that are the focus of so much development research. In focusing on neglected community economies such as volunteer, communal, reciprocal and household, they seek to generate new awareness about the importance of such economies to everyday life and sow the seeds for new subjectivities. To do so they draw from PAR techniques and ideas from assets-based community development (ABCD) to employ tools like photo essays and workshops (Cameron and Gibson, 2001; Kretzmann and McKnight, 1993). Their approach is informed by post-structural understandings of language, power and subjectivities as well as a 'post-capitalist politics', drawing on these devices to build on PAR and improve and reconceive participatory methodologies. Hence subtle changes in language and focus, from 'needs analysis' to 'portrayals of assets' for example, creatively nurture possibilities and opportunities rather than reifying often stultifying social norms.

Such research suggests that participatory approaches can creatively learn from the debates taking place and find new ways of pursuing Friere's (1972) original empowering goals.

AN ETHNOGRAPHIC APPROACH

Classically an ethnographic approach to fieldwork seeks to immerse the researcher in the lives and society of a particular cultural setting or group. Through this experience, the ethnographer (anthropologists originally) typically aimed to provide a rich and holistic account of the lives of peoples in these societies (Atkinson et al., 2007). In many respects, ethnographers provided the first qualitative development research, and many of the techniques developed by these pioneers (e.g. participatory observation,) continue to influence development fieldwork today, well beyond the field of anthropology. At the same time, though, it is clear that the classic ethnographic approach involving an extended period of living in a community (several years in some cases) is increasingly rare, even within academic anthropology, largely due to time constraints on development research and practice.

While there are numerous variations in the approaches adopted, ethnographic approaches to fieldwork are typically characterised by:

- long-term residence in the community;
- close relationships between researcher and community;
- local language acquisition by the researcher;
- a high degree of reflexivity; and
- a range of specific methods including interviews, participatory observation, surveys and the keeping of detailed field notes and journal.

There are some obvious strengths to this type of approach: the building of robust long-term relationships of trust between the researcher and those in the community;

the construction of a rich, deep and intimate knowledge of the society; and the way in which residence for an extended period allows the fieldwork focus to evolve. You may find the questions you took to the field shift to those that appear more relevant, to you or to your participants.

For many development researchers, an ethnographic approach to fieldwork represents the ideal: spending an extended period in the community; building meaningful relationships with participants who are centrally involved in the design and carrying out of the research itself; and seeking to ensure that the research will have a positive, empowering effect on communities. Unfortunately there are two problems with this portrayal. First, it somewhat romanticises the virtues of extended ethnographic fieldwork, when in fact many ethnographers find their fieldwork experience to be rather challenging and even tumultuous, as Gardner and Hoffman's (2006) collection of essays demonstrates. Second, in the world of scholarships, fees and shrinking resources – and even more restrictive, shorter-term timeframes for most development practice – the scope to carry out 'classical' forms of ethnographic fieldwork are increasingly limited.

Today ethnographic approaches have extended into other forms, including multi-sited ethnographic work (see Hannerz, 2012; Marcus, 1995; Salazar, 2011; Teaiwa, 2004). This recognises that localities do not act as a 'container of a particular set of social relations' (Falzone, 2009: 1) and that tracing linkages and flows between peoples and things across geographic space provides a richer understanding of contemporary, often transnational, lives than the classic locality based ethnographic enterprise. Despite the originality of the approach, such ethnographic fieldwork tends to use the same sorts of qualitative methods (interviews, participant observation, etc.).

INDIGENOUS APPROACHES

In recent times a number of indigenous scholars have called into question the dominant research paradigms, arguing that for too long the gaze of social science research has not only been aimed at indigenous peoples, their culture and their lives, but also that this gaze has been informed by Western ontological and epistemological understandings, with non-indigenous researchers constructing, interpreting and producing ideas about indigenous peoples (Hart, 2010; Martin, 2003; Nabobo-Baba, 2006; Smith, 2012; see also Chapter 10, section on 'Research with minority ethnic groups and indigenous people'). Instead indigenous scholars have argued for knowledge production which is led by indigenous peoples, and for recognition of indigenous knowledge, perspectives and understandings (Moreton-Robinson and Walter, 2009). Smith (2012) writes of the importance of re*writing* and re-*righting* the position of indigenous peoples in society.

While there is not one indigenous approach to social science research, what can be seen with indigenous methodologies is that most have a common philosophical base (Moreton-Robinson and Walter, 2009). This can be seen first and foremost by considering the notion of worldview. As McKenzie and Morrisette (2003) argue, the indigenous worldview is a worldview that emerges as a result of people's intimate relationship with the environment, and there are various metaphysical beliefs which shape this relationship and thus impact knowledge production.

The example in Box 4.4 is based on research in Fiji by Litea that was derived from and embedded within a Fijian worldview. This research sought to understand cultural constructs associated with the health and well-being of Fijian women, examining women living in Fiji and Fijians in New Zealand. The example provides an insight into a Pacific indigenous approach to research and the importance of respecting the relationship with the environment, or *vanua*. This relationship with the *vanua* is also an issue of ethics, and highlights the importance of reflecting on and responding to the researcher's own positionality.

Box 4.4   Ethical issues and collective responsibility of an indigenous researcher

Vanua in the Fijian context literally translates as 'land' but is defined 'as a people, their chief, their defined territory, their waterways or fishing grounds, their environment, their spirituality, their history, their epistemology and culture' (Nabobo-Baba, 2006: 155). In the context of research, a *vanua* methodology seeks to ensure that respect, humility and traditional Fijian cultural protocols are adhered to. In the Fijian context the first protocol involves addressing governance of the *vanua*. As an indigenous researcher, I (Litea) am never an individual but always part of a collective. Even though in the academy the study is considered my own, studying within my own cultural setting means many of the cultural obligations and protocols are concerned with establishing my place as part of the collective culture, binding me with the vanua. Any behaviour as a researcher that goes against my cultural values marks me and my family for a lifetime, as research within an indigenous worldview itself becomes part of the collective and reflects on the family as a whole. Adhering to the cultural protocols of the *vanua* safeguards my cultural position as an indigenous researcher.

One of the most important aspects of the collective nature of the *vanua* research methodology meant that to go alone into my own cultural setting would be an insult first to my immediate relatives, and to those receiving me at the village. Therefore, I had a group of relatives who I refer to as the 'cultural discernment' group. Their role was to ensure that how I conducted the research was culturally appropriate and ethical. However, the university ethics committee questioned the role of this advisory group. While there was no doubt in my mind that this approach was appropriate and ethical within the cultural setting, within the academy I had to substantiate my arguments with existing literature and to do this I drew on the concept of 'communal discernment', a term first coined by Gula (1998: 287) and cited by Angrosino and May de Perez (2003) when discussing ethical decisions in participant observation. Cultural discernment can be defined as a process in which a community or a group of people collaborate to ensure that the research process is appropriate and ethical within the cultural setting

(Continued)

(Continued)

(Meo-Sewabu, 2012). The process, however, was not necessarily simple as in my case the cultural context required an understanding of the complex systems of Fijian indigenous knowledge.

My cultural discernment group consisted of immediate relatives from the village and those living in urban areas. Every element within my research process was deliberated by my 'cultural discernment' group before I ventured into the wider village community. Every so often, other experts from within the village would be called in to discuss some of the concerns, but all ensured that the research methods and approach I was using in the village was culturally appropriate and ethical within the village cultural context. The group therefore changed in size according to who had the knowledge and the expertise on what was being investigated.

Such forms of collaboration around the research process are common in indigenous cultures as the ultimate responsibility for ensuring the cultural fit of the research in an indigenous context lies not with the academy but with the researcher. That is, if the cultural processes and protocols were not adhered to, or the researcher were to behave in a culturally inappropriate manner, the blame will forever rest on the extended family, clan, tribe and village the researcher represents or belongs to. This provides a very different set of epistemological assumptions around the relationship between the researcher and the social world they are interested in.

An important aspect of indigenous research is reciprocity. Battiste argues that reciprocity needs to be central to research with indigenous peoples because 'The reciprocal relationships embody both recognition of the custodians of knowledge and awareness of the associated responsibilities of the custodians and the receivers of knowledge' (2008: 505). This issue is often misunderstood by outside researchers studying indigenous cultures as they have sometimes assumed that 'poor' participants from 'third world countries' are desperate for money, and thus they assume that some of the power inequalities between the researcher and the researched may be alleviated by paying people for their time. Such universalist assumptions can be insulting to participants, and lead to poor research outcomes. Those embarking on indigenous research need to be very aware of local values and practices: whether to give gifts, and how, is culturally specific information. Reciprocity is often best shown in terms of relationships, of sitting around the kava bowl or building friendships and connections, rather than compensating participants with a token dollar.

Reciprocity and gift giving is an integral part of most indigenous cultures. All over Oceania, for example, reciprocity is the essence of communal and collective values, and is the glue that builds and binds the social capital of communities. Exchanges take place for weddings, funerals, births and birthdays, and occur not only within the village context but also wherever we live. Globally, the flow of money and cultural exchanges that occur are central to maintaining collective culture, and have been likened to that of exchanges within 'transnational cooperation' (Mafile'o, 2008; Spoonley, 2001). Within Oceanic cultures these exchanges, even for those in the Pacific diaspora, allows people to maintain a sense of belonging to their land. The continuity of these flows typically extends for decades and is based on the understanding that one day those giving will themselves be helped, without specific time boundaries.

Reciprocity in a Fijian worldview is also related to status and power relations. In Litea's research, the 'cultural discernment' group (see Box 4.4) decided that *tabua* (polished whale's tooth – a highly prized, spiritually significant item) and *yaqona* ('kava', an indigenous substance integral to Fijian culture) would be needed for the *sevusevu* (ritual offerings). As Litea and her mother (who accompanied her) had been away from the village for 20 years and 40 years respectively, they had missed many important events such as funerals of family members. Thus relatives provided five *tabua*, which they presented to the elders to acknowledge that they had missed paying our respects to those who had passed on. Other items we gifted during various ceremonies and visitations included eight *yaqona*, Western food items considered valuable in the village (as shipments take several weeks to get there), bails of cloth, laundry powder and soap, and church hymnals and Bibles. In addition, they travelled to the village assuming that everything they brought with them may not come back with them. Giving to relatives was centrally about maintenance of relationships, not about the value of individual items.

Reciprocity implies not only that gifts are given but also that knowledge derived from one's research is shared with the community. This should be an important principle of qualitative research generally, not just indigenous research (see Chapter 9, section on 'Reciprocity'). In the case of Litea's research, this sharing of data was conducted at the end of the village visit. She outlined the main themes of the material she had collected about women's health and well-being, and the women had an opportunity to view pictures taken over the course of the research. Women were also asked to discuss any issue they felt was inappropriate or did not want to be shared, turning the project into a co-constructed one.

ANALYSING QUALITATIVE DATA

While this chapter has focused mainly on data collection, the data collection process is not an end in itself: you also need to analyse, interpret and present the findings. We like to think of data analysis as having four stages, as noted in Table 4.3.

In qualitative research the process should be iterative, that is, the researcher can move back and forth between data collection and analysis (Mason, 2002; O'Leary, 2010). A skilled researcher continually analyses and reflects on the data they have collected, as indicated in column one and two of Table 4.3. Field journals often become a useful place for the 'scanning' or 'first cut' analysis of your data. You might find, for instance, patterns or questions emerging in the surveys or interviews you are conducting, and this can help sharpen the focus of the fieldwork on subsequent days (see Chapter 8). The process of transcription can also be used to simultaneously start your analysis by identifying themes that emerge and jotting them down as you transcribe.

The analysis process can be very challenging as the researcher needs to make sense of the often enormous amounts of data that have been collected from a multitude of sources. From this data they need to identify significant patterns and develop a framework for presenting, and hence communicating what the data reveals. You will be attempting to provide a convincing explanation, a well-reasoned and well-illustrated

Table 4.3 Data analysis stages

Data collection	Data organisation	Data coding (deconstruction)	Developing theory (reconstruction)
The first part of the analysis process.	Begin organising ideas while entering data.	Read raw notes and begin to apply some conceptual or thematic order to them.	Theoretical coding.
Write memos; reflect in your journal.	Transcribe as soon as possible.	Do this through a combination of description and analysis.	Ask questions of the data.
Catalogue and index material.	Read your transcriptions.		Compare and contrast codes.
Think about naming and numbering systems.	Use your indexing system.	Revisit your codes.	Find alternative explanations.
		Identify patterns in the data.	Examine fit between your data, relevant literature and theories.
	Start coding your data: use broad categories and find common threads.	Think of terms and concepts used in your research that draw from your literature review or theoretical framework.	Describe emerging theory.
	Compare transcripts.		
	Aggregate stories.	Think back to your research question(s).	
	Keep writing memos/ reflections.		

argument ultimately achieving the research aim and/or objectives, and answering the research questions (see O'Leary, 2010: Ch. 12; Silverman, 2006).

Recently there has been a shift by some researchers towards using computer programmes for qualitative data analysis; however, these programmes only help you manage your data, they do not fully analyse or interpret it – this is still the job of the researcher (see Chapter 12). Moreover, learning a computer programme can be difficult and time consuming and may not benefit your work at all, or may even give you a false sense of confidence about knowing your data. Unless you are dealing with a very large amount of data or working in a team which requires data collected by different people to be collated and analysed together, it is better to become intimate with your raw data and you do this by spending time reading and re-reading your transcripts, sorting and coding and resorting and re-coding your data.

ADDRESSING THE PITFALLS OF QUALITATIVE RESEARCH

In this chapter we have outlined the value of qualitative research and the various strengths of the approach; however, there are some acknowledged limitations or pitfalls. Note that these are often understood – sometimes misleadingly so – to be strengths of quantitative research. For example, some forms of qualitative research have been criticised for being less 'scientific' or valid in their approach, methods and, by implication, conclusions. One limitation of qualitative research involves the ability to generalise results to other populations. The depth of meaning and relationships sought by many qualitative researchers means a greater length of time is involved with a smaller number of participants than for other research methods. Allied to this, the focus of qualitative research on exploratory research and the often context-specific design in relation to the population group being studied means it is typically difficult to extrapolate findings to broader populations or to draw general or comprehensive conclusions.

For any research to contribute to knowledge it must be scholarly and rigorous, and over the years there has been much debate about rigour with respect to qualitative methods. Many qualitative researchers have argued that the criteria for determining rigour in research have largely developed in the context of quantitative methods, and it is problematic to transfer these criteria from one paradigm to the other. Hence specific criteria for determining rigour in qualitative research have been suggested (see Table 4.4). Instead of fixating on 'truth', for example, it is better to think about trustworthiness, or instead of validity we could reflect on the credibility of the research (Becker et al., 2006: 7–8).

Rigour is clearly influenced by, and will be assessed in relation to, the methodological decisions made by the researcher. Therefore if we subscribe to a participatory research approach, it is important that the finished product (a thesis, journal paper or book) provides evidence of participation by the researched throughout the research process. Techniques used by qualitative researchers to ensure rigour and credibility, transferability, dependability and confirmability include:

Table 4.4   Criteria for judging rigour in qualitative research

Criteria	Description
Credibility	The extent to which the findings are believable as judged by participants and others in the discipline.
Transferability	The extent to which a set of findings are relevant to similar settings to the one(s) from which they are derived.
Dependability	The extent to which a set of findings are likely to be relevant to a different time than the one in which it was conducted (different seasons, for instance).
Confirmability	The extent to which the researcher has not allowed personal values to intrude to an excessive degree (could another researcher from a different background come to the same conclusions?)

Source: Becker et al. (2006); Lincoln and Guba (1985); Morse et al. (2008); Shenton (2004)

- acknowledging potential biases through engaging in reflexivity such as use of a field journal and the explicit articulation of their own positionality;
- provision of a thick, rich description of the research context;
- participant checking of findings;
- peer review or examination of findings;
- triangulation of data methods and sources;
- the re-interviewing of participants; and
- using a mixed method approach to data collection.

Ultimately the real basis for assessing whether any research is rigorous ought to be about proper application of the research process and techniques: 'Badly or misleadingly applied, both quantitative and qualitative techniques give bad or misleading conclusions' (White, 2002: 512).

CONCLUSION

Qualitative research is a methodology employed in many differing disciplines where we seek to understand the meaning of social, cultural, economic and political phenomena. Meaning, however, is not only socially constructed, it is also situational and historically specific, and in order to understand the meanings attached to a particular phenomenon the qualitative researcher must really understand the local context. This is what ideally occurs when we conduct development fieldwork.

There are important reasons why qualitative methods often align well with development research, either when used on their own or applied as part of a mixed methods approach. In particular, qualitative research approaches provide development researchers with the means for making apparent the voices and concerns of the poor or marginalised, and give precedence to those voices which are not often heard (see Chapter 10). Qualitative approaches can also highlight the multitude of experiences (sometimes culturally specific) and interpretations by various actors in development. Qualitative inquiry has, further, informed critiques of development policy and practice, and helped to bring about fundamental changes in the ways in which development is practised.

Summary

- Qualitative research seeks to gain understanding of attitudes, behaviours, value systems, concerns, motivations, aspirations, culture or lifestyle.
- Qualitative approaches typically seek depth rather than breadth of understanding.
- Qualitative methods allow the voices of marginalised peoples to be foregrounded.
- Co-construction of knowledge, positionality, reflexivity and the relationships between the researcher and researched are critical to qualitative research.

- Techniques revolve around various interview formats, observations and secondary materials.
- Approaches to questions of rigour in qualitative research focus on credibility and trustworthiness of data.
- Participatory methods increasingly see communities involved in the co-construction of knowledge and the research process.
- Indigenous research methodologies are derived from differing worldviews and are constructed around relationships, reciprocity and trust.
- Qualitative data analysis is typically iterative and seeks recurring themes and patterns across the diverse materials.

Questions for reflection

- List three different social issues or questions for which qualitative methods would provide a more appropriate or better approach than quantitative methods.
- Mixed methods research can often appear to represent the 'best of both worlds'. What sorts of advantages might be associated with this approach?
- What issues may arise for a non-indigenous person doing research with indigenous peoples?
- What are some potential advantages of PAR, and what might some of the disadvantages be?
- Credibility and trustworthiness are ways of trying to ensure 'rigour' in qualitative research. How do you think you could go about assessing them?
- Pick a contemporary development issue that interests you. Think of ways you could design a research methodology and employ different qualitative methods to research this.

RECOMMENDED READINGS

Berg, B. L. (2007). *Qualitative Research Methods for the Social Sciences* (6th edn). Boston, MA: Pearson/Allyn and Bacon.

An introduction to qualitative research methods, showing new researchers how to plan, collect data, analyse and present their research.

Chambers, R. (2008). *Revolutions in Development Inquiry*. London: Earthscan.

This book provides really useful material on the basics of Chambers' qualitative approach to doing development research: that is, RRA, PRA and PLA methodologies and techniques. It includes extracts from his earlier writings alongside his current reflections, comments and critiques.

Cornwall, A. (ed.) (2008). *The Participation Reader*. London: Zed.

This edited book on participation includes discussions of what participation is, various methodologies and practices and the importance of collective action.

Denzin, N. K., Lincoln, Y. S., and Smith, L. T. (eds) (2008). *Handbook of Critical and Indigenous Methodologies*. London: Sage.

This book seeks to build on and extend qualitative inquiry by exploring the indigenous and non-indigenous voices whose research is informed by critical theories and/or indigenous perspectives.

Smith, M., and Humble, D. (2007). What counts as development research? Negotiating boundaries and borders: Qualitative methodology and development research. *Studies in Qualitative Methodology*, (8), 1–34.

Article exploring what counts as research in development and challenging predominant geographical conceptions of development research, arguing that qualitative approaches are crucial.

van Donge, J. K. (2006). Ethnography and participant observation. In V. Desai and R. Potter (eds), *Doing Development Research* (pp. 180–188). London: Sage.

This chapter provides an excellent introduction to ethnography and participant observation for development research.

NOTE

1. See also www.communityeconomies.org/Home.

5

SOMETHING OLD, SOMETHING NEW: RESEARCH USING ARCHIVES, TEXTS AND VIRTUAL DATA

SHARON MCLENNAN AND GERARD PRINSEN

Chances are you are reading this book because you are planning to do fieldwork. Before that fieldwork is done, it is likely that at some point you will find yourself following endless links through cyberspace or in a room full of filing cabinets, flicking through piles of yellowed paper. However, these activities shouldn't be considered separate from 'real' fieldwork, rather we argue that the dusty archive or an online community are themselves 'political locations' (Clifford, 1997: 84; Gupta and Ferguson, 1997: 35) and a 'social terrain' (Nast, 1994: 57) which reflect and recreate the wider power inequalities of the traditional field site (see Chapter 1 for discussion of what constitutes the field). This chapter therefore looks at the use of written sources, including 'old' paper-based and 'new' digital sources in development research as both an extension of the field and as a field location of themselves.

Because of the importance of off- and online archival and textual sources in development fieldwork, much of this chapter discusses the methodological challenges related to accessing and using existing data. This data includes the paper documents found in archives and the information posted on websites and on social media. However, the new online field presents a range of opportunities for the generation of data, for more interactive data forms of data collection (including online surveys and interviewing, and participant observation), and the collection of non-textual forms of digital data (video, audio and images). The final section of this chapter explores these, and their relevance to development research.

TEXTUAL DATA AND NON-ACADEMIC WRITTEN SOURCES

Most research includes written sources, perhaps because written sources tend to be more accessible, stable and verifiable when compared to unwritten or more personalised sources like interviews and observations. In addition, 21st-century fieldwork often includes the collection and use of digital and virtual data in some form. However, although the digital age has significantly changed the ways in which people and organisations store, transmit and access written information, there is much that is quite similar about old and new sources when accessing and processing existing data. Indeed, rather than simply discussing 'old' and 'new' sources, we find that there are three categories where the old and the new sit together (see Table 5.1).

The first category is the written materials that are carefully managed: the old archives and today's web pages and internet archives. The second is the unmanaged written sources, with the boxes of unsorted papers on the old side, and on the new side the tangled web of new social media. A third category comprises personal communications in the form of 'old' paper letters and 'new' email, blogs and private social media. In this chapter we will discuss the use of these three categories separately, as each has its own methodological challenges. Before we do that, however, we share a few methodological considerations that apply to all three categories.

CONTEXT AND PURPOSE OF THE WRITTEN RECORD

Perhaps the most important consideration when accessing and using written sources is the context and purpose of the written record. Why was it written? Who wrote it, and who was the intended audience? Why was its physical or digital repository created? Arguably, a text is less a factual record and more an indication of the worldview of the author (Jennings, 2006: 244). While you may be able to draw data directly from the source (e.g. the dates of events), for most sources the location, author and origin of the source will have a direct bearing on its usefulness and on how you interpret and analyse the information. Underlying all documentary research therefore is a concern with whether you can trust the overt message in the source, or whether the author has another agenda (Finnegan, 2006; Prior, 2011). This means active engagement with the record of all data.

This caution should extend beyond a consideration of what is written, to a concern with what is omitted (Zeitlyn, 2005: 415). This means thinking about what you have been given access to, what is obviously 'blacked out' or what is simply not written about. In online research, the process of exclusion and censoring is further complicated by the ease and speed at which online data can be deleted and changed,

Table 5.1   Textual data and non-academic written sources

Source	Managed	Un-Managed	Correspondence
Something old: offline data	Historical documents, reports, policy and budget guidelines, topical papers, records of work processes, official and private correspondence.	'Old boxes' and files of unsorted papers including those found in managed collections, and unofficial memos and communication inventories, shopping lists, document drafts, etc.	Official and private correspondence – may be managed or unmanaged.
	Found in the archives and offices of: <ul><li>Governments</li><li>Multilaterals</li><li>Religious institutions</li><li>NGOs</li><li>Private companies</li><li>Libraries</li><li>Media</li></ul>	Found in warehouses, storage rooms and back offices of: <ul><li>Governments</li><li>Multilaterals</li><li>Religious institutions</li><li>NGOs</li><li>Private companies</li><li>Back rooms and attics of homes</li></ul>	Found in: <ul><li>Archives</li><li>Offices</li><li>Warehouses, storage rooms and old boxes</li><li>Private collections and homes</li></ul>
Something new: online data	Internet databases and archived web pages (and linked documents) of: <ul><li>Governments</li><li>Multilateral agencies</li><li>Private companies</li><li>Religious institutions</li><li>NGOs</li><li>Social movements</li><li>Media</li></ul>	Social media sites Blogs <ul><li>Public accounts on Facebook, Twitter, etc.</li><li>Public web forums</li><li>Image and video-sharing sites</li><li>Abandoned and disused web pages</li></ul>	Email, private messages and texts, found in: <ul><li>Individual and organisational email accounts</li><li>Password-protected social media sites (e.g. Facebook, Twitter)</li><li>Membership-only web forums and email lists</li></ul>

and because the authors of the material may be aware that they are being 'watched' (Janetzko, 2008). In sum, you need to be critically aware of a written text's context and purpose when you use it for development research.

The concept of 'contextual integrity' (Bingo, 2011; Nissenbaum, 2004) is therefore important when processing data. This means being aware of the political purpose of the repository and of the values, etiquette and choice of words at the time in which the records were created. Can you interpret the words in the context of their creation? You should also be aware of, and explicit about, the political or conceptual perspective with which *you* are going to analyse the findings. For example, when Locatelli 'discovered' municipal archives in Eritrea, she was explicit about the possible choices. She could interpret the records as 'an account of everyday life', or 'a testimony of African customs and beliefs', or a source on 'the structure of colonial power', but also as 'evidence of social transformations during colonialism' (2010: 474). You will have to make similar choices.

ETHICS

While documentary research may appear to throw up fewer ethical challenges than face-to-face interviews or participatory methods, there are two key ethical considerations related to old and new documentary research. The first encompasses matters such as ownership, access and permission to use, while the second consideration relates to representation and fair use of material.

All researchers accessing written sources face challenges and questions regarding access and permission to use written sources. While this may be straightforward for documents in the public domain (such as those in archives or institutional websites), determining whether permission is needed, and who from, can be a complex process. This is particularly the case with restricted access and private documents (Denscombe, 2010), and for online sources where the creators of digital context are often accessible and in active control of the text in a way that the authors of traditional archives generally are not (Krotoski, 2010). This means that the question of consent is contentious. The core of the debate is the question of whether information posted on the Internet is considered public or private (Buchanan, 2011; Flicker et al., 2004; Grodzinsky and Tavani, 2010; Rosenberg, 2010; Sixsmith and Murray, 2001). In response to this question, the ethics working committee of the Association of Internet Researchers (Markham and Buchanan, 2012) state that the researcher has a greater responsibility to protect privacy and to get informed consent where the authors might reasonably expect that their posts are private. Conversely, if the author is posting with the belief that their work is public, then there may be fewer ethical obligations. The issues one of the authors of this chapter faced regarding research permission in online networks are discussed in Box 5.1. While these debates around research pertain predominantly to online research, we would also argue that this private/public divergence is something worth considering in all forms of documentary research.

Complicating questions of consent and privacy is the fact that it is very difficult, even impossible, to guarantee anonymity in online research. The ability to track IP addresses, the use of shared computers (often the case in poorer areas), and tricky questions around data ownership, all complicate discussions of privacy and confidentiality.

Box 5.1   Research permission in online networks

My doctoral research included the collection of data from an online network of small NGOs, including both membership and non-membership websites and forums. Following the recommendations of the Association of Internet Researchers (Markham and Buchanan, 2012), and Sixsmith and Murray (2001), I considered material from non-membership websites to be in the public domain, and as such, specific consent was not sought for its use. However I sought consent for the collection of data from websites that

> *required membership. This was complicated however by the nature of the network, which consisted of forums which were comprised of thousands of users. Obtaining individual consent from every participant was logistically impossible. To address this, I arranged initial access and permission through the network moderator, and then sent a message to all forums in order to ensure that participants in the network were aware of the presence of a researcher on the email list, and I sent regular reminders to 'catch-up' new members.*
>
> *Source:* McLennan (2012)

The second major area of ethical concern in documentary research is representation and the fair use of material. Modern technology makes 'copying and pasting' a breeze, and it is remarkably easy to select quotes quite purposefully (or perhaps subconsciously) to prove preconceived conclusions. As you write, you get to select and omit views. It is important therefore that researchers keep in mind the original reason for which the material was written, taking care with interpretation and representation of other's views and avoiding 'playing the ventriloquist' (Swadener et al., 2000: 3). Remember that it is relatively straightforward for readers to check the original sources of written material presented in a research article or thesis. In addition, you should remember that although you may be sympathetic to the cause of the people marginalised or misrepresented, you are not their spokesperson (see Chapter 10, section on 'Advocacy and activism').

LANGUAGE/ANGLOPHONE BIAS AND THE DIGITAL DIVIDE

When it comes to processing written sources in languages that are foreign to you, the overall guideline is: don't. Most people reading this book will be Anglophone and it is important that you recognise the limitations of your language when doing development research (see Box 5.2). Many of us endeavour to learn some of the basics of locally spoken languages when we do field research (see Chapter 8 for a discussion of language learning). However, unless you are fluent in these languages, you should depend on a third party for the adequate processing of texts written in these languages because the nuances of written language (such as the formal language of legal documents, or the informal language of social media) present particular challenges. Carlson and Duan (2010), for example, note that the stylised, colloquial Chinese in bulletin boards and blogs makes language a challenge for non-Chinese speaking researchers. Moreover, translating texts is a professional job, even more so if the texts are to be used for analysis or contextualisation in research. Prestigious journals may demand that the use of a written record in a non-English language requires a full transcription in the original language with the translation following (Carmichael, 2006; Zeitlyn, 2005).

Box 5.2   The Anglophone's blind spot – and blinded eye

English is written by less than 10 per cent of the world's population (Anderman and Rogers, 2003: 163). This leaves the Anglophone researcher of non-academic written sources quite blind to most of what 90 per cent of the people put to paper or screen. For example, a research on labour in 19th-century East Africa contains only two sources translated from Arabic or Swahili – even though agricultural commerce in that period was dominated by Arabic or Swahili speaking traders (Gazit and Maoz-Shai, 2010: 453). Similarly, in our (the authors') own field research in East Africa and Central America, we found that very few researchers acknowledge their blind spot for rich sources in Swahili, ةيبرعلا and Español.

Moreover, astute local actors may have selectively used local languages in their writing to blind prying colonial administrators and researchers. Freeman-Grenville, a prominent historian on East Africa who was fluent in Arabic, Swahili and Portuguese, was refused access to written sources in Arabic because the owners deemed the British lacked the required 'public enlightenment' (Freeman-Grenville, 1962).

This blind spot remains a concern in the online environment. While the 'digital divide' is arguably shrinking as digital and mobile technologies rapidly expand around the globe, there is still a considerable gap between what is available in English-language websites and what is available in other languages, which are more likely to be languages of the poor and marginalised (Dyson, 2011). Researchers need to remember that any material accessed online in English is still likely to be urban and elite-biased, and to exclude other perspectives (Mawdsley, 2006).

MANAGED WRITTEN SOURCES: ARCHIVES AND WEBSITES

Public bureaucracies, private organisations and literate individuals have produced large volumes of written records over the course of time. While much of it is discarded or boxed up and forgotten, it is likely that most of your research into written sources will take you to repositories where records are carefully – and purposefully – managed: the old archives and the new websites. While the two are quite different in appearance, they both present you with challenges in understanding the purpose of the collected written sources, finding what you want and, ultimately, interpreting the written sources you collect.

ARCHIVES

Archives that may be of use to development researchers include those of governments, multilateral organisations, religious institutions and NGOs (e.g. Eklund, 2010;

Gallaher, 2011; Rigg, 2006). These archives often contain rich data that reveals much about their relationships with local communities, the state, and with their international networks. Other organisations with potential useful archives are trade unions, political parties, cooperatives and even local chiefs (Locatelli, 2004; Maaba, 2001; Zeitlyn, 2005).

Before examining the mechanics of research in archives, it is useful to reiterate the importance of the context in which archives are created and managed. We noted earlier that archives can be as revealing for what they omit as for what they collect. Darwin notes that archives tend to be repositories of 'the view of the centre', leaving other people 'archivally voiceless' (1999: 556). Moreover, governments of all stripes throughout history have actively destroyed or concealed archives. For example, when the British colonial service saw independence coming in Uganda in 1962, orders were issued to burn 'sensitive' files in district archives (Tuck and Rowe, 2005: 404). Still today, the British government finds itself in legal and political problems over claims that certain archives did not exist, had been destroyed, were kept in the former colonies, positively lost, or could not be located (Anderson, 2011). Similarly, Norway's archives on the 'Oslo Peace Accord' went 'missing' in 2006 when researchers began suspecting that Norway was 'acting as Israel's helpful errand boy' (Waage, 2008: 62). All this leaves you as a researcher of archives to answer the question 'What is missing?' as much as enquiring 'What records are available?'.

Fortunately, many archives survive. Tuck and Rowe (2005) note how the wife of a District Commissioner spent months cataloguing the archives and 'would not hear of anyone touching them'. 'Her' archives later became a critical resource for Uganda's researchers. The nameless wife brings us to the first of three challenges in accessing archives: the not-to-be-underestimated importance of gatekeepers (see 'Gatekeepers' section in Chapter 9). While most archives are accessible to the public, you will still depend on the archivists, secretaries and administrators to actually get your hands on the records. Indeed, expressions of researchers' gratitude to named local archivists are ubiquitous (e.g., Mr Wani in Barrett-Gaines and Khadiagala, 2000; the unknown 'older gentleman' in Bjerk, 2004; Mr Mukungu in Howell, 2001; Mr Rutanga in McConnell, 2005; and Ms Seyum in Taddia, 1998). Barrett-Gaines and Khadiagala (2000) used the same National Archive independently of each other at the same time. One of them invested time, smiles and 'baked goods' in the relationship with the archives' staff and got what she needed, the other did not and didn't.

A second challenge in accessing archives is that many archives are still being used for operational purposes and will allow researchers only controlled access (Flinn, 2007: 169; Piggott and McKemmish, 2002: 3). Official records can be 'classified' for a few decades to ensure that they do not impact on today's government policies. Whether or not you get access to these records may depend on you couching your proposal 'in as non-controversial language as possible' (Diamant, 2010: 36). You may also have to file a request for access under the relevant legislation, such as the Freedom of Information Act in the UK and Australia. Filing such a request is an acquired skill; you need to couch your question broadly enough to capture the material you search, but not too broadly to be rejected as 'unworkable'.

The third challenge in accessing written sources for development fieldwork is that you are likely to be working with archives that are seriously under-resourced (high photocopying costs might be a way of addressing this, see Box 5.3). These archives may have been moved between different locations and in the process records have been misplaced or there is no longer a unified cataloguing system, and physically locating particular records may be a problem. Methods for dealing with this include becoming good friends with gatekeepers and using lateral thinking (Jennings, 2006; Zeitlyn, 2005). Under-resourcing may also mean that archives are hidden in closets, attics, and rooms that are 'uncomfortable, dark and dusty' (Barrett-Gaines and Khadiagala, 2000: 459) or without windows or light (McConnell, 2005: 474). The records you find may be damaged by water, termites or vermin, which may turn gloves and respiratory masks into research tools (Mann, 1999: 456)!

Box 5.3   Photocopying and scanning

Copying historical written records is a challenge. Assuming you have been authorised, there is the obvious temptation to photocopy as much as you can, but photocopying facilities in many fieldwork locations are limited. In addition photocopying may be charged up to €0.50 a page (e.g. Bjerk, 2004; Jennings, 2006; Schneider, 2003). For this purpose, consider buying a handheld scanner or look into mobile phone photo and scanning applications. It is important to note that most archives in developing nations are under-funded and often the photocopying services are an important source of income to maintain the archive. This may also explain why some archivists do not permit you to use your own handheld scanners or smartphone camera. Nevertheless, you may still be allowed to use you own scanner if you negotiate a fee along the lines of the photocopying fee. One of our students noted:

I took a handheld scanner to Ethiopia and it was definitely worthwhile. I knew from earlier fieldwork that most of the offices either had no photocopier or very old and expensive copying services. Often they would ask you to come back in a week to collect the few copies you had asked for. Now I was able to ask permission and scan the documents on the spot. (Amy Fraser, Master's Research in Ethiopia, 2012)

WEBSITES AND INTERNET ARCHIVES

While the Internet may sometimes seem chaotic, much of it is carefully controlled in much the same way as public archives. This includes internet archives (online databases) and managed websites, run by individuals and organisations including (but not limited to) governments and political parties, multilateral agencies, NGOs, businesses, social movements and media organisations. Unlike archives, however, these websites are subject to frequent and on-going changes. They are also usually interactive, presenting the face of an organisation, agency or business to the world. Websites that may be useful for development researchers include government websites (for data on population, economic indicators, health and education, etc.), political parties, multilateral institutions, NGOs, clubs and organisations, businesses, social movements and news sites (Mawdsley, 2006). In addition, an increasing number of development researchers are also using data from websites as a discrete data source, and are analysing the content and structure of websites for a variety of purposes.

Internet archives are great source of data for development researchers. These include historical and current statistics, public information regarding court cases, legal rulings and property information held on government sites, and the online collections maintained by offline archives (such as www.digitalnz.org, maintained by the National Library of New Zealand). They also include the news archives of media companies (e.g. the BBC archive at www.bbc.co.uk/archive), activist archives such as wikileaks (www.wikileaks.org) and archives of the Internet itself such as the wayback machine (www.archive.org) (Karpf, 2012).

Access to these sites is usually straightforward; indeed, this is likely the simplest source of data to find. Start by exploring the websites of organisations, businesses and individuals that deal with issues related to your research questions, doing general web searches on the names and acronyms in the references of your literature, and keyword searches on your research question. Searching will often turn up more information than you need, so start narrowly and broaden the search only as necessary (see Box 5.4).

Box 5.4   Searching the Internet

The Internet is vast and it is easy to get distracted, side-tracked or lost in a sea of links; however, there are some things you can do to improve the quality of your search results:

- Take some time to think through your research question and to work out a methodical search plan and some well thought-out keywords related to your research question.
- Familiarise yourself with the mechanics of Boolean searching: use 'AND' to combine terms, 'OR' to search for synonymous terms and 'NOT' to exclude terms.
- Use the 'advanced search' page. This gives you options to restrict by language (useful if you want to remove those pesky English-language sites!) or by date, by location, by file format (e.g., restricting to PDF documents may help you to locate articles and reports), to search for exact phrases, and to search within websites.

Source: Derived from Ó Dochartaigh (2012)

In terms of ownership and permission, collecting data from public websites is akin to using information from newspapers and magazines. As such it is public data and in most cases you probably will not need to get explicit permission from authors, but (unless there are good reasons not to) it is good 'netiquette' to check with website owners before collecting significant data from a site.

As with physical archives, the concept of 'contextual integrity' is vitally important in the analysis of websites. While physical archives may preserve a particular view of the past, websites have a clear focus on the present and often serve a public relations purpose. As the public face of an organisation, the material posted on the site is usually carefully written and may go through approval processes before being made publicly viewable. Some sites allow interaction (through comments and social media links), but these are almost invariably moderated. When using these sites in research it is therefore worth bearing in mind that what you see is rarely the complete picture of the organisation it represents (Murray and Sixsmith, 2002: 50). This means that you should not only be asking yourself once more the questions 'Why, and for whom, was this created?' and 'What is missing', but also 'How is this changing?'.

An associated question might be 'How can I safely store data I have collected'? Box 5.5 provides some pointers. (See also Box 6.5 for electronic devices that can help with your fieldwork.)

Box 5.5   Digital data storage and security

The decisions you make regarding the storage of digital data are both technical and methodological. Will you need to collect, analyse and store large amounts of data, or relatively few simple text files? Will you be collecting and storing data in the field, or will the data collection be carried out from your home or work PC? Technically, you will need to think about the storage options available to you (PC or laptop, USB, external hard drive, CD or the cloud?), the length of time data needs to be stored, the type of data to be stored, access issues and back-up options. Gaiser and Schreiner (2009) note that at a minimum, research data should be password-protected, while sensitive data should be encrypted.

On top of this, you need to decide whether to download and store individual posts manually, or use RSS or other subscription methods to collect and save whole feeds? Will you store the data in its original file format, or convert to plain text? Will the data be searched, processed and saved chronologically, or by author or theme? These decisions will be closely tied to the research question and methodology, which need to be planned carefully before data collection begins.

UNMANAGED WRITTEN SOURCES: OLD BOXES AND NEW SOCIAL MEDIA

The second category of textual data is the unmanaged written sources, the old boxes of unsorted papers and uncategorised documents and the tangled web of new social media. Using this data is more akin to treasure hunting. It looks, for example, for the piles of papers stacked in the attics and backrooms of warehouses and homes, the rambling Facebook pages, the forgotten filing cabinets and the long-forgotten posts on web forums.

OLD BOXES AND FORGOTTEN FILING CABINETS

Unmanaged written sources range from inventories and shopping lists to detailed records of work processes, and the documents vary in authorship and audience. As long as organisations and individuals are operational, they tend to safeguard their records. However, the control and management of these written sources often disappear once they cease to be active or once their operational function changes (e.g., a ministry merger, the sale of a business or death of an individual) and eventually the written material gets destroyed, boxed away or misplaced.

When considering the issue of access to written historical material that is 'boxed' away, the first challenge is actually locating the material. You may have to begin your search for historical records on your research topic with some clever investigating. For starters, you can identify the names and acronyms of the organisations, individuals or government departments that dealt with issues related to your research questions. These may be found in the references of your literature, by going through the archives of newspapers, and by using plain common sense. Then ask yourself, which ones would have kept detailed records? You will probably discover two principal sources: private sources (e.g., churches, companies, NGOs, individuals, etc.) and public sources (mostly government departments, but also newspapers and museums).

Accessing unmanaged private sources usually requires careful sleuthing. If you were, for example, researching how labour conditions in a particular industry changed between colonial rule and independence, newspapers from the years before and after independence would provide you with names of companies or shareholders. From there on, you could check out archival records like the companies register to identify which of these companies still exist or were sold to companies still active today, or the names of families that have continuously been involved with these companies. Then it is a matter of carefully approaching these companies and families, asking for a meeting to explain your quest for written historical material. If you approach these gatekeepers with care and respect, you are likely to find many of them keen to assist in your research by searching for the old boxes or calling on the children of the old uncle of their late father who is rumoured to have been a meticulous keeper of records.

Accessing unmanaged written material from public sources often takes you through different processes. If we continue with our example of the research on labour conditions in a particular industry, you begin by listing the government departments that may have dealt with labour issues at the time: the labour department, the tax department and so on. Although some of the records have been stored away in publicly accessible archives, they may well have been put in boxes that are either forgotten or not intended for perusal by the public. Accessing these boxes starts by studying records that *are* available for a reference to a title, event or name. Once you have found your sliver of evidence that certain historical records once existed and may still be around, you can approach the officials who keep today's archives, although you may find their response disappointing. After all, you are asking them to find what is not readily accessible and they may claim no knowledge of such records.

Probably the best you can do in the face of such a response is dogged persistence; come back another day and hope to find a more interested colleague, approach a more senior official, make a more formal request, or identify another department as an entry point (see, e.g., Halter, 2010: 117).

Assuming you have been smart, persistent and lucky, you might now find yourself looking at a few boxes with 'unmanaged' written historical records. The processing of these records raises many of the same challenges as the processing of managed sources, particularly the need to consider the purpose of the original writers and the context in which the documents were found. However, the 'search before you can research' process of finding data sources also brings up a matter of ethics in using archives that are under-resourced and poorly managed: you may have the thrill of *discovering* archives (Barrett-Gaines and Khadiagala, 2000: 462; Howell, 2001: 411; Roff, 2007: 551; Schneider, 2003). What should you do if you find these hand-written documents, these yellowed hand-typed reports? Sometimes, the gatekeepers allow you, 'for a small fee' (McConnell, 2005: 472), to take records away from the place in which they were found. When Gerard was researching in a library in Kenya in 2006, there were no photocopying facilities and records could not leave the premises, so he sat and hand-copied relevant texts. After three days, the gatekeeper offered the reports for sale. Gerard was tempted, but did not wish to deplete the collection (Prinsen, 2011: 59).

This dilemma is consistent with current debates on the preservation of archives which lean towards keeping, or placing, written sources in the context where they were created (Cook, 2006; Piggott and McKemmish, 2002) to ensure contextual integrity (Bingo, 2011). Moreover, there is increasing evidence of the importance in 'restoring memory' if marginalised and disempowered people regain control over their written records (Flinn, 2007; McClellan and Tanner, 2011). McIlwaine (2006: 228) reflects on another angle to this ethical issue: how verifiable is your research if you cite from an archive if the gatekeepers may never be able to retrieve the document again? On balance we would advise that you never remove archives from their original locations, and if you are lucky enough to access 'undiscovered' archives you could lend a hand by making a simple catalogue of your findings to leave with the gatekeeper. This is also a situation where a handheld scanner can be a very valuable tool (see Box 5.4).

SOCIAL MEDIA

The new social media of Facebook, Twitter and blogs may not seem to have much in common with old boxes of documents, and yet from a researcher's perspective there are many parallels. While the past decade has seen the explosion of dynamic, contemporary content on the Web, like those old boxes most internet posts soon slip into an untended web of disorganised posts and forgotten conversations. Searching, sorting and filtering this material can be as time consuming and tedious as searching boxes but, just as those old documents can turn up data 'treasures', searching the social web will have its rewards. The social web is also a wonderful medium for generating interactive data, which will be discussed in the next section.

First though, it is important to understand what social media is and how existing data on social networking sites can be useful for development researchers. The term 'social media' refers to internet-based technologies that allow the creation and exchange of user-generated content. This includes websites such as Facebook and Twitter, blogging sites, forums, newsgroups and social bookmarking, as well as multi-media sites that enable video and image sharing (such as YouTube and Flickr) and podcasting. These tools are usually free or low-cost, and have been lauded as heralding a new, more informal and participatory approach to information-sharing (Ashley et al., 2009: 8). This informal, participatory approach to communication defines the nature of the data posted online. Much of what is posted on social media sites is highly personal; however, a large proportion of postings discuss news and current affairs, politics and pop culture. Development organisations, development workers, volunteers and local people have joined this clamour of voices on the Internet and can be found blogging, tweeting and posting to myriad social media sites, both in official and personal capacities. These posts provide a rich source of information for research projects focused on development-related organisations, social movements and the media; and for those interested in contemporary events, politics, policy, popular discourse and communication.

Like the hidden boxes, the loosely organised, disparate nature of social media presents the researcher with an interesting mix of challenge and opportunity. But while the overarching challenges of gaining access, searching and filtering and processing the material are similar to those searching for the old boxes, the online environment presents specific challenges. Searching the maze that is the social web can be a 'disorientating, time-consuming and overwhelming experience' (Hookway, 2008: 107), and the dynamic and constantly updating nature of social media sites requires significant thought, planning and discipline on the part of the researcher.

The question of ownership is also a tricky one. Unlike the old boxes, the social media 'feed' or blog site usually has a clear owner, and as such there are significant ethical considerations. Although some cases may be akin to picking up a newspaper in the street – where social media posts are intended for a public audience – in many cases it is advisable to seek full, informed consent. However, this is an area of research ethics that is still evolving and there are conflicting positions (Buchanan, 2011; Grodzinsky and Tavani, 2010; Krotoski, 2010; Markham and Buchanan, 2012; Rosenberg, 2010). As such we advise care in the way in which these posts are used, and careful thought regarding the need for consent.

Finally, as Hookway (2008) notes, researchers need to consider the issues of trustworthiness. While websites may present the face of an organisation, blogs and internet posts may form part of the curation of individual lives. For example, blog posts may be consciously framed in order to showcase the bloggers 'desired qualities, such as "'good", "moral" and "virtuous"' (Hookway, 2008: 96). In addition, the anonymity afforded by the Internet means that it may be difficult to verify identities, events and 'facts' presented. In this case it is important to remember as discussed above – the context and purpose of the source, analysing it is as an indication of the worldview of the author rather than drawing data directly from the source.

CORRESPONDENCE AND PRIVATE MESSAGES

Old correspondence files and new email folders have much in common that make them different from boxes with documents and social media, as well as archives and websites. Correspondence and email reflect private conversations rather than public or official discourse – even though the authors often discuss matters of public or institutional interest. Moreover, because the authors and recipients often know each other quite well, these communications may contain elements of intimacy, trust or straight-talking that would be unlikely or misplaced in more official communications. For these reasons, correspondence and email may give you insights into the background or implications of the wider dynamics that are the subject of your research.

CORRESPONDENCE FILES

Correspondence files with letters between two individuals – either in a personal or functional relationship – are less common than official records, but when you can access them, they may provide valuable insights and a 'human perspective' to societal change. For example, correspondence between officials in Ethiopia is deemed by Carmichael to be 'free of overt propaganda, yet indicative of daily government praxis' (2006: 32). At the level of the people's daily life, Zeitlyn (2005) provides a revealing report on correspondence in the 2000s between parents and their children about school fees and the cost of living in Cameroon.

For you as a researcher, two practical challenges stand out when it comes to accessing this type of correspondence. To begin, finding private correspondence in developing countries is hard because in comparison with the richer parts of the world, there is simply a lot less of it. Fewer people were and are literate, and their private correspondence is suffering as much if not more than archives from the ravages of time. It is likely you will access private letters because either the authors want to tell their story (Peterson, 2008) or because a political movement such as South Africa's Black Consciousness Movement wishes to project its history (Maaba, 2001). In these cases, you need to be aware of the risk that the letters can be heavily edited. The second practical challenge with private correspondence is that you will often only find 'one side of the argument'. Howell, for example, realises he cannot fully assess the importance of a Bishop's correspondence in the 1950s 'without looking at records from the colonial end' (2001: 414). Similarly, you may find yourself holding only 'letters of reply', leaving you to deduce what the original letter actually stated (e.g., Triulzi, 2006: 49).

You also face particular methodological challenges when trying to process private correspondence. First, because of the intimate character, you may be led to believe the letters are honest – Gerber discusses the temptation 'to take for granted that what is written is a true account' (2005: 315). This, of course, is often not the case and the writer's motives need to be understood. Whereas an understanding of the politics of the day can assist you to identify motives behind official correspondence, an understanding of the relationship between the writer and recipient of private correspondence is also necessary to appreciate motives behind private correspondence. For example, farmers may exaggerate their harvest losses in their letters to officials to get aid, and parents may not talk of their hardship in order not to upset their children.

The other methodological challenge is that private correspondence, like official correspondence, also needs to be read in its wider socio-political context. At one level this means being aware that until quite recently, most people were illiterate and private correspondence most likely reflects views and experiences of a society's most powerful people. For example, Carmichael (2006) and Triulzi (2006) analyse letters from local elites to Ethiopia's central government against the backdrop of their power struggle. At another level, particularly relevant for Development Studies, private correspondence may also reflect a wider context of people from different cultures meeting. Correspondence from 19th-century British travellers through Latin America, for example, reflects the fact they were the first non-Iberians to visit newly independent states. They write about 'virgin territory' and 'nature unmediated by civilisation' – not because they wished to deceive readers, but because this was the lens through which most British people at the time looked at the 'New World' (Keighren and Withers, 2011: 1333). If you were to analyse correspondence of contemporary aid workers, what would be their lens? What is yours?

Finally, researching private correspondence carries unique ethical questions. Obviously, when the author-owner of private correspondence gives you as researcher access to his or her letters, consent is a rather straightforward formality. However, what if only one party in the exchange of correspondence gives you access to both sides of the correspondence and you cannot contact the other party? Here, again, the concept of 'contextual integrity' is helpful. In practical terms it means treating correspondence according the norms of the context in which the correspondence was written and sent. Rather than focusing only on whether correspondence can be shared publicly, the question is more how and for what purpose the letters were created, and you could assume that you could use the letters for similar purposes today: that is, you would treat letters between lovers with more confidentiality and a sense of privacy than you would the letters of complaint to the local council.

EMAIL AND PRIVATE INTERNET POSTS

The advent of digital technology has led to a proliferation of communication tools, including email SMS messages, mailing lists (such as Yahoo groups) and password-protected discussion forums. While there is clearly some cross-over with social media, the focus here is on messages that are intended for a restricted group, and which cannot be found by public searching. This includes many social media profiles where privacy settings may be set to 'friends' only, and postings that are accessible only with a password. Private messages are usually produced for a specific purpose. Email in particular usually has both functional purposes (giving discrete information such as instructions, questions and news) and personal purposes (such as greetings and personal updates). Mailing list messages and private postings to social media sites also tend towards the informal and personal. These messages are usually part of an on-going conversation or chain of messages that can stretch to multiple users and hundreds of messages.

Private messages are very useful data sources for research topics that seek to explore behind the curtain of official and public identities and perspectives, for research examining personal views, and for understanding the 'unsolicited everyday talk' that occurs online (Sixsmith and Murray, 2001: 424). In development research, these sources can be especially valuable in research with development organisations, documenting the history and progress of events and projects, and providing a record of decision making, organisational processes and stakeholder participation (or non-participation!). For example, Kendall et al. (2006) analysed the postings on an ICT policy email list to explore the way in which ICT for Development policy was formulated through discourse. This type of research is often complimentary to offline data collection, confirming or refuting the official history in published and archival material, and the unofficial 'remembered' history collected in interviews and surveys.

While these private communications can be a source of very valuable data for researchers, gaining access to them is likely to be a challenge. The nature of these private, and sometimes personal, communications means that they will not show up in an internet search, and they may not be offered by research participants. Indeed, you probably won't even know what, if any, useful data people may have stored in their email accounts or personal profiles. In addition, many organisations are likely to be very unwilling to give access to proprietary data, particularly if it contains confidential or commercially sensitive information (Blank, 2008). As with offline written sources, if you think data that will address your question is likely to be found in these types of sources, then you will need work out who the gatekeepers are (whose emails are you interested in, and what levels of organisational access will you need?) and actively seek access to the messages.

When accessing digital correspondence you will also need to think about the extent of access you will need. As with social media, you may have access to thousands of posts, many of which will be irrelevant to your study, and some of which may involve individuals who can't or won't give consent for their use. Make decisions regarding specific topics and timeframes early in the research and to stay close to them. Paradoxically, although you may have access to a large amount of correspondence, your research may be hampered by missing information, including deleted emails. Although it may be possible to dig, sorting and filtering messages and following the message chains to their origins can swallow up large chunks of time and you need to weigh up the benefits of doing this against the wider needs of the research.

Once useful material has been identified, the fact that these messages and posts are private and were never intended for public consumption has significant implications for research. In particular, the authors of these messages will likely have posted the messages in the expectation that they would remain private, and as such the authors retain ownership and control (see ethics discussion above). Therefore consent will need to be sought from all participants and, unless explicit consent is given, any potentially identifying information within email messages should be removed (Buchanan, 2011: 96–98; Murray and Sixsmith, 2002: 52) (see Box 5.1). In addition, as with the discussions of social media and offline correspondence, care needs to be taken with interpretation. Private correspondence may seem more honest but will still be framed in accordance with the priorities and worldview of the writer. In particular, at the beginning of this chapter we noted the implications of the digital divide for the use of written sources in development research. Until very recently, access to computers and the Internet was limited to elites and the well-connected, and this bias needs to be acknowledged when using material from email and internet-based discussions in development research.

INTERACTIVE ONLINE DATA COLLECTION

The increasing speed and reach of the Internet and the rise in internet-based communication technologies has had a profound effect on data collection and fieldwork. The Internet, email and mobile technology not only aid in accessing existing data as we discussed in this chapter, or the planning of fieldwork (see Chapter 6), or the communication with contacts in the field (see Chapter 8), these technologies have also proven useful as tools to interact with participants and to actually generate new data. Online tools such as email, instant messaging, VoIP (e.g., Skype) and video conferencing can be used for questionnaires and interviews, and survey websites (such as Surveymonkey) can provide even beginning researchers with powerful tools for collecting a range of quantitative and qualitative data. While internet research and internet-based methods are unlikely to be a substitute for on-the-ground and in-person research methods in poor or remote locations, they can be a useful source of information for research projects focused on development-related organisations, such as the online presence of indigenous groups (Dyson, 2011), or social movements such as the anti-globalisation movement (Van Aelst and Walgrave, 2002). However, there are some concerns as well as some significant advantages specific to interactive online data generation and collection.

The major advantage of online tools for researchers is in accessing participants, as the Internet opens up opportunities for researchers to collect data in areas or from people they may not otherwise be able to reach (Mawdsley, 2006; McCoyd and Kerson, 2006; McLennan, 2012; O'Connor et al., 2008). Collecting data online is often far safer and cheaper than travelling to remote or conflict-prone areas and, as McCoyd and Kerson (2006) note, can enable the researcher to include isolated, geographically dispersed and/or stigmatised groups in the research, potential participants who may otherwise be overlooked or ignored.

Internet-based research methods also allow repeat access to research participants, giving the researcher the opportunity to ask follow-up questions and to confirm findings and interpretations (Kivits, 2005: 47). In addition, the process of sending emails back and forth or of typing messages into an instant messaging program allows both the researcher and the research participant time for thought and reflection, and with typed responses there is no need to laboriously transcribe recordings and notes (Gaiser and Schreiner, 2009: 48; McLennan, 2012). Translation is easier too, particularly with email interviews, as responses can be carefully translated and reviewed before new questions are sent.

It is important however, to sound a note of caution as internet-based methods have some significant drawbacks. Most obviously in development research, internet-based methods may not be appropriate if you need to include the voice of the poor and most marginalised as, despite the increasing ubiquity of the Internet, its usage is still skewed to the West and the wealthy – the digital divide we discussed earlier.

There are also more general concerns related to the use of internet tools. Internet-based communications still feel less natural to many people, particularly to participants who may not be used to interacting online. The loss of visual cues and body language can make it very difficult to build the trust required for quality research in the online environment. It is therefore more difficult to build rapport and to use the traditional interview techniques (such as probing and reflecting) that are often necessary to draw out fuller, more nuanced responses. In addition, online responses are often shorter than responses to in-person questions, and the time between questions and responses can be lengthy, particularly for email interviews. In many cases the researcher's emails may be ignored, overlooked or forgotten by the participant, leading to long delays and in some cases to incomplete interviews. It is therefore important that you consider the use of internet tools carefully, weighing up the pros and cons in relation to your research aims and participants.

In sum, while internet-based methods may seem to be a good 'fieldwork' option for those who can't (or don't want to) travel, as with all topic decisions it is very important to ensure that your research question is a good fit with the methodology. The choice of internet-based methods should flow from the topic rather than vice-versa.

CONCLUSION

We consider the collection of archival, textual and virtual data as both an extension of fieldwork and as a field location themselves. These sources can provide the researcher with access to a variety of views and insights not accessible through traditional fieldwork methods, from information on events that happened decades or centuries ago, to viewpoints a researcher wouldn't normally hear, and to voices of participants in diverse and geographically distant locations. As such, these sources can provide data that compliments other fieldwork, or they may be even the major, or sole, source of data.

Although this data can be enormously valuable for many research projects, it is important to be aware of the pitfalls of written and virtual data. In particular, these types of methods commonly produce copious amounts of data (which paradoxically may be incomplete), they do not provide the researcher with visual and emotional cues, and there are often complex issues regarding access and ownership. This means that these methods should not be seen as an easy fall-back for those who cannot get to a traditional field site, or who would rather sit in front of a computer or box of documents than to get out and talk to people. The decision to use archival, written or virtual data is one that should flow from the topic and research questions, and not vice-versa.

The final point we want to leave you thinking about as you finish reading this chapter is the importance of considering the context and purpose of archival, written and virtual data. Unlike interview or observational data, which is collected specifically for the purpose of the research, most of the written sources referred to in this chapter are produced for other purposes within particular political, historical and cultural contexts, and in a broader global environment of power imbalances and of digital or technological inequality. The importance of considering this context when analysing each piece of written or virtual data cannot be understated.

Summary

- Archival and internet-based research can be seen as both an extension of the traditional fieldwork and as a field location of themselves, which are as political and as much a part of the 'social terrain' (with all pertaining power inequalities) as the traditional field site.
- The decision to use archival, written or virtual data should be closely related to the topic.
- While this data can be enormously valuable for many research projects, there are numerous potential pitfalls.
- Active engagement with the record is necessary in all archival, textual and virtual data as it is vital that researchers consider the context and purpose of the original writer when accessing and using written sources. Is there a hidden agenda? What is omitted?
- Access and ownership can be complex both on- and offline and determining whether permission is needed, and who from, can be a complex process. Key to these decisions is whether or not the original author considered the work to be public or private.
- Gatekeepers are of particular importance to archival and virtual research. Identifying the best person to give access to a locked storeroom or private online forum, and approaching them appropriately, can make or break a research project.

Questions for reflection

- We have argued that when it comes to the accessing and processing of information, the 'old paper-based' and the 'new digital' sources actually share similar challenges for researchers. Can you list at least two of these shared challenges for each of the following sources: archives and websites; boxes with paper records and social media; correspondence files and email folders?
- Describe how you would try to maintain 'contextual integrity' of the information that you collect in your research.

(Continued)

(Continued)

- What are some of the ethical issues that are pertinent to both archival and online research? Can you see any parallels between research using private correspondence and the use of online tools?
- Once you have collected some of the data for your research from written sources, look at your research questions and ask yourself explicitly, 'What information or whose views am I missing from these data sources?'.

RECOMMENDED READINGS

Buchanan, E. A. and Markham, A. (2012). *Ethical Decision-making and Internet Research: Recommendations from the AoIR Ethics Working Committee* (Version 2.0). Retrieved from http://aoir.org/reports/ethics2.pdf

Ethical guidelines for researchers collecting data online from the Association of Internet Researchers. This document includes discussion of the major tensions/considerations in internet research, and a comprehensive list of internet-specific ethical questions.

Finnegan, R. (2006). Using documents. In R. Sapsford and V. Jupp (eds), *Data Collection and Analysis*. London: Sage.

This book chapter focuses on the collection and analysis of existing written texts, including a good discussion of the need to consider the purpose for which the texts were originally produced.

Jennings, M. (2006). Using archives. In V. Desai and R. Potter (eds), *Doing Development Research* (pp. 241–250). London: Sage.

In this book chapter, Jennings provides a clear introduction to archival research for development researchers. It addresses practical considerations as well as disucussion of potential challenges and the ethics of archival research.

Mawdsley, E. (2006). Using the world wide web for development research. In V. Desai and R. Potter (eds), *Doing Development Research* (pp. 273–281). London: Sage.

This book chapter is one of the few resources specifically addressing the use of the Internet in development research.

Ó Dochartaigh, N. (2012). *Internet Research Skills* (3rd edn). London: Sage.

A guide to online research for social science and humanities students, including chapters devoted to social media and news, and governments, archives and statistics, which are very useful for development research.

Prior, L. (2011). Using documents in social research. In D. Silverman (ed.), *Qualitative Research* (pp. 93–110). London: Sage.

This chapter focuses on the ways in which documents are collected and analysed in qualitative research.

PART II
PREPARATION FOR THE FIELD

6

PRACTICAL ISSUES

MARIA BOROVNIK, HELEN LESLIE AND DONOVAN STOREY

Fieldwork is one of those undertakings for which one simply cannot prepare too much. Aside from the methodological and academic matters that you will need to consider, there are an enormous amount of practical issues to carefully work through as you plan to embark on what may turn out to be the experience of a lifetime. Being adequately and appropriately prepared will not only facilitate a positive dimension to your experience, but will also ultimately influence the success of your research project (Nash, 2000a; Robson and Willis, 1997).

This chapter discusses a number of practical issues and suggests ways in which you can approach them – from information on how to secure research funding to advice on what to pack and where to stay once in the field. That is not to say that you should read this as a blueprint for planning fieldwork. Ultimately, planning will be determined by your own choice of research project and by your personal attributes and qualities.

RESEARCH RESOURCES

Funding is rarely mentioned in accounts of development fieldwork, even though it may be funding even more than methodological or topical interests that will determine the nature of your fieldwork. After all, most of us plan to travel to a distant field site, thus until we can find the money to secure a flight, it will be very difficult to even begin our fieldwork!

EARLY CONSIDERATIONS REGARDING FUNDING

There are two key pieces of advice regarding funding for researchers considering overseas fieldwork: seek as many possibilities for funding you can, and apply early. It is important that you 'leave no stone unturned' (Barrett and Cason, 2010: 20; Nash, 2000b). Raising money can often be a lengthy process and many funding bodies only offer their grants once a year. Some donor agencies also require detailed and complex proposals. Soliciting the help of supervisors and peers is a useful first step to take in preparing grant applications. Work on budgeting the costs of your fieldwork early on, and identify what you need funding for – this also implies that you outline in your research plan, what, why and how you want to fund your fieldwork (Cheek, 2011: 253). Barrett and Cason (2010: 20) estimate that it can take up to a year to identify prospective sources and go through the application process. Simply writing or re-writing a really good proposal can take several weeks.

An important consideration is the kind of contractual agreement you will be entering into with the organisation that will provide funding, and whether the political, charitable or other affiliation of the chosen funding body is likely to determine the fieldwork's outcome (Brydon, 2006; Cheek, 2011). There are funding bodies that are explicitly tied to the very governments, military juntas and economic agencies that may have historically oppressed the people who will become your research participants. Conflicts of interest can thus arise (see Box 9.4). Sluka (2012a: 287), for example, explains the dangers of dealing with funding agencies whose agenda may be opposite to that of the fieldwork participants. He outlines the case of an American sociologist who only discovered on return from the field that his research on student groups in Chile was sponsored by a funding organisation tied to the American military. Investigating the sources of your funding and considering how your research participants view these sources may resolve such ethical dilemmas.

FUNDING SOURCES

Funding for development research can come from a variety of sources. Major institutional donors are governmental, private and non-governmental organisations such as the Economic and Social Committee for Overseas Research in the UK, and the Ford Foundation or the Wenner-Gren Foundation in the US. Such donors usually give large grants but have very strict and complex application procedures. Note that when they list funding criteria it is important to study such information carefully to ensure that you have the maximum chance of being successful. Applications are often 'scored' out of 100, so you need to ensure you address all of the requirements.

Other possible donors can include charities, service organisations (such as Rotary) and university grants committees. As smaller organisations they usually offer more modest sums of money, but often without the demands and complications of major donor agencies. Lists of miscellaneous donors can be found via libraries and university scholarships offices. University grants are typically subject to gaining ethical approval (see Chapter 9). Some students take a broader-sweep approach, writing 'simple, enthusiastic emails or letters to any prospective sponsor that seems even remotely interested in the research', prior to more formal applications for funding (Barrett and Cason, 2010: 20).

You should be aware that being successful with one application does not necessarily mean that your research will be bankrolled. Often, despite your best efforts at applying for funding, you may not be able to secure enough financial support to complete the kind of research project you had envisaged. In this case, it may be necessary to dip into your personal funds, or to revise your proposal to spend less time in the field, or to delay your fieldwork until you have secured adequate support. Or, you could consider linking to an already existing research project close to your chosen topic or site. Barrett and Cason (2010: 26) suggest enquiring with large donor organisations about researchers or institutions with larger contracts or projects in your area of interest that might be able to include you. In some cases the chief investigator might arrange employment for you or provide non-monetary forms of support such as supplying equipment or covering the cost of travel to your field site (Cheek, 2011: 251).

A final option to finance your fieldwork is to take out a loan. If you are fortunate, a supportive family member might be able to help; in such cases it is important to write up an agreement about the amount, and repayment conditions, and for you both to sign this. Alternatively, in many countries government-driven student loans can be used for research purposes. Whether it is a loan from a family member, a student loan or a regular bank loan that finances your fieldwork, the money will have to be paid back from your own purse. You are likely to ask for less than is probably needed, and you might be burdened with the pressure of finding ways to pay back the loan during the most important writing-up stage of your research (Barrett and Cason, 2010: 26). Despite these concerns, funding research through borrowing may well be an appropriate means when no other avenues exist.

ESTABLISHING CONTACTS

Creating a wide network of contacts will make your research interesting and successful. Crang and Cook argue that 'research *on* social relations is *made out* of social relations' (2007: 19). Start establishing contacts as early as possible, as this will help to facilitate access to the field site. You might also need to know someone very early on who can send you the documentation necessary to fulfil the requirements of your university human ethics committee or visa application (Hertel et al., 2009). This documentation could be a letter of approval from a local official or village elder and which is crucial in ultimately determining whether your application for research permission is granted.

WHO TO CONTACT

It is advisable that you contact a number of people in the organisation or community you want to work with as soon as possible to start a network that then can be carefully expanded (Desai et al., 2008; Devereux and Hoddinott, 1992; Wesche et al., 2010: 65). Make sure that one of your early emails or letters reaches someone of importance such as an NGO head, government official or village elder, as these people are more likely to have the power to both facilitate your access to the field and legitimise your presence once you are there (Binns, 2006: 15).

Along with members of the intended research community, it is also a good idea to contact other researchers currently in the field or recently returned (Crang and Cook, 2007). These early contacts can provide valuable information about the practicalities such as visas and cost of living, and can also lay the foundations for friendships and social support once in the field (Hubbell, 2010). Helen's contact with an American PhD student living in San Salvador, for example, provided her with a strategy to renew her one-month visa regularly by going across the border into Guatemala. It is also helpful to establish affiliations to academic institutions in your chosen field site (Hubbell, 2010: 332).

It is worthwhile writing to your consulate or high commission in the country concerned to see if they can put you in contact with relevant individuals and institutions. This has the additional benefit of informing them that you will be in the country doing research in a certain place for a specific period of time, information which could be used to keep you safe in the event of a crisis or natural calamity.

Finally, think about the language you will use during your fieldwork and whether you require research assistants or interpreters during or after fieldwork (Crang and Cook, 2007). Veldwisch (2008: 172) found that speaking to people in their local Uzbek language rather than in Russian, helped to build rapport with people who usually felt marginalised. During establishment of early contacts you could enquire whether your information sheet should be in local language, and how to find good fieldwork assistants and interpreters (see Chapter 8).

HOW TO ESTABLISH CONTACT

Once you have decided who to contact, you will need to give some thought to the best methods for establishing contact and introducing yourself. There are plenty of possibilities including traditional letters and phone calls, and a range of email, internet and mobile options. Although most government officials, NGOs or key contacts have access to email, internet servers are notoriously unreliable in many places and emails can easily be ignored or lost, meaning that your best efforts to contact individuals can go unnoticed. Hence in some instances it may be best to send a written letter, or even pick up the phone (especially if you have someone's personal mobile number), during the important initial contact stage. If your communications receive no response, keep trying as usually someone will eventually respond and could point out useful names and strategies. Starting contact through emailing NGOs well before she started her Master's research on organic agriculture in Cambodia proved successful for Alice Beban (2008: 69), who found that local organisations were enthusiastic about her study and helped her with accessing different rural villages.

What kind of emails or letters should you write to establish contact with people in the field? Lareau (1996: 203) believes that introductory letters should be short, direct and focus more on the needs of the researcher and the proposed role of the organisa-tion/individual contacted than on the academic or intellectual goals of the project itself. A summary of your research proposal can always be attached if you think the individual or organisation may want more details. Do not expect a flood of responses to your emails, phone calls or letters. Generally, the people whom you will most likely want to contact will be busy, and probably will not even directly read your requests. If you get a response, then great, but do not lose heart or take it as a portent of things to come if you do not hear back from someone. In fact, your attempt at contact may well be remembered once you have arrived and contacted the person directly.

A great way of establishing contact with the research community is to spend time with people of the same nationality before you enter the field (Barrett and Cason, 2010). Many different ethnic groups have associations in universities that organise social and cultural events, and your participation in such events can often lead to helpful contacts and advice. For example, before he decided to conduct fieldwork for his Master's thesis with returned workers and their families on Tanna Island in Vanuatu, Ed Cameron (2010) socialised and worked with a group of ni-Vanuatu seasonal workers in casual jobs in New Zealand vineyards. Having worked side by side proved invaluable for establishing contacts and building social networks in Vanuatu, and for developing a cultural awareness while still in New Zealand. In another example, Maria, one of the authors of this chapter, befriended a family from Kiribati before leaving for her doctoral fieldwork. Socialising with this family and their friends during special events in New Zealand helped with understanding cultural codes, especially for women, with choosing what to pack and what to wear, and with learning some of the language. Another possibility is to offer to do proof-reading for a student from the country you are going to in exchange for language lessons. Establishing such personal contacts can bring with it real long-term benefits and contentment.

Keep in mind that in many non-Western cultures, personal contact is still much more preferable than other forms of communication. Indeed, even experienced researchers find that the most successful way to gain interviews and material is to simply turn up at someone's office to make an appointment in person – or even to sit and wait for a meeting.

RESEARCH PERMISSION

Negotiating research permission can be complicated and time consuming, but is crucial for the success of your fieldwork (Barrett and Cason, 2010; Cornet, 2010; Eklund, 2010; Wesche et al., 2010). There are at least two levels of permission that you will need, from official authorities and from local gatekeepers. This section focuses on the former, while Chapter 9 will examine gatekeepers. Gaining official permission and the appropriate documentation to do your fieldwork may be as straightforward as filling in a research visa application, paying the fee involved, and waiting a few days or weeks – or it may be a much more serious impediment requiring months of attempted communication between yourself and the relevant authorities (see Box 6.1). Heller et al. note that in Uganda one author needed '33 approvals from four levels of government to carry out three months of fieldwork' (2011: 74). Gaining research permission was also an arduous process for Cornet, who was asked to provide various documents for the Chinese authorities:

> Ultimately, the list of required documents included: proof of a medical examination; a range of photographs of specific sizes; a resident permit; a copy of my diplomas (translated from Latin); a copy of my resume; a detailed research proposal in Chinese; a photocopy of my scholarship papers; proof of registration, a photocopy of the ethics approval from my home institution, and a letter from the director of the Southwest Minority Language and Culture Research Institute which stated clearly their responsibility in supervising my research during the entirety of my fieldwork. (2010: 140)

You need to consider the implications of your research and the site you have chosen, and may have to adjust your proposal should permission become an issue. For example, getting official permission to conduct research on the restrictive operating environment for NGOs in Ethiopia or on Pakistan's nuclear capabilities would be difficult, to say the least. Be realistic and do some homework on your (potential) topic and possible field sites.

Box 6.1   Perspiration and persistence: how to gain research permission

For me, studying Solomon Islands politics, a permit was mandatory. Unfortunately the process of getting the permit wasn't so simple. For every province I planned to visit (six in all) I needed letters of approval from the provincial government in question. I also needed letters from the MPs whose electorates I planned to visit. And then, when I had these, I had to submit an application, containing all the approvals, additional letters of support, and a form to the Ministry of Education for sign-off by the Minister. All of this in a country where internet access is limited, transport between islands expensive or difficult, the postal service slow, and provincial governments are often dysfunctional.

I got there in the end but it took two and a half months of perspiration, frustration, contact making, letter writing and polite reminding. And I succeeded mostly thanks to the help of some very kind, hard-working people. It's not a process I hope to repeat any time soon.

On the other hand, I did learn some valuable lessons: find out about permits early and allow time to get them. If appropriate, consider pursuing the application in-country – it's much easier in person. And where bureaucratic capacity is limited, personal contacts are critical, as is patience, and politeness.

Source: Terence Wood, Doctoral research in the Solomon Islands

Eklund argues that these difficulties around permissions are grounded in the concern of government officials and local gatekeepers 'with the motives of the researcher as well as costs and risks involved in the fieldwork' (2010: 134). Therefore, Barrett and Cason (2010: 49) advise it is always wise to consult with others who have been to the same 'field' you are going to, to see how best to gain research permission.

Issues may also arise for students going back 'home' to do their fieldwork. While 'locals' may have several advantages over foreign researchers, such as being conversant in political procedures, culture and having contacts, there may also be some disadvantages. They may be seen as a threat, as they have a greater opportunity to distribute their findings locally. For example, Mandiyanike (2009: 68) experienced difficulties dealing with officials in his home country Zimbabwe, even though he took great care with appropriate appearance and behaviour, and he worked on building a network within the bureaucratic system. The bottom line is to plan ahead and be realistic in where you go to do research.

Official approval is only the first step of many towards gaining legitimacy. Permission may need to be further granted from regional or local authorities (Cornet, 2010). A 'higher level' authorisation might help ease local resistance, but this may not always be the case. In some instances 'official' documentation may create a degree of suspicion when local groups are in dispute with national authorities. Local gatekeepers (see Chapter 9) may, in fact, be your most important people to approve your research because they 'exercise considerable authority and autonomy, depending on the local context' (Mandel, 2003: 203). On a positive note, working with a network of bureaucratic systems to receive permission for research can result in knowledge about government structures, and might even open doors to initial research contacts. This was Maria's experience during her fieldwork in 2012, as she found that the chain of authorities she had to contact in order to receive her research permit in Kiribati presented opportunities for interviews with government officials and participation in leadership meetings. Similarly, Heller et al. (2011) observed that once approval was achieved, authorities could become key informants and be supportive by arranging meetings or facilitating further networking.

HEALTH AND SAFETY

When preparing for development fieldwork, health and safety concerns are paramount. As Devereux and Hoddinott (1992: 14) stress, 'fieldwork can be an unhealthy occupation' and virtually every person who has conducted development fieldwork will have had some experience of illness and/or danger before returning home. There are various aspects or types of risks researchers face, including physical, emotional, ethical and professional risks (Lee-Treweek and Linkogle, 2000). However Heywood et al. (2012) concluded in their study on travel risk behaviour that many postgraduate students are not aware of or educated about the risks and preventative strategies they could apply before embarking on their research. This lack of knowledge and risky behaviour is illustrated by Hoffman's experience of a six-day fishing trip while studying how Mexican Caribbean fishermen make a living:

> My body was tested; it ached from the continuous swimming. I gained impressive wounds on my feet from my flippers, and the spikes of the lobsters pulped my soft academic's hands ... The actions of my companions also tested my conscience. I was obligated to participate in their lifestyle of looking for washed up packets of drugs, highly illegal fishing activities, and drug consumption. Yet all of this testing brought me to the realization that this was the work I had to do to gain the confidence of my subjects. (2006: 19)

While it may be unlikely that your research will involve such extreme participation, the vast differences between home and fieldwork environments (climate, lifestyle, food) makes it difficult to avoid uncomfortable experiences. This is not to suggest that fieldwork is necessarily dangerous. It would be unwise to wrap yourself in cotton wool on arrival and then expect to build rapport with locals who may well interpret your reluctance to try local food, venture beyond your neighbourhood or leave home without your first aid kit as a scathing indictment on their culture and way of life. The obvious approach to take is one of balance and flexibility. Experience as much as you can of the lifestyles of the people with whom you will be working, but make sure that you have taken the precautions that will mitigate against some of the more serious illnesses or issues that you may be faced with in the field (Barrett and Cason, 2010).

HEALTH PREPARATIONS

One of the first things you can do in preparing for a healthy fieldwork experience is to contact your general practitioner (GP) or your local tropical health centre.[1] These organisations have the most up-to-date information on country specific vaccinations and health conditions and can advise you on the kinds of immunisations and precautions that you will need to take before entering the field (Barrett and Cason, 2010: 31). Whatever your views or beliefs in conspiracy theories on immunisation, it is strongly advisable that you receive what is deemed necessary by medical authorities before entering the field. New and much more effective vaccines have replaced many that were less than satisfactory in the past. Some diseases are life-threatening and others can cause permanent damage to an individual's health.

Healthy preparations for fieldwork also include noting your blood group, and packing a comprehensive first aid kit (Devereux and Hoddinott, 1992: 14) (see Box 6.2). While not necessarily advocating self-diagnosis and treatment, a guide such as Schroeder's *Staying Healthy in Asia, Africa and Latin America* (2000) may prove an invaluable asset in the field. You should also obtain travel insurance, preferably the kind which will airlift you to your country of origin in the case of serious illness and will pre-pay costs rather than reimburse (Barrett and Cason, 2010: 31).

Box 6.2   First aid materials

In this kit you will need a range of items, depending on where you are going to be based. There are now excellent medical facilities in many cities of developing countries, so some of the items below might only be needed in more remote locations.

- basic dressing materials (Band-Aids and sterile pads);
- a crepe bandage (to use for ankle and knee strains);
- a thermometer (to keep an eye on levels of fever and to diagnose infection);
- antiseptic wipes and lotion;
- skin closure strips;
- medications for pain and/or inflammation such as paracetamol (acetaminophen) and ibuprofen;
- a broad-spectrum antibiotic;
- anti-malarial medicines (if required);
- antihistamine tablets for bites and allergic reactions;
- rehydration salts (to aid recovery when one has diarrhoea);
- rubber gloves;
- water purification tablets (alternatively, you might use a water filtration device);
- antifungal cream (tea-tree oil is a cheap and effective option here);
- scissors, safety pins, tweezers;
- several small syringes and needles for intramuscular injections (particularly if you are going to a country where HIV/AIDs is endemic – also attach a letter from your GP clarifying that you are not an intravenous drug user); and
- a small first aid manual.

Many of these items can be purchased straight from a pharmacy, but others, such as antibiotics, will need to be prescribed to you by your GP. You should note that some of these resources may be in demand in many communities – be wary about acting as a medical practitioner if you lack the requisite qualifications.

It is also very useful to find out what health concerns are endemic to the region you will be visiting, and in the season you are visiting (Barrett and Cason, 2010: 32). For example, if you are planning to conduct your fieldwork in a country prone to malaria, it is important that you thoroughly investigate the different kinds of malaria prevention tablets and insect repellents that can be used in your chosen field site, as well as carrying a mosquito net.

The old axiom 'prevention is always better than the cure' applies here. Getting comprehensive immunizations, preventing mosquito bites, having a good first aid kit, drinking clean water, keeping clear of old or unprotected food, and staying clean (especially one's hands) are all basic forms of prevention that can go a very long way towards a healthy fieldwork experience. Finally, while you may not be planning to initiate or establish sexual relations while in the field, it is essential that you make preparations to protect your own and other's sexual health. If you are planning to spend a period of time in a remote location, availability of condoms may turn out to be an issue. It is best then, to take a supply with you.

Along with these practical preparations for healthy fieldwork, Barrett and Cason (2010: 31) stress that it is also important that you prepare yourself mentally for what you may face in the field (see Chapter 7). Think about how you might cope with feeling sick and try to envisage what kinds of help or support you will seek if you are struck down with dysentery or some other problem. Devereux and Hoddinott (1992: 14) advocate building a sickness 'allowance' into your work schedule planning and stress that fieldworkers must be prepared to give themselves plenty of rest periods. In this way you are less likely to get run down and to make yourself vulnerable to contracting something debilitating.

SAFETY PREPARATIONS

Development fieldwork, especially when undertaken abroad, means taking risks and moving into a zone of uncertainty, and the consideration of these concerns begins with the selection of the country and region where you want to operate (Barrett and Cason, 2010: 90). There are strict ethical codes for postgraduate research in most Western universities that restrict research in regions with direct threats to a researcher's life. If you are permitted to conduct your fieldwork in a conflict or post-conflict zone or in a city known for violence, such as Port Moresby or Johannesburg, or among high crime communities, such as gangs or street children, safety precautions are clearly paramount. Sluka (2012a) suggests two considerations that need to be made when planning for fieldwork in dangerous or violent social contexts.

First, it is important to realistically evaluate the 'degree of danger' that you may be exposed to in the field and its potential sources. Here you might consider what level of risk you are prepared to take and the kinds of individual actions that would potentially lessen or increase such risk. Note that native researchers are not immune from dangers of fieldwork. Rashid and her research assistant decided to avoid some areas of the slum environment where they worked, particularly 'the seedier sections where heroin was sold' (Rashid, 2007: 380). Even if you are not going to an area to study conflict, violence or a dissident group, you may accidentally find yourself in the wrong place at the wrong time. Assuming that the majority of researchers would draw the line where their life is threatened, Sluka (2012a) stresses both the need for a plan of escape from the situation and recognition that you may have to terminate your fieldwork if the risks become too great. If you are a student, close contact with your supervisor can help you to make a sound decision regarding whether to terminate, delay or change the nature of your field research.

Second, before entering the field, discuss the potential safety risks of your proposed research with your colleagues, supervisors and any other potential research contacts. A check of your own country's travel advisories is a useful initial call. In addition, travel blogs, guidebooks and information from your high commission, embassy or consulate can be useful in building a mental picture of potential dangers or risks in the field.[2] Remember, however, that you are the one who is more likely to be cognisant with the current situation in the field, so try to trust your own judgement if the advice that ensues is alarmist or inappropriate. Bøås et al. advise talking to as many people as possible, including authorities and ordinary people, and 'if you feel uncomfortable in a certain situation, leave' (2006: 76).

Box 6.3 explains some basic security precautions for those doing field research in developing countries, which are particularly relevant to those going to a new country and location for the first time. In addition, Barrett and Cason (2010: 96) advise not to accept drinks from strangers, use camouflaged wallets and be prepared for unexpected circumstances.

Box 6.3   Going to the field with security considerations in mind

- Be stingy about revealing information about yourself (e.g., with taxi drivers).
- Write important financial and contact information including emergency contacts, numbers to cancel credit cards, embassy phone numbers, and doctors' numbers on a photocopy of the first page of your passport and hide it in your car, the false bottom of your backpack or bag, or your toiletries bag. Ensure that someone at home also has a copy.
- Do not conspicuously display a watch, electronic devices including phones and computers, camera or jewellery, as they distinguish you as an easy target. Use electronic devices in your hotel room, not in a café or on the street. Carry your laptop computer in your backpack or suitcase, particularly at airports and as you arrive at your accomodation.
- Ensure that you back up all your data by copying it to a transportable drive, emailing it to yourself or someone back home or saving to the cloud (see Chapter 5 for further discussion of data security).

Source: Hertel et al. (2009: 308)

When preparing for safe fieldwork it is also important to have some idea of what to expect in terms of everyday life, such as the behaviour expected at police or army checkpoints or 'no-go' areas at night. Building rapport and learning from research participants can also enable the researcher to put into practice appropriate safety mechanisms (Lee, 1995: 28–29). You will most likely find that as you get to know a new field location, you will be able to 'ease up' in some ways regarding safety precautions.

Female researchers should take particular note of the guidelines for women travellers and wherever possible plan to avoid those areas/situations where sexual assault is commonplace. As horrible as it may be to contemplate, women researchers are no more immune to sexual assault than any other women in a country and should be mindful of the increased risk of this that follows or accompanies violent social conflict in general. Once in the field, female researchers should also be aware of the advice of local people who have current knowledge of the dangers that exist in their own communities (see also examples provided by Barrett and Cason, 2010). During Helen's fieldwork in El Salvador, for example, she decided to abandon her plan to visit women participants in their homes in an isolated rural area upon hearing of the recent rape of a development worker in the vicinity.

Many accounts of fieldwork in violent settings speak of the fear engendered by the visibility of weapons (see, e.g., Lee, 1995: 28). Marianne Bevan (2011) experienced a mix of emotions when a police officer squad in Timor Leste asked her to photograph the group while posing with their weapons. Although she felt that the photo opportunity linked well with her research topic (on international policing and masculinities), the imposed masculinity also reminded her of her vulnerability as a female researcher and her exposure to assault. In such situations, Lee (1995) believes the researcher becomes a 'routine coward', or someone to whom recognising and avoiding potentially dangerous situations is second nature.

As is discussed in Chapters 7 and 8, anxiety and depression are common reactions to these stresses of fieldwork and should not be viewed as extraordinary or shameful. Recognising that health concerns may arise will aid researchers in considering strategies that could help them through trying times in the field.

PLACES TO STAY, OR NOT TO STAY

After travel, the most pressing logistical consideration will most likely be accommodation. Your choice of where to stay involves issues of cost, community acceptance or marginalisation, safety, security and wellbeing, and access to information. As Wall (2008: 138) reflects, 'how one situates oneself as a researcher' has a great influence on the outcome of fieldwork. You should therefore seriously consider several personal and professional implications about where to stay during your research.

COST

For most researchers cost is likely to be a primary concern during fieldwork. When you are on a limited budget, what you spend on a bed for the night is directly proportional to what you eat and do the next day, so the temptation is to cut accommodation costs. It would be tempting then to frequent the cheapest form of accommodation possible, but this too has its drawbacks. Staying in a 20-bed backpacker dormitory may be great socially, but it is hardly conducive to late-night reading or planning the next day's interview questions. Living in a 'tourist ghetto' is also likely to be distracting and will restrict productive work time to daylight hours (minus travel time). In some instances such areas are not particularly safe at night, and security for your gear may also be an issue. Finding a balance between cost and functionality is important, but there are other deciding factors: researchers will also, in most cases, want to be close to the community or activity they are studying, if not within it.

WHERE TO STAY – AND WHY

For those doing rural fieldwork or work in marginalised communities it is access to the research site(s) that will be the most pressing concern. Commercial accommodation is often limited in proximity to marginal or marginalised communities. So surely the best remaining option then is to live within your study area, even in the house of your key respondents? For some, while this would help offset logistical problems, open the door to late night research, and help build strong relationships and greater understanding, living within one's fieldwork site 24/7 can be emotionally overwhelming, physically draining and, in conflict situations, outright life threatening. Barrett and Cason argue:

> You have to be happy where you are living. There is nothing worse than coming home from a difficult day of dealing with bureaucrats or interviewing farmers or a fruitless day in the archives to a place that you find uncomfortable, dangerous or depressing. The trick is to find a place you deem acceptable financially and psychologically. (2010: 34)

Without a doubt, living within one's research site is potentially thrilling (at the personal level) and productive (with regard to data). Fitri (2006), for example, felt that adjusting to the family and community life of the family she and her spouse stayed with during her doctoral research in rural West Sumatra was an important aspect of building trust within the community. Living within a community can potentially bring rewards of acceptance and trust, both of which are invaluable for research. Especially in poorer or powerless communities, nothing perhaps conveys a message of commitment or acceptance more than living as part of a community. It may also have the consequence of disarming community suspicion, resistance or hostility. By literally 'being there' a much greater appreciation of issues and a context for data will eventuate.

The following example experienced by Wall (2008) in rural Uzbekistan shows how the choice of living *in* the village can provide opportunities within the community. Although this positioning does not necessarily lead to becoming an insider, it does mitigate some of the hierarchies involved with being an outsider in a research location (see Box 6.4). Despite your best intentions of living 'on site', you may well find yourself to be an outsider to a number of people in the community, such as those who are of a different class, caste or ethnic group from the people you are living with.

Box 6.4   Breaking down barriers between researcher and community

Upon entering the field, I made use of my 'tamorka' (household) plot of 0.12 ha attached to my house. This attempt to understand agricultural knowledge at the most immediate household level turned out to be incredibly rewarding, both professionally and personally .... From a professional research perspective it served as perhaps the best way of introducing my motivations to the community. Rather than entering the field with an agenda for what I wanted to teach or provide, instead I was deliberately making myself reliant upon the help and advice of the local community. This very quickly broke down barriers between those who had been suspicious of me and my work; it also reduced that I was a 'westerner' with superior knowledge.

Source: Wall (2008: 146)

Living in remote and/or poor communities is a serious commitment and needs as much forethought and preparation as possible. Access to food, telecommunications, outside news and the comforts of a hot bath or personal space may initially, and from home, seem like relatively minor inconveniences, but after weeks then months it can take on momentous proportions. Eating a bland, repetitive diet that one is unaccustomed to can lead to serious health problems. Sleeping on unwashed bedding in tropical overnight temperatures within airless rooms (the windows shut for safety in squatter settlements) can lead to feelings of being perpetually filthy. Being unable to find any space or time to read, reflect or plan might be very frustrating. Finally, living within one's research site may also involve continuous forms of reciprocity, in the form of financial contributions and/or in practical forms, such as baby-sitting, going along on shopping errands, or even taking an active part in karaoke (against your best judgment perhaps). Again, while these are potentially satisfying and productive encounters, they do need to be factored into your everyday existence outside of just being a researcher. Even the most ardent advocate of total immersion must be realistic, and find opportunities to get away even if for only a few hours.

Above all, be flexible and realistic when planning your accommodation. Your principal aim while in the field is to carry out your research aims to the best of your abilities, so choose a place to stay which allows you to do this the most effectively, and accept limitations.

WHERE TO GO AND WHEN TO GO

Discussing where to go may at first appear rather superfluous, given that some research is highly specific with regard to topic and location, or is 'home' for many international students. Yet for most first-time thesis students the reasons why such a decision is taken is often not so coherent. There is much to be said for starting from a position of some strength, and advantages of similar diet, language, educational systems and a location where your family or friends can more easily visit. A Master's student based in Australia may find the implications of aging on developing countries as relevant in the Cook Islands as in China. Thinking through why you are going, where and when may seem like obvious points, although students still opt for remote or difficult locations for reasons which are unclear to them. This is not to make the case against difficult or distant 'exotic' sites, but rather to encourage a coherent decision-making process linked to the requirements of research-based thesis work and minimising the risk of fieldwork failure (Barrett and Cason, 2010: 7).

Once you have more clearly thought through where you are going and why, the final issue is when? Again, there will be constraints on choice. Family and friends, finances and feeling prepared enough to go are some likely factors. Some disciplines, departments or your supervisor may also have preferences or stipulations regarding when in the research process fieldwork should be conducted.

There are also several destination factors that are context specific, and you must do the necessary background reading on where you are going. Climate is one issue to consider (Barrett and Cason, 2010: 7; Raybeck, 1996). Although many researchers might prefer to avoid the rainy season, Binns points out that it is important to weigh up the difficulties of doing research during this time against the consideration that 'if you avoid the rainy season you could actually miss much of the farming activity when people are working at their hardest, when food may be in short supply' (2006: 15). Other issues to think about are religious events or rituals (e.g., Ramadan, Christmas), national festivals, and associated holidays, election time, and any other foreseeable context for political conflict. Unless your research is particularly associated with such events, it may prove wise to avoid them.[3]

In her research in Indonesia, Fitri avoided going to West Sumatra during Ramadan 'when farmers in rural areas were not performing much farming activities' (2006: 131). However, research is still possible during such periods. This was the case with Loveridge, who gained 'a greater appreciation of the difficulties of conducting business and government during the Muslim month of fasting than would have been the case had she avoided it' (2001: 8). In the case of Master's research, you may have little flexibility with timing. It then becomes important to plan, to develop effective research strategies, and to integrate these into your methodologies.

PACKING

What you will need to take to the field will depend on the kind of environment you will be exposed to and the resources available in those environments. Packing goods that are difficult to come by may make the difference between a comfortable and successful fieldwork experience and one that is fraught with problems and difficulties. Plan considerably before you start packing. You will want to inform yourself about the visa requirements, currency, geography, climate, culture and history of the area that you are going to as much as possible. Google Earth is easy to download (www.google.com/earth/index.html) and will allow you to zoom in to the research area and to familiarise yourself with the general geography of the area. Your academic preparation should have included reviewing background information about the country and region that you are going to. It is also useful to browse the Internet for any relevant contextual information you can find, and to consider travel advice from bloggers familiar with the area.

Once you have a clear idea about the geography, climate and socio-cultural context, start packing accordingly. Make a list of essential travel documents: for example, passport, visa requirements, vaccination certificates, health and travel insurance, flight tickets and address book (see Binns, 2006: 17 for a comprehensive kit list). You will need to think about the currency and organise some cash. Barrett and Cason (2010: 35) suggest that you pack business cards with your contact details, your affiliation and title. In many cultures it is expected that you will present your business card when you introduce yourself, and they can be useful for following up after you left the field. It might also be useful to have an international student identity card available and paper with academic letterheads that affiliates you with your academic institution.

Pack clothes according to the specific social and cultural context in which you will be working. Travel lightly and leave behind any 'unmanageable large wardrobe', articles that require special care (Barrett and Cason, 2010: 39). Whether you are a male or female researcher, you should solicit advice on appropriate dress in your destination area and take this advice seriously: if local women always cover their shoulders and wear skirts or dresses at least knee length, then do the same; if it is not acceptable for men to wear short pants, then pack some pairs of long pants. Usually it is better to aim to look professional rather than a bedraggled backpacker who has been on the road for many months (Desai et al., 2008). Make sure that you have items that display respectful manners.

Clothing that is light and dries easily is preferable to items that may take hours to dry in damp or cold climates. While cotton is breathable and a good choice of fabric to wear close to the skin in tropical environments, there are many forms of clothing manufactured with light new synthetic fabrics that are ideal for fieldwork. Binns (2006: 17) advises students to pack basic items such as a towel, underwear, shirts, socks, trousers and shorts, togs (swimming costume), pullover or fleece, waterproof jacket, hat, belt and glasses and/or sunglasses. You might like to pack spares of items such as prescription glasses or contact lenses so that you have extra on hand in the event of loss or breakage.

Another essential item to pack is footwear. Well worth the investment is a good pair of water-resistant sandals or boots. Wherever you plan to conduct your fieldwork you will most probably be doing a great deal of walking. It is therefore essential that you have comfortable and hardwearing footwear. A variety, including a pair of smart shoes, training shoes, sandals, lightweight walking boots and plastic slip-on sandals, is suggested by Binns (2006: 17).

It is also important to pack malaria prevention equipment and clothing. A mosquito net and full strength Deet (N,N-Diethyl-meta-toluamide) insect repellent are essential preventative items, as are items of clothing that can be worn out at night to completely cover your arms and legs (i.e. long-sleeve tops and long pants). Check if the area you are travelling to has incidence of dengue fever, and if so, make sure that in outside areas you are always covered with insect repellent as there is no other prevention available. See also Box 6.2 on first aid materials.

Toiletries and related personal items that most people find useful during fieldwork include lip salve, toothbrush and paste, deodorant, soap, shampoo, flannel, razor and razor blades, shaving soap, comb or hairbrush, sun-protection cream, ear plugs and tissues. Equipment you might also want to consider packing are: string, pegs and a small piece of soap for your laundry, luggage keys, coat hangers, sheet sleeping bag, penknife and scissors (remember not to put in your hand-luggage), small backpack, filtered water bottle, short-wave radio, clock, torch, mirror, pens, pencils, notebook and maps (see Binns, 2006: 17). Note that even if you intend to voice record your interviewees, it is handy to pack a good notebook.

As you will be seen as a researcher from an overseas or Western university, assumptions will be made in the field about your relative wealth and status. It is best, therefore, to avoid packing too many valuable items as these symbols of wealth (such as expensive digital devices) may be stolen or act to place you in a more vulnerable position (see also Box 6.3). Keeping a small-change purse containing a limited amount of money is a good idea in many contexts as it can be easily given away if need be and appears less flashy than a bulging wallet (Barrett and Cason, 2010: 93). Be aware that although you might see yourself as a serious researcher, to some you will simply appear as another wealthy tourist to target.

Although they may at times draw unwanted attention, it is important to consider research tools, such as computers, camera or digital voice recorder, necessary for you to conduct successful fieldwork. Try to minimise the number of electronic devices you travel with, and choose devices that can multi-task (see in detail Box 6.5). For those whose needs may be limited to finding information and making calls, a smartphone might suffice, and it can be used as a camera, voice recorder and portable scanner (Welsh and France, 2012). Make a list of the computing and communication tasks you anticipate doing in the field and the functions that are most important to you, and plan your electronic packing list accordingly.

Box 6.5   Electronic devices in the field

In recent years, the type of equipment carried by researchers has changed dramatically – and it will change again the future. No longer do novice researchers arrive armed only with a notebook packed with essential phone numbers and addresses and a pen. However, before packing electronic gadgets for fieldwork it is important to stop and think about what you will really need, and to consider the risks of carrying electronic devices to the field.

(Continued)

(Continued)

- *Laptop computer:* Having a laptop in the field has considerable advantages, as data can be entered and backed up on the go, and communication is made easier, but consider leaving your laptop behind if travelling to remote areas with limited power and internet access, or to areas where humidity or dust are likely to play havoc with sensitive electronics.
- *Mobile phones:* These are very useful for communication purposes but also – in the case of smartphones – as web browsers, cameras, voice recorders, GPS and hand-held scanners. Before packing, check if there will be mobile access as data connections are still patchy in many parts of the world. A simple non-smartphone may be all you need and these can usually be bought very cheaply once in the field.
- *Tablet computer:* These can be a good alternative to a laptop if you want to share photos or videos with participants in the field, and are great for storing (and reading) PDFs and other documents. Many tablets now can be used for basic photography and scanning, and as voice recorders. However, unless you have mastered touch-screen typing, data entry can be more difficult than on a laptop, and they are more conspicuous, bulkier and more awkward to use on the go than a mobile phone. If you don't need a smartphone or full sized tablet a smaller device like an iPod touch can be used to access maps and other local information, update social media or take short notes on the run.
- *Cameras:* Most researchers take photos in the field: for personal use, as a memory trigger during analysis and writing, and as a data source. However, think about whether or not you need a separate camera; if you only intend to take a few snaps for personal use, this could be done with a mobile phone or tablet. However, if you are a keen photographer, or want to take photographs as part of your research methodology, think carefully about the type and size of camera you need.
- *Hand-held scanners:* If your research data is likely to include collecting documents from institutions, printed media or archives you might consider investing in a hand-held scanner. These can quickly and easily turn paper documents into digital files for easy storage and analysis. However, if you only anticipate collecting only a few documents this way, the camera apps on modern electronic devices may be sufficient for most jobs. (See also Box 5.3, Chapter 5).
- *Digital voice recorders:* The digital voice recorder is now a standard item of equipment for researchers, and if your research plan includes significant numbers of interviews it is advisable to get the best you can. However, voice recordings can now easily be made on laptops, mobile phones and tablets so consider how many interviews you plan to do, and where these are likely to take place, as you may find other devices will do the job just as well. If interviewing in places where there is background noise, buy an external microphone to ensure audible voice recordings are made.
- *Adaptors, converters, chargers, batteries and surge suppressors:* Before leaving, investigate the kind of outlets and voltage in your destination country, and purchase the correct adaptors and converters. A good surge protector is highly recommended in some contexts, as are rechargeable batteries. Double-check all your chargers and cables before you leave.
- *Storage devices:* Before leaving for the field it is important to seriously think about your storage needs. What data will need to be stored? What are the storage options available to you?

Are there strict privacy requirements (e.g., medical data, sensitive information) or large volumes or file sizes to consider? Many researchers now back up data to online data storage services including Dropbox, Google Drive, iCloud or Mega). However, the usefulness of these services needs to be weighed against privacy and security concerns (see Chapter 5). It is advisable to pack a couple of USB storage sticks small enough to squeeze into a pocket of your bag. These may come in useful for saving data on the fly. If you think you may need to store large amounts of digital data consider packing a portable hard drive for back up.

Source: Contributed by Sharon McLennan

It is not your automatic right as a researcher to take photos or videos, and you should reflect with care on any decision to do so. It is important to understand that visuals are not 'objective', but that they are bound within the social context and discourses that surround them (Crang and Cook, 2007: 105; McEwan, 2006: 232). There has been controversy and debate about the use of visual tools and the way they can exhibit or expose. Box 6.6 summarises some of the ethical concerns to consider before deciding to use videos or photographs as research tools. The National Geographic Society (2013) states that photography of people and their land is an act of trust and must be done with respect and with an understanding of the laws and traditions of the people involved. When taken respectfully, photographs 'taken in the field – correctly filed and annotated – can usefully complement the writing of field notes' (Crang and Cook, 2007: 106). Similarly, videos can demonstrate the immediate situations of marginalised groups in a community and, when used carefully, could have quite empowering effects in action or participatory fieldwork (Crang and Cook, 2007: 120; McEwan, 2006: 232; Wiles et al., 2008).

Box 6.6   Using visual tools ethically

- Come to a good understanding of the cultural setting of your fieldwork before taking photographs or films. In different cultural contexts people have different perceptions of what is appropriate in visuals and what is not.
- Explore carefully if there could be any reasons why individuals may find photographic or filmic practice offensive, harmful or distressful and make a sensitive judgement call in each individual situation.
- Every image should respect the dignity of the subject(s).
- Participants must be fully informed in advance about plans for photography or filming as part of a research project, including intentions for use of the material. Participants must give their consent.

(Continued)

(Continued)

- Participant-oriented, collaborative research is often the best way to avoid harm, as it provides participants with some control over the capture, and use, of visuals.
- Do not use photographic or filmic material covertly.
- When material is published, readers and viewers should be shown the wider context in which visual images are embedded, in order that they gain a more meaningful understanding of the situation.

Source: Compiled from Pink (2007) and Crang and Cook (2007)

Finally, do not forget to pack some appropriate gift items. These are useful in providing reciprocity for information given and kindness bestowed (see Chapter 9, section on 'Reciprocity').

Above, we have simply outlined certain items that we feel would be invaluable for fieldwork. You may come up with others specific to your topic or your region of study, or decide that many of the items we have suggested are superfluous to your requirements. Again, and as in all cases with fieldwork planning, the choice is ultimately yours.

CONCLUSION

As you will have gathered from reading this chapter, planning for fieldwork is no simple exercise. There are many decisions to be made about such issues as when to go to the field, which funding organisations to target, and who to contact with regard to research permission and clearance. In this chapter we have attempted to make your decision making a little easier by outlining the options available and by drawing on our experiences and those of other researchers as to what has worked or not worked in the past and why.

The key points we have made on the practical issues associated with preparation for the field can be summarised by the following statements: begin preparing for fieldwork as early as possible (particularly with regard to obtaining funding); permission for research may need to be sought at several official and unofficial levels; fieldwork can be an unhealthy occupation which requires careful physical and psychological preparation; do some homework when choosing field sites and seek a wide range of opinions on this (keeping your personal security uppermost in your thoughts); and be flexible and realistic when it comes to thinking about where you will stay in the field and what to pack. Above all, this chapter has argued that preparing for the field is an integral part of fieldwork itself.

Summary

- Planning the practical aspects of your fieldwork is as important as preparing methodological approaches.
- Start planning early. Listen to expert advice.
- Be prepared to be flexible in your approach and to expect the unexpected.
- Consider carefully how you will finance your research, and what sources of funding are appropriate; check the requirements of funding agencies early.
- Choose the location and timing of your fieldwork by weighing up academic enquiry and methodology with practical, health and safety issues.
- Create a large network of contacts, and start approaching them prior to fieldwork. Use a variety of methods (e.g., email, phone calls), and do not give up when there is no immediate response.
- Make good use of published and internet resources to understand the geography, history, political, social and cultural situation of your research location.
- Put your own health and safety first: prepare for difficult situations, be flexible in your timing and movements, and leave if situations become threatening.
- Especially when you are planning on using visual methods, such as photography or filming, consider the ethical implications and consider cultural and personal circumstances, as well as issues of representation and context, to avoid possible harm.
- Pack wisely and with knowledge of the fieldwork site.

Questions for reflection

When preparing for your fieldwork you might want to ask the following questions:

- What kind of preliminary contacts can I draw on when choosing my research site?
- How expensive will the research project be and how will I finance it? What funding sources are available and what are their requirements?
- What is the political, cultural and geographical situation in the area?
- What are the visa requirements in this area? Whom will I need to contact to fulfil these requirements and how long is the research permission process likely to take?
- Are there any academic institutions or experts nearby that I could link in with?
- How can I best prepare for my health and safety, and avoid danger?
- What particular methodological tools will I use and, therefore, what equipment will I need to pack?
- What kind of clothing is appropriate (considering culture, weather, geography)?

RECOMMENDED READINGS

Barrett, C. B., and Cason, J. W. (2010). *Overseas Research: A Practical Guide* (2nd edn). Milton Park: Routledge.

Book providing practical advice to students undertaking overseas research, including advice on how to prepare for the field, how and where to find funding for fieldwork, personal safety and security and so forth.

Crang, M., and Cook, I. (2007). *Doing Ethnographies*. Los Angeles, CA: Sage.

A text aimed at students using ethnographic field methods in their research. Covers getting ready, ethnographic methods, and analysis and writing.

Hertel, S., Singer, M. M., and Van Cott, D. L. (2009). Field research in developing countries: Hitting the road running. *PS: Political Science and Politics*, 42(02), 305.

This article provides practical advice for graduate students undertaking fieldwork in developing countries, including goals, preparation, research methods and practical issues.

Howell, N. (2007). *Surviving Fieldwork: A Report of the Advisory Panel on Health and Safety in Fieldwork*. Washington, DC: American Anthropological Association.

This text provides a comprehensive overview of the dangers faced by fieldworkers.

Nash, D. J. (2000a) Doing independent overseas fieldwork 1: Practicalities and pitfalls. *Journal of Geography in Higher Education*, 24(1), 139–149.

This article provides a good introduction to preparation for overseas fieldwork.

Schroeder, D.G. (2000) *Staying Healthy in Asia, Africa and Latin America*. Emeryville, CA: Avalon Travel Publishing.

An excellent resource on health for those in the field.

Sluka, J. A. (2012a). Danger in fieldwork: Dangerous anthropology in Belfast. In A. C. G. M. Robben and J. A. Sluka (eds), *Ethnographic Fieldwork: An Anthropological Reader* (pp. 283–296). Malden, MA: Wiley-Blackwell.

Book chapter discussing danger in fieldwork, including recommendations for researchers. Particularly relevant for those doing research on politically sensitive issues, or doing research in areas of conflict or post-conflict societies.

NOTES

1. An excellent online source of health information is the US Department of Health and Human Services' travellers' health website: www.cdc.gov/travel/yellowbook.pdf.
2. In any case, you should inform your high commission or embassy of your intended research.
3. This is not, however, a promotion of 'development tourism'. Chambers (1997) offers an excellent critique of the shortcomings of research which 'sticks to the tarmac', avoids rainy seasons, and stays within the comfort zone of researchers, thus avoiding the realities of life for many in developing countries.

7

PERSONAL ISSUES

HENRY SCHEYVENS, REGINA SCHEYVENS AND BARBARA NOWAK

Researchers embarking on development fieldwork for the first time are often, understandably, nervous. Yes, you will face many challenges; yes, you may have no experience in the communities/countries where you will conduct fieldwork; and yes, you may have no idea of how others you require information or assistance from will respond. If we let our imaginations run loose, the fears we can dream up are endless. However, Wolcott (2005: 88) advises us to 'Rest easy', pointing out that almost all researchers whose interests lead them to do development fieldwork return with invaluable experiences and more than sufficient data to complete their inquiries. A person undertaking fieldwork for the first time will lack experience, but brings with them a fresh perspective. Although at times it will be difficult for us, our understanding and appreciation of life in the places we research will usually benefit from these experiences. This is also true for students from developing countries conducting 'home-based' research in unfamiliar territory (see Box 7.1).

Box 7.1   Thugs, drugs and other challenges of doing research in a Bangladeshi slum

Rashid talks about the challenges and negotiations with powerful gatekeepers which were required so that she could conduct research in a Bangladeshi slum:

The slums of South Asia ... are not idyllic places. Violence, along with a climate of fear and insecurity, is part of everyday life in Phulbari. The violence involves gang warfare,

(Continued)

(Continued)

police raids, and overt oppression of residents by local leaders and the state. It also involves domestic abuse, fights between neighbors, and fights among gamblers and drug addicts. Doing fieldwork in a slum is stressful and involves constant negotiations with gatekeepers at community and individual levels to be able to conduct interviews.

She gives a specific example of her negotiations with one of the *mastaans* (thugs):

Kabir listened and then, without smiling, addressed me:

'Sister, as long you study what you say you are interested in, then there should be no problems. But if you do have any problems, just let Hashem know. He will sort it out for you. We will learn from you, and you will learn from us.'

Kabir's permission to work in Phulbari, however, came with a warning 'not to investigate anything other than women's health.' Otherwise, he said, we 'could be in trouble.' As it turned out, this section of the slum had a thriving heroin business run by these same leaders and supported by the police and other local political leaders. In return for seeking their permission and sticking strictly to the topic of reproductive health, we were offered support and protection.

Source: Rashid (2007: 371, 374–375)

Venturing into the unknown raises unique concerns for each individual. Thinking in advance about the kinds of issues we might face, and how we might deal with these, can help us to avoid unnecessary problems and to develop response mechanisms to cope with difficulties. Issues that might be considered 'personal' also affect those we interact with, therefore our planning must consider the well-being of others and not just ourselves. This chapter thus discusses the following personal issues: creating a good impression; desirable personal traits; preparing for discomfort and depression; and taking families or partners into the field.

CREATING A GOOD IMPRESSION

Having the ability to create a good impression is indispensable to social science research. Permission is needed for most research (see Chapters 6 and 9), usually from university ethics committees, and often also from others such as governments, village councils, and the people we interview. To secure this permission, we need to be able to impress upon people that our research is needed, that we have the skills and determination to conduct the research, and that we are trustworthy. If people trust us, they are more likely to be willing to share information as well as their thoughts, experiences and ideas.

How can we create a good impression? First, we need to show that we know our subject well, that we are knowledgeable about and interested in general issues in the country/localities where we will be conducting fieldwork, and that we are well-organised. If at interviews we ask people questions that the readily available literature would provide answers to, or if the flow of our questions has no clear logic, we will not create a good impression. Through your explanations and questions, show people that you know the subject and make the best use of the time you have with them. When you gather additional material during interviews and meetings (e.g., reports), read this well and incorporate the new information into your next interviews. Also, make an effort to learn at least basic greetings and some expressions in the local vernacular as this will be greatly appreciated (see Chapter 8 for further discussion of language issues).

Second, we must be able to impress upon others that our research problem and the questions we have formulated are worthy of investigation. As researchers, one of the most difficult issues we grapple with is whether we are asking the right questions, and from whose perspective? In addition to consulting with your supervisor on these issues, check the websites of organisations (e.g., government departments, NGOs, universities) for people who could advise you on refining your research topic and questions. Also, check whether there are any groups or discussions that you could participate in on sites like LinkedIn or Facebook, or via email lists specific to your discipline (e.g., the Association for Social Anthropology in Oceania (ASAO) has an active listserv). Through the process of discussing our research topics with knowledgeable people prior to departure, we refine and gain greater confidence in our research. This confidence will be evident to others in the fieldwork country and will encourage them to engage further with us.

Third, in order to establish a comfortable dialogue for those you meet with, be flexible. We cannot control every aspect of our research and indeed, if we seek to do so by stoically refusing to budge from a pre-determined research plan, we might miss other opportunities to learn. Many people embarking on development fieldwork find that open-ended interviews are ideal: here you need to find a balance between being organised by preparing a logical set of questions in advance, and flexible by responding to new information that you learn during the course of the interview (Arendell, 1997: 342). There are times when our participants will determine what questions are or are not appropriate to ask, and what methods we should or should not use. For example, Rashid and her research assistant began doing social mapping in a slum, but decided to jettison this exercise when one of the residents mistook their intentions and muttered, 'Yes, they are making a map. They are going to send it abroad to the original owners who live abroad! They want their land back. The slum people are going to be evicted' (Rashid, 2007: 374).

Fourth, dress well and be polite. Before travelling abroad you should educate yourself on the subject of appropriate behaviour, dress and cultural norms of the country you are visiting. As suggested in Chapter 6, travel guidebooks and websites may provide useful guidelines and speaking with nationals or expatriates will help. If you are a student who will be travelling to Nigeria for the first time, why not see if there are any Nigerian students at your university who would be happy to meet you for a coffee and share their experiences of culturally acceptable behaviour and protocols? While it may be appropriate for students at Western universities to dress casually on their home campuses, you should always dress neatly when approaching outside organisations (Apentiik and Parpart, 2006: 37). Polite behaviour is something we should have already cultivated, but it is also important that we are able to show we can listen carefully. We won't create a good impression at interviews or meetings if we repeat questions unnecessarily or interrupt answers.

Fifth, you are more likely to create a good impression if you demonstrate a genuine interest in the people you are talking to, their culture and their country. Mandel writes that one woman who participated in her survey and interview 'insisted on tape that the reason she had been willing to help me was because I had demonstrated an appreciation and respect for their culture, and that I had not presented myself as an authority' (2003: 6). You can plan to use your 'non-research' time in a country by engaging in some experiences that will provide insights into the people and their society. While undertaking fieldwork in Bangladesh, Henry took time off to attend a one-day international cricket match. By following the national side, he was showing interest in something outside the poverty and natural calamities that more commonly draw the attention of the international media. He was taking interest in something that Bangladeshis might be proud of, not ashamed of, and he had a topic of conversation that helped develop rapport with his research participants.

DESIRABLE PERSONAL TRAITS

As suggested above, certain personal traits make good fieldwork possible. They enhance the fieldwork experience for our informants and us, and will likely improve the quality of data we are able to collect. Reflecting on her fieldwork experiences in Indonesia, Moser (2008) found that while the colour of her skin, gender, age, economic status, position as an outsider, and other ways in which she might be labelled were important, her personality (and emotional intelligence) was more significant to the results of her research:

> I found that it was aspects of my personality, such as my social skills, my emotional responses to and interest in local events, how I conducted myself and the manner in which I navigated the personalities of others that were the main criteria by which I was judged. This in turn affected my access to certain people, the degree to which they opened up and shared their stories and views, and ultimately had an impact upon the material gathered. (2008: 383)

Despite its significance to our research, the issue of the researcher's personality is seldom a topic of discussion in university courses: we study others rather than ourselves. While desirable personal traits cannot be taught, perhaps those who are willing can make the effort to cultivate them. Wolcott observes that the 'human-relations aspect of fieldwork is enhanced for those to whom such qualities as empathy, sympathy, or at least every day courtesy and patience come naturally' (2005: 80).

First, researchers should have an *open mind*. Two dangers present themselves: we may idolise a foreign people and their culture or, conversely, we may consider them in some way inferior. When we come across something unfamiliar, rather than condemning it, we should seek an explanation for what we have observed. This requires certain strength of character. It is easy to become frustrated living in another culture where people have different customs, norms, values and world views. In one country it is rude to be even two minutes late for an appointment. In another country, as long as you arrive within half an hour of your appointment time, this is acceptable. Rather than judging which system is 'best', accept that there is difference and that difference is sometimes a good thing. For example, despite your best efforts the unreliable public transport system might make you very late for an important appointment.

A *willingness to learn* depends upon preparedness to surrender long-held views and beliefs, or to expect the unexpected. Lewis, recalling his fieldwork in Bangladesh for his doctoral research, wrote that 'no-one ever answered my questions the way I expected them to, but, if they had there would have been little point in asking them' (1991: 57). For Wolcott, a willingness to learn is being receptive to new information: 'A fieldworker must rely on his or her ability to surrender to what the field observations actually reveal rather than prematurely to superimpose structure on them' (2005: 183).

Expect to practice *patience and tolerance*, particularly if you are dealing with officials. It may be common practice, for example, to give extra money to a bus conductor to secure a seat near the front. We may see this as bribery; locals may view this in the same way Americans view tipping – money provided for service rendered. Chapter 5 described a similar situation whereby you are more likely to get access to archival data if you cultivate a friendly relationship with the relevant official: for example, regularly bringing refreshments to share. Remember also that people of our host countries have to live all their lives with what for us are only very short-term frustrations. If they can be tolerant, we can too.

In addition to the normal daily challenges of living and moving about, we may find that the values and views of those we study are very different from our own, and this may be an on-going source of irritation and even anger. Attitudes to women may not appear 'progressive', people may seem disinterested about political troubles in their country (more likely, they might prefer to avoid 'unpleasant' conversation topics for your benefit) and so on. You should consider that for locals your views or behaviour might be equally perplexing. Your informants may wonder how your partner or husband could allow you to travel abroad alone, or why you don't have any children. Weaver (1998) instructs travellers to developing countries to 'travel in a spirit of humility and with a genuine desire to learn more about the people of your host country.'

Researchers need to cultivate *understanding* for the people, organisations and topics they are studying. Rather than listening closely to what people are telling us and focusing on understanding why they hold a particular view or their organisation has a particular policy, we can become engrossed in explaining our own concerns and viewpoint. As Apentiik and Parpart sagely advise, 'seek first to understand before being understood' (2006: 4). As outside researchers we are generally in the 'field' for a relatively short period of time. The commitment of the organisations and individuals we study may span decades. We return to our world of relative luxury to write our reports or dissertations and, separated by distance, it becomes easy for us to criticise. Chambers (1983) has pointed out that in Western universities we seem to be praised more for criticism than for writing about success.

Discretion is needed when we find we disagree with the views of the people we are interviewing or their organisation's policies. This does not mean that you cannot hold strong opinions about your subject matter. Hage, for example, records his emotional response to Israel's bombardment of Lebanon in 2006 that killed a man who had been assisting his research and the man's two children: 'There was, needless to say, an overwhelming feeling of anger and hatred towards Israel – and I whole heartedly shared this anger and hatred' (2010: 131). Hage explains that he was constantly negotiating between being emotional and being analytical.

During periods of frustration *tact* will serve the researcher well. It is important to take care with issues such as when to speak out, when to hold one's tongue and how to phrase what you wish to say. If we have concerns, we should try to present them in a constructive, non-threatening fashion.

Researchers also need to be *determined*, because our frustrations may be many. Our research may fall far behind schedule, the mosquitoes may seem to be our personal tormentors, we may suffer illness, and we may have much less privacy than what we are used to. Determination is also needed to overcome periods of self-doubt (Wolcott, 2005: 87). We may at times lose faith in ourselves, in our methodology, in the value of our fieldwork and in our competency (see Box 7.2). Being determined must be counterbalanced with a preparedness to pull out of fieldwork that is not worth persisting with, dangerous, or if personal troubles are too great to cope with.

Box 7.2   An overriding feeling of bothering people

When I was in the field I would intermittently feel depressed or lonely. These feelings would get mixed with feelings of incompetence. Why was I there? What was I doing? Why in the world would these people want to talk with me, someone who constantly bothered them asking them dumb questions? I would think to myself: 'Here I am, a rich American woman, hassling very poor people who work very hard to try to ensure their families' health and well-being. People who go off to work at 6 in the morning and sometimes earlier, and come home late in the afternoon, don't want to be bothered by someone asking them dumb questions! All these people want to do is relax and be left alone. The last thing they wanted was to see me coming to bother them!'

When I felt like this I learned to relax and not stress myself. I would stay close to my house and read. I read voraciously when in the field. All the classics I should have read at university! After a few days of time out, I would start to regain my confidence and would slowly return to visiting with people, just talking; I would ask questions later – and I did.

Source: Nowak (1987)

Researchers need to be *emotionally prepared for rejection*. A few villagers refused to answer Lockwood's surveys, some arguing that they were pointless (Lockwood, 1992: 171). A problem that researchers may face is that their intended fieldwork site may be 'over-researched' from the perspective of locals, with competition for community consultation time coming from consultants and government officials as well as other research students. The locals have had enough of outsiders requesting information with no obvious benefit to them. This situation seems to occur mostly when there is something unique about the site, or some type of development innovation is being undertaken that is attracting a lot of interest. Before deciding your research site, consult widely to avoid over-researched areas.

It is not only communities that can be over-researched; people in the civil service who deal with development assistance may also feel that they are over-scrutinised and that outsiders demand too much time of them (see Box 7.3). Wrighton (2010), when conducting research for her Master's thesis, found Government officials in the small Pacific Island country of Tuvalu to be so much in demand for meetings with international development agencies that it compromised their ability to complete their regular work. Native researchers are also not immune from being seen as burdensome:

> [Some departments] have been saturated with researchers to a point where they can no longer accommodate them e.g. when I approached the Ministry of Finance, I could hear somebody whispering to his colleague, 'Oh no, not another researcher'. (Solomon Islands researcher: personal communication, 2012)

Box 7.3   The problem of over-researched projects or communities

So many consultants, not enough action, say Niueans

Niueans say they are being 'over consulted'. Researchers working on the Niue 'Sustainable Living Community' project report that people are overloaded by the many consultants that call for meeting after meeting. The researchers say the common complaint from the local people is that they are tired of review after review where not much happens after recommendations are submitted.

Most of the year a steady stream of consultants pass through the big raised coral atoll with a small population (1,700). They come from government, regional and international agencies delving into every imaginable aspect of life on the island.

Source: Niue Economic Review/PINA Nius Online, April 21, 2002

As researchers, we should not be put off easily, even by people who may initially be reluctant to meet us because they are under much demand from 'other outsiders'. Our challenge is to make an effort to understand the situations that the people we hope to meet with are in, then to present our research to them in a compelling manner. Even people who are very busy may find it refreshing to meet with an outside researcher who does not bring with them an organisational agenda and is prepared to listen. For example, when one student did research on corporate social responsibility and thus had to interview senior people from a major bank at their Sydney headquarters, she concluded the interview by thanking the participant (a director of the bank), who said: 'No, thank *you*. I really like talking about this stuff' (Marchant, 2012: 76).

PREPARING FOR DISCOMFORT AND DEPRESSION

During the course of fieldwork you can expect at times to feel homesick, to miss the company of your friends and family, to miss the pastimes you would normally enjoy, and to feel 'disoriented' (Davies, 2010: 80). Yet another source of 'fieldwork blues', as these moments of depression are sometimes referred to, is stress: the stress of introducing yourself to strangers and strange organisations, the stress of forever being careful with how you behave and what you say so as not to offend, and stress resulting from culture shock (see Chapter 8). Expect 'good days' and 'bad days'. In interviews with 16 PhD students, Pollard (2009) recorded that their negative feelings during fieldwork included: alone, ashamed, bereaved, betrayed, depressed, desperate, disappointed, disturbed, embarrassed, fearful, frustrated, guilty, harassed, homeless, paranoid, regretful, silenced, stressed, trapped, uncomfortable, unprepared, unsupported and unwell. Don't be surprised if you experience some of these things, but also remember that fieldwork can be very exciting, stimulating and rewarding.

It would seem normal to want to avoid hardship or discomfort during fieldwork. However, often those experiences that are the most difficult for us provide important opportunities for learning about the daily struggles of those at our research sites. Thus while you might not have to use public transport in Rawalpindi, Pakistan, to understand women's reluctance to use the crowded mini-buses you will likely gain a much deeper appreciation of barriers to women's mobility by riding mini-buses for a few days yourself rather than observing from afar.

As researchers we need to regularly reflect on what we observe and experience, and to monitor our emotional responses to a broad range of issues from behavioural norms to politics. Keeping a field diary, a personal account of experiences and emotions, can assist with this reflection process (see Chapter 8). Reflexivity is essential for all fieldwork, but it must be monitored by the researcher to ensure that it is constructive: that is, contributes to the research process by enhancing self-awareness rather than encouraging excessive brooding (Moore, 2009: 181).

To collect information, especially to undertake interviews, requires considerable energy. It would not do to place ourselves in so many trying situations that we end up jaded to the point that our ability to observe and gather information are adversely affected. Before departing for fieldwork, it is worth considering both how to make research enjoyable, rather than just a testing experience, and how you might re-energize yourself during periods of research. Having fun is important to research: if you become continually depressed, not only will your research suffer but others around you who feel in some way responsible for your welfare (even if you do not realise this) will feel they must have done something wrong. Your key informants, even those living in difficult circumstances, will be trying to enjoy life. So make some time available for things you enjoy doing. Go for a walk, chat with people you come across, take photos, read books, make yourself a good coffee, listen to music, compose emails to tell funny stories to your friends back home (but be careful not to be unprofessional by 'unloading' using social media which may have a wide reach – see Box 8.4), or do whatever you find relaxing or fun, within cultural bounds. The possibilities are many. A group of geographers found they had come up with a variety of ways to deal with the 'down days' during their fieldwork, including taking Saturdays off, cooking a nice meal or watching a movie (Heller et al., 2011).

Periodic withdrawal from the 'field environment' is also a common way of managing down periods and disorientation. For some, the privacy of one's own room or hut might be all that's needed (Davies, 2010: 83), whereas others doing fieldwork in remote locations might find that a visit to a large city provides a much needed break, a change in diet and access to modern communication and entertainment facilities. Those involved in long periods of research may wish to return home for a short while or have their loved ones visit them. Alternatively, some may want to take their loved ones to the field with them, as discussed below.

FAMILIES AND PARTNERS IN THE FIELD

The above discussion assumes that researchers are undertaking fieldwork as individuals, but this is not always the case. We now turn to the subject of researchers who are in close relationships and/or who are raising families. Deciding whether to take one's partner and/or children into the field is not always an easy task, but it helps that this issue has been debated quite openly in the literature since the mid-1980s (Barrett and Cason, 2010: 38–42; B. Butler and Michalski Turner, 1987; Cassell, 1987; Cupples and Kindon, 2003; J. Flinn et al., 1998). There are advantages of having one's family present during fieldwork, but there are also drawbacks. Problems can include financing the travels of family members, the logistics of organising for a larger group, loss of income and professional identity for the partner of the researcher, consideration of health and safety, children's education, comfort needs of all family members, and general household maintenance.

The length of fieldwork might be a factor in determining whether or not the researcher's family joins him or her. For relatively long periods of fieldwork, the researcher's partner may have to resign from their employment. When a family accompanies a researcher, more often than not they will need to find accommodation separate from other households. This can potentially interfere with data collection for those involved in participant-observation who would otherwise have lived with a local family. One possible solution may be for the partner or family to join the researcher near the field site for a brief holiday in the middle or at the end of their fieldwork. This way, the family can see the environment the researcher worked in, thus gaining an appreciation of their loved one's experiences.

While some of the complications of having family present can be difficult to resolve, there are also some real benefits of having family members accompany researchers into the field. The family can be a great means of emotional support to the researcher, enable researchers to be more productive by eliminating 'down time' associated with loneliness, and the presence of family members might also provide an entrée into parts of the community that might otherwise have been off limits to the researcher.

Below, separate sections are devoted to discussing issues associated with bringing partners and children to the field.

PARTNERS IN THE FIELD

Whether a partner should accompany the researcher into the field is a question that needs to be treated very carefully. There will be drawbacks and advantages for both the research and non-research partner regardless of what decision is made. Whether one's partner is male or female you should discuss with them what their role will be during the period of fieldwork. They may be able to assist you with everyday living, with your research and also emotionally, being a sounding board when you've had a challenging day. However, they too must be prepared for the difficulties of living in a very different setting from that which they are accustomed. Undertaking tasks such as laundry, cooking and shopping are often more time consuming in the field, yet critical for maintenance of good health. Tasks that modern appliances make easy can take on several orders of difficulty when a partner has to adopt new skills to complete them. Doing laundry, for example, may entail hauling water or carrying the laundry to the water source and then hand-washing with a bar of soap. Such tasks are repetitive, time consuming and require a lot of energy. Is your partner prepared to take on these responsibilities?

Other activities partners might become involved in include acting as a research assistant by transcribing interviews, taking photographs, cataloguing documents or scientific samples such as soil or cultural artefacts, and maintaining research equipment such as cameras, generators or computers. Partners can also become a second set of ears to hear things that the researcher might be restricted from hearing. They might find themselves talking with local villagers and doing supplementary research. For example, in a Muslim country a wife might assist her husband by talking with local village women who would be off-limits to a male. In such cases it is essential that one's partner is fully briefed about ethical issues such as informed consent and confidentiality (see Chapter 9).

While having a partner present can certainly be rewarding, the researcher must be prepared to spend time and energy meeting the needs of their partner. The partner may not be so enthralled by the researcher's fieldwork and they may find life in a strange setting very trying. The researcher must be willing to 'put down their digital recorder/notepad' in order to spend time with their partner.

Some researchers may find their personal relationships significantly challenged during field research. In the case of Yamagishi's research on males working in 'host clubs' in the largest sex district in Japan, she had to face the derision of her Canadian boyfriend:

> At the beginning he [the boyfriend] seemed to be accepting. But his complaints gradually surfaced six months after I started my fieldwork. The situation escalated and he began to sound more offensive, humiliating and even abusive toward the end of our two-year relationship ... he began to say things like 'Are you still 'collecting' data?' 'When will you stop going to meet 'your man'?' 'Will you ever stop your 'research'?'. (2011: 106)

The question of whether to take one's partner might be further complicated for homosexual researchers. Disclosure of one's homosexuality is more likely if the partner accompanies the researcher into the field. In a community that is not accepting of homosexuality, being open about one's sexual orientation could threaten the research programme. Nevertheless, a researcher is asking the community to be open and honest about their lives, thus ethically shouldn't the researcher do the same? Evelyn Blackwood (1995) pondered this issue during her stay in Sumatra. Her solution was to tell most community members she was engaged to be married and that her fiancé was back home, without disclosing her homosexuality. However, Blackwood found playing the 'deceptive' role of a heterosexual woman to be a real strain (1995: 59). Some gay and lesbian researchers choose a research project or a research location that is accepting of their sexuality (see Burford, 2010) or provides concealment.

Regardless of sexual orientation, field research can place a relationship under strain. To the question of whether or not fieldwork put stress on their marriage one anthropologist replied, 'Only until we got a divorce' (Howell, 1990: 168). The non-research partner might feel 'left out' by both their partner who is focused on research and by the local community who might not be welcoming. The partner is now in a foreign place possibly without some of the comforts of home and little knowledge of what is expected. Yet it is taken for granted that they will remain in full control of their emotions as well as provide for their partner's emotional and physical needs. The rewards for the researcher may be in the form of financial assistance and a furthering of their career interests. Their non-research partner may wonder at times what is in it for them.

While trouble may be brewing for couples who go into the field together, trouble may also lie in wait for those who decide that the non-research partner should remain at home. There are always difficulties in separation. Stress might develop for the partner who remains at home if they are left to do all the parenting and housekeeping, especially if this compromises their career. The close bond between couples is often temporarily disrupted due to long periods of fieldwork, and despite their enthusiasm for being reunited, on their return they may have to allow each other time to re-adjust to being part of a relationship.

CHILDREN IN THE FIELD

Deciding whether or not to take children into the field is another difficult decision to make. No one wants to be separated from their children for an extended period of time, but no one wants to place their children in a vulnerable or difficult situation. Cupples, who was accompanied by her two children (aged 4 and 7) while conducting fieldwork on single motherhood in Nicaragua, is one of a number of female researchers who have been accused of being irresponsible for putting their children at risk by taking them to the field: 'I felt a significant amount of irritation at the moral judgement of my behaviour and the concomitant lack of concern that millions of the world's children are at risk of premature death every day because of poverty and preventable disease' (Cupples and Kindon, 2003: 214). When making the decision as to whether she and her children would accompany their anthropologist husband/father on a two-year field trip, Patricia Hitchcock felt that:

> We all had very real needs that could be met only if we stayed together. The children needed a father. Two years apart would bring John home a stranger; none of us would be able to understand what he had been through or what he was thinking or writing about. To me, this would not be a marriage. (1987: 175)

Most researchers who have written about taking children into the field remark that they believe it humanises them to the community (Cassell, 1987; Flinn et al., 1998; Mose Brown and de Casanova, 2009). As well as reflecting on 'the benefits of a baby's disarming presence', Goldade, doing research on labour migrants in Costa Rica, noted that taking on the subject position of 'mother' or 'father' can also lead to research insights: 'having Sonia [the baby] brings me a deeper understanding of working motherhood, the situation many of my informants face' (2006: 54). Similarly, with children present the researcher is seen as having something in common with others in their research area, with families and family obligations.

For a woman, in particular, going into a fieldwork situation and leaving her family at home is something incomprehensible to people from many cultures. It makes the researcher look quite strange. When Cornet (2010) was doing research with women and men from the Dong minority group in China, she found that her lack of ability to communicate in their native language, Kam, was a major impediment to accessing women's voices. Women often kept their distance and used specific strategies to avoid participating in her research: for example, asking their husbands to answer a question for them, claiming they had poor Mandarin, or that they had nothing useful to contribute. It was only when Cornet brought her 8-month-old child into the field that the barriers came down: this facilitated a connection with village women, and made them more comfortable in her presence.

Nevertheless, having children present can pose serious challenges that should not be treated lightly. While infrequent, there are cases when children of researchers in the field have died (see e.g., Hitchcock, 1987 who writes about the death of her son in Nepal). Others can get very sick. Anyone contemplating taking children in the field must include consideration of their health and sanitation (Barta et al., 2009). In her thesis, Trisia Farrelly explains how she accepted the help of a traditional healer to treat her sick son who had been ill with diarrhoea for two weeks. The healer, stating that the boy was the victim of black magic, massaged him with oils then came to collect him to be brought to a church in the evening. Here, a charismatic healing session took place. Farrelly reflected, 'To this day I am very glad Jacob slept through most of this because if not, I fear he may have been quite traumatised ... The group of people cried, shook and wailed in waves together as they commanded the evil spirit out of my baby son' (2009: 41). When her son started vomiting the next day, Farrelly decided to take him to the nearest hospital for more conventional treatment.

Time is another critical issue. Children, by their very nature, are demanding of attention. They have needs that parents must fulfil, and this may include home schooling if they are in the field with you over an extended period of time. Hopefully they will be in a situation where they can strike up friendships with local children. Whether or not this is the case, toys and books can be a great comfort and distraction for children adapting to a new environment, so consider packing such items (Barrett and Cason, 2010: 36). No matter how much thought you put into preparing for your children to be with you in the field, however, they are not necessarily going to always be happy about being there with you:

> Although my children were usually absorbed and fascinated by life in Nicaragua, at other times they were homesick and stroppy, and resented the lack of space, the mosquitoes, and having to wash in cold water. They reminded me that it was my choice and not theirs to travel to Nicaragua. (Cupples and Kindon, 2003: 215)

Having families in the field will also typically mean that you need to prepare nutritious, substantial meals. It is much easier for a fieldworker when on their own to find a local household willing to provide a place at their 'table'. Having a family in the field usually means time must be spent on domestic chores including shopping, cooking and cleaning. The exception is societies in which hiring domestic help is the norm for many people. Thus, for example, Cupples (Cupples and Kindon, 2003) found that it was much easier to get assistance with childcare for her two children during fieldwork in Nicaragua than when at home in New Zealand.

Prior knowledge of the field situation will aid in considering whether to bring your children with you. Speaking with other researchers who have been in the region or local residents can help in your deliberations. Bringing children into a situation that is not only physically but also emotionally challenging will be stressful to all. Hugh-Jones (1987: 29) suggests that it might be best for the field researcher to travel ahead and set up the field site before bringing their children over. Established friendships between researcher and some community members may well help in the children's transition (Hugh-Jones, 1987). However, for single parents, there may be no choice but to either take their children with you or simply not do fieldwork.

You must not only consider how having children present might impact on your research but also how the overseas experience might impact on them. Although researchers might be reluctant to take children with them, especially if they are very young, the experience can be very positive for the children (Whiteford and

Whiteford, 1987: 118). It can help to enhance children's cross-cultural understanding and language skills, for example. While Cupples warns of the danger of idealising accompanied fieldwork, she acknowledged that there were benefits to her and her two children from the experience:

> The main long-term benefit for us as a family was that my children became co-participant observers of life in Nicaragua. My professional life is not separate from my personal life. I am glad my children understand what my research is about and can understand the sense of on-going responsibility I feel towards my research participants. (Cupples and Kindon, 2003: 216)

Farrelly conducted field research in Fiji, accompanied by her young son and her husband. In the following extract from her field diary, and her reflection on this in her thesis, she notes that while having her family with her was wonderful in many respects, it also presented a number of challenges (see Box 7.4).

Box 7.4　The pros and cons of having family in the field in Fiji

June 6, 2004

Having J here has been a blessing and has also been much, much harder than I had thought. The sleep deprivation has really been affecting us. Trying to attend night activities is hard as we have to get up early in the morning for J. We both take turns attending to J in the morning because we have to try to keep him as quiet as possible in our room while the others sleep. Plus it is still dark and there is nowhere else to play ...

Had a great day with J today. The children ran him up and down the beach showing him bright green fish they had caught, sea slugs and a snake. He was captivated by a variety of beautiful shells. A. wanted him to feel the current as he walked through the stream running into the sea ... The children just couldn't leave J alone – pinching him and kissing him at every opportunity. I wonder if this fascination will get old with time.

As this diary entry shows, there are advantages and disadvantages particular to bringing a family to live with research participants in the field. This has been recognised by other anthropologists and social researchers (e.g., Cupples and Kindon, 2003; Flinn et al., 1998). The benefits include a greater opportunity to become subjectively saturated in the culture and to gain more insights into family life. Conversely, the disadvantages of research with children include finding time for research and for private family time. This was a very real struggle for our family. While I appreciated having Matt there to take the load off me as far as my parental responsibilities were concerned (washing and drying cloth nappies, cooking, and general childcare), I was constantly aware that this was not actually his 'thing' at all. He never wanted to be a near-solo full-time parent and parenting in such a different and challenging environment was twice as hard as parenting at home in New Zealand. Other parents and children in Boumā often encouraged our one (and later two) year old son to behave in ways we felt were unacceptable (e.g., to hit other children and to kill chicks). We were constantly fighting an uphill battle with our own discipline and boundaries for our son. Some days the heat made the simplest chore almost impossible and we came to fully embrace the Fijian expression *cegu mada* (please rest).

Source: Farrelly (2009: 38–39)

CONCLUSION

Fieldwork is an adventure. Like any adventure, we cannot foresee all the challenges we will face, nor the outcome of our endeavours – the best we can do is to prepare for the adventure as thoroughly as possible. A variety of desirable personal traits that make good fieldwork possible have been raised and should be pondered before commencing fieldwork. In particular, researchers need to have an open mind and we should continually reflect upon our reactions to local customs and the people we meet. We also have to present ourselves as professionals, and convince those we seek assistance from of the merits of our research programme. Creating a good impression will be aided by efforts to build rapport, a broad knowledge of our host country, organisations and communities, and a genuine interest in the people we meet. There are both pros and cons to taking families and partners into the field, and individual researchers need to reflect on these matters. By thinking in advance about these personal issues we can make the research experience more rewarding for both our participants and ourselves.

Summary

- Fieldwork is an adventure, and it is normal to feel a little anxious especially if conducting research for the first time.
- Rest assured that most researchers whose fieldwork takes them to new environments return with invaluable experiences and more than sufficient data to complete their inquiries.
- You will be more likely to create a good impression if you prepare well, have a genuine interest in the people and places you are going to, and are organised.
- Desirable personal traits for those conducting fieldwork in developing countries include empathy, tolerance, patience, open-mindedness, courtesy, discretion and a willingness to learn.
- Expect to occasionally experience discomfort or even 'fieldwork blues', and consider strategies to help you through these times: for example, sharing a meal or movie with acquaintances or taking a short break from your research site.
- Conducting fieldwork with family members around you can be distracting, but it can work well if planned for carefully and if you accept that there will be tensions at times.

Questions for reflection

- What do you think you will need to do to 'prepare well' for fieldwork?
- Reflect on your personal traits: do they align closely with the traits listed in the 'Summary points' above, or are there things you might need to work on?
- Thinking of your own research site, what things can you put in place to make adaptation easier and to help you through any periods of 'fieldwork blues'?
- Reflect carefully on whether you are the sort of person who is quick to criticise and quick to judge. If so, you should think about how you can ensure that you will be open-minded about what you find when you conduct your research.
- If you have a partner and/or children, write up a table which lists the pros and cons of taking your partner and/or your children to your field site. If it is not possible or appropriate for them to join you, what alternative arrangements could be made (e.g., for you to visit them or them to visit you during field research)?

RECOMMENDED READINGS

Davies, J. (2010). Disorientation, dissonance and altered perception in the field. In J. Davies and D. Spencer (eds), *Emotions in the Field: The Psychology and Anthropology of Fieldwork Experience* (pp. 79–97). Stanford, CA: Stanford University Press.

Book chapter exploring the emotional responses of anthropological researchers immersed in unfamiliar environments.

Flinn, J., Marshall, L., and Armstrong, J. (eds) (1998). *Fieldwork and Families: Constructing New Models for Ethnographic Research*. Honolulu, HI: University of Hawaii Press.

An edited text with a range of good examples of the benefits but also potential difficulties of bringing families to the field.

Heller, E., Christensen, J., Long, L., Mackenzie, C. A., Osano, P. M., Ricker, B., Kagan, E., and Turner, S. (2011). Dear diary: Early career geographers collectively reflect on their qualitative field research experiences. *Journal of Geography in Higher Education*, 35(1), 67–83.

Student reflections on field research experience, including discussion of ethics, gatekeepers and research fatigue.

Moser, S. (2008). Personality: A new positionality? *Area*, 40(3), 383–392.

Discusses limitations of recent discussions of positionality, and argues for more attention to the impact of personality and emotional intelligence on field research.

PART III
IN THE FIELD

8

ENTERING THE FIELD

SHARON MCLENNAN, DONOVAN STOREY AND HELEN LESLIE

ENTERING THE FIELD

The preparation is done, the flight has finally landed, and you are on the ground, ready for fieldwork. You may be full of excitement and anticipation at the prospect of finally doing the research that you have been meticulously visualising and planning for months or even years. Alternatively, you may be paralysed with the kind of fear, self-doubt and uncertainty that is commonplace for first-time researchers. To some extent experience can be an advantage in coping with the demands of research as 'fieldwork is a cumulative and synthetic affair in which the best work of any scholar builds on past experiences, good organization and careful preparation' (Veeck, 2001: 34–35). The difficulty is that, for many, this is their first taste of research, or even their first overseas experience.

The anxiety that often accompanies this initiation affects almost all researchers, both those going 'away', and those going (or staying) 'home'. For those who will be conducting fieldwork across gender, ethnic, class and national divides, visions of the 'exotic other' may shape beliefs and expectations of the field. For those researchers who are going home to conduct their research, anxieties may be related to one's multiple roles as a researcher, member of an extended family, absent friend, newly crowned 'expert' and so on. Whatever you may anticipate when embarking on development fieldwork, at a personal level your fieldwork experience will always present some challenges. If the researcher has at least rudimentary language skills, initial contacts and a place to stay, this can offset initial anxiety. Preparing well (see

Chapter 6, and Box 8.1) and being open-minded and flexible can help you to thrive in the fieldwork environment.

Box 8.1   The value of a preliminary visit to the field

If you have the time and funding to make it possible, a preliminary visit to the field has significant practical and methodological advantages, assisting in formulating networks and helping smooth fieldwork logistics. Apentiik and Parpart (2006) note that a preliminary visit can help the researcher to overcome anxiety about the 'gap between preparing for the field and the exponential leap into the field itself', allowing the researcher to 'hit the ground running' as many of the obstacles to beginning fieldwork will have already been cleared.

   This was true for Sharon, one of the authors of this chapter, who was able to visit Honduras for a month at the end of her first year of her PhD candidature, ahead of a longer visit for data collection in the second year. During the 'pre-fieldwork' visit Sharon attended a conference in Honduras where she introduced herself and her research, and conducted some early interviews. She also spent time looking for accommodation for the following year and for a school for her daughter, and made contacts with a university department who offered her office space. All this made her arrival for the main fieldwork visit much easier, enabling her to concentrate on data collection much earlier.

ARRIVAL

For some researchers doing development fieldwork for the first time, getting through the first day is an achievement in itself. Haanstad writes of 'physically encountering the field with all its infinite possibilities and probable terrors' (2006: 225) which led him to seriously question his sanity. While your experience may not be so dramatic, stories abound amongst researchers of failed meetings, shattered expectations and all-consuming panic on their first day in the field. Helen, one of the authors of this chapter, had the following experience of travelling to her field site:

> The bus to San Salvador was slow and excruciatingly stuffy. We passed the body of a dead man lying unnoticed on the side of the road. The person who was supposed to meet me at the bus station had not turned up. I sat on my luggage in the crowded and dirty station and fought hard to quell the rising panic.

Meanwhile when Donovan, another author, first arrived in a Manila squatter settlement where he would be based for his research his journal entry read:

> Arrival at house a real shock. The access road consisted of rail tracks dotted with small fires. Terrifying. Trains pass regularly! They toot all the way through to clear lines of people, they give the house a real shake and the dog howls.

He had a feeling of 'this is it' and a desire to get the very next plane home. After two weeks Donovan was still despondent ('the dogs barked all night and the train got on my wick'), and yet a week later problems of sleeping in had emerged!

Expectations and well thought-out plans often go awry in development fieldwork precisely because everyday life in your new environment might be characterised by uncertainty. Airports and public transportation terminals can be confusing, over-whelming and a good place to get ripped off. Buses and other forms of public trans-port might arrive late or not at all, emails signalling your arrival are sometimes not received and, despite the fact that your research is the most important thing in the world to you at the time, your plans are often a low priority for other people. Don't lose your cool – or confidence. Entering into an argument at immigration over a three-month visa which should have been six or getting agitated at the late arrival of someone to meet you will not get you far, nor will moaning about these problems when you finally arrive at your destination. Creating a poor first impression may be difficult to undo even after an extended period of fieldwork. Remember, your field-work is – obviously – not just about you. While your arrival may be the biggest event of *your* calendar, this may not necessarily be the case for others.

Even when plans and expectations end in disarray on your first day it is important to 'ride out' this period. This is the start of the process that Kleinman et al. (1997) describe as researchers gaining control of their projects by first allowing themselves to lose it. For some this loss of control or vulnerability will be more difficult to cope with than others. A useful starting point in this quest to remain calm is to sit back and take stock for a few moments. In the weeks ahead there will be plenty of time to get official permission and to orientate yourself to your surroundings. Getting through your first day will not only give you a sense of well-earned achievement, but will also begin to equip you with the tools that you will need in what will be your new home and workplace for a period of time.

THE MORNING, AND WEEK, AFTER

For those new to a fieldsite, once safely ensconced within a research community or in your guesthouse/hotel, it is a good idea to jot down some brief notes detailing your initial impressions and the ways in which these impressions meet or do not meet your expectations. This form of reflection will be useful later in the research process not only as evidence of how you have adapted, but also to provide an outlet for any frustrations you feel.

After you have had a good night's sleep (or two) and begun to recover from jetlag and the disorienting experiences of arrival, it is important to start to get to know your environment. Go for a walk around the vicinity of the guesthouse/hotel and try to ori-ent yourself in this new place. Ingold and Vergunst (2008: 68) note that 'the repeated action of putting one foot in front of the other necessitates contact with the ground and, often a state of being attuned to the environment', and as such walking is the best way to start to understand a place. Going for walks on your first few days is a great way to familiarise yourself with this new environment and to begin to get your bearings.

At this stage you should also be in touch with your local contacts, particularly if they were not able to meet you on arrival. Call or visit to arrange meetings. Binns (2006) also suggests using your first week in the field to visit government offices, NGOs and higher education institutions, where you may be able to discuss fieldwork objectives, access local reports and other data, and to talk about logistical arrangements for your fieldwork.

It is important to note that some researchers enjoy a 'honeymoon' phase early on in the research. The excitement and enthusiasm that accompanied the planning phase of the research often intensifies on arrival. Irwin (2007) notes that in this stage everything is 'new, exciting and fascinating'. However in his seminal work on culture shock, Oberg (1960: 143) argues that this 'Cook's tour type of mentality' does not normally last when people remain in the field for longer durations and have to cope with everyday life, and that this is when discomfort, or even outright hostility, can occur. It is particularly common for researchers to experience some type of 'culture shock'.

CULTURE SHOCK

Culture shock has long been recognised and discussed, particularly in the context of anthropological fieldwork. Agar summarizes the impact of culture shock as:

> [T]he shock comes from the sudden immersion in the lifeways of a group different from yourself. Suddenly you do not know the rules anymore. You do not know how to interpret the stream of motions and noises that surround you. You have no idea what is expected of you. Many of the assumptions that form the bedrock of your existence are mercilessly ripped out from under you. (Cited in Wolcott, 2005: 87)

While the term 'culture shock' conjures up images of wild-eyed and desperate researchers to whom fieldwork, and the people who constitute the field, have become a source of anger and frustration, for many the experience of culture shock is more subtle. In addition, it is also often incorrectly assumed that Western researchers will be most likely to experience culture shock when doing development fieldwork: as Box 8.2 indicates, it is also an issue for researchers, such as international students, returning 'home' to do research.

Box 8.2   Culture shock and cultural identity in returning researchers

Culture shock has traditionally been seen as something that is experienced by outsiders entering an alien environment. More recently, as more researchers from the developing world have chosen to conduct their studies abroad, there has been an increasing awareness of the culture shock faced by returning international students, including 'reverse' culture shock or 're-entry shock' (Wild, 2007: 13), and challenges related to changing identities.

Reverse culture shock is related to the process of 'readjusting, reacculturating, and reassimilating into one's own home culture after living in a different culture for a significant period of time' (Gaw, 2000: 83). It is common for students to find that they have changed during their time away, and so have friends and family, and this can be disorienting and stressful. Returnees may also find what was previously familiar is now confronting. For example, Gill (2010: 369) notes that Chinese postgraduates returning home were unsettled by the crowdedness, pollution, the lack of respect for personal space, the chore of gift exchange and the general feeling of competitive pressure they encountered on their return.

Students returning home as researchers also commonly experience cultural identity issues, including conflicts between their newly assumed identity as a researcher and their home cultural identity (S. Gill, 2010). Sultana notes that that despite strong family ties to her field sites in Bangladesh she was 'acutely aware of my class and educational privilege. As such, I was simultaneously an insider, outsider, both and neither' (2007: 377). Balancing the expectations of family, friends and community with academic expectations and roles is an early and on-going challenge for many, as Ronicera Fuimaono notes:

I arrived home at the time for a family funeral, so I was unable to start my fieldwork immediately ... The situation is one of the realities of undertaking home-based research, since it is inevitable for us (Samoan researchers) to be caught up with family, and cultural obligations ... It was very difficult for me to adjust back to study mode in such circumstances, which made me realise how much I needed the support of people who I am close to ... who encouraged me to remain strong and focus on my fieldwork. (Fuimaono, 2012: 71)

Ronicera's account highlights the importance of local support. Explain your situation to those you are close to, and try to identify people at home who understand what you are trying to do, and who can provide encouragement and support when the re-entry shock, the family or community pressure or the stress of balancing multiple roles threatens to overwhelm you.

DETECTING AND DEALING WITH CULTURE SHOCK

A fellow researcher once described culture shock as a feeling of helplessness. Others have described it as a sense of drowning or a feeling of being totally out of control (Goopy, personal communication, 2002). In fact, culture shock is a label that can be applied to a whole range of responses to the forms of stress discussed above, from a 'terrible longing to be back home, to be able to have a good cup of coffee and a piece of apple pie' (Oberg, 1960: 178), to more serious problems including irrational fears, sleeping difficulties, anxiety and physical illness (Irwin, 2007). Depression (sometimes called 'fieldwork blues') is also a very common manifestation of culture shock during development fieldwork, particularly if a researcher is unaccompanied and planning to be in the field for some time. It may occur as a result of feelings of loneliness, cultural alienation and isolation, or be brought about through the numerous physical health problems that often befall fieldworkers: 'few experiences are more depressing than sweating out a fever on a bed thousands of miles away from home' (Devereux and Hoddinott, 1992: 15).

If you do begin to feel depressed during your fieldwork, or if you are beginning to feel as though you are losing command of your thoughts and feelings, it is important to acknowledge that you may be experiencing culture shock. Remind yourself then that culture shock is not a mental illness, that you are not in fact 'going crazy'. Rather, you are having a normal reaction to a situation or series of events over which you have very little control. Accept these feelings, and give yourself space to deal with them.

A good place to start is to give yourself some 'time out'. While dependent of course on where you are conducting your fieldwork, finding things that are familiar can often help dilute feelings of cultural alienation. After listening to harrowing stories of war trauma suffered by El Salvadoran women, Helen would often need to give herself a break from the intense emotional investment that came with conducting such interviews. As shallow as it seemed to her at the time, she found relaxation and solace at a nearby air-conditioned mall. Here, she would catch the latest B-rated action thriller, or sit in the food court and eat some manner or another of highly processed and fatty food! Music, books and social media may also alleviate homesickness (see Box 8.4).

You may even find yourself with a unique withdrawal: that of isolation from academic support structures, such as fellow students – and even your supervisor. You may yearn for an opportunity in which to critically discuss what you are doing with others. Ways of offsetting this may be to spend some time exchanging ideas with your supervisor or fellow students via email, Skype or social networking sites, making some contacts at local educational institutions, or even with NGOs based in the region. While it is important to maintain ethical principles in discussing your research, some time out to discuss the context of your work may be helpful in releasing some mental energy and generating ideas. Similarly, diaries or journals may also serve this purpose (Heller et al., 2011, and Box 8.3).

Box 8.3　Diaries and journals

Keeping separate personal and research diaries are often recommended as a very effective way of developing your ideas, recording experiences and letting off some emotional steam. Monchamp did just this, and found that in the early days in the field the research diary was sparse while his personal journals were 'filled with long rambling entries of endless self-doubt as to whether this whole fieldwork idea was even remotely a reasonable undertaking' (2007: 2). Donovan also kept both a personal (the 'green book') and a reflective research diary while doing his PhD fieldwork in the Philippines: the latter was dubbed the 'blue book' because of its colour, not how it made him feel. The blue book was used as an evolving 'think pad' for research design, methodology, listing (changing) goal and linking ideas and information. Thus, the blue book helped Donovan to think through ideas and have them recorded and was particularly helpful in the initial period of research (re)design (see Chapter 2) and methodological orientation. Subsequently, the research evolved through the pages and gave him a written record of changing directions, ideas and propositions. At the time he thought this record would be useful when he returned to write up the research, but in fact it was most valuable while still in the field. Some of the ideas became important, others not, but the real value lay in the writing of them at the time (Storey, 1997).

Finally, while culture shock is an uncomfortable experience, Epprecht (2004) argues that it is part of the field learning experience. He contends that culture shock disorients students from a 'parochial' worldview, and forces them to take on a more mature and global perspective. While you may not appreciate Epprecht's position when you are in the middle of a bad bout of 'fieldwork blues', it is worth reflecting on during and after the fieldwork. What have you learned – or un-learned – through this experience?

BEHAVIOUR DURING FIELDWORK

Very much related to the issue of culture shock, and dealing with it, is the minefield that is maintaining appropriate behaviour whilst conducting development fieldwork (see also Chapter 7, section on 'Desirable personal traits'). As Binns (2006) notes, when in the field you are a guest of the local communities, and it is important to be polite and friendly in your work. However, the whole notion of 'appropriate behaviour' is complex because it is tied up and intertwined with cultural constructions of morality, gender, class, ethnicity, socialisation processes and individual personalities (Ellen, 1984: 100–104). Thus, what may be considered appropriate behaviour for a researcher may be seen as down-right rude or offensive to the individuals or society with whom he or she is interacting (DeVita, 1990, 2000). As development fieldwork involves forming relationships with others (Brown, 2009: 16; Devereux and Hoddinott, 1992) and contemporary fieldwork processes pay overt attention to the subjective (de Laine, 2000: 2), there is no avoiding the need to critically examine the ways that we behave during fieldwork. This includes 'off-duty' behaviour. As Brown (2009: 214) notes, in the field the researcher often loses the luxury of separating their personal and professional selves as their self-presentation and reputation are often important for obtaining and accessing information. This means that decisions regarding leisure activities, drug and alcohol use and sexual relationships should be made very carefully (see Chapter 9).

In this globalised world of instant communication the need for researchers to pay attention to behaviour during fieldwork extends to the use of social media. What you put out there is in the public domain and can get back to the community or institution you are working with. Think carefully about the photos and updates you post and who they may become visible to (see Box 8.4).

Box 8.4   Social technology in the field: some guidelines

There was a time, not that long ago, when supervisor and student parted ways for the duration of fieldwork; however, internet-connected devices including laptops, tablets and mobile phones have revolutionised travel and fieldwork. Now almost constant contact can be achieved. These devices also make such diverse activities as checking bus timetables, accessing secondary data and chatting with friends at home much easier. However, while it is possible, and even tempting, to keep communicating with supervisors and friends at home, this may not necessarily benefit your research at all times as a degree of self-reliance and working through issues yourself remains an essential part of good fieldwork. Indeed, some would argue that the overuse of social media is detrimental to fieldwork. For example, Huesca (2013) argues that the unchecked use of social media and mobile phones during overseas study undermines cross-cultural growth and understanding. He noted that students find it easier to 'hunker down' behind a computer screen in their bedroom, to rely on Google maps for directions rather than asking a local, or to entertain themselves with streaming movies and music rather than getting to know neighbours or visiting local hang-outs. These devices, designed to connect us to the wider world, can therefore have the inverse effect, distancing researchers from the people and the place they are actually living and working in.

Beyond disconnecting us from the world immediately around us, social media, which enables messages, photos and video to be spread widely and rapidly, has the potential to negatively impact research relationships. Even with very careful attention to privacy settings, social media postings can 'leak' out and become visible to research participants and sponsors (and family back home). Messages intended for one audience can cause social ructions when shared with another (e.g., through a friend's well-meaning 'share' or photo tag), and wrongly placed or misunderstood messages may have unexpected impacts on the research.

In order to deal with these risks we propose a few simple guidelines:

- *Review your online profiles before arriving in the field:* It is important to present yourself as a professional researcher, so check your public profiles for posts that may give the 'wrong' impression. Hide or delete posts (or whole profiles or feeds) where necessary, and remove tags on pictures you would rather your research participants did not see. Consider having a completely private profile, page or site for family and friends at home, and a professional and public one (for those times when your research participants want to 'friend' you).
- *Limit your use of social technology while in the field:* Think carefully about why you want to connect. Your priority is your research and learning, and your experience of the field, not embellishing your Facebook feed. Decide on places and times when it is appropriate to connect, and limit non-essential activities (such as texting friends at home, personal blogging and Facebook updates) to those times. Treat every status update, tweet, blog post or other Internet posting as public and don't post anything you wouldn't want a research participant to see.

- *Do not post any research data, or information about research participants:* In general it is not a good idea to post any research data anywhere, although as the world becomes increasingly connected it is likely you may find yourself in online discussions with participants. This is where a public, professional profile is advisable. Keep posts and comments professional, and do not discuss – or allude to – confidential research data.
- *Avoid the use of social technology in sensitive situations:* If your research is sensitive, in a politically unstable region or a location where Internet usage is closely monitored, it may be advisable to completely avoid any social media postings while in the field. Weigh up the potential costs and benefits carefully, along with your own security and that of your participants.

HOW TO GET ON WITH OTHERS

Getting along with others in a mutually pleasing fashion is a skill that cannot, unfortunately, be easily learnt, and may be hampered by factors such as sex, age, wealth, ethnicity, religious and political philosophies (Gaskell and Eichler, 2001) and the labels that communities may ascribe to you and your research (Hammersley and Atkinson, 2007: 63). Nevertheless, practising qualities such as sympathy, empathy, kindness and even courtesy and patience will certainly facilitate a smoother fieldwork experience (Wolcott, 2005: 80). Hammersley and Atkinson (2007) note that the value of pure sociability and the skills of 'small talk' cannot be underestimated as a means of building trust. Particularly desirable personal traits worth cultivating include tolerance, patience, discretion and tact (see Chapter 7).

For those researchers who find these interpersonal skills difficult to master, it will be a relief to know that, in the words of one anthropologist, 'foot in the mouth is not fatal' (Flinn, 1990). The generosity and goodwill with which many fieldwork participants greet awkwardness and even downright blunders is a constant source of amazement to researchers. Indeed, in the event of a mishap laughter may be the most appropriate response (DeVita, 1990, 2000). Personal 'weaknesses' may also prove to be strengths in some cultural contexts. Successful fieldwork for Flinn (1990), a self-proclaimed shy person, was facilitated not by her innate confidence or ability to be flexible, but rather by her qualities of modesty and quietness.

'Getting on with others' also involves understanding that, as much as you need your personal space and time out from being the centre of attention, your local contacts and research respondents may also feel this way at times. Developing an awareness of when people are jaded from your questions or would like some privacy from your presence is an important tool. You should have some appreciation how others see you and when to make yourself scarce.[1]

CULTURAL SENSITIVITY

Cultural sensitivity is the individual's ability to acknowledge biases and to be non-judgmental when interacting with other cultures (Scaglion, 1990). Researchers must be constantly mindful of the ethnocentrism or cultural baggage that they carry with them wherever they go (Hammond, 1990). However, putting aside your cultural biases in an attempt to enter the field unencumbered is an unrealistic expectation for any researcher, and it is impossible to learn everything there is to know about another culture. Even the most experienced and sensitive individual will occasionally make cultural *faux pas*. Despite this, it is reassuring to know that the immediate embarrassment and perhaps even offence caused by these mistakes are unlikely to seriously undermine the research or researcher, although, as was Trisia's experience (see Box 8.5), it may take some time to regain trust.

Helen's experience of riding buses in El Salvador is one case in point. After months of having to clamber over passengers who would stubbornly position themselves in the aisle seat of the bus, she had jumped to the erroneous conclusion that since the war had ended, Salvadoran people had become individualistic and self-preserving. One day when she was chatting with her Spanish teacher, she discovered that Salvadorans purposefully position themselves in the aisle seat in the hope of avoiding an unwanted, gun-wielding companion (robber or kidnapper) taking advantage of the space available next to them. Thus, to her embarrassment, she learnt a valuable lesson not only about her own ethnocentrism but also about the ways in which Salvadoran people daily negotiate the culture of violence in their society.

Such sensitivities are also an important part of actual data collection. So although Wuelker (1993: 165) has argued that non-Asians interviewing Asians are 'fiascos', others have noted that with sensitivity and care cross-cultural research is possible (Jones, 1983; Wesche et al., 2010), and that it may actually 'open up the possibility of multiple interpretations and dialogue' (Shope, 2006: 163) (for more discussion on this, see Chapter 1).

WORKING WITH RESEARCH ASSISTANTS

Depending on factors such as the size and scope of your research and the amount of funding you have available, you might find it necessary and indeed useful to hire a research assistant (RA), interpreter or cultural advisor. These individuals can be an enormous asset during fieldwork. Not only can they provide help with the nuts and bolts of data collection (surveys, interviews, etc.), but also with the more intangible aspects of fieldwork such as building rapport with research participants and assisting with travel and safety requirements (Binns, 2006). The right research assistant can thus be seen as an 'ambassador at large', guiding and screening the research process so that the researcher is able to make the most of their fieldwork experience (Devereux and Hoddinott, 1992: 27).

Devereux and Hoddinott argue that if you were to draw up a job description for an ideal RA it would probably include:

communication skills, good knowledge of English (or French, or Spanish) as well as the local language(s), a perceptive intelligence, inexhaustible patience, unfailing dependability, and an ability to get along with all elements of the local population. (1992: 27)

While it may be impossible to find someone who fits such a bill, there will always be individuals who, despite a lack of one or two of the above qualities, will make excellent RAs. It all depends, of course, on the kind of assistance you will be requiring. If you need your RA to act as an interpreter, then you will obviously need someone with fluency in both your first language and the local language(s) in which you will be working (see the discussion on interpreters below). Likewise, if entry into the research community is your primary concern, then a RA who is well known and trusted by the community will be important.

RAs can be drawn from a variety of sources, each of which will have their own advantages and disadvantages. Some researchers will seek an educated individual (e.g., a teacher, student or public servant). This way you can be more confident that the RA will be able to understand the nature of your research. Educated assistants may be difficult to find, however, and may have more constraints on their time than less-educated individuals (Devereux and Hoddinott, 1992: 27). They may also have their own agenda and understanding of what constitutes good research (see Beban, 2008: 67 for an example of this).

For some balance between education and accessibility, many researchers seek RAs from high schools; Veeck (2001: 36) concurs, suggesting visiting the local high school for the most cost-effective and loyal interpreter you could imagine. Indeed, students are perhaps less likely to paraphrase or analyse the responses and to give clear verbatim translations. However, this must be balanced against the availability of students and the nature of the research project. Sensitive research topics or very technical research will require a more mature or educated RA.

Often a researcher will opt for an individual from the local community to act as their RA. Local knowledge can help prevent embarrassing and sometimes costly blunders, and can be invaluable when identifying possible research participants. However, a local RA has the potential to dominate the form of data collected by directing the researcher to their own friends and family. This can be problematic, particularly if the researcher wants to access an alternative group and collect broad rather than specific data on the research community (Ellen, 1984: 118).

Ethnicity, age, status and sex are also important considerations when selecting an RA. Choosing an assistant of the opposite sex can have its advantages, as Heyer (1992: 206) discovered during her fieldwork in Kenya and India, where male RAs offered her more protection in awkward situations and often counterbalanced the fact that she was a woman conducting fieldwork. Conversely, male RAs may not be granted access to the private worlds of women participants as easily as women RAs. When Razavi (1992: 158) was conducting her fieldwork in rural Iran, for example, she found that the reservations of her women participants 'disappeared immediately' once she had dispensed with the male RA she had employed.

Whether you decide to employ an educated outsider or a RA from the local community, it is important to think about the positionality of your RA. All RAs have a position in relation to the research participants, and this may have a significant impact on the research, and sometimes unexpected consequences (Turner, 2010). You need to be alert to any signal from research participants that may signify discomfort with the RA, and as much as possible work at developing relationships with your participants who are independent of the mediation of the RA. As Farrelly's experience shows (see Box 8.5), all may not be as it first seems, even with the most highly recommended advisors (or assistants).

Box 8.5   Finding a suitable cultural advisor

In the first year of my PhD, I worked hard to secure a suitable cultural advisor for my fieldwork in Fiji. I eventually found a Fiji government representative (Vili[2]) willing to help. He agreed to introduce me to the communities and guide me through local cultural protocols. My one-year-old son and I travelled to Taveuni where I had arranged to meet Vili at a local hotel. However, days later he still had not made an appearance. I was very concerned as I had little money to spend hanging around in tourist accommodation but I understood that an eivalagi/palagi (outsider) could not simply turn up at a Fijian village unannounced and unaccompanied. I would be expected to present a sevusevu[3] to each of the four village chiefs. In addition, it was a requirement of the Massey University Ethics Committee and my scholarship that I consult with a cultural advisor. It was a relief, though slightly puzzling, when he turned up four days after we had planned with barely an apology. Regardless, after five days in the villages, I felt that Vili had proved invaluable in helping me navigate my way through the complex web of cultural protocols necessary to make my presence known and my research intentions and requests understood. My concerns returned, however, on the evening Vili left the island. The taxi driver who had driven him to the airport returned to request a taxi fare, even though I had given Vili cash for this purpose.

The next point of concern occurred in an interview with one of the turaga ni 'oro[4] about two months into the fieldwork. His wife waited until the end of the interview to tell us that her husband was most upset that I had not followed the correct protocol by coming to him when I had first arrived. I was mortified and could not apologise enough, but I was also disappointed that Vili had not guided me through this process. The friendly greetings that had met the charismatic Vili during his stay misled me to believe that he was loved by all. This was not the case. Many of my participants were later to divulge that they did not trust me when I arrived and that this was purely due to my association with Vili. They assumed that, like Vili, I was being paid a lot of money to work for the Fiji Government. They told me that Vili had been an officer with a government department alleged to have stolen thousands of dollars' worth of donated equipment from my participants. Consequently, it took at least three months to shake off Vili's negative association with me and to start building enough trust and rapport with my participants to begin meaningful fieldwork.

Source: Farrelly (2009)

One of the most important factors to successful fieldwork will be the personal relationship you develop with your RA. This was certainly the case with the relationship that was forged between Helen and her RA, Natalia, during fieldwork in El

Salvador. Reflecting on the experience, Natalia wrote that she felt 'so good to have collaborated in what you are creating ... I feel proud ... Thanks for the "ego-boost"' (personal communication, 1998). Collaborative research may prove more than an 'ego-boost', however, and give local researchers an opportunity to gain experience and develop research skills. Daviau (2010) notes the potential to build capacity among Lao research assistants as one of the key positive outcomes of his fieldwork, while Khan et al. explain how (2007) becoming a research assistant can be a transformational and mutual learning process. However, as Chloe and Vi, research assistants interviewed by Sarah Turner (2010: 216), pointed out, there is a 'very careful balancing act required between friendship, professionalism and avoiding the appearance of arrogance'.

It is important therefore to spend time with your RA before you launch into interviews or observations and develop some kind of professional relationship early on. Spend some time thinking about what you want from your RA and what you are prepared to offer them, including both professional assistance, mentoring and material remuneration. Problems of setting wages, conditions and expectations are common (Barrett and Cason, 2010: 82–86; Robson and Willis, 1997: 70–72), even among researchers going home. For example, a Namibian PhD student found that recruiting research assistants in Windhoek and Oshakati was one of the most challenging tasks he had to grapple with during fieldwork (see Box 8.6).

Box 8.6 Recruitment of research assistants: dilemmas facing a Namibian researcher

Like many indigenous researchers, I initially assumed that hiring research assistants was going to be the easiest task but it turned out to be one of the most difficult ... I found myself in trouble because my research assistants expected me to pay them like an overseas researcher or large organization. This was far beyond my budget and it cost me time to negotiate a local rate.

The University of Namibia assisted me by providing a list of experienced enumerators from which 6 were selected ... however our first meeting sparked difficulties over the amount they were to be paid per questionnaire. They wanted to be paid the average amount that the National Planning Commission, the University and UN agencies paid. I argued that I was an individual/indigenous Namibian and it was unfair for them to ask what they would of the UN. As part of my defence, I also raised the issue of cultural obligation, which forced some compromise because as a Namibian I should not have been expected to pay at all. Nevertheless, they rightfully countered because we were in Windhoek everything depended on money.

Source: Sikabongo (2003)

LANGUAGE ISSUES

Unless you are conducting home-based research within your own social group or have prior experience of the research vernacular, you will find it necessary to learn at least some local language.[5] While language learning is difficult for many researchers and there is seldom space for developing language fluency within most postgraduate programmes (Veeck, 2001: 34; Watson, 2004), language learning has great personal and professional benefits. Knowledge of the local language helps the researcher to gain an understanding of different viewpoints, enabling richer and more textured data to be collected and facilitating sensitive and appropriate fieldwork, while generating greater opportunities to interact and enjoy the company of others in the researched community (Devereux, 1992: 44; Watson, 2004: 61). In development research, language learning is also an important first step in addressing the cultural and linguistic biases of English. While you may not achieve full fluency during a short fieldwork trip, as Watson notes, the process of learning languages can be 'part of gaining and understanding of these different viewpoints and experiences, and can help to facilitate sensitive and appropriate fieldwork, in many different contexts' (2004: 62) . By contrast, a lack of local knowledge can lead to inappropriate or even invalid data and can generate feelings of frustration and low morale.

HOW MUCH LANGUAGE?

The 'gold standard' for researchers is full language skills (Bujra, 2006); however, this may be unrealistic or difficult for many researchers. Devereux (1992: 44–45) argues that it is important at the outset of fieldwork to weigh up the costs and benefits of language fluency before any decision regarding language tuition is made as although there is much to gain from language fluency, the costs in terms of time and money spent on the endeavour are generally high. This means that it is important to reflect on your specific circumstances. If, for example, you are a person who finds learning other languages easy and who plans to collect data from observation and interviews over a prolonged period, then it is probably a good idea to learn the vernacular as intensely as possible. If, however, you are a person who finds language learning difficult or plan to collect quantitative data over a short time period, then a basic understanding of some of the important vocabulary and cultural norms (Devereux, 1992: 44–45) and the assistance of an interpreter will probably suffice. Overall, your willingness to learn the language will mean more to your research participants than your ability to handle the subjunctive tense.

USING INTERPRETERS

As was the case with Helen's fieldwork in El Salvador, many researchers who do not have sufficient command of the vernacular in which to conduct research employ a

RA to act as their interpreter. Having an interpreter on hand gives the researcher the ability to understand and also some flexibility to take notes during interviews, but has the disadvantage of receiving information second-hand, and it creates significant distance between the interviewer and interviewee (Watson, 2004: 61). This can be problematic if the interpreter decides to 'filter' the interview (2004: 61) and to omit or change elements of the interview to prevent potential embarrassment or because they believe the information is irrelevant or of little use to the research topic (Devereux and Hoddinott, 1992: 25). This is why, as discussed above, the careful selection of a RA/interpreter is of vital importance, and even a small amount of language ability is important as it will enable you to recognise when research participants are straying from the questions and should give you the confidence to be able to detect possible misinterpretations of the participants' responses (Heyer, 1992: 204).

To address, and hopefully avoid, some of the problems associated with interpreting it is also important to communicate carefully and clearly with your interpreter, ensuring they understand the nature of the research and the reasons why you want to ask particular questions. During your initial meetings discuss in detail both the nature of the research project and the role of your interpreter. Here you need to clearly state whether you require your interpreter to translate literally or whether you would prefer a more concise translation.

Finally, if you decide to audiotape your interviews, rather than asking your RA to translate on the spot while you take notes, it is worth considering asking your RA to transcribe, then translate, the interviews. This will prevent another interpretation or possible misinterpretation of the data and will ensure that you are correctly representing the knowledge and understanding your research participants bring to the research process. Note, however, that this would involve more of their time and thus increase the cost to you of their service.

CONCLUSIONS

Arrival and adaptation in a new fieldwork setting provide both personal and professional challenges to researchers. Even with considerable planning one is more often than not faced with challenges upon of arrival into a foreign setting. Initial shock and confusion might be followed by a more delayed testing period of adjustment and cultural acceptance. There are, however, ways in which to prepare for and deal with these pressures (see Chapters 6 and 7). It is also important to accept that there will be some difficulties, whether you are a returning researcher, going to your home country, or entering a completely new environment. A thorough research design, an initial strategy for adaptation, keeping contact with supervisors, mentors, and local support people, using diaries, learning some of the language, being flexible and having realistic expectations will all go some way to helping you through the demands that will present themselves at different stages of your fieldwork. As a final note, most researchers find that their life is inevitably enriched by their fieldwork experiences.

Summary

- Almost all first-time researchers experience some level of anxiety on arrival in the field.
- Even if your plans and expectations end in disarray on your first day it is important to 'ride out' this period. Although it may seem chaotic, this is the start of the process of gaining control of your research project.
- Allow yourself a day or more to rest, recover and orient yourself to your new surroundings before beginning research tasks.
- Culture shock is common amongst fieldworkers, both those going into new environments and those returning to do research at home. This is a normal reaction, and plans to cope with it include time out, contact with loved ones and keeping a personal diary.
- While the notion of 'appropriate behaviour' is complex and culturally constructed, a polite, friendly demeanour and careful thought to off-duty and online behaviour will go a long way towards smoothing the fieldwork experience.
- Research assistants have an important role to play in many research projects. It is important to choose them carefully, being aware of their own positionality and limitations, and to think about what you are able to offer them, including both professional assistance and mentoring, and material remuneration.
- The 'gold standard' for researchers is full language skills but this is unrealistic for many researchers. It is, however, both respectful and to your advantage to learn some of the local vernacular, and to choose an interpreter who speaks the local language as their first language.

Questions for reflection

- What are your expectations of your arrival and first day in the field?
- How might you deal with culture shock?
- What do you think you might learn from the disorienting effects of arrival and the discomfort of culture shock? How might this be of benefit to your research?
- What does the term 'appropriate behaviour' mean for you, and what would it look like in your field site?
- How are you going to manage social media while in the field?
- What are your priorities when recruiting a research assistant? Where might you find one in your field site?
- How can you improve your language skills and cultural understanding both before fieldwork and in your early days in the field?

RECOMMENDED READINGS

Bujra, J. (2006). Lost in translation? The use of interpreters in fieldwork. In V. Desai and R. Potter (eds), *Doing Development Research* (pp. 172–179). London: Sage.

This chapter highlights the implications of researching with an interpreter and provides some practical advice on negotiating relationships and choosing an interpreter.

DeVita, P. (ed.) (1990) *The Humbled Anthropologist.* Belmont, CA: Wadsworth.
DeVita, P. (ed.) (2000). *Stumbling Toward Truth: Anthropologists at Work.* Prospect Heights, IL: Waveland Press.

These two edited volumes offer honest and humorous examples of how researchers cope with the challenges thrown up during cross-cultural fieldwork.

Devereux, S., and Hoddinott, J. (1992) The context of fieldwork. In S. Devereux and J. Hoddinott (eds), *Fieldwork in Developing Countries* (pp. 3–24). New York: Harvester Wheatsheaf.

This chapter provides an excellent overview of the issues facing researchers during fieldwork and prove that some issues do not change a lot over time.

Gardner, A., and Hoffman, D. M. (eds) (2006). *Dispatches from the Field: Neophyte Ethnographers in a Changing World.* Long Grove, IL: Waveland Press.

Written by graduate students during their fieldwork, this collection of essays gives an insight into the challenges faced by students arriving in the field for the first time.

NOTES

1. Or, as Van Maanen bluntly states, an understanding of why and where one's presence is likely to bring forth an 'oh fuck, here he comes again' response (Van Maanen, 1988: 36).
2. Pseudonym.
3. A *sevusevu* is a ceremony involving the offering of a *waka* (kava root). This is accepted in the customary way and is a symbol of recognition and acceptance of one another.
4. Village headman. All official business should go first to the *turaga ni 'oro*. It is his role to then pass this information on to the chief.
5. Still, language may well be an issue for researchers returning to their own country. Ite (1997: 80–81), a Nigerian, relied on English to communicate with respondents as she could not do so in the local dialect.

9

ETHICAL ISSUES

GLENN BANKS AND REGINA SCHEYVENS

> Just imagine how easy it would have been for you to have done your thesis in the place where you live, if you didn't have to travel to the other side of the world to learn about other experiences … I just think about you, how you leave your children, live in a risky situation, because it's dangerous here, how you have to travel so much, to be able to interview us … I admire this idea of yours and I feel like I've won a prize to have been included in this written work. (Carla Martínez, research participant, 24 May 2001, cited in Cupples, 2002a)

Fieldwork in developing countries and/or with marginalised people can give rise to a plethora of ethical dilemmas, many of which relate to power gradients between the researcher and the researched. Combined with this are complex issues of knowledge generation, ownership and exploitation. Ethical issues which arise in relation to cross-cultural situations thus need to be considered and questioned seriously by all scholars pondering fieldwork in the developing world, and ethical principles should in turn inform all stages of research, from the inception of a research project through to writing up results.

However, for many graduate students in particular, 'ethics' has come to be equated with a gruelling test to write an ethics proposal acceptable to the powers that be within their university. This is not what ethics is fundamentally about. Doing ethical research in a foreign or cross-cultural setting, as indicated by the starting quote for this chapter, requires building mutually beneficial relationships with people you meet in the field and acting in a sensitive and respectful manner. There is also a moral imperative which should inform Development Studies research (Sumner, 2007). As Madge asserts, 'ethical research should not only "do no harm", but also have potential "to do good", to involve "empowerment"'(1997: 114). Corbridge (1998: 49) similarly argues that the interdependencies of the world economy mean that those of us who are privileged should be 'attentive to the needs and rights of distant strangers'. Furthermore, he suggests that Development Studies scholars have an obligation to inform development practice, specifically, 'to provide plausible alternatives to existing social arrangements or patterns of development' (Corbridge, 1998: 42).

In this chapter, we explore the typical principles under which university ethics committees operate, before moving on to explore a much wider range of ethical issues likely to present themselves to students in the field, including questions of who sanctions one's research, balancing the expectations of different stakeholders, reciprocity, deception and the dilemmas associated with sexual relationships in the field. These warnings should not, however, necessarily deter researchers from engaging in development fieldwork. As noted in Chapter 1, there can be many benefits from cross-cultural research and there are ways to do research in a responsible manner and to avoid harming our research participants.

ETHICS IN RESEARCH

What do we mean by ethical issues in field research? John Barnes writes that ethical decision making in research

arises when we try to decide between one course of action and another not in terms of expediency or efficiency but by reference to standards of what is morally right or wrong. (Barnes, 1979, cited in May, 2011: 61)

Decisions based on ethics are not determined by how successful the researcher will be but rather by whether the research is just or not, and the extent to which the research takes the participants' needs and concerns into account. The research process must ensure the participants' dignity, privacy and safety, and must 'give back' to them in some ways. We see this as constituting 'ethics from the bottom up' (see Box 9.1), which is equally as important as official university ethics procedures. What we are most interested in discussing in this chapter is not deliberately unethical behaviour such as falsifying or fabricating data, misappropriating funds or plagiarism, rather, decisions involved in negotiating field research which are less obvious such as avoiding harm to those involved in the research.

Box 9.1   Ethics from the bottom up

- Considering local needs/concerns when identifying our research topic.
- Showing respect for the knowledge and traditions of the communities we work with.
- Following research protocols in the country concerned, and cultural protocols on permission from communities.

(Continued)

(Continued)

- Building mutually beneficial relationships with the people we meet.
- Acting in a sensitive and respectful manner.
- Ensuring that our research is of value to those who give up their time to participate in our study.
- Sharing the findings of our research with our research participants in an accessible manner, and allowing for dialogue or feedback.

The principles discussed in Box 9.1 are particularly important if one is to ethically conduct research with indigenous peoples (see Chapter 4). Battiste (2008: 503) asserts that there must be space for indigenous control over the research process and products.

There are two models of ethics prevalent in social science research (Denzin, 1997). The first is an absolutist ethical model premised on a set of principles or codes that direct research practice (de Laine, 2000: 23) which must be adhered to under all circumstances. There is no flexibility regarding the ability of the individual to make ethical decisions based on situational and personal circumstances. In other words, there is no ethical relativism. The second model, originating from a post-modern position, argues for flexibility in ethical decisions. This model contends that the rational objectivity required in the first model is a false reality. Supporters of this model maintain that researchers are not apolitical, neutral observers but rather fully involved, self-aware, interacting people who are (or should be) ethically fully informed, therefore responsible for their actions. Proponents argue that research should not necessarily benefit the researcher, rather, it should empower participants and solicit positive change. Researchers should be knowledgeable about professional codes of ethics, but in the end ethical decisions should be based on reasoned beliefs regarding the 'goodness' or 'correctness' of what to do. Ethical decisions, then, are reached on an affective rather than intellectual basis (de Laine, 2000: 28; Denzin, 1997: 276).

To this perspective others counter that 'a loose and flexible system involving "anything goes" so easily opens the research door to the unscrupulous' (May, 2011: 63–64). However, even professional associations with codes of ethics recognise that flexibility is critical. The American Anthropological Association's Statement of Ethics, for example, says:

These principles address *general* circumstances, priorities and relationships ... that should be considered in anthropological work and ethical decision-making. The individual anthropologist must be willing to make carefully considered ethical choices and be prepared to make clear the assumptions, facts and considerations on which those choices are based. (2012: 3),

Both absolutist and relativist ethicists believe fieldwork must be concerned with ensuring that the research will not have negative implications for the participants.

There are a variety of 'good practices' discussed below that the researcher should remember, many of which follow ideas intrinsic to participatory development. The ethical guidelines developed for the Royal Melbourne Institute of Technology's (RMIT) Timor-Leste Research Program provide a good example of this, centred on partnership and building local research capacity (see Box 9.2).

Box 9.2   RMIT's Timor-Leste Research Program: ethical objectives

- To build innovative knowledge about East Timorese society that is applicable, socially progressive, accessible and widely distributed in both Timor-Leste and globally, including both within and beyond Universities;
- To ensure that our research program is transparent and accountable in Timor-Leste, and involves locally-based partners wherever possible;
- To build the research capabilities of East Timorese communities, organisations and individuals, and emerging researchers from Australia and internationally;
- To include a diverse range of East Timorese voices in data collection and written outcomes.

Source: RMIT (2011)

OFFICIAL ETHICS PROCEDURES

Ethics approval from a university review board or ethics committee is typically mandatory before fieldwork can be undertaken. This is not always welcomed by researchers, who bemoan that the 'recent increase in the extent and range of university bureaucratic controls over research with human subjects often conflicts with, and may unduly delimit, the academic imperative to pursue research' (Casey, 2001: 127). This increasing ethical oversight in development is related to the broader application of ethical guidelines from the bio-medical sciences, where the researcher works in a highly structured, objective relationship with their research subjects. The breaking down of the clear separation between researcher and researched (through greater use of participatory tools and approaches) in much current development fieldwork therefore presents a challenge to these more traditional ethical standards and guidelines (de Laine, 2000: 4).

Problems can arise for students and other researchers seeking ethics approval if the committee or board does not include anyone with experience in conducting research in cross-cultural settings. Further problems are likely if the ethics board takes an absolutist stance by adopting a code of ethics with specific requirements that must be adhered to. Ethical relativists argue that a research situation is continually evolving, that context is important and flexibility must be worked into the process. They would contend that formulating ethical procedures based on a code of ethics is helpful as a starting point, but rigidity – the inability to shift one's procedures and ideas – might lead to unsuccessful research results and possibly even harmful situations for the participants or the researchers. This is particularly the case with qualitative or ethnographic-style fieldwork where research themes, questions and relationships can evolve through the process. Kaupapa Māori research prioritises relationships and takes this flexible approach (see Bishop, 2008), and this is what Mackintosh (2011), who is non-Māori, tried to be true to when conducting research among Māori communities in New Zealand. However, she felt her university's ethics procedures did not support this approach: 'I felt uncomfortable trying to fit, mould and squeeze my thesis proposal into an ethics application that was not open to indigenous methodologies' (2011: 40).

This section outlines typical concerns of university ethics boards, as well as raising examples of difficulties some researchers have had in adhering to the codes developed by such boards. While there are variations, three critical ethical concepts that must be guaranteed by the researcher are typically of particular interest to those sitting on ethics boards: informed consent; privacy, including ideas of confidentiality and anonymity; and conflicts of interest. Further concerns should be safety of the researcher (Chapter 6) and ways of managing stress and personal difficulties (Chapters 7 and 8).

INFORMED CONSENT

Informed consent is when a potential participant freely and with full understanding of the research agrees to be part of the project. It is premised on the notion that the person has a complete and thorough understanding of the aims and processes of the research project, what the research will be used for, such as policy formation and publications, and who will have access to the information gathered. Knowledge of the research comes from the researcher honestly explaining what the research is about and providing an opportunity for the participant to ask questions about the research at any time. These are the standards for which all development research should strive, although in practice this may be more complex than it appears – and indeed Boden et al. note that in some situations this process can be described as little more than an 'empty ritual [that] embeds a fantasy of respondent control' (2009: 741).

An essential aspect of ethical research is ensuring people's right not to participate and that they are fully cognisant of this. Such consent should be given without duress or pressure. 'Gatekeepers', discussed below, can be a problematic element in ensuring free and informed consent by research participants, especially in hierarchical organisations or communities. Another critical aspect of informed consent is the knowledge of the right to withdraw from the study at any time with the understanding that the information provided will be removed from the pool of collected data.

The researcher should also honestly and as fully as possible advise the people requested to contribute to the study about any potential harm or benefits the researcher believes might come to them as a consequence of their participation. This could mean physical harm by others fearful of what might be revealed, loss of liveli-hood, or loss of opportunities. No matter what the potential ramifications might be, the researcher needs to disclose them, although as Boden et al. (2009) and Bosk and de Vries (2004) point out, this can be problematic when many risks may be hard to anticipate. One risk might arise from not protecting confidentiality in research notes, discussed further below.

Informing potential participants typically occurs via an 'information sheet'. Most university or institutional ethics committees require inclusion of the following infor-mation, which should be phrased in language that is simple and easy to understand:

- a description of who the researcher(s) is/are;
- a comprehensive statement of the purpose of the research, including who is being approached to participate and how they are being selected;
- the expected duration of the research, and approximate time required for participants who agree to be interviewed, fill in survey forms and so on;
- the nature of the research procedures and the role the participant will be asked to play;
- a complete and, as far as possible, an honest discussion of the potential harms and benefits that might result from participation – discussion should also point out that a decision not to participate in the research will have no negative impact on people;
- a discussion of how data will be stored and the precautions taken to ensure privacy issues and who will have access to the data;
- what will be the final product(s) of the research in terms of publications and reports, and who will have access to this/these;
- researcher (and supervisor, where relevant) and university contact details.

Along with the above points, the information sheet should also include all the basic rights of the participant, such as the right to:

- decline to answer any particular question;
- withdraw from the study (for which most researchers specify a timeframe);
- ask any questions about the study at any time during participation;
- ask for the recorder to be turned off at any time during the interview;
- provide information on the understanding that the participant's name will not be used unless they give permission to the researcher;
- be given access to a summary of the project findings when it is concluded. (Massey University Ethics Committee, 2013)

Some ethics committees suggest and even require that the researcher removes him-self or herself from the initial phase of requesting assistance from potential partici-pants by having a third party make contact and pass on the information sheet. Committees reason that people might feel pressured if the researcher makes the initial contact. They also suggest that potential participants have an opportunity to read the information sheet and consent form at their leisure before committing themselves. Depending upon the research and the cultural context within which one

is operating, this process may or may not be possible or desirable, and would need
to be considered for each project (Laws, 2003: 239).

While ethics boards or committees generally encourage translation of the information sheet into local languages, they do not always recognise that in cultures with a
strong oral tradition, and/or where a large proportion of the community to be studied
is illiterate, what is written on a piece of paper may have very little meaning for potential participants. It is often more advisable for the researcher to sit down with potential participants and introduce themselves informally first: family, experiences, country
you come from, interests and so on, to try to establish a rapport. A full explanation
of the research could then be provided, covering the points made above in relation to
information sheets. Finally, the community to be studied should have time to reflect on
the proposed research before deciding whether to participate in the research.

In conjunction with the provision of an information sheet, ethics committees usually
also require the use of 'consent forms'. The consent form spells out the participants'
rights (mentioned above). At the bottom of the consent form is a place for the participant to sign if he or she agrees to participate. In some cases, participants may be
very wary of signing a form which could end up in the hands of authorities, especially
where military regimes have made people suspicious of official documents. Others
argue that seeking written informed reinforces an inappropriate relationship of power
between the researcher and the research participants that can undermine the trust and
relationships that the ethical researcher needs to do good qualitative research:

> [T]he enforced requirement to contractualise, to give legal force, to certain aspects of the
> researcher–respondent relationship will inevitably transform those relationships in ways that
> neither respondent nor researcher will necessarily deem desirable or generative. (Boden et al.,
> 2009: 741)

Box 9.3 explains how a researcher working with an Aboriginal community was
challenged by an elder who was asked to sign a consent form.

Box 9.3   What is best for cross-cultural research: an 'informed consent form' or a 'letter of commitment'?

*In spite of repeated assurances that such a document [informed consent form] was
designed to protect participants' interests (i.e., primarily to ensure confidentiality and
anonymity), one aboriginal elder I attempted to interview refused to sign anything,
mocking the formality of the language with which the form was written. The participant
was far more interested in having me sign the document – in having me put my promises
in writing (which I gladly obliged). … this experience raised the question as to whether an
informed consent form – a standard ethical protocol – is culturally appropriate for use in
some contexts, in this case with aboriginal elders.*

> *In hindsight, use of the form felt insensitive in light of the negative historical connotations associated with the signing of treaties, of which First Nation elders are, perhaps, more acutely aware. However, a Letter of Commitment seems a reasonable means with which to address the challenge. Such a document, while closely following the content of the original Informed Consent, would assert the researcher's promises to the participants, and would be signed by the researcher alone. Participant consent would then be secured verbally. This implicitly acknowledges and seeks to address postcolonial power relations, ensuring mitigated vulnerability on the part of both researchers and informants.*
>
> *In the interim period since this research project took place in 2001, the Carleton University Research Ethics Committee has developed a different aboriginal research protocol. Researchers are now required to prepare a script, and to proceed with oral consent. The name of the Informed Consent form itself has in some cases been changed to Permission to Interview. This shift has occurred in recognition that aboriginal culture is a largely oral culture that places paramount importance on a system of honor. Thus, the imposition of too much paperwork may jeopardize the research relationship.*
>
> *Source:* Ballamingie and Johnson (2011: 717)

Most ethics committees or boards now recognise that where culturally inappropriate or where there are good reasons not to record a person's consent in writing, consent can be given verbally. However, they will usually require that this be documented (e.g., on a tape recorder). Not all researchers agree that this is appropriate in every context, as recording conversations or statements can be as intimidating for some as writing it down. We would argue that in certain circumstances, informed consent should be achieved verbally in an informal, undocumented way. For example, this may be appropriate where potential participants are illiterate, but ashamed to admit so. Another option which can, depending on the circumstances, make ethical sense is to obtain informed verbal consent for the interview at the beginning and formalise the consent (by use of a written form) at the end of the process. At this point the participant will be in a better position to understand the nature of the research being carried out, be able to reflect on what they have said and whether they want this to be included in the research project, and, importantly, they will know the researcher better. As a researcher, it is imperative to be sensitive to the context and the participant's individual and cultural history.

Additional issues regarding informed consent arise when one is doing research via the Internet (Berg, 2007). What is appropriate from an ethical standpoint will depend on whether the author of online content regards their material as public or private. (See Chapter 5, section on 'Ethics' for an extended discussion of this issue.)

Ethics boards and committees usually have particular guidelines about obtaining consent for research involving vulnerable populations such as children or the intellectually disabled (Berg, 2007: 78). In such circumstances, the consent of a parent or guardian is usually required.

While we have exposed some problems associated with the application of informed consent, we do not disagree with the principle of informed consent. Rather, we would argue strongly that, as the American Anthropological Association Statement of Ethics states, 'It is the quality of the consent, not the format, that is relevant' (2012: 7). Discussing consent to participate reminds people of their rights and it is also an excellent mechanism to avoid researcher complacency. However, research is a dynamic and continuous process so informed consent at all stages of the research cannot be guaranteed by a pile of signed consent forms handed out early in the research process. Relationships between the researcher and participants can evolve as might the socio-political environment within and outside the community, and hence 'It is best to think of consent as an on-going process' (Laws, 2003: 239), with Lederman arguing consent is something 'to be negotiated throughout a long-term relationship, as a substantive part of the research itself' (2006: 486). And importantly, participants can (and in our experience do) also withhold consent by avoiding interviews or through their silence.

ANONYMITY AND CONFIDENTIALITY

The terms 'anonymity' and 'confidentiality' are often used in different ways – and sometimes interchangeably – by different researchers and institutions. In the research context, anonymity typically means 'we do not include information about any individual or research site that will enable that individual or research site to be identified' (Walford, 2005: 84) in research outputs (e.g., theses or articles). In its purest form, anonymity can only be guaranteed where the individual researcher has no knowledge of the identity of the participant – such as can occur through postal surveys. More typically for qualitative fieldwork, the identity of individuals is concealed through the use of pseudonyms. The rationale for anonymity is to protect the individual or the community from possible negative associations or harm that could arise from the published research. This can be more vexed than it appears. For much qualitative research, disguising the research location is difficult: if we are working on the impacts of a particular development project, for example, this context is an important element of the research itself, and the location will be easily identified by knowledgeable readers. In such instances the researcher needs to clearly explain to participants at the time of interviews the degree to which their privacy and anonymity can be guaranteed (e.g., how the information contributed will be separated from the master list which matches pseudonyms to real names).

It would also be wrong to assume that all participants want anonymity. Consent should allow for the disclosure of participants' identities if they so desire (see Tilley and Woodthorpe, 2011). Participants can feel proud of being included in a research project and want acknowledgement of their contribution in your writing. However, even though individuals or communities may want such acknowledgment, the researcher might decide that disclosure of their identity is inappropriate in terms of future harm if, for example, it is associated with potentially damaging material. In other instances, such as asking a local government official for his or her opinion of a nearby forestry project that is being developed, you can identify this official when citing his or her response as long as a) you have received consent to do so, and b) they are speaking in their capacity as an official.

'Confidentiality' is a broader term which recognises that a researcher may be entrusted with sensitive or private ('confidential') information, and that the source of this information either does not want the information made public at all, or does not want their name connected with it (Wiles et al., 2008). This might include, for example, details of problematic social relationships within a village setting, or information on dubious internal government decision-making processes. If such information did become public – either intentionally via a research publication, or accidentally such as by leaving electronic or hard copies of transcripts in a publicly accessible location – and they were able to be traced back to the source, it could bring censure or harm to your source. Therefore the researcher has two threads of ethical responsibility here: first, to ensure as far as they can that any field notes, electronic media or transcripts are stored in a secure place and password protected; and second, that where confidential information is cleared to be used, the source of the information is protected (hence anonymity). In assuring participants of the confidentiality of material they provide, you must also be prepared to destroy information that someone has provided you with if asked to do so during or after the information is collected. Sometimes this occurs if a participant decides what they have said is inflammatory or just problematic.

CONFLICT OF INTEREST

Development research, as we have noted above, is based around relationships of trust and loyalty with participants, research sponsors, supervisors, universities and professional organisations and societies. These trust relationships can be put at risk by conflicts of interest. Some of the most acute conflicts arise over the issue of funding connected with research. As Cheek notes, 'accepting funding for … research affects the nature of relationships between the research participants and the researcher' (2005: 403).

Therefore funding accepted from host governments, from corporations, universities or even scholarships can impose obligations on the researcher which may clash with their primary responsibility towards their research participants. Researchers may feel torn between or constrained in critiquing the policies or activities of a government or company when this same institution has been instrumental in funding the research in the first place (see Box 9.4). The Association of American Geographers argues that in these situations

[t]he guiding principles in relations with sponsoring and funding organizations should be openness and disclosure. In many cases, ethical issues related to funding can best be avoided by discussing possible conflicts or concerns with officials at the agencies and institutions that fund research at

the time funding is sought, rather than after problems appear. Geographers should be prepared to reject funding from an agency if agreement cannot be reached that enables the geographer to behave ethically. (2009: VI)

Box 9.4   Financing fieldwork: managing a conflict of interest

One of us (Glenn) has worked for many years as a researcher on the social, economic and cultural effects of mining in Melanesia. Over the course of this period the fieldwork for this research has been funded from a range of sources: his various universities, the Papua New Guinea government, donors such as NZAID, international institutions such as the International Institute for Environment and Development and the World Bank, and most significantly, a number of the mining companies themselves.

Managing the ethics and potential conflicts around these various relationships, especially in the context of the communities where Glenn has worked, has required a high degree of openness, transparency and negotiation. On the one hand, being very clear with communities and participants about who is funding the research, why it is being done and what it is going to be used for has been critical in building local relationships of trust. On the other hand, being very clear with the funding body (and especially mining companies and government) that research entails a primary obligation to respect the research participants, to publish and to return research to the participants has sometimes been difficult. Building the latter into the formal contracts for consultancy and contracted research is one way that this has been addressed and is increasingly accepted by the funders of such research, although it typically still requires some negotiation and, significantly, also relationship and trust building.

Funding of course is not the only potential conflict of interest that is likely to confront a researcher. On the issue of conflicts of interest, the American Anthropological Association's Statement of Ethics states:

Anthropologists must weigh competing ethical obligations to research participants, students, professional colleagues, employers and funders ... while recognizing that obligations to research participants are usually primary ... These varying relationships may create conflicting, competing or crosscutting ethical obligations, reflecting both the relative vulnerabilities of different individuals, communities or populations, asymmetries of power implicit in a range of relationships, and the differing ethical frameworks of collaborators representing other disciplines or areas of practice ... Anthropologists must often make difficult decisions among competing ethical obligations while recognizing their obligation to do no harm. (2012: 9)

Researchers can often find their values (e.g., around human rights or privacy) challenged by the ways in which these concepts are understood and practised in other societies. Exposing the cultural assumptions that we as researchers carry with us can be uncomfortable, but an empathic approach to the different values that your participants may hold is likely to be more productive for both yourself and your research partners than blunt confrontation over these.

Conflicts of interest can also arise in the case of students conducting home-based research, such as what Karra and Phillips (2008: 547) describe as 'auto-ethnography'. Those who wish to return home to work after their studies in a Western university are completed may find it particularly difficult to pursue topics in which concerns about their government's processes and policies may arise (Mandiyanike, 2009). They may also find that barriers are put in the way of their research simply because they are not trusted by local authorities, who 'perceive them as potential political adversaries, as radicals' (Cernea, 1982: 134).

It is often a good idea to talk through the potential for conflict of interest in your research with your supervisor or a colleague, as they may be able to identify issues which are not apparent to you, or they may be able to suggest a way of handling such conflicts. A solution can sometimes be easier and less traumatic than simply abandoning a particular piece of research, and might mean altering the direction of the research, for example, or not accepting financial assistance from some sources. Often such solutions can improve the quality of the research process.

THE VALUE OF OFFICIAL ETHICS PROCEDURES

The problem with Institutional Review Boards and qualitative research is that they are such a distraction from the real difficulties we face and from the real ethical dilemmas that confront us that we may not recognise and discuss the serious and elemental because we are so busy with the procedural and bureaucratic. (Bosk and de Vries, 2004: 260)

As Bosk and de Vries note here, in comparison to the social injustices we may be investigating, the concerns of ethics boards can sometimes appear quite trivial, if not totally misplaced. It certainly may seem that our academic institutions are at times more concerned with their image and protecting themselves from the potential threat of litigation rather than allowing research into important social issues (see Hammersley, 2009: 218). In this context it is no surprise that Lederman writes that 'Intentional and unintentional evasion and active cynicism about IRBs are predictable responses when regulations appear to make no sense' (2006: 487).

But it is also unfair to portray ethics committees or boards as simply one more hurdle that the researcher needs to cross. At the very least, submitting an application for ethics approval should force you to think systematically about your research and the well-being of your informants, and to articulate some of your assumptions around the cultural context in which you expect to carry out your work. Nevertheless, before sending in an application for ethics approval you should consider what the board is likely to be concerned with, not just what you regard as the important ethical issues. Seek advice from your supervisors or colleagues who have experience submitting ethics applications. No matter how critical you believe your research is, it will not receive approval from the ethics board unless they are satisfied with the way you address the central ethical issues discussed above.

Going through formal ethics channels does not mean you will know all the ethical dilemmas you will face, nor does it mean you will necessarily have the tools to deal with them (Hammersley, 2009). Likewise, because so much of our fieldwork is built on managing personal relationships, formal bureaucratic ethics procedures alone cannot make unethical research(ers) ethical.

GATEKEEPERS

In the social science research we generally describe as gatekeepers 'individuals who directly or indirectly facilitate or inhibit researchers' access to resources such as people, institutions, information and logistics' (Bonnin, 2010: 183). Gatekeepers are significant as they can either help, or hinder, the research process (Cornet, 2010).

In many instances, before they even reach their field site researchers will have to apply to and receive permission from government agencies which can control who does research on what topic. Receiving a research visa or the official stamp of approval from the government is likely to be just the first stage in negotiating your research with various gatekeepers. Beyond this, gatekeepers might include village headmen, community religious leaders, librarians in charge of an archive, heads of kin groups or households, government officials, or the personal assistants of company executives.

Often it is *local* gatekeepers who will need to be satisfied before an adequate level of fieldwork can be undertaken. In some cases this will be informal 'permission' – people's consent will be indicated by their degree of participation and enthusiasm for you and your work. This is perhaps the most important and relevant permission you will be granted and will continue to strive for and negotiate even on a daily basis. In other communities this may be more rigorous, involving a further set of ethical guidelines and commitments. Examples of this may be found in Polynesian cultures, where chiefs or local *Kaumatua* (Maori elders) need to be satisfied regarding the merits, ethical issues and future implications of your research. The requirements of such gatekeepers, coupled with the formal requirements of governments, may necessitate considerable foresight, awareness and planning on the part of the researcher, especially at the Masters level where time can be very precious. While sometimes onerous, consulting with a number of different gatekeepers can be beneficial when starting out with your research as this can establish trustful relationships. As a group of early career geographers concluded after reflecting on their fieldwork experiences, 'often those we initially considered gatekeepers turned out to be facilitators of the research process rather than obstacles to accessing respondents and resources' (Heller et al., 2011: 73).

Gatekeepers commonly try to influence the direction of the research by directing you to speak only to certain people or to visit certain 'star' projects that are known to perform well. This is what Fisher (2011) found when she went to New Delhi to research transnational municipal networks involved in climate change (see Box 9.5). Meanwhile, during Bonnin's (2010: 185) research in Vietnam, she became aware that RAs can play a powerful gatekeeping role, particularly when they are employed as translators, as in this role they are the researcher's 'main means for dialogue and interaction' with the communities they are studying:

some of my state-assigned assistants were not helpful connecting with Hmong and Yao I wished to speak with ... I felt that the demeanour of my assistants was off-putting or disrespectful to informants due to a lack of cultural sensitivity, such as cutting informants off while talking, making facial expressions that signalled a lack of interest, speaking sharply, fondling informants' garments or trade wares, or showing discomfort at the setting (we would often squat on the floor in market stalls during interviews). (Bonnin, 2010: 185)

Box 9.5 How gatekeepers can attempt to manage the researcher and the research process

My work on/with the network began in June 2008 when I first approached its Delhi headquarters to discuss the possibility of conducting research, which could be both part of my PhD and fill any research needs they might have. Despite a positive email exchange with the Executive Director, when it came to a first meeting in New Delhi, on the appointed day (which took several attempts to set up) I was unable to meet with the man himself. I was already in a taxi when he phoned to say something had come up, and passed me on to his deputy. By the time I had arrived, I had been again passed down to the two most junior project staff. These two staff became my primary contacts within the organisation and my gatekeepers to the others.

... staff members shaped the type of research relationship I would have with them through delegating me to deal with the junior staff, limiting access to other staff, and having little interest in developing a wider relationship.

... Two cities were suggested by staff members as my primary case studies, which I duly visited. These were the cities most engaged with the organisation and seen as 'best practice examples'. On the other hand, I was actively discouraged from going to certain municipalities where there was very little going on.

Source: Fisher (2011: 459)

Gatekeeping controls sometimes conflict with the needs and rights of the researcher and/or the researched. Many researchers have reflected on to whom they are obligated: the government official in the capital city who granted you research permission, the local administrator who vetted your research and introduced you to various contacts, or to the people who you lived with and learned from? In most cases, we would suggest your primary obligations are to those you are researching. Researchers often feel conflicted, however, if their research unearths information which paints their gatekeepers in a negative light. If the researcher decides to go ahead and publish their findings, this might lead the government to tighten up restrictions on future researchers. Ideally, you do not want to jeopardise fieldwork opportunities for others; however, if researchers do not speak out against the injustices witnessed, then Scheper-Hughes (1992) would argue that they are condoning them. The researcher's position is a position of privilege which should be used to help those in need.

RECIPROCITY

Before, during and after fieldwork it is important to consider what you can give back to those who have given up their time and provided you with assistance. Typically we will gain far more from our fieldwork than those who participate in it (Patai, 1991; Wolf, 1996). We return to our home universities, write our dissertations or research papers, and will most likely seek employment or promotions based on our newly gained information and qualifications. But what is in it for those we study? After three decades as an anthropologist, Wolcott concludes very frankly that 'I have no evidence that my own research ever helped anyone I thought it might help or intended to help' (2005: 128). Unless our research is policy oriented and unless we have built linkages with institutions that are committed to act on our findings, or the research process has been empowering for the communities we have been working with, our research will benefit us far more than our informants.

This should not necessarily deter us from embarking on our research programmes, and nor does it make our research unethical. The understanding you gain from fieldwork could lead you down various avenues of activism (see Chapter 10, section on 'Advocacy and activism'). Later in life we may find ourselves in positions in which we can influence development policy or practice, or inform others in positions of power of the insights we have gained. We should not therefore become immobilised by doubts about the legitimacy of fieldwork. It is salutary to note, though, that existing research quality evaluation systems implemented at many Western universities put additional pressure on staff to 'perform', preferably by publishing in A-ranked journals. Those who invest their energy into these endeavours can sometimes gain more recognition and reward within the academy than those who focus on 'giving back' to the communities they work with. Researchers working for social justice are likely to be involved in hours of work that do not lead to 'quality' academic publications (Smith, 2012: 206).

GIVING BACK VIA THE RESEARCH PROCESS

There are various ways that you can give something back and these should be considered before fieldwork begins. You can give something back through the *process* of research (see also Chapter 1, section on 'Responses to the crisis of legitimacy facing Western researchers' and Chapter 4, section on 'Participatory approaches'). The research experience can be rewarding for your informants when you act in a manner which conveys genuine respect for them and their knowledge. Visiting poor households/individuals that would normally be ignored by distinguished visitors (a category you will most likely be placed in, despite any unease you may feel about this) could help raise their self-esteem. You may even develop mutually rewarding relationships that could last a lifetime.

In terms of specific research activities, some suggest that collecting oral histories from participants can validate their knowledge and increase their self-esteem (Francis, 1992). It is even better if researchers then share a record of these histories with participants in a suitable manner (e.g., laminated booklet). Interview processes can also 'give back'. Box 9.6 provides an example of how Helen Leslie sought to assist women in her research project on post-conflict El Salvador. Her main activities included participation in self-help groups facilitated by the organisation and conducting in-depth interviews with individual women participants of the self-help groups. Leslie used the interview process as a way of giving participants the opportunity for further reflection on, and thus redefinition of, their gendered experiences of the war. Many carried the guilt of the loss of family members and their inability to care for their children during war-time crises such as *guindas* or flights, where they were forced to hide out in the mountains in an attempt to save their own and their families' lives.

Box 9.6 The therapeutic value of interviews for women in El Salvador

I hadn't really considered the therapeutic value of my in-depth interviews with participants, but as I began to conduct my interviews it became apparent that they were, in fact, constructed as having therapeutic value to the women. Many experiences which were considerably traumatic for participants were recounted in the course of the interview process and these would induce much emotion on the part of the participants, my research assistant and myself. Some time for reflection on gender issues raised in the self-help groups was also part of the interview should the participant desire it and these opportunities, along with the process of expressing emotion, often resulted in women feeling that a great burden had been lifted off their shoulders in terms, for example, of the guilt they felt for transgressing society's notions of the role of a 'good' mother during the conflict.

Source: Leslie, cited in Scheyvens and Leslie (2000: 128)

In an interesting initiative, when doing home-based research in Nigeria, Amadiume (1993) found that by running an essay competition for school children she could both verify her research findings and instil in them a sense of pride in their culture and history.

Outside of data gathering activities there will be other ways to give something back. You should consider participating in local activities and learning local customs that show you value the culture of those you study. A visitor to the village of Lesu in New Ireland was told the following about the anthropologist Powdermaker, who had previously done research in the area:

> You know, when she [Powdermaker] came here she was so dumb. She did not even know how to speak. She was like an infant. She knew nothing. But now, ah, all is changed. She speaks and she understands us; she knows our magic; she can dance with the women; she has learned our folk tales; she knows how we garden and the different ways we fish; she has been to our feasts … Ah, she knows much. Who is responsible? I am. (Wax, 1979: 255)

If you are doing research in remote areas, then at the very least you are likely to be a distraction from the boredom of village life (Goward, 1984: 109). And, as you blunder your way through the vagaries of cross-cultural research, you may also provide a source of amusement.

PROVIDING GIFTS AND PRACTICAL ASSISTANCE

Gift giving is another means of showing appreciation to those who have assisted you or given up their time to speak with you. It can be, however, a very delicate issue (see Chapter 4). Bleek (1979: 201) argues against giving presents on the basis that they serve to reaffirm existing socio-economic inequalities, but van Binsbergen believes that gifts or services are appropriate when they are to express one's commitment to evolving relationships, not to 'buy off the informant's envy or one's own feelings of guilt' (1979: 207).

Before departing for fieldwork, discussions with nationals or other researchers who have conducted fieldwork in your study country may help. You should seek local advice after arrival as well. In other instances, it may only be during the course of fieldwork that you will become aware of what gift giving gestures are appropriate.[1] Near the end of two separate village-level studies in Bangladesh, Scheyvens (2001) paid for dinners of high-status food for the field staff of the development organisations he was researching. It was only through discussions with the management of these institutions that he became aware that this was an appropriate gesture of gratitude. For some of his informants who were impoverished women, he offered to take photos and send to them prints as soon as possible. He found that some women would put on their best saris before having their photos taken, suggesting that they valued this opportunity. Of course, such a gift is not going to help these women in their daily struggles. Researchers face the dilemma that the gifts they offer may be little more than a token of their visit.

Before giving a gift careful thought should be given to the nature of your relationship with your informants and the type of offering. Gift giving that results in a patron–client relationship (i.e., one in which the receiver expects and becomes reliant on further gifts) can be very problematic. What informants might hope for and what is reasonable can present another quandary.

In some instances you may be able to offer certain practical services. Razavi (1992) found she could provide practical assistance during the duration of her field-work by transporting locals in her car. Lewis (1991: 62) had access to a photocopier and was able to give out maps of village plots that were normally not accessible to locals. Other researchers may be asked to help to write grant applications, in order to help the communities they are working with. This is one of the activities that Polly Stupples continues to assist with, several years after she completed her field research (see Box 9.7).

Box 9.7   'Reciprocity' during research with an NGO in Nicaragua

The director of the artists' organisation (and my primary research collaborator) was always pleased to talk with me about what was going on in the project. To her I was a useful sounding board who was unconnected to either the internal politics of the organisation or the wider political context for art-making in the region. I provided a fresh perspective.

I also contributed considerable time to helping to write funding applications, translating documents between Spanish and English for donor evaluations, and occasionally taking photographs which were used in funding applications or in other documenting processes. This process was not one-way. Later on I sent conference paper drafts back to the project director in Nicaragua who gave me frank and rigorous feedback that helped to refine my understanding. There was a genuine sense of exchange.

Source: Stupples (2012)

When she went to Kampala, Uganda, to research young men from neighbouring countries who had fled war or insecurity, Lammers (2007) also found that local expectations clashed with her initial convictions about 'helping out'. Before leaving the Netherlands, Lammers had decided that she would not give assistance to any-one in need, as she had read this would distort the research process and also entrench power relations which situated her as the wealthy foreigner. However, once she started her research she soon changed her mind: 'To me this was, first of all, a matter of ethics: is there a valid reason to say no when requests for material, financial or legal assistance come from people in life-threatening circumstances?' (Lammers, 2007: 75). Lammers thus provided assistance in a wide range of ways: giving money for passport-sized photos, emails and letters of recommendation for those seeking official status as refugees; buying household items such as blankets; paying school fees and medical bills; and doing advocacy work for refugees via

Makerere University. She concluded that making economic contributions was a form of social engagement, as reciprocity is central to building trust in human relationships. She also suggests that it actually benefited the research process for her to be a generous giver:

> My experiences in Kampala confirmed that, firstly, trust was indeed a precondition for open conversation, and secondly, that trust was only generated when I was prepared to enter into a personal relationship that involved sharing and giving ... Being prepared to give or contribute not only is a matter of personal ethics, but also is in keeping with the prevalent social rules. Therefore being prepared to give when this is expected or needed – instead of keeping one's distance in the name of objectivity – will most likely contribute to the level of trust and as such positively contribute to the research process and its outcom.e (Lammers, 2007: 77)

Note that just because you clearly see yourself wearing a 'research' hat does not mean that is how others will perceive you: if you have skills, or connections, or specialist knowledge, those you develop relationships with might want you to apply them in a way which could directly assist them. This is what Boesten discovered when conducting research with impoverished HIV-positive men and women in Tanzania:

> The fact that I was not there to develop a 'project' ... did not alter those expectations. Rather, for many local Tanzanians it meant that there was scope for me to set up projects and pressure was exerted to help develop such projects and seek funding. Considering the poverty and need of the people involved, their willingness to work for the community if provided with the means to do so, and the idea of 'giving something back' as part of an engaged participation in their activities, I became involved in developing ideas and proposals for fundraising. This was facilitated by my participation in a small British NGO with a local office in the region, called Village-to-Village (V2V). (2008: 11–12)

FEEDING BACK RESEARCH FINDINGS

At the very least, reciprocity should include researchers feeding back their research findings in appropriate ways. This should not, for example, solely consist of a promise to participants that they will have access to an electronic version of your thesis via a library website two years hence. If possible, start the process of feeding back findings before leaving your field site. Seriously consider providing oral presentations of your preliminary research findings: for example, at a workshop in a community you have studied or at the office of an organisation that has assisted you. Such opportunities can also be invaluable for providing feedback on your data and analysis. Do note, however, that sometimes your closest research collaborators could be upset by what you have found, as occurred with Jenkins (2007; see also Box 9.8).

Box 9.8 Feeding back findings: the possibility of causing offence

From the outset, I have been committed to the process of feeding back to research participants and giving access to publications arising from the research. However, my initial analysis, in the form of a conference paper, which I sent to Esperanza on my return to the UK, was considered by the organisation to be unduly negative. In particular, Maria (the Integra [health promotion] project director from Esperanza [a Peruvian NGO]) did not consider that my interpretation of a situation of polarisation between the NGO and the promoters was accurate. This situation has led to an uneasy relationship between myself and Esperanza since my return to the UK, with minimal contact between us. This is difficult on a personal level – as I considered Maria a friend – and on a practical level – as I have been unable to obtain any constructive criticism or input into the analysis from the organisation. Part of this reaction may well be due to the organisation's worries about the impact on its funding of a negative portrayal of its work. ...

The difficulty I had in generating a constructive engagement with the NGO around these sensitive issues reflects the heavy workloads of NGO staff and their need to prioritise more practical and immediate concerns as well as illustrating the perception of foreign researchers as transient individuals who often make little long-term contribution to the work of the NGO.

Source: Jenkins (2007: 97)

TRUTH AND DECEPTION

The subjects of truth and deception cut at the core of the ethics of fieldwork, and thus not surprisingly have been at the centre of some rather emotive debates. On one side are those who insist that it is essential to be absolutely honest with participants when you expect truthfulness from them. Purveyors of another view argue that 'truth' is a relative concept: even researchers who are strong advocates of telling the truth may choose to withhold some personal information about themselves, which could be seen as deception, and participants certainly are known for manipulating information and telling untruths or partial truths when they feel this is in their interests. There are also those who believe that partially concealing the truth can be more sensitive to research participants (see Adams and Megaw, 1997: 220–221), thus supporting the idea that to be open and truthful at all times could undermine not only the research objectives but also the well-being of research participants. In this regard it is apt to keep Bulmer's (1982) statement in mind: 'Ethics say that while truth is good, respect for human dignity is better' (cited in Bulmer, 2001: 45).

Many researchers in practice sit somewhere between the absolute and partial truth camps. Under most circumstances they are honest, but they may lie to participants if this could improve their access to research information. For example, a single female researcher may feel that a lie about her marital status is justified if it allows her access to important information or events in the field, or if this enhances her sense of safety, especially if the 'lie' causes no direct harm to participants.

Of course, whether or not lies cause harm can be difficult to ascertain, as noted by Raybeck, who commences a chapter in his book on fieldwork in Malaysia entitled 'Shady Activities and Ethical Concerns' by stating that

> many ethical decisions require a degree of compromise ... While I hope to have done 'right' in each of these instances, I lack full confidence that this was always the case. As you will find, several of my decisions involved obfuscations, some concerned temporizing, and still others included outright lies (honesty is *not* always the best policy). (1996: 116)

Certainly telling lies, whether about one's marital status, class or religious background, may cause little direct harm, but in some cases 'the guilt for those deceiving their respondents with whom they are attempting to create a bond of empathy may cause considerable anguish' (Wolf, 1996: 11–123). Furthermore, supporters of the 'absolute truth' camp would probably suggest that to begin your research with a lie establishes a bad precedent. A number of researchers have found that when they have been truthful, the negative reactions they expected have not been forthcoming. Schrijvers (1993: 148), for example, describes her initial reluctance at revealing the true nature of her blended family, lest she met with disapproval. Yet when she did later reveal to the Sinhalese villagers that she was divorced, and that her partner was not the father of her children, to her great surprise 'our scandalous past did not damage our good reputation. Rather, it helped us to be viewed as more or less 'normal' human beings, people who, just like most villagers, had undergone some serious difficulties in their personal lives'. Further, 'People were most amazed that Peter, who was not the children's own father, behaved like a real father towards them. This greatly increased his moral reputation!' (1993: 149).

Another situation in which researchers may feel compelled to conceal the whole truth is when dealing with gatekeepers who are protecting their own interests:

> Informed consent may be seen as an obstruction to access gatekeepers can use to protect their interests. In response [ethical] relativists may recognize that something less than full disclosure or lying is necessary to combat 'exploitation' and for promotion of the greater good of the group. (de Laine, 2000: 24)

We might also need to be aware of whether our research relationships are being developed in an ethical manner. If we attempt to 'win over informants' (sometimes called 'building rapport') in order to draw closer to them, and thereby to gain information valuable to our research, Wolcott suggests that this could be seen as a form of 'seduction' (2005: 140). The problem lies with the extent to which we might exploit these personal relationships. Thus de Laine (2000: 76–77) talks about deception which stems from befriending participants. They note that friends may be told private information which is never intended to be included with one's research data.

Researchers who are friends with their research participants may become privy to intimate information, such as who is having an illicit affair with whom, who is the actual biological father of a person, or who is involved in illegal activities. What will the researcher do with this information? Is it acceptable to include it in notes or to discuss the information with others? The researcher has a possible conflict of interest, which is the result of his or her dual role as researcher and friend. To publish the information might be viewed as a deception to the person who spoke with the researcher in the role of friend not researcher (de Laine, 2000: 77). Clare Madge confronted such issues of disclosure of information from 'friends' when returning from fieldwork in The Gambia (see Box 9.9).

Box 9.9   What to do with 'privileged information' from fieldwork 'friends'

During my year's stay in The Gambia I learnt much 'privileged information' through my personal relationships with individuals, informally chatting or through daily participation. However, after becoming a friend, I did not feel that I could suddenly become the detached stranger on my return to England and use such information for my academic advancement. For example, I learnt much privileged information about the use of herbal medicines for 'women's' complaints, but although one aspect of my study was the role of herbal medicines to rural Gambians, I did not use the information about women's herbal medicines in my thesis. To do so would have been to betray the trust of my friends, as in this context knowledge is linked to power; I may have disempowered them through the use of such information (I was sending the villagers a copy of my thesis so anyone could have gained access to that medicinal knowledge).

Source: Madge (1997)

The subject of covert research is more fraught than issues of how much information will be disclosed. According to Berg,

a major argument for covert ethnographic research is the sensitivity of certain topics that might make it impossible to do research by other means. Naturally, in making such a case, you must additionally justify the undertaking of such research by some actual social or scientific benefit. (2007: 178)

It is also true that our research may confront people because it could expose something illegal or morally unacceptable, not because the research isn't valuable: 'The presence of a researcher is sometimes feared because it produces a possibility that deviant activities will be exposed' (Rashid, 2007: 380). In such a situation, someone might choose to proceed with their research, within certain parameters. This was the case with Chok who, when researching employment conditions in the globalised economy, was faced with the dilemma: 'How is one to be an "ethical researcher" when investigating unethical practices?' (2012: 56). Given the lack of openness that organisations have to independent researchers in Singapore, Chok spent a lot of time negotiating access to her field site (i.e., hotels): 'I finally obtained approval from my [Australian] university ethics committee to undertake covert research, framed as "direct participant observation"' (2012: 57). This led Chok to apply to work as a cleaner for an international hotel group without revealing to them that she would be studying issues such as the working conditions and rights of employees. This method of study certainly provided unique insights:

> A day after my first (and only) shift as a night kitchen cleaner for a five-star hotel, the skin on my right hand starts to peel. This is the direct result of cleaning with industrial strength chemicals without gloves – which I was not given; neither were the two other women I was working with... From that one night of work, I not only gained information in quantitative terms (e.g. wages, contract terms, gender ratio) but was also enriched with qualitative insights on subcontracting recruitment processes and modes of interaction between supervisors and contract workers and among contract workers themselves. (Chok, 2012: 55)

Despite Berg's openness to covert research, he asserts that in no case should you progress with covert research if this might abuse the rights of the participants in your research or in any way cause them harm (Berg, 2007: 178).

Issues of truth and deception, like issues of ethics generally, are not as black and white as they may at first appear. Researchers need to be guided by their conscience, which should ideally be strongly influenced by what is in the best interests of those being researched. Regularly considering how we might respond to issues of truth and deception if we were the ones being researched might help. De Laine (2000: 29) suggests that we ask 'Would I want others to do this to me?'.

SEX AND SEXUALITY[2]

There are many viewpoints on the issue of sexuality and fieldwork, especially sexual relations between a field researcher and someone from their field site, from those who propose that fieldworkers put sex on hold for the duration of their work lest they behave in a culturally inappropriate manner, to those who say that sex is a normal act of human expression and it would be dishonest for the fieldworker to inhibit themselves from behaving in a sexual manner in the field. Indeed, as Malam found when researching the Thai beach scene on Koh Phangan, the community *expected* that she would be sexually active: 'my sexuality was a topic of continuing gossip and speculation among some men and women on the island' (Malam, 2004: 179). We do not wish to push any single viewpoint on readers, but rather to make you aware of the gamut of ethical issues involved.

The potential for misunderstanding in cross-cultural contexts, and the unequal power relations between the researcher and many of their participants, means that sex in the field can be both exploitative and unethical. Fieldworkers need to be aware, for example, that sex can take on unanticipated meanings in cross-cultural settings. There may be extremely conservative attitudes to homosexual relationships. While in most Western countries sex outside of marriage is acceptable, this is not the case everywhere. And in some cultures establishing a sexual relationship with someone brings with it the commitment of a long-term relationship and ties not just to the individual, but to their extended family (Killick, 1995: 90).

The contributors to Kulick and Willson (1995) note, however, that sex in the field need not be seen as inherently problematic and unethical, and advocate for more openness and debate about expressions of sexuality in the field. Mazzei and O'Brien recently commented on the continuing lack of openness, despite sexuality being a pervasive issue: 'Though rather seldom discussed in formal academic settings, field-work is rarely devoid of the sexual and romantic overtures that occur in non-field interactions' (2009: 375). That the issue of sexuality is rarely raised in accounts of fieldwork may be linked to ethical concerns surrounding positionality, racism and exploitation which many researchers want to avoid discussing (Kulick and Willson, 1995: 19).

It has been suggested that to choose to get close to our participants and share their lives in a multitude of ways *except* sexually may itself smack of racism:

> The taboo on sexual involvement in the field serves to maintain a basic boundary between ourselves and the Other in a situation in which our goal as ethnographers is to diminish the distance between us ... Refusing to share in sexuality across cultural boundaries helps to perpetuate the false dichotomy between 'us' and 'the natives'. (Bolton, 1995: 140)

However, some researchers have been concerned that sexual attraction to one's research participants may be equated with neocolonialist exploitation (Cupples, 2002b): for example, they do not want to perpetuate the image of the foreign male wishing to 'possess' or 'exploit' the exotic, Eastern female (Killick, 1995: 80). Such concerns need not be limited to male researcher–female participant interaction. Morton (1995) exposes her attraction to Tongan males, whom she describes as 'tall, muscular, handsome, and extremely charming', and bravely reflects on the 'possible overtones of racism' inherent in her attraction, particularly when, in the case of one partner, she and he could not communicate well because of language differences.

Conversely, some researchers find that when in foreign field settings they become 'asexual', with all thoughts of eroticism put on hold. We call this the traditional 'no sex, we're fieldworkers' approach:

> There seems to be a kind of unwritten, unspoken, and, for the most part, unquestioned rule about the ethics of sex in the field that all anthropology students somehow absorb during their graduate education. That rule can be summarized in one word: *Don't.* (Kulick and Willson, 1995: 10)

Some of this is no doubt motivated by a fear of breaking cultural rules about 'respectable' behaviour and being admonished or rejected by the community who they are reliant upon for their research data. However, we should not assume that by avoiding sexual activity we will receive greater acceptance and respect in a community. Gearing found that the opposite was true when she had a relationship with a man she met during fieldwork in St Vincent:

> Contrary to my expectation that my relationship with my boyfriend would provoke comments about my 'loose morals', several of my female neighbors told me they were glad 'I had a man about the house', and that they had been concerned about my living alone. My previous 'standoffishness', demonstrated by living alone and not having a boyfriend, had been a cause for worry and comment. My Vincentian neighbours let me know in subtle ways that by being in a sexual relationship I was finally acting like a normal adult. (1995: 200)

It is important to note here that in Gearing's case, the community's acceptance of her relationship was at least partly based on the fact that she had followed traditional Vincentian protocol of a 'courtship' with her boyfriend, and he had introduced himself to other community members when courting her, rather than behaving in a clandestine manner. Where there is respect for cultural norms, such relationships need not be exploitative or oppressive.

Less comfortable are situations where the feelings are not reciprocal. There have been many instances where researchers have had to stave off unwanted romantic or sexual advances from those living in and around their field sites, sometimes due to assumed associations between Western womanhood and promiscuity, as Malam (2004) found when researching the Thai beach scene. Meanwhile, Gearing (1995) had difficulty dealing with unwanted attention from males in positions of power – some of her gatekeepers – in St Vincent. Mazzei and O'Brien argue that this can be particularly challenging for female fieldworkers because 'Of course she does not want to embarrass or demean the source of advances, but such situations can undermine her overall credibility within the field environment as well as her sense of self' (2009: 375). Foreign males are also sometimes pursued quite aggressively in the field, as Farrelly (2009: 40) observed in Fiji and Gurchathen experienced in Liberia (Henry et al., 2009). Thus males and females may face similar dilemmas in how to respond to unwanted advances, and how to stay safe. Where there is any threat of sexual violence, researchers need to seek help immediately and potentially remove themselves from the field site (see Chapter 6, section on 'Health and safety').

Finally, as researchers we should consider whether we are in some way playing on our sexual positioning in order to collect data – and if yes, whether it is ethical to do so (Mazzei and O'Brien, 2009). The field researcher may display various forms of charm to build research relationships, gain access to institutions or individuals, and to get information. For example, when conducting research on single motherhood in Nicaragua, Cupples reflects on 'taking advantage of being fashioned as an object of desire in order to further my research project' (2002b: 387). As with other issues regarding the researcher, it is important that we actively reflect on our positionality in relation to our behaviour throughout the research process.

CONCLUSIONS

This chapter has unearthed a range of ethical dilemmas commonly faced by Development Studies researchers, from dealing with powerful gatekeepers to hiding truths from research participants, from ensuring reciprocity in relations with participants to deciding whether to follow up on one's sexual interests in the field. While to some, their own strong moral convictions may place them in the 'ethical absolutist' camp and make responses to the above dilemmas clear cut, many researchers find themselves adopting an 'ethical relativist' position, which means they are constantly debating, negotiating and reflecting on such dilemmas in the course of their fieldwork.

Only one thing is clear: while satisfying the requirements of a university ethics committee may encourage you to think through some ethical concerns before engaging in fieldwork, it will almost certainly *not* prepare you for a range of other ethical dilemmas which will crop up once you are actually doing your research. Many fieldworkers have found that their informants are far less interested in the formal design and goals of the research than the character and disposition of the researcher, building a trusting relationship with the researcher and understanding how the research might contribute to their own lives. Thus while a general code of ethics which covers informed consent, confidentiality and conflicts of interest can provide you with useful guidelines, in many cases it is your personal characteristics – ideally, a combination of integrity, maturity and sensitivity to the local cultural context – that you will need to call on to guide you (de Laine, 2000: 28; see also Chapter 7, section on 'Desirable personal traits').

Summary

- The research process must ensure participants' dignity, privacy and safety, and must 'give back' to them in some ways. We see this as constituting 'ethics from the bottom up' (see Box 9.1).
- Development researchers will have their proposals screened by their institution's ethical review board or committee. While this may take some negotiation, and may lead to some frustrations, it can be a useful exercise to go through – approach it positively!
- Don't expect the formal ethics review process to prepare you for the 'real-life' ethical dilemmas you will encounter in the field.
- The relationships you develop with gatekeepers are important as these people can both help and hinder the research process.
- Before, during and after fieldwork it is important to consider what you can give back to those who have given up their time and provided you with assistance.
- Sex in the field is not inherently problematic, but researchers need to be aware that ethical issues often arise due to the potential for misunderstanding in cross-cultural contexts, and the unequal power relations between the researcher and many of their participants.

Questions for reflection

- Are you an ethical absolutist or relativist? Justify your stance, and explain how this might influence your field research experience.
- Beyond getting research permission from your institution, what ethical issues might you face 'on the ground' in your intended research site?
- How are you going to gain the 'informed consent' of the people or community you are hoping to carry out research with? What form will this consent take?
- What types of gatekeepers might you come across in your research (e.g., officials at different levels, leaders, receptionists), and how could they both hinder and help with your research?
- Can you identify specific ways of 'giving back' to your research participants through a) the process of conducting research, b) practical assistance, and c) sharing of the research findings in appropriate ways?
- Knowing the location of your field site and likely participants, are there circumstances under which you feel it would be appropriate to engage with 'sex in the field'?

RECOMMENDED READINGS

Brydon, L. (2006). Ethical practices in doing development research. In V. Desai and R. Potter (eds), *Doing Development Research* (pp. 25–33). London: Sage.

This book chapter covers ethical practices in fieldwork including consent, funding, power and context, with a section on 'Deviations from the ideal', pp. 30–32.

Chok, S. (2012). The visible/invisible researcher: Ethics and politically sensitive research. In C. M. Hall (ed.), *Fieldwork in Tourism: Methods, Issues and Reflections* (pp. 55–69). London: Routledge.

Book chapter which provides an excellent example of challenges faced by a researcher who gains work as a cleaner in a five-star hotel as part of her methods in employment conditions in the global economy, and how and why she chooses to engage in activism.

Dowling, R. (2000). Power, subjectivity and ethics in qualitative research. In I. Hay (ed.), *Qualitative Research Methods in Human Geography* (pp. 22–36). Melbourne: Oxford University Press.

A succinct and clearly written chapter which introduces the reader to university ethical guidelines, while also drawing attention to the need to move beyond these guidelines and take a stance of 'critical reflexivity'.

Heller, E., Christensen, J., Long, L., Mackenzie, C. A., Osano, P. M., Ricker, B., Kagan, E., and Turner, S. (2011). Dear diary: Early career geographers collectively reflect on their qualitative field research experiences. *Journal of Geography in Higher Education*, 35(1), 67–83.

Student reflections on field research experience, including discussion of ethics, gatekeepers and research fatigue.

McEwan, C. (2011). Development and fieldwork. *Geography*, 96(1), 22–26.

Article outlining ethical issues in development fieldwork for researchers and students, particularly in relation to power and privilege.

Sumner, A. (2007). What are the ethics of Development Studies? *IDS Bulletin*, 38(2), 59–68.

Discussion of ethics in development studies and development research, defines ethics and reflects on the particular ways in which researchers have thought about ethics in development studies.

NOTES

1. Chapter 11 provides a further discussion on gift giving with relation to leaving the field.
2. Chapter 7 has touched on some issues of sexuality (see the section on 'Families and partners in the field' which includes a discussion on homosexuality).

10

WORKING WITH MARGINALISED, VULNERABLE OR PRIVILEGED GROUPS

REGINA SCHEYVENS, HENRY SCHEYVENS AND WARWICK E. MURRAY

By now you will be well aware that fieldwork in the developing world can present difficult practical, ethical and personal challenges. When the subjects of research are marginalised groups,[1] the challenges look even more foreboding. How should you behave when you are interacting with people who are obviously much poorer than you, or who are minority ethnic groups, lower-class women, or children? How will they react to you? We must be sensitive if we are to carry out ethical and worthwhile research involving marginalised peoples. hooks (1990: 151–152) indicates that for too long research on the marginalised has been carried out in an oppressive manner:

> Often this speech about the 'other' annihilates, erases: 'no need to hear your voice when I can talk about you better than you can speak about yourself. No need to hear your voice. Only tell me about your pain. I want to know your story. And then I will tell it back to you in a new way. Tell it back to you in such a way that it has become mine, my own. Re-writing you, I write myself anew. I am still author, authority. I am still the colonizer, the speak subject, and you are now at the centre of my talk. Stop'. (1990: 151–152)

The challenge for researchers is to 'find ways in which the marginalised can enter our discourses in their own genres and their own terms so that we can learn to hear them' (Krog, 2011: 384). Effort should also be made to ensure that our research is not merely a self-serving exercise. This can be achieved in various ways, from nurturing respectful and friendly relationships with our participants, to forms of activism, as will be discussed later in this chapter.

Another group with whom we have to take special care in our research are the privileged – those who are rich and/or powerful. While some people may feel that research involving the poor is more of an immediate priority in Development Studies than research targeting the rich, this overlooks the importance of understanding the culture and practices of those occupying powerful positions, who, due to their positions, may have potential to do considerable good. Research on powerful institutions can help us gain a deeper understanding of how the lives of the poor are structured by decisions made within institutions – such as the International Monetary Fund (IMF) or World Trade Organization (WTO) – seemingly so distant from them. 'Studying up' is therefore now considered a highly credible form of research as it allows us to gain a greater understanding of how differentiation and power are reproduced.

While a section of this chapter is thus devoted to researching the elite and powerful, the first four sections will examine special considerations for researchers working with groups whose members are often marginalised or vulnerable: that is, children, women, minority ethnic groups and the poor. We realise that there are other marginalised social groups with whom researchers may come into contact – the physically or mentally disabled and the aged are obvious groups not specifically discussed due to space constraints – but we try to make up for this somewhat by suggesting general principles to apply when working with disadvantaged and vulnerable groups (see Box 10.5). In choosing to focus on these groups we also do not wish to suggest that children, women, minority ethnic groups and the poor are universally oppressed, nor that men, adults, majority ethnic groups and the very rich are universally oppressive. Rather, members of the former social groups are *more often* in less powerful positions, and thus we must face up to our responsibilities as researchers to ensure that our research is carried out in ways which uphold their dignity, does not exploit them, and accurately portrays their voices and their struggles.

Building on the discussion in Chapter 9, it is important to remember that all researchers need to be self-aware and reflexive when working across ethnic, class, age and gender lines. Wolf expresses that all social scientists should 'critically and self-consciously examine their positionality' (1996: 35) and consider how this impacts on the research.

Those of us who are motivated by emotional responses to poverty, human rights abuses and other social injustices need to consider carefully how we present ourselves to the subjects of our study. Our attitude towards people who face economic and other hardships should not be so shrouded by pity that we fail to see things of value in those we study. Neither should our attitudes to the elite be clouded by mistrust or anger before we have even met them. It is a problem if we view our informants not as people who lead multi-dimensional lives – laughing, crying, celebrating, grieving and hoping, just like the rest of us – but as people we feel a need to help or that need to be taught something or to be taken down a peg or two.

This chapter therefore provides an examination of the importance and concerns associated with research involving both the marginalised *and* the privileged. Our aim is to help researchers prepare for the challenges of such research so that they are able to work in a responsible, sensitive manner and gain a deeper appreciation of the lives of these people and their interaction with development processes.

RESEARCH WITH CHILDREN AND YOUTHS

In development research the trend has been to consider children indirectly, if at all: 'Choosing to study children in development is in itself a major challenge to the researcher, for it is often not considered a worthy subject. It is rather a category taken for granted – seen but not heard, acted upon but not with' (Bowden, 1998: 282). In addition, contemporary researchers are very aware of the ethical issues associated with doing research with children: the safeguards university ethics committees put in place around research with those under the age of 16 or 18 most likely deter many researchers from examining the experiences and perspectives and of younger people.

In this chapter we have identified children and youths as an important, less powerful group in society whose voices deserve to be heard so that their interests can be served. We also acknowledge that they make up 40 per cent of the world's population, with particularly high proportions of young people in the developing world, thus they should not be ignored (van Blerk, 2006). We support the current trend among social researchers which views children as meaningful actors in their own right, authorities on their own lives, who can speak for themselves and express multiple ideas and opinions (Kellett, 2009; Valentine, 1999). Below we consider appropriate ways of working with children and youths.

The guidelines for researching children and young people in Box 10.1 provide some pointers regarding ways to ensure that research minimises harm and maximises benefits to them, including suggestions as to how involvement in the research can be made more fun and interesting for our participants (van Blerk, 2006). It is also vital that children's rights are respected in the research process (Kellett, 2009). Perhaps the most important guideline for those conducting research with children to abide by is to allow sufficient time to build trust and rapport. This can be achieved through repeated visits in which the research proposal is carefully explained, before any actual data collection goes ahead.

Box 10.1   Guidelines for research involving children and youths

- Clearly explain the purpose of the research to children and young people in terms they can understand, and what their participation will involve. Also inform their parents or guardians and, where appropriate, the wider community.
- Allow sufficient time to build rapport with young participants – this is vital if you wish to develop their confidence and encourage active participation from them.
- Give children and young people the chance to opt into the research without pressure from parents or friends. Assure them that they can withdraw from the research at any time.
- Find ways of enabling children and young people to exert some control over the research: for example, giving them control of the tape recorder during interviews so they can turn it off if they feel uncomfortable.

- Assure the children and young people's privacy and confidentiality and their right to remain anonymous in the research.
- Consider working with children in small groups rather than individually, as it can be less threatening and give them confidence to be with friends.
- Consider training children to be researchers: they can prove to be very effective at accessing the experiences, and views, of other children, and can be empowered by the experience of being a researcher.
- Ensure that participation in the research is enriching for your participants: for example, if interviews could be intimidating, use child-friendly research methods such as making posters, drawing, story writing, keeping oral or written diaries, or role play.
- During long research sessions such as workshops, provide recreational activities such as singing or dancing, to rejuvenate children's energies.
- Consider appropriate ways of providing feedback and inform all participants as to when feedback will be provided.
- Show appreciation for young people's participation but do not raise unrealistic expectations among participants.
- Provide acknowledgement of young people's involvement in your research.

Sources: Robson (2001: 137, 138); Matthews and Tucker (2000: 302–308); Haque (1998: 77–78); Laws (2003: 252–254); Kellett (2009).

Swanson (2008) had a unique means of building rapport with children when she moved to Ecuador to conduct research on women and children who beg and sell on the streets as she brought her pet dog, Kiva, with her. The children enjoyed playing with Kiva and this facilitated the building of research relationships for Swanson, such that 'the level of depth I attained concerning young people's experiences with poverty and injustice would have been difficult to obtain without her' (2008: 62). However, she also had to deal with the uneasy fact that her dog was more 'privileged' than those who were her research participants.

There are a number of innovative methods used to conduct research with children, from drawings to diaries, role play to mapping (Boyden and Ennew, 1997; van Blerk, 2006: 55). When the Tanzanian government wanted to access children's views regarding a poverty monitoring system they devised some unique tools:

Quantitative questions were asked verbally, qualitative questions were framed through role-playing scenarios and nuance of opinion was captured by drawing opinion lines on the ground and getting children to indicate where they would place themselves on such continuum lines. For example one question of teachers put a definition of kind, listening teachers at one end and strict, disciplinarian teachers at the other end of the line. (Kellett, 2009: 39)

Using visual methods seems to be a particularly valuable means of encouraging child-led participation in research, as Mizen and Ofosu-Kusi (2012) discovered when they conducted research with children living on the streets in Accra, Ghana. They asked them to take photographs of one or two days in their working lives, and these photos were then discussed with the researchers, leading them to conclude that 'photographs can contribute distinctive and novel sources of insight into working children's lives and a powerful, humanising media of dissemination' (2012: Abstract).

It is suggested that researchers should pay particular attention to accessing the views of less confident or less articulate children, particularly girls (Gordon, 1998; Matthews and Tucker, 2000: 300). Researchers overcame this problem in Nepal by encouraging girls to sing songs, which helped to make them more comfortable and gave the researchers insights into girls' present perceptions and future goals (Johnson et al., 1995, cited in Gordon, 1998: 67).

Robson (2001) found that her research, which was intended to reveal the difficulties facing young people caring for sick relatives in Zimbabwe, was seen by some to be harmful because some participants became distressed. However, she felt it was valuable in highlighting the voices of young carers from Zimbabwe and could lead to positive interventions in the future. Similarly, Evans conducted research with young people caring for family members affected by HIV/AIDS in Tanzania. She reflected that there were participants who, despite feeling distressed at times during the research, valued the opportunity to reflect on their experiences of their caring role, as no one had ever asked them about this before. In addition, Evans focused the interviews around resilience: that is, identifying sources of support the young people had been able to access (Evans and Becker, 2009: 80–81).

When the research subjects are children, it is also very likely that the researcher could be viewed with suspicion and seen as a threat to the safety of those they are studying. Thus Matthews and Tucker (2000: 301) make the important point that you must inform authorities beforehand and carry identification and copies of any research permission documentation with you.

Some researchers are now using children to conduct research (Kellett, 2009: Ch. 6). Heyer (1992), for example, employed school children as research assistants in her work in Kenya, asking them to keep time budget diaries of their own households and those of their neighbours. It is important in such cases to be clear on how the children will benefit from involvement in the research, and to reflect on ethical issues associated with employing, or 'using', children (see Alderson and Morrow, 2011).

Despite the depth and breadth of ethical issues concerning research with young people, if we exclude them from research we may marginalise them further. Overall, there is definitely a need for more sensitive, well-thought out development-related research with children and young people because

children need allies … and vulnerable, invisible, poor, minority children … in the global South desperately need allies with long-term commitment in both academic and political worlds. (Robson, 2001: 140)

RESEARCH WITH WOMEN

Even if you are not conducting research on a specific gender issue, it is likely that your research will involve women since they comprise around half of the popula- tion. Often in development research you will want to search out women's voices at least in part to help triangulate your findings (Momsen, 2006: 4). That is, to ensure that your conclusions are not based on the views of a narrow group of respondents you might seek to include women and men, young and old, educated and non- educated in your study.

As suggested in the introduction to this chapter, women are not all vulnerable or dis- advantaged in relation to other members of society; however, societal structures which vary from culture to culture mean that many women do face specific forms of oppression in their daily lives and are less able, in general, than men to be able to access resources to improve their quality of life. They also often lack political voice. Many researchers are aware of the need to consult women, especially because past research efforts so often ignored women or misrepresented them (Momsen, 2006), and such misinformation was often used to inform development policy and practice (Rogers, 1978; Tomm, 1989).

However, there are often difficulties associated with research involving women in the developing world. It may, for instance, be very difficult for the researcher to gain access to poor women, partly because they are often extremely busy so time to sit and talk may be restricted to the late evenings when it might not be appropriate – or practical – for a researcher to visit women's homes. In addition, women are rarely given roles as official spokespersons for a community, thus they are not the first people outsiders are likely to encounter (see Chambers, 1983, on the 'people bias' that often occurs in development work and research). Women's freedom in public domains might also be constrained, meaning fewer women attend community meet- ings, or, if they do, they sit quietly at the back without expressing opinions or asking questions. In more remote communities there may be genuine surprise and suspicion in the minds of community leaders if a researcher asks to speak to women. If such permission is granted, men may 'loiter' when focus groups or interviews with women are held, at least until they feel comfortable that the issues being discussed are either not threatening to them or are 'only' women's business.

Even when means are found of talking to women, some may be reluctant to express themselves in front of an outsider due to mistrust or low self-esteem, or just that they are not used to being asked their opinion (Momsen, 2006). As noted by Keesing, a sense of inadequacy can certainly influence what women will tell a researcher about themselves: 'Reflexive autobiography is possible only when subjects believe that their own lives are important enough to deserve recounting, and when social support is provided' (1985: 37). It is perhaps not surprising, therefore, that a male researcher working with women in a traditional society in Papua New Guinea found that most women preferred interview sessions at night, in contexts where the lighting was dim. Some women admitted to the researcher that they felt more relaxed than they would during the day as they did not want him to look at their faces or to identify who was talking (Lagisa, 1997).

Development research with women can also be sensitive if it reveals aspects of women's disadvantage, or if it examines a deeply personal issue. Critical research examining gender inequities in household decision making or gender-based violence, for example, can inherently challenge the status quo. If the purpose of such research is made public, it may upset power brokers within a society and others who benefit from women's disadvantaged position. For example, Box 10.2 shows how Rashid (2007) sometimes had concerns for her personal safety as well as that of her research participants when conducting research in Dhaka, Bangladesh, on the sensitive subject of reproductive histories.

Box 10.2   The challenge of accessing adolescent slum-dwelling women in Bangladesh to talk about their reproductive health

We carried out our surveys in the morning, when most husbands were at work and women were busy cooking, washing, and cleaning. If the husband was at home, we would explain our study objectives and seek permission from him first. In four cases, the husbands were at home and denied us access to their wives. One of the men just said no. In another case, a husband walked into the room to find his wife in an interview with me and proceeded to hit her. I ran outside to get help, and the landlady [a senior leader's wife] intervened, calling the husband 'a heroin addict' and threatening to slap him. He left the room quickly, and I ended the interview, not wanting to cause any further trouble for the young woman.

Source: Rashid (2007: 378)

Difficulties in conducting fieldwork with women should not provide an excuse, however, for researchers to avoid engaging in such research. It is possible to create contexts in which either socially repressed, introverted or less accessible women are willing to open up their private worlds to view (Keesing, 1985). As long as researchers are informed of and sensitive to local socio-cultural contexts, the difficulties discussed above can often be overcome, and women can become very enthusiastic participants (see Box 9.6):

> For people who do not usually have the opportunity to voice their concerns, research can be very positive and enabling in itself because it can encourage such people to articulate their needs. (Pratt and Loizos, 1992: 17)

Even those concurring with the above conclusion may be less certain about the place of men conducting research with women in developing country contexts, or, indeed, if women should conduct research with men. A number of writers suggest benefits arising from same-sex researchers and participants, with Oakley (1981), for example, arguing that female research participants respond more freely and openly to a female researcher. Challenging questions about men's ability to do research with women, or their right to represent women's voices in their research outputs, have led to reluctance on the part of many male researchers to directly engage in research with women in development contexts. Some have changed their research topics accordingly, or employed female research assistants to conduct the necessary research with women.

In other cases, however, males have gone ahead and carried out very good development research with women. One example is research for a Master's thesis which was conducted in Lihir, Papua New Guinea (PNG), by a male PNG student. Lagisa examined women's involvement in decision making regarding a major mining project which was in its construction phase, and considered the initial impacts of the mining development on women's lives. Most of Lagisa's fieldwork consisted of group interviews, as it would have aroused suspicion had he attempted to talk alone with village women with whom he was not formally acquainted. Many of the women were quite shy and unused to talking with those from outside their village area; however, they participated actively in these interview sessions, somewhat to the surprise of Lagisa. As he later reflected, this may have been due to the fact that they felt he could help them to overcome some of the disadvantages they were facing because he had access to the mining authorities (Lagisa, 1997: 106). In addition, Lagisa's position as a man helped him to gain insights into local gender relations and male perceptions of females, especially through participant observation. When staying with one family, for example, he witnessed an argument between a woman and her husband which occurred when the wife, an employee of the mining company, came home late. The husband was upset that food was not ready, so he scolded his wife, saying:

'What sort of work do you people do that you come home this late? Do you remember that we have children to look after? Tell whoever your boss is to remember that some of you are mothers and should come home early to cook for the family ... if you come home late again I will come and physically abuse you and your boss.' (cited in Lagisa, 1997: 158–159)

This provided a poignant reminder to Lagisa of the burden of the double day that female employees of the mining company faced, and the ways in which men's attitudes impeded women's development. It is unlikely that the man quoted above would have spoken to his wife in this way had the researcher staying with them been female or from a foreign country.

It therefore should not be assumed that men will be unable to conduct effective research with women, nor the reverse. Neither should it be assumed that women researchers will be able to build better rapport than men with female participants, or that they will be likely to gather more meaningful data. As Mazzei and O'Brien note, 'status group memberships such as gender are not destiny for building access and rapport during fieldwork' (2009: 358).

RESEARCH WITH MINORITY ETHNIC GROUPS AND INDIGENOUS PEOPLE

Anthropologists in particular have a long history of conducting research with minority ethnic groups[2] and indigenous peoples.[3] Other social scientists have often found that their interest in topics such as the creation of national parks, cultural tourism, human rights or the impacts of logging or mining has also brought them directly into contact with these groups. It is clearly important that research gives voice to the interests and concerns of minority ethnic groups and indigenous peoples, especially where these groups still face political repression or subversion of their rights. In the past it was assumed that those hailing from Western academic institutions had a 'right' to engage in such cross-cultural study. The power relations inherent in this research were not considered important enough to warrant comment. Now, however, strong political awareness of minority ethnic groups, combined with a good deal of self-reflection on the part of academics (as discussed in Chapter 1) has led to important changes in the ways in which such research is carried out (Smith, 2012).

Many indigenous groups, in particular, remain wary of outside researchers because their historical experiences have been framed by imperialism, their knowledge colonised for the benefit of Western science (Smith, 2008). Insensitive outside researchers will simply not be tolerated:

> We've had enough of your 'conspicuous innocence'. We have been pathologised by Western research methods that have found us deficient either as genetically inferior or culturally deviant for generations. We have been dismembered, objectified and problematised via Western scientific rationality and reason. We have been politically, socially, and economically dominated by colonial forces and marginalised through armed struggle, biased legislation, and educational initiatives and policies that promote Western knowledge systems at the expense of our own. We know better now. (Louis, 2007: 131)

Most of us are familiar with the term 'research problem', but Smith turns the meaning of this term around to suggest that to indigenous peoples, research *is* the problem:

> [I]ndigenous peoples are deeply cynical about the capacity, motives or methodologies of Western research to deliver any benefits to indigenous peoples … Because of such deep cynicism there are expectations by indigenous communities that researchers will actually 'spell out' in detail the likely benefits of any research. (2012: 122)

As Chapter 1 asserted, too often researchers have been preoccupied with their own agendas and have offered little that is of benefit to those they are researching: research has been a one-way process of extraction of information. This leads Krog (2011: 381) to ask: why are we who record and write up the knowledge of marginalised peoples called the 'scholars', while they are seen merely as the 'raw material'? A researcher may have received the government's permission to conduct research, but not that of the community they plan to work with (see Box 9.5), and they may have given the community no opportunity to influence the questions being asked or the way in which the research is conducted. Because of such concerns some governments have put in place specific rules about working with ethnic groups within their borders. For example, in the Pacific Island country of Vanuatu, the Vanuatu Cultural Centre takes a pro-active role in initiating research ventures, encouraging training of and research by indigenous people, and ensuring that communities get tangible benefits from research, not just a copy of the completed thesis or an academic paper.[4]

Concerns about outsiders dominating research projects have led to the call that research on ethnic minorities or indigenous groups should be conducted by members of the groups concerned. As Smith explains with relation to New Zealand Maori:

> Increasingly ... there have been demands by indigenous communities for research to be undertaken exclusively by indigenous researchers. It is thought that Maori people need to take greater control over the questions they want to address, and invest more energy and commitment into the education and empowering of Maori people as researchers. (2012: 180–181)

Indigenous researchers have notable advantages when their upbringing gives them knowledge of indigenous customs, languages, values and systems (Krog, 2011: 384). In their study of impacts of healthcare reforms on minority ethnic groups in Canada, Khan et al. (2007) found that research assistants were able to develop deep and sincere relationships with research participants due in part to shared language and cultural identity. There can, however, be significant constraints to research being conducted by indigenous researchers. Missbach (2011), for example, finds that after the devastating Indian Ocean tsunami in 2004 and the cessation of armed conflict in 2005, Aceh became a 'social laboratory' for foreign researchers that contributed greatly to their careers. She suggests this occurred at the expense of local Achenese researchers who were mostly only involved in data gathering and not in the analysis and interpretation of data due to 'a general lack of structural conditions for publishing, such as under-funding, lack of access to major academic literature, and language barriers' (2011: 373).

One possible way around this is to encourage more collaborative research, particularly where Western researchers can gain access to grants to support fieldwork carried out with indigenous researchers. Such collaboration can also be important in terms of mentoring indigenous researchers, particularly when they also contribute to the research design, analysis and writing up. Introducing research collaborators into fieldwork does bring complexities, but these can be offset by benefits for the research. In line with the discussion in Chapter 1 on the value of cross-cultural research, it is also important to note that differently positioned people can bring unique insights to a research project. Certainly a collection of works by indigenous anthropologists in 1982 suggested that there is value in work done by both indigenous researchers and foreign researchers, thus exposing 'the superficiality of the belief that the cure for the excesses of colonial anthropology lies in its replacement by indigenous anthropology' (Madan, 1982: 16). In addition, it cannot be assumed that shared ethnicity will always make researchers 'insiders' when they conduct research (see Narayan, 1998).

In Box 10.3, Cram (2001) suggests a set of practical ethical considerations that can inform those wishing to do research with indigenous communities. This is based on examples provided by Linda Tuhiwai Smith of how Maori communities describe respectful conduct, trustworthiness and integrity at a day-to-day level. These are principles which Mackintosh (2011), who is non-Maori, sought to apply when she conducted research on how the concept of universal human rights was being interpreted and used by a Maori development initiative. Mackintosh reflected deeply on her positionality, concluding that non-Maori have an obligation to carry out research that is 'culturally appropriate, provides space for self-determination and that has empowering outcomes' (2011: 37).

Box 10.3   Indigenous principles to guide researcher conduct

Aroha ki te tangata: A respect for people – allow people to define their own space and meet on their own terms.

He kanohi kitea: It is important to meet people face to face, especially when introducing the idea of the research, 'fronting up' to the community before sending out long, complicated letters and materials.

Titiro, whakarongo . . . korero: Looking and listening (and then maybe speaking). This value emphasises the importance of looking/observing and listening in order to develop understandings and find a place from which to speak.

Manaaki ki te tangata: Sharing, hosting, being generous. This is a value that underpins a collaborative approach to research, one that enables knowledge to flow both ways and that acknowledges the researcher as a learner and not just a data gatherer or observer. It is also facilitates the process of 'giving back,' of sharing results and of bringing closure if that is required for a project but not to a relationship.

Kia tupato: Be cautious. This suggests that researchers need to be politically astute, culturally safe, and reflective about their insider/outsider status. It is also a caution to insiders and outsiders that in community research, things can come undone without the researcher being aware or being told directly.

Kaua e takahia te mana o te tangata: Do not trample on the 'mana' or dignity of a person. This is about informing people and guarding against being paternalistic or impatient because people do not know what the researcher may know. It is also about simple things like the way Westerners use wit, sarcasm, and irony as discursive strategies, or where one sits down. For example, Maori people are offended when someone sits on a table designed and used for food.

Kaua e mahaki: Do not flaunt your knowledge. This is about finding ways to share knowledge, to be generous with knowledge without being a 'show-off' or being arrogant. Sharing knowledge is about empowering a process, but the community has to empower itself.

Source: Cram (2001; based on Smith, 1999)

RESEARCHING THE POOR

The majority of researchers conducting fieldwork on development-related topics will come into contact with people who are much poorer than themselves, some of whom may have difficulty in sustaining even a basic livelihood. This applies both to Western researchers and to researchers from middle- or upper-class roots in developing countries who have not been directly exposed to various forms of deprivation or oppression before: all of us are 'relatively privileged' (McEwan, 2011: 23). Wolcott rightly observes that during our university education we are protected from some of the harsher realities of life: 'All those statistics we read – poverty, illness, accidents, violence, abuse – may suddenly materialise for a fieldworker whose most traumatic experience to date had been a ticket for speeding' (2005: 87).

There is danger in using concepts such as 'poor' and 'marginalised' uncritically in a way that portrays people as entirely helpless, leading the researcher to fail to see the complexity of their lives. Researchers, through their methods and questions, can show genuine interest in the knowledge, skills, resources, connections and other strengths of the poor. In addition to gaining a more accurate depiction of their lives in this way, this also allows the poor to see that their ideas and experiences are valued, in a context in which they might otherwise place the researcher on a pedestal, thinking 'You are educated abroad and know more, what do we poor know?' (Sultana, 2007: 379).

A particularly challenging issue to address is how we should respond if our fieldwork brings us into contact with people who are struggling to meet even their basic survival needs. Here we are not talking about gift giving as an expression of gratitude (as discussed in Chapter 11), but whether we should provide assistance for humanitarian reasons to people who are destitute. When Henry (one of the authors of this chapter) conducted PhD fieldwork in Bangladesh, his subjects were poor village households who were already participating in programmes initiated by local development agencies. Because these organisations were attempting to instil in programme participants a sense of self-reliance, Henry felt it inappropriate to offer material assistance. Instead, he informed these organisations of his findings and made recommendations that he believed were practical. However as Boesten (2008: 14) points out, communities looking for more immediate benefits may not be satisfied by the researcher's explanation that the findings will be channelled into policy.

Encounters with severe poverty, such as that described in Box 10.4, can be a difficult experience and it would be wrong to paint the search for an appropriate response as an easy task. It is useful to be aware, however, that if you give generously to one person or household, you will likely be approached by others.

Box 10.4 Twenty-five times the price for two eggs

On one occasion, Henry's interpreter was very moved by the impoverished state of one household they visited. As a Bangladeshi national who had participated in similar village level studies before, poverty for the interpreter was not an unusual sight, indicating just how extreme the hardship was in this household. The household owned a few ducks and the sale of eggs provided one of its sole sources of cash income. The interpreter offered to buy two eggs and paid about 25 times the usual price for them. The following day an elderly couple, hearing of this incident, approached the interpreter for a loan.

Source: Scheyvens (2001)

Some argue for 'no giving' on the basis that giving when there is a power differential between the giver and the receiver exacerbates the power differences, or could bring the researcher too close to those they are researching, thereby affecting the research itself. Lammers (2007: 75–76), who worked with destitute refugees in Uganda, started her field research with this conviction, but later rejected it. She not only became involved in advocacy work for the refugees, but also paid for document services such as passport pictures and letters of recommendation, and also school fees. While she recognised that this affected her relationship with them, she also observed that many of the refugees were disappointed with the 'empty promises of researchers' who had come before her: 'We have seen so many of them, it makes no difference, we tell them what they want to hear' (2007: 76).

When charity is inappropriate, in some instances you may be able to offer practical services (see Chapter 9, section on 'Reciprocity'). Razavi (1992) found she could help by transporting locals in her car; Lewis (1991: 62) had access to a photocopier and was able to give out maps of village plots that were normally not accessible to locals; and Lammers (2007: 75) decided to always combine her meetings with participants with a meal and to pay for their transport. Providing practical assistance, in a way that preserves the dignity of those we research and is appropriate in their society, is the idea.

Be aware that people may have expectations that are unreasonable and which you cannot meet without compromising your research. In Tanzania, Boesten (2008: 11) found that the common practice of development organisations paying people sitting fees for participating in seminars and projects led her participants to expect payment for being involved in her research. It is also difficult if you choose to compensate a selection of people involved in your research. Boesten found that paying some local people to write diaries about their daily experiences living with HIV was successful to the point of encouraging them to go around their communities gathering information, but this also generated jealousy from community members that were not paid, and this combined with other factors ultimately led her to withdraw from the field research (2008: 13).

In terms of data collection, there are a number of other issues you should consider when researching the poor. Poor households may be forced into activities that are frowned upon within their societies and may hide these from the researcher. Lewis (1991: 57–58), for example, examined the practice of *kutia* in which a poor farmer takes a loan from a rice mill owner to buy rice for husking at the mill, but he found that his informants were reluctant to reveal whether they had taken loans from informal moneylenders. The village rice mill owner was happy to discuss these loans, however.

Those undertaking social surveys will have to familiarise themselves with indicators relevant to local contexts, which will in turn depend upon having a good understanding of what matters to one's respondents. In North America and Europe, weekly household income may be a good gauge of socio-economic status. In villages in Pakistan, however, how many times the household eats fish or chicken per week – or month – may be a better indicator. Reading studies by government agencies, research bodies, NGOs and so forth that have been undertaken in the country or area you are researching should help you to identify useful indicators. Also note that sensitivity is needed in many instances when asking questions about income, for two reasons. First, sources of income are likely to be so erratic for people living from day to day that asking them to estimate how much they earn daily or weekly may be inappropriate, and for agricultural day labourers there is also the problem of seasonality. Second, asking about a poor person's meagre income may simply reinforce their feelings of ineptitude as providers for their families.

This section concludes with Box 10.5, which provides principles regarding research with marginalised groups in general. The principles draw attention to the way in which research is conducted, the respect accorded to the participants, and the potential benefits of the research for them.

Box 10.5   Principles regarding research with marginalised groups

- The research must be based on respect for the knowledge, skills and experience of people in the group being studied.
- Marginalised groups are active subjects rather than passive objects of the research.
- The research questions should be centred around issues of interest and concern to the group being studied.
- The researcher's participation with the marginalised group should be characterised by committed involvement rather than impartial detachment.
- Research findings should be shared with the marginalised group in a means deemed appropriate by the group, for example: public meeting; workshop allowing for discussion, feedback and modification of findings; summary sheet; report; not necessarily a thesis or academic papers.
- There should be positive outcomes of the research for the marginalised group, and any anticipated negative outcomes should be eliminated if possible.

Source: Adapted from Hall (1992, cited in Martin, 2000: 193–194)

RESEARCH WITH THE ELITE AND POWERFUL

In 1986, Maurice Punch noted that 'researchers have rarely penetrated to the territory of the powerful and many field studies still focus on lowly, marginal groups' (1986: 25). In a ground-breaking special issue of *Geoforum*, Cormode and Hughes (1999: 299) argued that the lack of attention accorded to elites can be attributed to at least two factors. First, researchers of development often hold a political commitment to working with the less privileged in society. Second, gaining access to elite groups is often difficult, and this is amplified when the data being sought is qualitative.

Development Studies is gradually overcoming what was a relative silence with respect to researching the elite. At least three linked points can be offered as to why we should study the elite:

- The gap between the elite and the non-elite is getting wider globally, and some elements of the elite increasingly determine social and economic outcomes (Cormode and Hughes, 1999). In Development Studies, we need to understand what drives the elite. Some researchers have thus argued the need for richer, ultimately more ethnographic interpretations of the motivations and rationale of the elite (Conti and O'Neil, 2007; Herod, 1999; Hertz and Imber, 1993).
- Understanding local outcomes in developing areas requires an understanding of how elites act as vessels of global scale processes and imperatives and how power relations in given territories influence outcomes on the ground.
- It can be argued that the elite and non-elite are two sides of the same coin. For coherent representations we need to understand both sides. As Lindisfarne argues, 'anthropology from below works only if it includes looking up' (2008: 23).

Thus, for example, Conti and O'Neil explain the relevance of research with the dispute resolution mechanism of the WTO to those of us interested in global development:

The pool of informants included employees of the WTO Secretariat and member nation trade delegations, private attorneys and former WTO appellate jurists. Almost all are lawyers; some hold academic appointments as well. Some are current or former diplomats. While these persons are not the world's richest, they occupy a critical site in the political and legal structures of the global economy. Through their decisions to litigate, the specific strategies and evidence that they deploy, and their skill and judgment, they influence how the WTO regulates inter-state relations. In turn, their actions influence the daily activities of millions of people around the globe. (2007: 64)

But why all this fuss? Is there anything inherently different about researching the elite? Cormode and Hughes suggest that there certainly are different issues to consider:

Researching 'the powerful' presents very different methodological and ethical challenges from studying 'down'. The characteristics of those studied, the power relations between them and the researcher, and the politics of the research process differ considerably between elite and non-elite research. (Cormode and Hughes, 1999: 299)

In general there are two sets of overlapping issues which are specific to researching elites: practical issues and issues of positionality.

PRACTICAL ISSUES IN ELITE RESEARCH

Gaining access to the elite, be it representatives of a corporation or Fijian chiefs for that matter, can be particularly problematic. Why should such people, for whom it is often said 'time is money', grant an audience to a student or any other researcher? At the conclusion of a 90-minute interview with a partner in one of the world's top 10 largest law firms, Joseph Conti was told by the friend who had arranged the interview, 'Wow, you got a thousand dollars worth of his time!' (Conti and O'Neil, 2007: 71). There is perhaps a feeling in business circles that academics are some-what, well, 'academic' (in the sense that everything is hypothetical), and that exchange with them is likely to produce little of practical use. This can, however, be turned to the researcher's advantage, as being perceived as non-threatening can help win access to information that might otherwise be considered sensitive.

The lack of seriousness which interviewees may accord an encounter, or their scep-ticism regarding the researcher, can often lead to last-minute cancellations and many interruptions during the interview process (Mullings, 1999; Szarycz, 2010). Pursuing personal interaction under such circumstances can be frustrating. It is very important that personal contact is made, however: letters and emails are commonly ignored. Warwick (one of the authors of this chapter) constructed a questionnaire for 30 mul-tinational fruit export companies as part of his PhD research and sent it out by post. He received three replies, two of which said that the companies could not help! When these companies were approached again through telephone calls and informal drop-ins, virtually all of them agreed to grant personal interviews (see also Chapter 6, section on 'Establishing contacts'). This was undoubtedly assisted by being extremely nice to administrative staff such as personal assistants and secretaries – an important skill worth cultivating. Not only did access rates improve, the quality of the data was far richer through the use of open-ended interviews which retained some of the closed-ended attributes of the original questionnaire. It is essential when negotiating access to strike a balance between impersonal and personal interaction.

Many researchers become despondent in the face of low response rates or rejec-tion of one's attempts to set up meetings with elites. For example, Conti describes a particularly humbling experience when trying to solicit an interview for research on the WTO: 'I was denied the interview and told to call back when I "had better questions"' (Conti and O'Neil, 2007: 70). It is important that we are not defeat-ist in the face of such responses, however. Szarycz (2010: 165) advises that those attempting to contact elites develop a technique which Joan Cassell, in her research on American surgeons, describes as 'brute persistence and blind compulsivity', and 'a certain imperviousness to rejection' including 'pushing, and trying, and hoping, and smiling, and pushing some more' (1988: 94–95).

The use of networks is an important way of achieving access and gaining the co-operation of interviewee. It can be helpful to devise a flow chart which traces all of the individuals who put you in contact with other individuals in different institu-tions (Herod, 1999). A very good way of starting an interview is to say 'I was given your name by …'. Likewise, some contacts may 'phone ahead' for you. This will help establish your legitimacy, reduce the perceived threat, and may also please the interviewee in that it is implied that they are recognised within their relevant net-works. This is particularly useful in societies where personal links are paramount. In many Pacific Island nations, for example, without explicit names you would be very unlikely to gain access to an organisation. Meanwhile in Chile, the age-old system of *pitutos*, which constitute networks of semi-formal contacts that interact reciprocally, must be understood for the researcher to operate effectively. Warwick found that the only way to gain access to local civil servants in the countryside was to quote the name of a friend who worked for the Ministry of Agriculture in Santiago who had an established system of *pitutos* across the country.

A further practical issue you might face often occurs when interviewing senior people within development organisations: encouraging them to 'open up' might be your greatest problem. Such officials can be frustratingly guarded and reticent about the interview process, largely because they are expected to conform with presenting a particular institutional message to outsiders. This can be the case particularly after periods of organisational change, or when they have tightened up funding requirements or moved their aid policy in a new direction: just the types of things you might wish to explore in your research. When researching elites associated with medical tourism in India and Thailand, French PhD students Bochaton and Lefebvre (2011) discovered that at times their respondents would take control and turn the interview into a public relations exercise. The marketing directors and managers they interviewed were 'trained for this type of exercise' and thus it was no surprise that they delivered a consistent message: 'medical tourism is positive for the country, its economy and its healthcare system' (2011: 77). Bochaton and Lefebvre concluded that the researcher needs to be very aware of the power of the interviewee during elite research if they wish to come away with rewarding data: 'we had our own agenda for the interview, but so had our interviewees' (2011: 77).

Similarly, Desmond faced a number of barriers when researching elites in Ireland's biotechnology industry during a period of political sensitivity and public debate. She describes one interview where she was made to wait for some time, was not allowed to voice-record the discussion, and was made to move room twice during the interview: 'The interview proper lasted approximately 20 minutes, from which the information received could best be described as a series of sound bites, that is, segments of well-rehearsed stories already in the public domain adding nothing new to my understanding of the debate' (2004: 266).

During interviews, you might find that you need to be emotionally tough to negotiate the 'micropolitics of the researcher encounter' (Conti and O'Neil, 2007: 63). It is not uncommon to feel despondent after being 'talked down to' by research participants (2007: 63). What Desmond (2004) learned on reflection about her research with biotechnology proponents was that some of her subjects were 'destabilised' by the presence of a critical social scientist and this might account for attempts to disempower her during the interview.

However, not all elite interviewees will try to obstruct your research. Just as we have to be careful not to essentialise the poor as oppressed/depressed/powerless, we have to be careful not to essentialise elites we may encounter in development research as the oppressors/jubilant/all-powerful. Some of our respondents could have a strong commitment to issues of equity and social justice, as Conti found among WTO officials (2007: 79).

A final practical issue is that, just like non-elites, the participants in research may wish to see copies of the work you finally do. You will usually have power over the final writing up of your work – but this is not always the case. If you are somebody who becomes critical of the elite within the context of a particular study, this may present a problem. It is possible to be selective with what you choose to feed back to the groups you worked with, but usually it is best to be as critical as you feel you should be based on the evidence you have before you (see the section on 'Advocacy and activism' below).

Note, however, that there can be long-term implications from such academic honesty. Discussing research on powerful institutions in the aid and development realm, Mosse (2005) speaks of 'anti-social anthropologies', referring to the fact that people from development institutions might not like what our research has to say, and colleagues with whom we formerly had friendly relationships could turn against us (see Box 10.6).

Box 10.6   Elites questioning the legitimacy and accuracy of academic research

I worked as an anthropologist-consultant on a development project from its initial design in 1990 until 2001 ... the DFID agreed to support a study of the project experience from my particular anthropological perspective. This would be a critical analysis of policy and administrative rationality and modes of expertise in aid and development. (p. 938)

Mosse then wrote a book about the project, which received a range of responses:

[M]ost who responded to the drafts over eighteen months – especially my social development and field staff co-workers – in fact gave strong endorsement to my analysis, describing it as 'balanced', 'truthful', 'insightful'. However, my attention became preoccupied with those key actors (including UK technical consultants and those in managerial positions) who took strong exception to my 'too negative and unbalanced' account, which was 'unfair and disrespectful', 'out of date', and even 'damning of all our work'. This group, represented by a UK consultant and DFID Project Adviser, disagreed fundamentally with my conclusions and wanted the book re-written. Such a reaction should disturb any ethnographer; the more so for me because these were my close colleagues, co-workers over thirteen years. (p. 941)

Source: Mosse (2005)

POSITIONALITY IN ELITE RESEARCH

As discussed in the introduction to this chapter, it is important to examine our positionality in relation to our research subjects, but we should be aware that notions of 'insider' and 'outsider' are more accurately understood as existing on a continuum, rather than being binary opposites. With respect to elite research, most authors agree that the problems of self-positioning are considerable; however, how they should be dealt with is contested.

In the context of foreign elite research, Herod (1999) argues that being an 'outsider' and playing up this aspect of one's identity can actually work in the favour of the researcher. As a foreigner doing research in Eastern Europe he was surprised by the seriousness with which he was taken. In particular, the fact that he had come from many miles away (the US) combined with the notion held amongst the interviewees that he was a 'foreign expert' acted in his favour. 'Outsiderness', he argues, was perceived in this particular situation as non-threatening and even encouraged small-talk. Furthermore, as an outsider he felt more comfortable asking for things to be clearly explained and in this way was able to maintain a crucial critical distance.

In the context of elite research in Jamaica, Mullings (1999) takes a different stance to Herod. She argues that with the central goal of encouraging participation the optimal strategy was to attempt to occupy 'shared positional spaces'. Towards this end she posits that it is good to present yourself to elites as a temporary insider – someone who knows the ropes of the particular issue under concern and is therefore an intellectual equal. She also argues that as a black, female, US resident researcher in Jamaica, it was advantageous to put various aspects of her identity to the fore at given times. There can be little doubt that your gender, race, nationality and sexuality has the potential to influence the research process to the extent that you make these things visible and how they are perceived by the interviewee. Ultimately Mullings argues for cultivating insiderness for elite research:

> [R]ecognising that the information that we as researchers receive will always be partial makes our claims circumspect and our stance more reflexive. This is a consideration that is particularly important for researchers whose identities rest upon axes that are not only different, but in many circumstances may be disempowering. Identifying aspects of difference which may stultify dialog and seeking spaces where some level of trust can be established, to me, is the only way that researchers can gather information that is reliable. (1999: 349)

Gazit and Maoz-Shai (2010) were very aware of issues of both studying-up and studying-across (where the researcher shares a similar background or experiences with respondents) when doing home-based research on governmental violence organisations (e.g., military, police) involved in the Israeli–Palestinian conflict. Their positionality and perceptions of respondents about their loyalty had major impacts on issues such as access to respondents and their openness in interviews:

> [W]henever a researcher studies a governmental organization within his or her home country, the structural components of their personal and social background become fundamental variables that intervene in the research process [especially] ethno-national and citizenship affiliation, military past, their relationship with the academic community, and their gender. (2010: 290)

Particular issues may arise for researchers like Gazit and Maoz-Shai who are studying elites in their home country. Here, the power differentials noted earlier could lead to long-term implications for the researcher if, for example, they upset someone with authority through the process of their research, whereas the foreign researcher can usually just leave: 'When undertaking at-home research, researchers can never be "out of the field" because they are socially and personally embodied in the field' (Gazit and Maoz-Shai, 2010: 289).

A central issue, whether we are foreign or native researchers, is how we represent ourselves to gain access and information (see Chapter 9, section on 'Truth and deception'). Of critical importance perhaps is striking a balance between being an insider and an outsider and cultivating the ability to represent oneself according to the situation. You must be able to move up and down the 'sliding scale of intimacy', as Herod (1999) calls it. Is this tantamount to deception? In the sense that one puts particular axes of identity on display at a certain time to achieve self-interested goals, perhaps so. However, who does not alter their speech register, their appearance and their behaviour in different social situations?

In many cases, as noted earlier in this section, work will involve interviewing both the elite and non-elite. One issue is that elite groups may actually be able to prevent access to the non-elite if they are not satisfied that what you are doing is in their interests. Another issue for the researcher is working out how to scale hierarchies successfully and ethically. Moving up and down power structures presents particularly salient problems. For example, Mookherjee struggled with the tensions inherent between the two main groups in her research, leftist activists in the cities and poor landless women who had, many years before, been subject to rape during the Bangladesh war. These tensions came to the fore when Mookherjee discovered that the narratives of rape survivors had been appropriated by the left-leaning intellectuals for their own purposes (Mookherjee, 2008).

Overall, the researcher has to remain flexible and learn to improvise where necessary. Recognising that one's positionality is inevitably and necessarily ever-changing, and learning to cultivate shifts where this is required is perhaps the first step in being able to negotiate these tricky problems satisfactorily. We must also be wary not to underestimate our ability to negotiate in the research process with elites, nor overestimate the power of the elites we research.

ADVOCACY AND ACTIVISM

Research with marginalised or privileged groups, as discussed above, is often driven by a concern for matters of social justice. How to take the next step – to use one's research to actively promote change – is a matter to which we now turn.

ACADEMICS AS ACTIVISTS

A range of academics explicitly state their commitment to effecting positive change via their research. Chatterton et al. (2007), for example, designate themselves as 'academic-activists', whereby they choose research projects associated with social struggles and do their research in conjunction with other activists. Routledge, meanwhile, asserts that the activist geographer 'is concerned with action, reflection and empowerment (of oneself and others) in order to challenge oppressive power relations' (2010: 388). While not labelling herself in any way, Kobayashi shows similar commitment when reflecting on her research with the Japanese-Canadian community: 'I am deeply convinced that no social scholarship is independent of political action, and I am personally committed to acknowledging my research as political and to using it most effectively for social change' (1994: 78).

It is not the norm to find such strong convictions espoused by academics, although publication of texts devoted to emancipatory research (Truman et al., 2000), the politics of anthropological fieldwork and 'taking sides' (Armbruster and Lærke, 2008) and participatory action research (Kindon et al., 2007) suggest this is becoming more common.

Many researchers of development issues are motivated at least in part by their moral conscience. The field of development studies has been particularly influenced by Friere's (1972) work, which suggests that research should be an empowering process for participants, an opportunity for education and a stimulus for social action (Humphries et al., 2000: 7). Development researchers want not just to better understand the world, but to enable people to improve their living conditions and overcome inequalities. This is what Mellor refers to as 'researching for change' (2007).

In doing research with the poor, many development researchers find themselves in a position where they can help to effect a change for the better for their participants by virtue of their social positioning and associated power. Mookherjee's research with poor, landless women who had been raped during the Bangladesh war, led her to advocate on their behalf for reparations: 'the least I could do was to deliver my friends' letters, put forward their views to specific individuals and lobby them by virtue of the symbolic capital and privilege I had as a foreign researcher' (2008: 82).

For those wanting to become involved in advocacy, for example lobbying on behalf of disadvantaged peoples or challenging those abusing positions of power, their research is a means by which they can gain greater knowledge to be better advocates. Appadurai (2006) argues that such research should be done in conjunction with everyday citizens, who need information so they can make good decisions and claim their rights. This is exactly what Appadurai and colleagues have sought to do via a not-for-profit organisation, PUKAR, which they set up in Mumbai. PUKAR works with young people based on the belief that 'developing the capacity to document, to inquire, to analyse and to communicate results has a powerful effect on their capacity to speak up as active citizens on matters that are shaping their city and their world' (2006: 175).

There are types of research which go beyond gathering of data and are a form of activism in themselves. Action-based research, involving the researcher intervening in the community being studied and observing the changes that take place, is one example. Many social development interventions have evolved from this approach. The well-known Grameen Bank model of micro-credit delivery emerged from experiments by Professor Muhammad Yunus and his students dating from the second half of the 1970s (Counts, 1996).

PARTICIPATORY RESEARCH

Participatory research is another method of inquiry whereby, when conducted properly, the research process is a form of activism:

> Participatory methods are a step towards ... creating meaningful connections with researchers in the South, ensuring that fieldwork is collaborative and engaging with local researchers at each stage of the research process, from project formulation and design to publication. (McEwan, 2011: 24)

Boesten (2008) identifies feminist social research, engaged anthropology and participation in development as three approaches to participatory, non-extractive research. Under these approaches participants play a role in the collection and analysis of data, and on the basis of their findings engage in action to transform society (Cohen-Mitchell, 2000: 146).[5] Thus researchers who adopt a participatory stance inherently take on responsibilities with regard to their research:

> Supporting or enabling participation in the strongest sense becomes a political act through establishing partnerships between the researcher and the researched, whereby ownership, empowerment and responsibility for accountability are shared throughout the research process. [Thus] PR [participatory research] can play an important role in fostering or stimulating community activism at both the individual and collective levels. (Dockery, 2000)

Cohen-Mitchell's research with disabled women in El Salvador led to collective action when the women she was interviewing on an individual basis expressed a keen interest in meeting as a group: 'they saw a support group as a place to share and solve problems, and also do community outreach to identify and incorporate other disabled women' (2000: 163).

The research setting can make it more, or less, possible to engage in activism, as discovered by Bonnin (2010). During one period of fieldwork in the Philippines on female home-based workers, she was able to do advocacy work via a community organisation which supported informal sector workers. However, when later she conducted research among market traders in the highlands of Vietnam, being an activist was more difficult because she found herself in a rather constrained environment where the state kept a close eye on international NGO activity and there were very few independent civil society organisations.

In PAR (Participatory Action Research – see Kindon et al., 2007) researchers 'work closely with groups to identify needs, plan action research projects, consult and then strive collectively to "action" their findings' (Chatterton et al., 2007: 216). This can be very empowering for some participants, encouraging them, for example, to stand up to a power company that has been over-charging them, or to lobby a politician about inadequate services in their area.

Chatterton et al. are concerned, however, suggesting that researchers need to actually be prepared to take action in association with their research topics, because 'too many times, participatory researchers are more interested in the "R" than the "A" in PAR' ... [they need to] 'live up to the challenge of delivering transformative social change' (2007: 217). Similarly, Weber-Pillwax warns that 'PAR was never intended to be used as a research methodology outside of research conducted with a community of people who desire and are willing to work for some transformation or change' (2009: 48–49). The comments of these authors should challenge those who, quite casually, think it might be interesting to use a few participatory research tools as part of their data gathering activities. All researchers should reflect carefully on their own research philosophy and whether they truly want, and have the capacity, to do participatory or action-based research.

PRACTICAL CONSIDERATIONS REGARDING EMANCIPATORY AND PARTICIPATORY RESEARCH

If as a researcher you are motivated by a desire to conduct emancipatory or participatory research, there are issues you should consider. The personal gains can be very rewarding, in particular, giving you the sense that you are able to 'make a difference'. Yet your enthusiasm for 'changing the world' may need to be tempered if you are to carry out effective research:

> Contributing to social change involves deliberate attempts at mobilising opinion in a particular direction. If the conclusions, however, are predetermined by the activist's own predilections and ideas, without taking into account the situation, perceptions, and wishes of those on whose behalf we seek to help bring about change, we can easily end up either being irrelevant, pompous imposters or authoritarian manipulators. (Kishwar, 1998: 293)

Researchers choosing to conduct action-oriented or participatory research need to be led by practical considerations, not just by their ideals. Advocacy and activism will require time and effort outside that directed towards attaining academic qualifications: if your first priority is to write your thesis, will you really be able to take a participatory or action-based approach? In addition, in the case of both types of research, strong institutional support in the study country is usually necessary: will you be able to establish appropriate connections and collaboration? Be aware that while engaging in local actions can make a valuable contribution to some people or causes, it may change people's perception of you and your roles, and there may be associated expectations of what you do with your time. Thus Mellor advises:

> The researcher involved in change-oriented research, far from taking a neutral approach, would need to be clear on the boundaries and limits of any potential action and what ethical and political issues are involved. (2007: 188)

For example, if you are considering advocating on behalf of your informants, you will need to address the issue of representation (see Chapter 12, section on 'The politics of representation'). The question of 'who speaks for whom?' is often raised in relation to cross-cultural studies and needs to be treated carefully (see the quote by hooks (1990) in the introduction to this chapter). It is the task of the researcher to interpret these struggles in the peculiar social and political context that has given rise to them; not to superimpose inappropriate conceptual frameworks drawn from their own experiences and societies. Interestingly, the poor or otherwise marginalised groups who have no effective voice in their societies do not seem to be as concerned as academics are with the issue of representation. If you are in a position to bring their concerns to the attention of decision-makers, then with the exception of politically sensitive situations when this could lead to further oppression, they most likely will wish you to do so. An extreme postmodernist viewpoint becomes an easy excuse for not engaging in advocacy.

Researchers may be in a position to advocate by disseminating research findings through various channels. Writing reports for development organisations is one possibility, which is further discussed in Chapter 11. This will require work that in no way directly contributes to your qualifications or career; hence you may be tempted to keep putting this off. However, if your findings are to have any impact, the sooner you report on them the better. Postgraduate students can tell their supervisors that they are writing a report and ask them to allow for this when judging the progress that is being made on writing up. Writing reports for non-academic institutions requires special skills. The report should be free of jargon, succinct and make at most a few clearly argued points, supported with sufficient data from your fieldwork. If you are advising a change in policy or practice, then consider carefully how to do so in a constructive fashion. You are not merely engaging in academic debate. Any criticism could be taken very personally, though sometimes this may be impossible to avoid (see Box 10.6).

If you are advocating a change in development policy or practice, there may be a temptation to overplay data that supports your views and understate data that does not. Our arguments will be all the more persuasive if they are based on a rigorous investigation rather than if we are only willing to see those facts that concur with our views. We must thus be prepared to listen carefully to the multiple, often contradictory voices of those we are studying:

> We should not assume that because we subscribe to an ideology that we believe is in the best interests of the people whose lives we are looking into, or because we genuinely believe we have their interests at heart, this will automatically give us greater insight into their situation, or that our perceptions are necessarily superior to their own regarding the possible solutions to their problems. (Kishwar, 1998: 310)

CONCLUSION

This chapter has examined the difficulties, and rewards, that can stem from research involving marginalised and/or privileged groups. The ethical and practical constraints associated with conducting research on these groups should not provide us with an excuse to avoid such research; rather, this should force us to reflect carefully on our motivations for research, to conduct our research in a sensitive manner, and to ensure that our research will have beneficial outcomes – particularly for those who are marginalised.

Some commentators suggest that participation in the research process can, in itself, enhance the capacity of citizens (Appadurai, 2006), and be an empowering experience, especially where it seeks to elicit and project previously silenced voices (Acker et al., 1991; Humphries et al., 2000; Pratt and Loizos, 1992). And when poor people are aware that the researcher has travelled from afar specifically to speak with them, not just those of higher social status in their communities, it can enhance their self-esteem (Scheyvens and Leslie, 2000). Cotterill (1992) also asserts that research can be therapeutic, and Opie (1992) claims that this is especially true if interviewers encourage participants to analyse their experiences and to understand how the system that disadvantages them can be challenged.

This chapter has also argued that those interested in emancipatory research should not shy away from research focusing on or involving elite groups. If we do not understand the motivations or actions of those with power we will struggle to conceive of ways to dismantle privilege and build more equitable societies. As Taylor asserts, 'Understanding global inequalities is a key stage in the process of overcoming them' (1992: 20).

Finally, as development researchers who unearth information on inequality, injustice, problematic development programmes and processes, we might feel a moral obligation to do something beyond collecting and analysing data and presenting it in academic forums. Academics are increasingly being called to use their privileged position, their knowledge and their social capital to ignite social change via activism and advocacy. Another way of making a genuine contribution to the communities we study is to conduct our research in participatory ways, so these communities share in the design, data collection and analysis, and can use this knowledge to inform future decisions. This is sometimes the most effective means of 'giving back' to those who allow the field researcher to intrude in their lives for a period of time.

Summary

- Ethical issues are often brought to the fore in research with children, the poor, women and ethnic minorities, but they are not insurmountable: if we plan our research with care, such research can be rewarding for both researcher and participants.
- Research with the marginalised should be based not on pity but on respect for the knowledge, skills and experience of people in the group being studied.
- Marginalised groups should be treated as active subjects rather than passive objects of the research.
- All researchers need to be self-aware and reflexive, especially when working across ethnic, language, class, age and gender lines. However, our different positioning does not normally need to preclude us from doing research.

- 'Studying up', that is, explicitly including the powerful and privileged in our research, is now considered a highly credible form of development research. This allows us to gain a greater understanding of how differentiation and power are reproduced and used as tools to exacerbate marginalisation of the weak.
- Efforts should be made to ensure that our research is not merely a self-serving exercise. This can be achieved in various ways, from nurturing respectful and friendly relationships with our participants, to forms of practical assistance or activism.

Questions for reflection

- What child-friendly methods could be incorporated if your research is to involve children?
- What principles should you keep in mind when working with groups who are marginalised or vulnerable?
- What is your positionality regarding the research (i.e., ethnicity, class, nationality, gender, age, marital status, sexuality) and how might this influence your ability to conduct research with the following: poor women, lower-caste people, indigenous people, NGO managers, government officials, heads of corporations?
- How will you respond if your fieldwork brings you into contact with people who are struggling to meet even their basic survival needs?
- What are some of the pros and cons of being an activist or advocate as well as an academic?
- If you want to do participatory research, how will you share the research process with participants: design, data collection, and analysis?

RECOMMENDED READINGS

Alderson, P., and Morrow, V. (2011). *The Ethics of Research with Children and Young People: A Practical Handbook* (2nd edn). London: Sage.

This book breaks down the process of researching with children and young people into stages, and includes discussions of ethical and methodological issues.

Armbruster, H., and Lærke, A. (eds) (2008). *Taking Sides: Ethics, Politics and Fieldwork in Anthropology.* New York: Berghahn.

Edited book highlighting questions of politics and ethics when conducting field research. It is particularly relevant to researchers concerned with social justice and political activism.

Conti, J. A., and O'Neil, M. (2007). Studying power: Qualitative methods and the global elite. *Qualitative Research,* 7(1), 63–82.

Article discussing power relations in research with global elites, highlighting the difficulties and ways they can be negotiated. The authors suggest research with elites should be informed by feminist methodologies.

Humphries, B., Mertens, D. M., and Truman, C. (2000). Arguments for an 'emancipatory' research paradigm. In C. Truman, D. M. Mertens and B. Humphries (eds), *Research and Inequality* (pp. 3–23). London: UCL Press.

A useful starting point for those wanting to ensure their research has emancipatory potential.

Kindon, S. L., Pain, R., and Kesby, M. (eds) (2007). *Participatory Action Research Approaches and Methods: Connecting People, Participation, and Place*. Milton Park: Routledge.

Book focusing on effective ways of implementing participatory action research. Both the potential and pitfalls of PAR are acknowledged.

NOTES

1. 'The marginalised' in this chapter is a term used to embrace groups which have been socially constructed such that they lack access to power, resources and privileges in society in relation to other groups.
2. The term 'minority ethnic groups' does not necessarily refer to numerical minorities; rather, it is used more broadly to include ethnic groups which are politically, socially and/or economically marginalised. Indigenous peoples in many countries, including Canada, the US, Australia and New Zealand, can also fall within the category of 'minority ethnic groups'.
3. See also Chapter 4 for a discussion of indigenous approaches to research.
4. For a copy of the full Vanuatu Cultural Research Policy, see www.vanuatuculture.org/resources/national-filming-policy/73-the-vanuatu-cultural-research-policy.
5. We are referring here to an *approach* to research. Participatory research should not necessarily be equated with application of some PRA tools, as discussed in Chapter 4.

PART IV
LEAVING THE FIELD

11

ANYTHING TO DECLARE? THE POLITICS AND PRACTICALITIES OF LEAVING THE FIELD

SARA KINDON AND JULIE CUPPLES

Arriving and leaving are two universal human experiences (Maines et al., 1980). For development fieldwork we are encouraged to spend a great deal of time and effort preparing to arrive in our field site and research in appropriate and ethical ways. But how do we prepare for leaving? Shokeid argues that 'the stories of departure ... and the ... dynamics of fieldwork journeys are as important as the opening narratives' (2007: 222). Despite this argument, leaving has received little academic attention until recently (e.g., see Binns, 2006; Hammersley and Atkinson, 2007; Shokeid, 2007; Wolcott, 2005).

There is a great deal to think about in terms of research design, ethics and methodology before we set off for and while we are in the field. Yet arriving and leaving, or 'getting in and getting out' (Iversen, 2009), are intimately connected processes and one should not be thought of without the other. Arriving, how our research work evolves, what relationships and commitments are made, the kind of person we become to our participants and others over time, and contingencies like mistakes, conflicts or betrayals, all influence how we are able to leave and how we can write once back at university. All phases of the research process influence the experience of leaving.

Leaving involves us in both a physical relocation and a sociological transformation. We leave a specific geographical place with which we have become familiar and distinct social spaces and relationships in which we have performed particular identities. Then through acts of analysis, writing and re-presentation, the field and the meanings of the space and the relationships formed in it become actively transformed. Leaving the field is therefore not a benign or passive phase of research. It plays a dramatic part in shaping our experiences and understandings.

We should not naively assume that we can walk away at the end of fieldwork (Ortiz, 2004). Thinking *before* we arrive in the field about what we hope to achieve with our academic work, what relationships we may establish and what commitments we might realistically be able to meet upon our departure is critical to the pursuit of ethical and rewarding research.

It is often harder for us to extricate ourselves if working with vulnerable or marginal groups (see Chapter 10) than it is if working with people in positions of power or people more like ourselves (Ortiz, 2004). We will also form other types of relationships while in the field, and we will be returning to university and another set of personal and professional relationships. The clearer we are about the power relations and expectations between ourselves and these different people as we prepare to leave, the easier it is to avoid misunderstandings, negotiate changes in relationships, and end our fieldwork with goodwill.

Leaving is but a further stage in the on-going interplay between ourselves and the people or issue we are investigating (Shaffir et al., 1980). As Bailey (1996: 86) has reflected, '[w]e don't so much terminate our field relationships as continue them in another form over greater distances' (see also Bailey, 2007; Stebbins, 1991). With the rise of social media like Facebook, the continuity of these relationships is increasingly possible, though not always desirable. With or without social media, we remain psychologically and emotionally connected to the field even when we have left it physically. It may therefore be more useful to think of our return to university as *expanding* the field, rather than leaving it completely.

It is also important to remember that, as David Maines et al. (1980: 273) have noted, 'the problems, concerns, and ease of field exiting are not uniformly distributed across research settings', and what actions or decisions are appropriate will vary according to the specific geographical, cultural and institutional contexts in which we are working. This chapter is not and cannot be a 'how to' guide to leaving the field.

What we offer here is some 'food for thought' from our own experiences and those of our colleagues and postgraduate students based in New Zealand and in the UK. This wide range of experiences comes from 'Western' researchers carrying out fieldwork outside of their countries of origin or with indigenous people in a postcolonial context, and from researchers carrying out fieldwork in their own countries in Asia, Latin America, the Pacific or Africa and returning to 'Western' universities to write.

In the following sections we look at the reasons for leaving the field and factors that can influence our experiences of leaving it. We then explore a range of possible feelings that researchers may experience and discuss strategies for managing them and departure from the field. We focus on exploring researchers' ethical responsibilities to participants and others and provide some handy reminders about practical considerations.

REASONS FOR LEAVING

For most researchers, the process of leaving a research site is inevitable. It is a methodological imperative. However, when, why and how we leave can vary enormously depending upon the nature and type of our research, the context and the relationships we have formed during our fieldwork. In particular, *why* we leave often has a huge influence upon *when* we leave, *how* we leave, and *how we feel* about leaving. It also informs the feelings of the people we leave behind.

In many cases, why and when we leave is related to pragmatic reasons or external factors (Letkemann, 1980): the time allocated for fieldwork is up, our funding or research permits have expired, we need to submit our thesis or provide reports to funding agencies, or we may need to get back to meet other personal obligations.

Hopefully, we also leave because we reach 'theoretical saturation' (Glaser and Strauss, 2007). Our fieldwork yields diminishing returns (Taylor, 1991) as we hear the same information over and over again, or there are no new people to talk to about our topic. We can narrow our topic, clear the decks and consolidate our data relatively easily (Barrett and Cason, 2010).

Alternatively, we may find that no new information is generated because our research design and methodology aren't working. Our relationships and/or approach don't enable us to get below a superficial understanding, or may actively work to prevent us get detailed information. We need to try other approaches or leave our field site. Sometimes fieldwork may not be a positive or rewarding experience.

We may also realise that it is time to leave because we have become so immersed in our field site that it is becoming difficult to analyse it with any clarity (see Box 11.1; Ortiz, 2004). We may be losing our sense of self in the immediate cultural context and putting our ability to do research and write about it at risk.

In other cases, we may have to leave unexpectedly because aspects of our personal or field circumstances change. There may be a death or illness in our family or amongst our research participants that requires our attention. We also may become ill and need evacuation at short notice. There may be personal or institutional responses to events or information 'exposed' through our research, and permission (informal or official) for us to remain and work may be revoked. Or there may be a 'natural' disaster, political upheaval or civil unrest which forces us to leave. All these scenarios are possible.

Box 11.1   Knowing when it is time to leave

The final months of fieldwork are generally the best and most productive: the months of laying groundwork pay off in the increasing intimacy and comfort in your relationships and in the depth of the insights you are able to reach. This fact made me ever more reluctant to say that my research was 'finished'. I kept extending my stay at the factory; it became something of a joke, as the older women would tease me about my parents, whose 'neck

(Continued)

(Continued)

must be sooooo long,' the expression one uses to describe someone who is waiting impatiently. 'You must have found a boyfriend,' they would tell me, or laughing, they might suggest, 'Why not find a nice Japanese boy and settle down here?' I laughed with them, but I continued to stay on as research became more and more productive, until one event convinced me that the time to depart was near. At a tea ceremony class, I performed a basic 'thin tea' ceremony flawlessly, without need for prompting or correction of my movements. My teacher said in tones of approval, 'You know, when you first started, I was so worried. The way you moved, the way you walked, was so clumsy! But now, you're just like an ojosan, a nice young lady.' Part of me was inordinately pleased that my awkward, exaggerated Western movements had finally been replaced by the disciplined grace that makes the tea ceremony so seemingly natural and beautiful to watch. But another voice cried out in considerable alarm. 'Let me escape before I'm completely transformed!' And not too many weeks later, leave I did.

Source: Kondo (1990: 23–24)

FACTORS INFLUENCING EXPERIENCES OF LEAVING

Leaving will be simpler if we have adopted a topic that is not contentious, if our research design and epistemology has required us to remain somewhat distant from our research participants (an observant outsider), or if our fieldwork has been short and functional.

If we undertake a survey of government or NGO officials in a capital city, for example, we may be involved in interviewing and also be responsible for the co-ordination of local research assistants who administer the survey. Our research interactions are likely to involve a series of short encounters with a range of relatively well-educated people. Here, the acts of arriving and leaving can occur within a relatively short time period associated with each interview and we remain clearly positioned as outsiders. Our obligations may be limited to the professional realm such as providing a summary of research findings.

Leaving our research assistants, however, may be more challenging and require different strategies if we get to know them quite well (see Chapter 8). Some of the strategies discussed below may be more appropriate to the changing nature of our relationships with them.

If our research design and methodology involves us in periods of ethnographic or participatory work where we become more involved in the lives of our participants, we may occupy a more ambivalent position as insider/outsider. In situations like these, leaving can be complicated. We, along with our participants, may 'forget' that we have to leave to write about our experiences, and participants may place greater expectations upon us as a result of our longer and/or deeper involvement in their lives (Ortiz, 2004). Our obligations may extend well beyond the period of fieldwork (also see Chapter 12 for a discussion of these aspects). A summary of these factors is provided in Box 11.2.

Box 11.2   Factors influencing experiences of leaving

- Nature and topic of research.
- Epistemology, research design, methodology and methods adopted.
- Length of time spent in one place.
- Degree of immersion in the field.
- Nature of research and other relationships formed.
- Degree of similarity or difference between researcher and participants.
- Commitments and obligations made to research participants.
- 'Success' or otherwise of fieldwork.
- Funding regime.
- Expectations and feelings of family members and friends.
- Perception and feelings associated with returning to university.
- Cultural norms and expectations associated with leaving.
- Time available for the leaving process.

Sources: Iversen (2009); Ortiz (2004); Reeves (2010); and the authors' own experiences

---

Not surprisingly, leaving is always going be problematic for researchers working within less affluent areas and/or vulnerable groups (see Chapter 10). Here, power relations with our research participants are most unequal (Huisman, 2008; Ortiz, 2004), our topics are potentially sensitive, and there is often an implicit desire for change as a result of our work. We may be operating within finite funding and time regimes that make extensions to our fieldwork or return visits impossible. Such problems give rise to a range of feelings and emotions associated with leaving which we discuss in the next section.

FEELINGS/EMOTIONS ASSOCIATED WITH LEAVING

There are many feelings, emotions and psychological challenges associated with the processes of disengaging and leaving (Davies, 2010; Pollard, 2009). As researchers, we establish multifaceted relationships with the places and people in whom we are interested, particularly if we spend a period of extended time in one place. We develop a familiarity with another culture (or a specific part of our own culture), experience different aspects of ourselves and often, though not always, come to care about the people and places where we are based. The complexity of these relationships often makes it hard to define their exact nature and how we feel about them. This complexity complicates the imperative we have to leave (Bacchiddu, 2004; Ortiz, 2004; see also Box 11.4). Below are some of the most common emotions experienced when ending fieldwork and leaving field sites. From our perspective, the important thing is to recognise them and find ways to work with them, rather than pretend that they don't exist, or wish that they would somehow go away.

RELUCTANCE OR RESISTANCE

Leaving presents us with both a psychological and a tactical problem (Shaffir and Stebbins, 1991). We may find that we do not want to go because we have become immersed in the field (Wax, 1986). This immersion might be based on the genuine passion for our research or personal connections that have been formed (or renewed, in the case of home-based research). However, we may be involved in 'compulsive data collection' (Kleinman and Copp, 1993 cited in Ortiz, 2004: 268): anxiously striving for 'continuous coverage' and assuming (usually incorrectly) that more data will result in a better thesis. We feel reluctant to leave because we are on the verge of getting the 'full picture' (see also Box 11.1). Yet we will usually have more than enough data with which to write, and can never know everything (see Chapter 12).

In addition, the perceived pressures (e.g., thesis writing) and grey weather awaiting us on return to university may fuel our reluctance. It can be worth revisiting our research design and methodology with our supervisors at this point to help think through how to work with our data upon return to university (Gallaher, 2011).

ANXIETY, DISAPPOINTMENT AND/OR SHAME

Depending upon how our research process has gone, how our various relationships have developed, or how we have responded to being in the field, we may feel anxiety, disappointment or regrets as we get close to leaving (Pollard, 2009). Perhaps significant people refused to talk to us, or critically important information was not accessible, or unpredicted events circumvented our plans. Anxiety may also emerge as we grapple with the implications of leaving respondents or participants who have shared intimate or distressing stories and want them shared. We feel concerned about how to write these dimensions into 'factual accounts' and best represent our sources (Bennett, 2004).

Such occurrences are very common but can produce a sense of shame associated with what we perceive to be our 'failure' in the field, especially if we have made a decision to go back to university earlier than originally planned (Pollard, 2009). In these cases, it is helpful to remember that we have acted to the best of our knowledge at each stage of our fieldwork and that 'everything is always clearer in hindsight'. It may also help to share our experiences with other graduate students. Being realistic, remembering that as researchers we are always vulnerable and accepting the limitations of our work can help us to find ways to integrate 'negative' aspects productively into our writing. These dimensions will add greater depth and nuance to our theorisations of our topic and field site.

GRIEF, SADNESS OR LOSS

As Binh and Mizna note in Box 11.3, grief, sadness or loss often accompany leaving: relationships and routines change irrevocably, and we return to other ways of living and being (Bacchiddu, 2004). We may not want to leave the freedom from university pressures or our identity as a 'researcher' with its unique status and opportunities. We may have developed familial-like connections, or a particularly intimate relationship with someone in our field site. These can complicate the leaving process and prove emotionally traumatic.

Alternatively, we may feel sad because our participants and others we have come to know do not seem to care much about whether we stay or leave. They may be familiar with researchers or development workers and their cycles of arrival and departure.

Box 11.3 The difficulties of leaving: Binh and Mizna's experiences

Before New Zealand, I had never been away from home for a long period. After becoming familiar with Wellington, I had to prepare to return to Vietnam for three months of fieldwork.

Within this period, time flew by extremely quickly, especially as I had so much fun with my family and friends. One day, I realized that I had only a couple of weeks to go. I had to chase participants for interviews and documents and I became more sad about saying goodbye to my loved ones. I experienced a lot of stress. I needed to quietly relax to calm myself. I tried to focus on the excitement I felt about going back to New Zealand and the fact that I had only one year left to complete my degree. I told myself that I might not have another chance to write a thesis. I comforted myself with the thoughts that Vietnam was where I belonged and would return to live forever, and that time would fly by when I had to concentrate on my thesis. By thinking in this way, it was easier to leave.

Then, anxiety about my research started to occupy my mind. I wondered if I had sufficient data and how to analyse it. My concerns increased when some participants expected my thesis to solve their organisation's issues and challenges. I wondered how would I be able to satisfy their desires and not disappoint them.

(Continued)

(Continued)

> *Two days prior to my departure, I went alone to a quiet place where I could breathe deeply and witness my feelings. This moment helped me to recall something helpful: 'That life is full of ups and downs, lows and highs. Life means choice after choice, no matter how hard, and every single choice has two faces. So just go and see where I can go'. When the plane took off, I felt more comfortable and a sense of relief. I would fulfil my Masters. It would be a precious gift for the reunion with my beloved.*

Source: Binh Li, Master's research in Vietnam

> *I had gone to the field prepared with a busy schedule, forgetting that going back home to the Maldives for fieldwork also meant spending time with family and friends. Amidst boat rides, plane trips, spending days in different communities and catching up with family and friends, the time passed quickly. It was soon time to leave and saying the final goodbyes to family was particularly hard.*

> *I am grateful that despite the loss they feel, my family has always been supportive of my quest to seek an education, but underneath their supportiveness are also fears that I will not return home. Amidst these are also other concerns about when we will be able to see each other again. I did not know it then but this was the last time I would see some family members. Perhaps these are fears that every student studying so far away from home negotiates. I felt thankful that I had been able to return to do fieldwork.*

> *As the plane lifted and I got further and further from home I felt excitement too about the thought of returning to my 'other' home – Christchurch – where my husband and son would be waiting for me. They have been such an important part of my PhD journey. Having my immediate family there at the end of a full day of study has given me a sense of normalcy and a positive distraction from getting too embedded in my research work. Having them with me helped me recover faster from the homesickness I felt from leaving my family back in the Maldives.*

Source: Mohamed (2012)

GUILT

As we begin to recognise the extent of our emotional attachments to people with whom we have spent a great deal of time, or as we come to comprehend the expectations our research participants have of us, we may experience guilt. If we have been based in one place for any period of time, research participants may implicitly insist that our lives continue to mesh with theirs. They may expect us to live up to our personal commitments permanently (Ortiz, 2004). Such expectations, as Barrett and Cason (2010) mention, may prompt us to feel that our research is 'never over', and we may feel guilty if we want it to be.

Participants may also be unhappy with the removal of privileged status gained through their role in our research, or they may be saddened at the loss of us as a confidant, friend, ally or lover (Huisman, 2008; Ortiz, 2004; Watts, 2008), or feel cheated, manipulated or duped by our changing interest in their lives (Shaffir et al., 1980). Some of them may be dealing with harsh consequences of their associations with us (Mies, 1983 cited in Hays-Mitchell, 2001: 320). With increasing access to forms of social media, research relationships can also persist long after we have left the field, and it is wise to plan for how to manage them as part of our exit strategies.

RELIEF

Relief may be particularly acute for researchers working in their own culture where 'the schizophrenic life style [of repeated cycles of cultural immersion and withdrawal] may be methodologically useful but emotionally draining' (Posner, 1980: 211). For those researchers working in locations and cultures different from their own, we may also feel relief at being able to leave behind the potentially overwhelming confrontation with difference represented by our participants and their lives and the cognitive dissonance it produces (Davies, 2010).

Relief may be the most significant feeling for anyone whose research has 'turned to custard', for whom the experience of living and working in another culture has become associated with feeling 'cloistered or trapped', or for whom fieldwork has been unpleasant or traumatic in some way (Pollard, 2009). Leaving can provide relief from the various 'withdrawal strategies' we may have instituted in an effort to 'steady the self' while in the field, such as claiming to understand our participants' worldview in a short space of time, spending lots of time alone, writing and revising field notes, writing long emails home or spending time on social media or Skype to friends and family elsewhere (Davies, 2010: 84–85).

Even for researchers who have enjoyed their field experiences, relief may be associated with being beyond the grasp of powerful key participants or gatekeepers (Watts, 2008). Such feelings may also be accompanied by guilt as we face the explicit recognition and experience of our privilege and ability to leave. Reorienting our focus on to how we can honour our experience and participants through writing can be one way to accept our changing situation.

SATISFACTION/ACCOMPLISHMENT

So far most of the feelings and emotions we have discussed can be painful or difficult to negotiate; however, many of us are also likely to experience a sense of accomplishment and satisfaction associated with the completion of fieldwork, which can be extremely rewarding (Roth, 2001). It can be helpful to write a 'gratitude diary' either during fieldwork or upon completion, in which we record successes and appreciation. It can help to focus on the positive dimensions of our fieldwork and put some of the more challenging aspects into perspective. As we prepare to head back to university, fieldwork can also position us as an expert in our particular topic or site. Invitations to share our preliminary findings with others in our field can provide a sense of intrinsic satisfaction and may result in external validation. Thinking about how to celebrate our achievements alone or with others and how to give thanks before we leave is also important and may also help to provide some closure to this part of our lives.

ETHICAL CONSIDERATIONS AND EXIT STRATEGIES

There is no correct way to leave a field site and no singular exit strategy. It is often easiest to manage departure where external factors determine the end of fieldwork, such as the expiration of funding or visas, personal crises or changes in the research environment (see Letkemann, 1980). However, when we are involved in longer-term research, our hosts and participants are likely to construct kinship relationships for us, which imply particular responsibilities and appropriate actions from us (see also Huisman, 2008; Ortiz, 2004; Watts, 2008).

ETHICAL CONSIDERATIONS

Ideally when leaving, we have time to engage a situated ethics (Doucet and Mauthner 2002, cited in Watts, 2008: 10) and develop the best and most appropriate processes for the specific contexts and relationships in which we have become embedded. However, as we may not have this luxury, so integrating processes for managing information and confidentiality as we go may be prudent. Trying to imagine what information we will need when we come to write about the places and people involved in our work and making a checklist of key facts and figures, people names, positions and/or institutional history can help minimise anxiety about leaving and protect us if we have to leave suddenly (Barrett and Cason, 2010; Gallaher, 2011; Taylor, 1991).

Participant fears about how we will represent them and the issue of confidentiality must also be resolved before leaving the field (Watts, 2008; Wolf, 1991). They are best dealt with face to face periodically throughout our fieldwork. Clarifying the use of real names or pseudonyms with our participants as well as the use of any images in which they appear is crucial. Such clarification may involve arranging to share interview transcripts or drafts of our emerging analysis to check accuracy and issues of interpretation before or after we return to university (see also Chapter 12).

Considering the different relationships we have with our research participants and other friends or 'relatives', their expectations of us, and the local cultural patterns associated with leaving and the ending of relationships, can help guide our actions. For example, if working with a small community or community organisation in some places in the Pacific, it will be appropriate to throw a feast upon departure. However, in other parts of the region, the onus may be on the participants to throw the feast and for researchers to give gifts. Elsewhere, it may be appropriate for us to receive gifts given to us and to reciprocate how and where possible (see Box 11.4).

EXIT STRATEGIES

It may be appropriate to adopt a gradual exit strategy with participants who have been directly involved in our research or with those whose participation has been more indirect, progressively reducing the frequency of contact with them through cycles of arrival and departure. Such 'periodic leave taking' can remind participants of our 'visitor' status in their lives and be a useful strategy for generating more information as our absence can provide an opportunity to ask 'catch up' questions upon our return (Gallmeier, 1991). It may also help to lessen the concerns of 'being used' that can arise if participants have become friends over time (Hall, 2009).

A gradual exit involving periodic visits before the final visit can also enable new relationships based on diminishing frequency of contact to replace former relationships based on regular personal contact (Bacchiddu, 2004). These visits can be used to share interview transcripts or draft analyses as a means of giving something back and signalling to participants the changing nature of our research relationships.

Box 11.4   Wrapping-up research and giving thanks: Lauren's experience

Looking back on my departure from my research in one of Nicaragua's poorest and most sparsely populated municipalities, I felt unsurprisingly that there was much more that I would have liked to have done – less so for my research than for the families and individuals that had helped me. Despite all of the efforts I had made in preparation for the trip, I hadn't thought to prepare for the outward journey, which I learned is an important consideration in ethnographic research.

Towards the end, I was overwhelmed by the generosity of the people with whom I had built respect and friendship. One woman insisted I take a large bag of typical Nicaraguan pastries she had baked. One man took it upon himself to personally connect me with the members of his community and welcomed me into his home to stay whenever I would visit. Despite all he had given me, he then also entrusted with me a book of poems that, to me, seemed to be an inspiration for his deep involvement in civic issues. Another person crafted me a goodbye gift with his woodworking skills. Some of the people I would often sit and chat with in the evenings even accompanied me to Managua to say goodbye before my flight.

Having brought only what would fit into a backpack for my three months in Nicaragua, I had very little in the way of material possessions to give back as gifts. Instead, I made a

(Continued)

(Continued)

concerted effort to connect with each of the people I had come to know in the course of my research. For some, I made dinner. Others I caught up with over locally made ice cream or frozen treats. When I arrived home, I sent a care package with little items for the children at the local library, and a personalized photo album documenting the pictures of the family I had been welcomed into while researching one of the more remote communities.

Source: Sinreich (2009)

Periodic or return visits can be problematic if local situations change or new avenues open up for possible research. Participants may want us to take up new causes or lines of enquiry, or become confused about the nature of their relationships with us as we begin to distance ourselves from them to write. They may also express anger or frustration about how we have represented them in our work in the meantime (Rupp and Taylor, 2011), or request that we share aspects of our work or selves that we consider to be private, such as research diaries or social networking addresses (Hall, 2009). Thinking through what information we feel we can share and why ahead of time can reduce stress if we are unexpectedly presented with such requests before or shortly after leaving.

Alternatively, it might be more appropriate to 'drift off' from the field, moving loosely in and out of our research site without an apparent 'formal goodbye' or final visit (Rupp and Taylor, 2011). This approach may be acceptable in the context of work or research involving relatively short visits to field sites or when conducting a more formal survey. It may also be appropriate in some longer-term participatory work (Kindon, 2012). The informality of drifting off 'suspends' rather than 'terminates' the research. Such a strategy works well if we are able to easily maintain physical contact with our research site and participants, but is perhaps less appropriate where we have to relocate over large distances or return to another country at the end of fieldwork.

In other contexts, sharing writing and explaining the process of writing are useful strategies to close relationships reciprocally before we leave (see Box 11.5).

Box 11.5   Negotiating responsibilities to research participants by sharing our work: Monica's experience

For my Masters fieldwork, I chose to return to Valparaiso, Chile (a city in which I had lived for over a year on a student exchange), and to interview friends of mine who had become fathers at a young age and did not live with or near their children.

Interviewing friends brought issues of responsibilities to participants into sharp relief, as I was acutely aware that the ways I represented these men and shared my interpretations with them would likely affect not only the research process itself but also the relationships that, essentially, had allowed the work to emerge in the first place.

As a result, I chose an iterative interviewing process, involving a series of interviews with each man. I transcribed each interview verbatim and presented it to the participant at our following meeting. In doing so I tried to create opportunities for discussion of what had gone before, how we interpreted it, and how they wanted to be represented in the final report. Later, I also put together a Spanish-language summary of the research, which I sent to participants for feedback and permission before distributing through Latin American research and NGO networks.

Perhaps unsurprisingly, participants' responses to these 'opportunities' were diverse. One man quickly became bored of poring over transcripts, and told me that because he trusted me as a friend, he didn't need to know or see what I was writing, as he was confident I would do him justice. He did, however, seem to value the deepening understandings of his own fatherhood that emerged in our interviewing spaces. Another participant was concerned solely with the number of swear words he had used in his interviews, and asked me to edit them so he didn't sound so 'crass'. Another went over everything I gave him word for word, giving thoughtful and challenging feedback and correcting my Spanish grammar as he went; he also ended up volunteering to proofread the entire Spanish summary of the work for me.

I often, too, felt awkward talking about things like researcher responsibility and representation, in the context of our friendly and informal conversations. However, sometimes those conversations led to some really important insights and clarifications for both of us. The experience served to remind me: if in doubt, don't assume, just ask!

Source: Evans (2010)

Alternatively, to signal an official end to fieldwork a more formal exit strategy and closing event like a presentation can be useful. Such an event is particularly important where we know disseminating information will be difficult or impossible upon our return, or our participants are illiterate and have limited access to communicative technologies (see Box 11.6). Another approach is to run a workshop in which preliminary findings are presented to diverse stakeholders involved in the research. In small groups, they can then discuss the findings and provide feedback on the perceived accuracy and validity of the research.

Box 11.6   A quick and formal exit strategy: an example from Costa Rica

In 1990 I worked for four months with a small women's jam-making co-operative in central Costa Rica with my friend, Carol Odell. We undertook an analysis of current and future business practices using a verbally-administered questionnaire and interviews. We knew we had a finite period of time in the field and would not be able to return with a report so before we left, we presented our 'findings' orally and in the form of cartoons with simple accompanying text in Spanish. We followed this up with a leaving party for anyone involved in our research work and lives. At these formal events we were able to give something back to participants and practise culturally appropriate ways of saying goodbye with exchanges of gifts, stories and tears.

Upon return to England, we wrote a report for sponsors. This was not sent back to co-operative members, although we did keep in touch with letters and photographs for a number of years.

In 2008, I renewed contact with the co-operative and revisited the women with a Masters student of mine who carried out further research with them in 2009. I felt that the earlier work and the appropriate exit strategies had helped to sustain goodwill and affection over the intervening years. They enabled the renewal of relationships nearly 20 years later and the extension of support to my student. This time around, the exit has become more gradual with on-going correspondence through Facebook.

Source: Sara Kindon, Acosta Women's Association, Costa Rica

In all cases, leaving is generally smoother when we are clear about the implications of our particular epistemological and methodological choices for *how* we might leave (Gallaher, 2011; Iversen, 2009). Negotiating a realistic and understandable research 'bargain' – what each party will be expected to do and not do – with our participants (direct and indirect) at the beginning of our fieldwork and renegotiating this regularly throughout our stay also helps.

MANAGING ON-GOING ETHICAL RESPONSIBILITIES

Our presence in participants' lives can be complex and our roles and identities as researchers might not always be fully understood. Thinking about the implications of these misunderstandings as our fieldwork draws to a close can help us monitor what expectations might be raised by our departure. Being flexible enough to respond to participants' expectations ethically and to be honest about what is possible, as well as allowing sufficient time to meet our obligations, is important. Also thinking ahead about keeping in touch, sending back published material (see Chapter 12) or returning to visit are critical and should be seen as part of conducting ethical research and aiming for more reciprocal research relationships.

For example, participants might expect us to give them gifts, or our belongings, or do some networking or fundraising for them when we get back to university. Others might expect us to share our preliminary research findings with them before we leave. They might expect us to keep in touch via letters, email, social media sites, or send them copies of published material. Some may ask us to send them money. People might ask us when we'll be back. There are ethical implications if our participants receive clothes, money, photos or gifts and are therefore favoured over other members of the same community. Our actions can also impact on future researchers in the same communities (see Box 11.6). However, it important to understand the cultural context in which requests for fundraising and gifts are made. In some cases, these requests constitute a way of saying goodbye and should not therefore be a source of anxiety.

Overall, we need to be realistic about what we can commit to, and if there is any possibility that we might never get around to things when back at university, it is best to do them while we are still in the field. It is important that we do not make promises we cannot keep and that we keep the promises we do make.

PRACTICAL CONCERNS

Having considered the emotional, cultural, academic and ethical dimensions of leaving in the previous sections, practical matters may seem relatively straightforward. However, they can cause a great deal of stress and last-minute panic and anxiety if we haven't planned enough time for them within our fieldwork schedule. In Box 11.7, there are a number of questions about logistical matters associated with leaving.

Checking our information, organising packing, transport, flights and gifts can take a lot of time, especially if we are also trying to leave appropriately (as discussed in the section on exit strategies) and cope with our feelings about the whole process (as discussed in the earlier section). From our experiences, leaving enough time for personal priorities such as visiting places or doing things specific to the cultures in which we are working is very important in terms of managing stress and easing our transition out of our field sites. Unfortunately, these aspects are also often the first things to be sacrificed when time gets tight. Planning ahead and leaving enough time to accommodate our ethical and academic responsibilities alongside our personal desires is important and will enable us to feel more satisfaction upon our departure. In addition, it is quite likely that people with whom we have been working will want to do things with us before we leave, so planning a timeframe that can accommodate last-minute requests or invitations is also worth keeping in mind.

Box 11.7   Practical questions to ask when leaving

Managing information

Last minute checks on data:

- Have I got everything I need in terms of essential contextual facts, figures or photographs of key places and people that I might need?
- What are the residential and email or Facebook addresses and telephone or mobile numbers for people with whom I want to keep in touch or send information?
- Have I finalised confidentiality agreements with participants and friends about the use of their information and images in my work (thesis, teaching, and publications)?

Exporting information:

- Have I got digital files and back-ups of my research data?
- How safe is it to carry other forms of data with me?
- How will I ensure it's protected, secure and accessible when I get to university?

Personal priorities

- How long will it realistically take me to say thanks or goodbye to everyone I want to/need to?
- How much time can I leave open to respond to last-minute invitations or requests?
- How long will it take, and what will it cost to have photos printed before I leave (if I intend to give these away)?
- How much can I afford to spend on gifts for those I worked with (if appropriate), and/or contribute to NGOs or other organisations?
- What places or things do I want to visit or do before I leave?
- What presents do I want to take back, how long will it take me to find them and what are they likely to cost?
- What might some of the ethical issues be associated with buying particular goods?
- How am I going to carry or send gifts?

Packing, travel and taxes

Packing, shipping and weight allowance:

- How am I going to get materials (and any gifts, etc.) back to university?
- How much can I carry with me on the plane?
- What goods can I or can't I import?
- How long will air-freight or sea-freight take to arrive? How much will it cost?

Confirming plane bookings and getting to the airport:

- Is it necessary to confirm my flights and if so, how many hours in advance do I need to do this?
- What time do I need to be at the airport and how long will it realistically take me to get there?

Departure tax:

- How much do I need to keep for my departure or other taxes?

Source: Adapted from authors' own experiences

CONCLUDING REMARKS

Leaving is a dynamic, challenging and critically valuable part of any fieldwork experience. It is also essential. It informs our understandings of our research site, impacts upon our on-going relationships with participants, and indirectly affects the future relationships they may have with other researchers. More fundamentally, it confronts us with our own privilege as educated researchers, and demands that we consider the ethical praxis of our work.

Ultimately there is no 'right' way to negotiate the complex web of human relationships that make up the field (Cook, 2001; Hyndman, 2001; Katz, 1992), and no one

ETHICAL
- Write and/or present findings before leaving
- Give participants information they can use
- Be clear about what happens now
- Clear issues of confidentiality
- Make only promises you know you can keep

EMOTIONAL
- Anticipate personal transformation
- Accept feelings
- Write/and or talk about your feelings
- Review/summarise your information
- Change activities/take a break

PROFESSIONAL
- Accept closure and get organised
- Plan time to show appreciation
- Establish ways to share your work
- Negotiate ownership/authorship
- Communicate clearly
- Collaborate
- Check data/fill gaps

FLEXIBLE REALISTIC
ORGANISED
LEAVING THE FIELD
PRAGMATIC
CLEAR

PERSONAL
- Acknowledge feelings
- Plan time for you and others you care about
- Be clear about what happens now
- Write and/or talk about the process
- Honour obligations
- Set limits

PRACTICAL
- Plan ahead to organise logistics, packing and gifts
- Make time for you and to present your findings
- Remember to confirm travel and save for taxes
- Work out how to stay in touch with people

Figure 11.1 Leaving strategies

Source: Adapted from participatory diagrams generated in a workshop that Sara Kindon facilitated for postgraduate students and staff in the Development Studies Research Group at the Department of Geography, University of Durham, 14 March 2002

formula for leaving the field. The questions at the end of this chapter provide a useful starting point for consideration.

Each fieldworker, the nature of his or her research, the types of relationships formed and the contexts in which he or she is working will vary, demanding different approaches and strategies. What we face in common are emotional as well as intellectual responses to leaving, and the imperative to negotiate the implications of our presence in people's lives and our departure from them in realistic and ethical ways (see Figure 11.1). This chapter has given you some insights and tips about how to prepare for leaving – the rest is now up to you.

Summary

- Leaving the field is as worthy of consideration and planning as arriving and starting fieldwork.
- Thinking about leaving *before* arriving is valuable to our research design and ability to negotiate productive and respectful relationships.
- Experiences of leaving are interwoven with all other phases of research.
- Leaving has pragmatic, emotional and ethical dimensions, which influence our experiences of it and can generate helpful insights as we write.
- Developing appropriate leaving strategies for different relationships and cultural contexts is important to meet our ethical responsibilities to our participants, others in the field site and to future researchers.
- Planning adequate time to leave is important within research design. Factoring in time to celebrate as well as to respond to others' requests is crucial.
- We never completely leave the field. It expands through our on-going psychological, emotional and academic connections, and gets reworked through our writing.
- Thinking carefully about our on-going connections and obligations after leaving our field sites is essential, especially with the increasing availability of information digitally and the advent of social media.

Questions for reflection

- How and when will I know it is time to conclude my fieldwork?
- Drawing on others' fieldwork and leaving experiences, how do I wish my own experience to end?
- What will I do and how will I leave if my research doesn't go according to plan? If I have to leave unexpectedly, how will I get help?
- What kind and how much writing do I want to have done while in the field?
- How much of my analysis (transcripts, emerging ideas) do I want to have shared or discussed with my research participants before leaving?

- What methodology and theoretical framework will I use to guide my data generation and analysis?
- How will I leave the professional and/or personal relationships I have established with research participants and/or others in my field site? Do I wish to cultivate on-going associations, or should all relationships be research-dependent and end when the fieldwork ends?
- How will I manage the social, political and ethical implications of my research? Will I be able to return to my field site, when and in what capacity? What commitments (practical, emotional, academic) can I realistically make and maintain at the end of my stay?
- What do I want to share with my supervisor, family and friends *before* leaving that may help them to help me as I adjust to university life?

RECOMMENDED READINGS

Gallaher, C. (2011). Leaving the field. In V. J. Del Casino, M. E. Thomas and P. J. Cloke (eds), *A Companion to Social Geography* (pp. 181–197). Malden, MA: Wiley.

Book chapter outlining approaches to leaving the field, particularly in regard to data analysis and writing up.

Hall, S. M. (2009). 'Private life' and 'work life': Difficulties and dilemmas when making and maintaining friendships with ethnographic participants. *Area*, 41(3), 263–272.

Article discussing some difficulties and dilemmas that occurred through friendships formed with participants in an ethnographic research project. It includes attention to ethics, sharing and issues that arise from social networking

Ortiz, S. M. (2004). Leaving the private world of wives of professional athletes: A male sociologist's reflections. *Journal of Contemporary Ethnography*, 33(4), 466–487.

A reflexive account examining the impact that collaborative relationships and compulsive data collection can have on the process of leaving fieldwork relationships.

Pollard, A. (2009). Field of screams: Difficulty and ethnographic fieldwork. *Anthropology Matters*, 11(2).

Research paper describing a range of difficulties and feelings as experienced by PhD students doing ethnographic research.

Reeves, C. L. (2010). A difficult negotiation: Fieldwork relations with gatekeepers. *Qualitative Research*, 10(3), 315–331.

Article discussing research on the lived experiences of sex offenders, focusing on how access was gained, the completion of fieldwork, and issues associated with leaving the field.

12

RETURNING TO UNIVERSITY AND WRITING THE FIELD

JULIE CUPPLES AND SARA KINDON

Leaving your field site and returning to university to write your thesis is essential if you are to receive the degree for which you are enrolled. Many researchers take time to prepare themselves for fieldwork, thinking very carefully about research design, conduct in the field and how data will be collected but, like the leaving process discussed in Chapter 11, pay relatively little attention to the writing phase.

This relative lack of preparation for writing stems in part from how this period has been referred to simplistically as 'writing up'. Yet writing an article or thesis on a development topic is a challenging and potentially ethically fraught process which implicates the author in complex politics of representation. It can also be exhilarating and satisfying as you get clear about what you know and how best to communicate that to others.

Writing is an embodied and emotionally driven practice (DeLyser, 2010) in which data are analysed and transformed through processes of 'writing in' (L. Berg and Mansvelt, 2010) or 'writing through' (Crang and Cook, 2007). How and what you write is no less central to the epistemological consequences of your work than how you approach your time in the field, who you talk to and what kind of research materials you collect or generate. You will learn as much from writing the field as being in the field. These processes are entangled, inseparable and mutually constituted, because as you write the field, you continue to performatively bring it into being.

This chapter considers the practical, ethical, epistemological and emotional dimensions of returning to university to write your thesis. It outlines the things you need to consider in order to get started, it explores ethical issues surrounding the politics of representation, it encourages you to think carefully about theory and how you will manage your post-fieldwork relationships. It also provides you with some help in handling the emotional complexities of writing, along with some practical tips on how to become a writer.

GETTING STARTED

Without forethought or writing drafts while in the field, returning from fieldwork to write up your research can appear to be a rather large and daunting task. Spending some time organising your material through the writing of drafts before you leave your field site can support your capacity to start or resume writing when back at university (see Chapter 11). Writing is not a simple and unproblematic process, but there are some strategies that can help you not to feel so overwhelmed once back at your university desk.

First, it is worth bearing in mind that although you might be leaving one physical location (the field) to return to another (university), the field is not only a bounded physical location but also a space which is actively constituted through the social and spatial practices of the researcher and his or her relationships with participants and place. So when writing back at university, the field will continue to 'leak' (Cook, 2001: 104) into your drafts and everyday life. The field site itself will be further constituted as a result of this process. Some students, because of lack of time or equipment in the field, might need to devote some of this time to transcribing interviews. If you find yourself in that situation, try to confine your transcribing to two or three hours a day and then to move on to other activities, especially writing. Also recognise that transcribing itself is analysis, and not something that has to done before analysis can begin. Listening to the words of your participants takes you back into the field and brings the field into your university workspaces. It advances your thinking on how such material might be theorised.

Second, it is important to recognise, as Crang and Cook write, that even if you return from fieldwork with a mass of data, it is 'not as if you will be trying to create order out of chaos. The way that the data has been constructed means that it is far from "raw". It has already been partly analysed, made sense of, ordered in the research process' (2007: 132). In other words, you have probably done more work than you think you have and there is no need to panic.

Third, just as analysis is something that has been taking place throughout your fieldwork and cannot be temporally confined to a post-fieldwork period, it can be valuable not to separate writing from analysis. While some scientific disciplines separate these two activities, development research and scholarship often proceed quite differently. You are unlikely to have completed your analysis and worked out your arguments in advance of writing. You might start a chapter or section without knowing what your conclusion will be, but the act of writing enables you to construct the argument.

As DeLyser (2010) remarks, writing should be thought of not only as a means to communicate research to others, but also as a research method in itself. In other words, 'writing is the means by which the research is constituted' (Berg and Mansvelt, 2010: 341). It can therefore be worthwhile to start writing before you (think you) are ready, writing rough drafts at first. The act of writing will help you to elaborate an analysis. Revising and reworking your drafts will then help you move from a process of writing to know what you think, to writing to communicate your ideas to others. Most scholars, even very experienced ones, need to produce several drafts of a piece of work before it is ready for submission or publication.

This early period after return involves making other important decisions about your work. If your work is qualitative, does it require close reading or more formal coding? Are you are going to do the analysis manually by using some combination of folders, index cards, highlighters pens, Post-it notes or piles of paper, or by using a software package such as Nvivo, Atlas.ti or Ethnograph? There is no right and wrong on such matters. Your choice depends in part on the quantity and kind of material you have, what kind of thesis you are writing, the kind of software licenses available to you financially or institutionally, and your own personal preferences. In many cases, software packages are more useful for large team projects where different researchers need to access the same material, and are less useful for individual ethnographies or theses. Software does not do the analysis for you; it merely helps you to organise the material. If this is your first piece of research, there is a strong argument for doing it manually so that you learn how to analyse. If you are contemplating using coding software, attend a workshop on the software and seek advice from colleagues, supervisors or postgraduate students who have used the software successfully. Other important decisions for students relate to how you are going to interact with and make use of your supervisors. Good relationships with supervisors are often crucial in setting goals and deadlines and maintaining motivation. While supervision arrangements vary widely between departments and institutions, it is important to communicate how you would ideally like to be supervised and the frequency, length and style of supervision meetings. If you established a supervision agreement before leaving for fieldwork, now is a good time to revisit it. In general, it is reasonable to expect drafts of your work to be returned promptly by supervisors and for them to be specific about their criticisms. You must *not*, however, rely on your supervisor to motivate you and guide your research.

If you are doing a PhD, you might also need to decide what kind of PhD you are going to write. You may have the option of doing a thesis by publication instead of a conventional monograph. The advantage of this route is that if you manage to publish three or four journal articles by the time you complete your thesis, they will enhance your ability to find employment post-thesis. However, getting material submitted or accepted by journals can take time and you face more editorial constraints than you do with a monograph-style thesis. A compromise position is to write a conventional thesis and submit some portions of it for publication along the way.

Writing a thesis involves a great deal of reading and decisions about the literatures that are most useful to you. It is not only fieldwork experiences and materials that will shape your thesis. What you read and how you use what you read to build and construct your argument will influence the kind of thesis you ultimately produce. If you are struggling to find an argument or a way through your material, doing more reading and considering others' analyses will help you. Take care, however, not to read *instead of* writing as this can slow down your progress considerably.

The pressure to complete the writing process in a timely fashion has intensified in the context of the neoliberalisation of higher education – a process that is well developed in many parts of the world, especially in the UK and Australasia. Contemporary funding arrangements in many places mean that academic staff are under pressure to ensure that their graduate students complete theses within a certain timeframe. Your university is likely to demand frequent progress reports to ensure that you have realistic targets and are on track to meet them. For most students, who have borrowed money to study or who are living off a scholarship with a fixed end date, finishing on time is financially prudent and often essential.

Having said that, upon your return consult with your supervisor to determine what time might be needed to digest, process and reflect upon what might have been a life-changing experience for you. Making time to adjust to a new work rhythm and find your place again in the university setting is vital for your well-being. If starting to write immediately feels right, go with it. If not, use the time to organise your materials, re-read your field notes or your interview transcripts, and read pertinent scholarly or theoretical material. All these activities will facilitate the writing process, enable the intensity of fieldwork experiences to settle and the theoretical potential of your material to emerge.

THE POLITICS OF REPRESENTATION

When it comes to writing, almost all researchers across the social sciences and humanities are faced with complex questions surrounding the politics of representation. Most university ethics committees focus on the dynamics of fieldwork and on how participants will be treated during interviews or other research activities. Yet writing is just as ethically challenging, as you will be producing a long-lasting written record of those participants and the place in which they live that if done badly could have negative consequences for them, yourself and other researchers.

Development researchers today write in the aftermath of an extended critique of the practice of ethnography (see Clifford and Marcus, 2010; Van Maanen, 2011) and a growing tendency to write the messiness of fieldwork into research accounts. There is now a large and ever growing body of reflexive and critical literature on these matters that must be acknowledged, as you reflect on the specificities of your own fieldwork experience.

Such acknowledgement is particularly crucial if we are writing about groups of people who have endured long histories of colonialism, slavery, racism or neocolonial development interventions. If you have worked in low-income communities or with groups who are marginalised, stigmatised or discriminated against, it is important to write in such a way that acknowledges that marginalisation but does not exacerbate it. One strategy can be to write about the struggles and agency of marginalised groups in ways that recognise their dignity and contribute to their empowerment (see Chapter 1). Such writing can contribute in some small way to bringing a different kind of (third) world into being, to doing development differently or even to moving beyond development as a dominant discursive frame. Embracing that opportunity and recognising that you occupy a privileged space as a researcher can be a source of both motivation and inspiration as you negotiate writing challenges.

Thinking about the intended audience(s) for your work is also important as you revise and rework earlier drafts. Defining and thinking about the needs of your intended audience(s) will help you to decide what to include and how to include it. You may find that you are writing for competing and quite different audiences. Development researchers are usually attempting to reach at least three different audiences: other academics in their field of study or discipline (including supervisors and examiners); development practitioners working for aid agencies or NGOs; and people in the region or community in which they have worked. Even if you focus primarily on your academic audience, the breadth, diversity and interdisciplinary nature of contemporary development studies make that challenge substantial. While speaking to multiple and competing audiences is something that must be attempted, 'we can never tailor our ethnographies to match the interests of all our potential audiences simultaneously. No single text can accomplish all things for all readers' (Hammersley and Atkinson, 2007: 201).

Alongside writing considerations, the visual representations of our fieldwork and the ways in which we are going to use photos, maps, slides and videos need care. How a subject is represented and contextualised will facilitate particular kinds of interpretations by readers (Goin, 2001). With the digitalisation of theses, it is now getting easier to include video clips or other media. The inclusion of videos or photos of 'third world' places or peoples in Western publications, while satisfying to the reader or invaluable for illustrating certain points, can be politically tricky. If it is not done with care, we can open ourselves to accusations of Othering, exoticism or aestheticising suffering (see Chapters 1 and 9). Photos and videos of people are particularly problematic as they might breach confidentiality. Making return visits to our field site to seek permission to publish photos might be a practical impossibility. It is therefore best to clarify issues of confidentiality and permission to use and publish photos or video footage before leaving where possible (see Chapter 11).

Writing a thesis based on development fieldwork usually means enacting specific forms of self-censorship (Hammersley and Atkinson, 2007). The extent of this need varies dramatically depending on the context in which you are working. You must exclude material that could harm, offend or distress participants or complicate future research in this area by you or other researchers. It is best to write as if all participants are potential readers so that you can reflect upon the possible ramifications of your representational strategies. It is likely that there will sometimes be aspects of your fieldwork or events that took place which you cannot write about, even if that material has substantial theoretical or methodological potential. Many development researchers are comfortable with producing written criticisms of the World Bank, Monsanto or the Colombian government, but cannot for ethical reasons criticise the NGO or civil society organisations that provided them with transport, office space or access to participants, even if they have misgivings about some of their actions.

While many of your participants will never read what you write about them, or perhaps care how you choose to represent them, some will.

USING THEORY AND STYLE OF WRITING

Using theory and developing an appropriate writing style are tricky issues for some fieldwork-based researchers. While many go into the field knowing the broad theoretical framework (Marxist political economy, feminism, ethnomethodology, semiotics, poststructuralism) that has informed and shaped the choice of topic and the research design, some students struggle to explain how they are going to theorise the material generated. As an emerging academic, it is both an opportunity and a requirement that you theorise, bringing your analysis to bear rather than simply describing what you observed or letting your participants 'speak for themselves', however empirically rich your material might be and even if giving a voice to marginalised or silenced perspectives is central to your methodology.

There are usually many ways to theorise a set of research materials and it is up to you, in dialogue with your supervisors and in collaboration with the scholarly works you are reading, to decide which theoretical approaches have the greatest explanatory power. Effectively, writing involves adding one or more layers of analysis to the empirical material generated in the field. What that means in practice and how it will look in your final thesis depends on your research questions, your discipline or field of study, the level of degree, your intended audiences, your career aspirations, your skill as a theorist and your knowledge of particular bodies of literature.

While the question of theory faces all social scientists and those working in the humanities, development scholars are often faced with an additional challenge: that of trying to negotiate between what might be the trendy Anglo-American theory or 'big names' and local and indigenous theory and knowledges which might not have been translated into English or be part of your disciplinary canon (see Box 12.1). It may, however, be appropriate to use European thinkers to make sense of development dynamics in Guatemala or the Philippines without reference to local or indigenous theories. The main thing is to think about and provide a rationale for the epistemological implications of your theoretical choices.

Box 12.1   Weaving together indigenous Latin American and English language literature

When completing my PhD working with an Indigenous (Mapuche-Pewenche) tourism initiative in Chile, my home country, it became clear that I needed to take into account literature being produced in English and published as books and journal articles, as well as the work of Indigenous and/or Latin American intellectuals and activists, often published in Spanish in less far-reaching books, journals, reports, magazines, websites and so on. I was trying to work from a decolonising stance, and therefore it was crucial to consider actors, perspectives and knowledges often marginalised or not taken

(Continued)

(Continued)

seriously. Doing so shaped not only the methodology, but also motivated me to include the work of scholars and activists that in different ways have engaged in the decolonisation of knowledges, and who according to Claudia Zapata (2006) occupy a marginal space within academic (and often also political) debates in Chile, and even more so in international contexts. For me this meant engaging with their work in terms of the 'factual' information they provide, and with their theoretical contributions.

However, being fluent in both languages was not all I needed to do. Trying to 'bring into conversation' these different literatures posed important challenges. I wanted to avoid falling into the trap of comparisons, measuring one in relation to the other, or even worse, re-creating a binary that would set them up as two opposed, clearly defined entities. Instead, I was more interested in weaving them together to expand conceptual and analytical tools to facilitate more nuanced understandings and the search for alternative (and critical) ways of thinking.

Although not easy, weaving together discussions with diverse origins and trajectories proved to be highly intellectually stimulating and beneficial. It allowed my thesis to engage in discussions not often applied to the topic of my research, to provide interesting and innovative insights to different disciplines like geography, development and indigenous studies, and to promote dialogues between lines of work that often run in parallel tracks. Moreover, I believe integrating these different literatures has contributed towards the decolonisation of academia and to moving beyond the tendency to see the experiences and knowledges coming from the 'Global South' as case studies that interpret or affirm Western knowledge, while considering only the West as capable of generating theoretical and general geographical knowledge.

Source: Palomino-Schalscha (2011)

Writing also means making choices about voice and style to communicate in a way in which you feel comfortable as author, is appropriate for your discipline and is engaging for readers. It can be a struggle to make academic writing accessible to multiple audiences. While writing clearly is always something to be aspired to, it is equally important not to simplify the complex. Complex problems often require complex conceptual language, and some academic writing correctly assumes that the reader will have some specialised knowledge and familiarity with a conceptual language (DeLyser, 2010). The best work is both accessible and theoretically sophisticated, and you can learn much from authors who do so (Andrea Cornwall, Arturo Escobar and Stuart Hall constitute good examples and are authors with whom many Development students are familiar).

Understanding properly the theoretical and methodological orientation of your thesis is important, as it will determine what it is you are able to write. As Gallaher

(2011) notes, a common mistake made by students is to assert causality or make definitive or generalised conclusions when their methodology does not permit it. An example of this mistake may be claiming that women in your field site are powerful leaders and basing your information on the comments or actions of a handful of individuals. Thinking carefully about what kind of material you have generated and what it does or does not enable you to say is one of the most important tasks you face as an academic writer. Your account can only ever be a partial and fragmented one, shaped by your own experiences in the field, your observational, sense-making and analytical skills, and your own professional, political and personal motivations. It is advisable therefore to write 'vulnerably' (Crang and Cook, 2007), by 'using less forceful language' (Gallaher, 2011: 194), and/or to consider 'playing with' the conventions of thesis writing to open up space for critical engagements with the writing process alongside the content of your writing itself (see Box 12.2). It is a strength if your written accounts and conclusions contain some ambiguities, some unanswered questions and a degree of open-endedness.

Box 12.2 Alternative forms of writing: Jamie's story

I found transitioning from my fieldwork in Bangkok back to life in Wellington a real challenge. My fieldwork had been long and difficult, but also immensely rewarding. I had been researching the experiences of MSM (men-who-have-sex-with-men) development practitioners, and my participants shared many stories about the constraints they negotiated doing the kind of work that they saw as important for their communities. I noticed in transcripts that many of my participants spoke about how they creatively negotiated the constraints they faced by emphasising the collateral benefits they acquired from participating in such projects. These stories resonated with me deeply, and had parallels to some of my own experiences as a Masters student studying development studies. Throughout my research I negotiated the heterosexism that structures the development industry and development studies itself.

When I returned from fieldwork I began to explore how I could both analyse the material I had generated in Bangkok and make the constraints of queer students in higher education visible in the representation of work. Ultimately, I took up a queer representation methodology in my thesis. This involved using both the margins, and the centre of my pages to bring these two related concerns into dialogue. I also engaged per formative writing and poetry, and grafitied my thesis before its examination. My decision to write and represent my thesis in an alternative way was a risky one, given it is expected that students should 'pass' (in both senses of the word). But in this case the risk paid off, with my examiners commenting on the strength of my representational strategy, and the poems being published in an academic journal. I encourage other students to be intentional with the writing and representation of their theses – writing doesn't just carry your research, it is your research!

Source: Burford (2010)

REFLEXIVITY AND POSITIONALITY

One of the most dramatic shifts observed in written accounts of development fieldwork is what we might refer to as the 'reflexive turn' or the now almost ubiquitous attention to positionality. Up until a couple of decades ago, development fieldworkers and ethnographers used to write themselves out of the written account, writing in the third person as if their knowledges and observations were detached, impartial, disembodied and objective. Today researchers devote substantial portions of their theses and published work to considerations of how their gender, age, race/ ethnicity, sexuality, motivations or beliefs, parental status and mode of accompaniment have shaped the research process and the kinds of knowledges constructed (see inter alia R. Butler, 2001; Cupples, 2002b; Cupples and Kindon, 2003; England, 1994; Falconer Al-Hindi and Kawabata, 2002; Ng, 2011; Sultana, 2007; Sundberg, 2003).

Part of reflexivity is also acknowledging the failures of fieldwork, the things that didn't work out so well and the ethical compromises you found yourself making. For example, many development researchers find that they cannot keep the commitments made to their institutional ethics committee (see, e.g., Box 4.4). Many find how ill-equipped such processes are for dealing with the twists and turns of development fieldwork: you couldn't get signed consent forms because of local anxieties about officialdom or you gave people money or gifts even though you stated you would not. It can be valuable to bring these complexities to light as you write, as they often provide lessons for others as well as helping you to understand how you came to know what you know.

The reflexive turn has produced richer and more honest accounts of fieldwork, revealing how all knowledges are situated and embodied in specific ways. Readers gain important insights into the position from which you write and into the epistemological foundations of your project. However, too much or ill-considered reflexivity can come across to readers as distracting and self-indulgent (Fife, 2005), and hyper-self-reflexivity, while valuable in addressing some power relations, often does not distinguish between levels of complicity or adequately account for the institutional constraints faced by development researchers (Kapoor, 2004). Kobayashi (2003) notes that while reflexivity is an important way to account for the power relations that underpin research, in many cases it is taken too far and we must discriminate between the reflexive information that supports our research goals and is useful to share from that which does not. Some reflexive accounts are little more 'a privileged and self-indulgent focus on the self that ... ends up distancing the writer ... from the very people whose conditions she might hope to change' (2003: 348).

One way around the dilemma posed by the reflexive turn is to recognise, as Myers (2010) writes, that representing self and representing others is not a binary, as when we represent others, we are also representing ourselves. Focusing on your participants in a self-aware way that does not deny your embodied presence in the field can go a long way towards being reflexive without being solipsistic. Such an orientation can offer an alternative means of writing social experience by making connections between your own experiences and wider social theory and debates.

EMOTIONAL ISSUES

Moving back and forth between your field site and home or university presents emotional challenges. The fieldwork experience might have changed you in significant ways and you might be struggling with new identities and subjectivities – you might even feel that you are not sure who you are any more – and that can make it hard to readjust to everyday life at home or back at university. You might find it hard to communicate the intensity of your experiences to family and friends back home or even to find other people who are interested in or care enough about your work or who understand what you have been through. If you did your fieldwork in your native country, you might be missing friends and family there as you face the pressure of completing a thesis.

As you write, you might find yourself 'working through the emotions of field-work' (Bennett, 2004: 420) and returning, trying to decide to what extent feelings of sadness, distress or elation experienced during and after your fieldwork should be addressed in your writing. It is reassuring to consider that even supposedly 'negative' emotions such as anger, guilt, anxiety and disappointment can often help you to explore the politics of your research and how to write about it. They are common and normal, and often indicate some of the most exciting avenues to explore in writing and theorising your work.

Many students from Euro-American societies who do research in Africa, Asia, Latin America or the Pacific expect to experience some kind of culture shock when they travel abroad to do their fieldwork, as discussed in Chapter 8. However, coming home or returning to university might also entail a reverse culture shock or reverse dissonance (Davies, 2010). Bacchiddu vividly describes this experience after completing fieldwork in Chile:

> Once back in London, I experienced a sense of intense displacement: an incident of what could be called reverse culture shock. I was totally unprepared for it. Just like I had felt out of context at the beginning of my fieldwork, I was again feeling the same – but this time I was on supposedly familiar ground! The experience was so powerful that I felt paralysed. I was incapable of dealing with the immense crowds that animated the streets, the noise of traffic, the waste of electricity, water and paper. I did not know who I was, and in what language I was organizing my confused thoughts. [...] I felt I had lost myself in a world that did not belong to me, and I was unable to find my old self – indeed so much had changed in the meantime; more than anything I had changed. (2004: 5)

If we experience such emotions, peer support can become crucial (see Epprecht, 2004). Finding out what kinds of support your department or institution provides can help, or setting up your own support networks can make a huge difference to your experience with writing. Such groups can provide you with a space to share your fieldwork experiences with others, reflect on ethical issues and have your achievements in the field validated. Talking through your understandings and ideas can often clarify what it is that you are trying to write.

You can also find much support online. Social media, blogs and email discussion lists can be valuable tools for connecting with peer support networks and can be good for students who are in small departments with few graduate students or in departments where other graduate students are not working on development theses. Joining a group such as Postgraduates in Latin American Studies (PILAS) on Facebook or reading and sharing insights on a blog site such as thesiswhisperer.com can be a valuable way to share experiences and thesis and post-fieldwork survival strategies.

BECOMING A WRITER

Learning what kind of writer you are and can become is one of the most enriching aspects of thesis work. Many students confront a lack of confidence in their ability to write. These feelings if not properly managed can easily lead to procrastination, yet as DeLyser (2010) has described, writing is a habit that must be practised and nurtured. You might have to set aside a small amount of time at the same time every day to write until it becomes a habit. And it is worth reading books about writing and talking with your colleagues, supervisors and postgraduate students to gain ideas about the ways in which you can both write and approach writing.

It is very common to experience what might appear to be long periods of lack of productivity (when you struggle to write anything at all) as well as periods of productive processing and then productive generation of words. As you draft each section or chapter, you might find for example that the writing goes very slowly for three or four weeks, then you experience a kind of break-through in which you manage to find your way through to the argument and writing accelerates. Drafting and trying to write with what appears to be limited success in the early stages is not necessarily a waste of time. The trying helps you to develop your argument and ideas and paves the way to faster and clearer writing later. You may also notice that when you've been struggling with something for a while, you suddenly have a moment of inspiration while taking a shower or doing exercise. This illustrates that the trying was not in vain and your brain has been processing while you've been doing something else. Keeping a small notebook on hand for these 'aha!' moments becomes essential to capture your newly distilled realisations, and helps you maintain the momentum you need to finish your thesis.

If you are struggling to write, there are many strategies you can adopt to get started. One approach is to break the writing up into small and manageable chunks of either time or word count. You can sign up to an online programme such as 750words.com (to get you writing 750 words a day) or the pomodoro technique that encourages us to stay focused on writing in 25-minute segments (pomodorotechnique.com). There are other means to motivate writing, such as making a commitment to presenting your preliminary research findings in a departmental talk or at a conference (Barrett and Cason, 2010). Joining or starting a writing group can also work wonders for motivation, tenacity and clarity. It is a good idea to think of ways of rewarding yourself for sticking to deadlines, such a night out or a weekend away for completing a chapter draft on time.

Box 12.3 summarises some of the ideas raised up to this point in the chapter.

Box 12.3 Strategies for adjusting to being back at university and writing

- Expect and prepare for return culture shock.
- Think about how your fieldwork experience may have caused your identities to shift, and what the implications may be for being back and writing.
- Keep in touch with participants in field sites via letters, email and social media (where appropriate) (see also Chapter 11).
- Work out personal support networks and find people with whom to talk about your work and experiences.
- Join a graduate email discussion list or Facebook group or a university/department social or support group for students in which ideas can be shared.
- Continue to write some kind of research journal upon return in which ideas and feelings can be documented.
- Write before you think you are ready and be prepared to draft and redraft.
- Read books and blogs about the thesis journey and the experience of writing.
- Read different kinds of theses in development studies to see how others approached writing.
- Establish a regular writing habit alone and/or with others.
- Give yourself little rewards for sticking to deadlines.

Source: Bailey (2007) and the authors' personal experiences

MANAGING POST-FIELDWORK RELATIONSHIPS

Being back at university and writing your thesis means also managing your post-fieldwork relationships, a process often characterised by tensions surrounding conflicted identities. After completing fieldwork with Bosnian refugees, Huisman struggled to balance the need to complete her thesis in good time with her desire 'to move slowly, cultivate relationships within the community, and give back to the community in a meaningful way' (2008: 379).

Managing these relationships involves exploring at least four issues. First, what kind of on-going relationships are you going to have with participants? Second, how are you going to share your research findings, including your thesis and subsequent publications? Third, beyond completing your thesis, how are you going to publish your work? Fourth, are you going to return to the field to share findings, do further research or visit friends? You might not know the answers to these questions immediately but they are important issues to consider.

While some researchers sever all ties with research participants once the research is completed (Duval, 2011), others maintain long-term friendships. Friendships with participants might allow much more interesting knowledges to be generated, but might also place you in an ethically compromised position when writing. Internet, email and Facebook make it easier to remain in contact with participants but also complicate relationships. Even if you maintain a professional distance from your participants during fieldwork, they might later send you a friend request on Facebook, which if accepted (and it is not so easy to ignore or decline) means that they and you gain access to a range of personal information about each another and you could inadvertently breach their confidentiality to your other friends (see Hall, 2009; Ortiz, 2004; Tilley and Woodthorpe, 2011). Hall (2009) suggests making use of privacy settings as a way through these issues.

Alternatively, if you embark on an academic career after your thesis, working in your field site could become a long-term activity and it will be important to consider how best to nurture what may become lasting research relationships. Returning to the field is theoretically and ethically valuable. It enables you to communicate the importance of your research relationships to participants and build on earlier knowledges as you continue to work together. Return visits facilitate the possibility that new reflections and insights from participants can be incorporated into subsequent publications and that you can gain new insights by participating in other roles (see Box 12.4).

Sharing research findings with research communities is important but there is no single right way to do it. Sharing also raises its own ethical problematic: it is important to think about the possible impact on the 'informational economy' of your field site (Hammersley and Atkinson, 2007). Are the less quoted participants going to feel less valued than the more quoted ones? Will circulating findings generate expectations that cannot be met? Evidence of publications or reports might lead a researched community to believe that you are going to take up respondents' causes or that you have the power to influence policy or other outcomes.

Box 12.4   Giving back to indigenous communities: Simon's story

My doctoral fieldwork involved regular visits to small-scale Maori vegetable growers in tandem with a series of community meetings to establish what became the National Maori Vegetable Growers Collective. I was soon elected onto the inaugural committee – not an unusual occurrence with Maori organisations where you're politely but firmly co-opted into helping with development strategies. My main role in the early days was as editor of a regular newsletter (still, I'm sure, the most widely read of my publications). We continue to meet two or three times a year, hosted by communities for one or two nights and being shown their gardens, hearing the histories, catching up on gossip. Although I am Maori myself, being a university researcher will always position me somewhat as an outsider and one of my challenges is to manage expectations: PhD candidates might be top of the student pile but are pretty much bottom of the research ladder!

This collective became an audience not just for my research insights but a succession of postgraduate students, Maori and non-Maori (including some very good international students). Traditions of face-to-face contact, clear and honest communication, and the cultural skills of being among diverse, curious, often intimate communities are, I think, paradoxically more necessary in today's digital world.

I'm still on the committee of the collective 8 years later, and the necessary travel is sometimes funded by the university (if it coincides with other tasks), but more often it is funded by whatever airpoints I have and from my own pocket. There is some scope for 'auditing' these relationships under the New Zealand PBRF [Performance Based Research Fund] system but there is a general institutional ignorance as to the value of such networks. To this community, the university is just one of many colonial organisations: there's no need to apologise for its lack of a more formal presence. Maori, like other Indigenous peoples, play the long game.

Source: Lambert (2008)

Sometimes sharing cannot be done at all. Van der Geest's (2003) thesis based on fieldwork in Ghana contained information about illegal abortion practices. Giving pseudonyms to participants and the village where he worked could not protect confidentiality, as long as he was identified as the author of the work. His only solution was to write under a pseudonym and not share the thesis.

As theses become increasingly digitised and as more people in Africa, Asia and Latin America gain access to the Internet, sharing copies of theses or published articles is becoming easier. There is no doubt that passing on theses or other published material can be hugely beneficial and much welcomed by research communities. You have to also be aware that even if you don't pass on your thesis, somebody in your research community might find it online and circulate it to others. Assuming that your participants are going to read your work, even if the majority never have any wish to do so, is a useful ethical strategy to adopt. You should also be prepared for the possibility that your participants will not like what you write (see Mosse, 2006; Rupp and Taylor, 2011; Sluka, 2012b), and think about how you might respond to that.

PUBLISHING FROM RESEARCH

Publishing is a personal, professional and political issue. It may validate your fieldwork and enable the knowledge generated to circulate more widely. When shared with participants, it can endorse their struggles and challenges.

However, where, for whom, how and in what language(s) you publish are not straightforward decisions. While academic journal articles published in English might be of little use to research communities, they may be essential for your own career progression: getting an academic job after completing a thesis might depend on publishing in the 'right' journals. Alternatively, you might feel compelled to make your work accessible to wider audiences and to fulfil commitments to research participants. Such commitments, while worthwhile, can slow down your 'outputs' in academic journals or increase your workload as you attempt to do both.

One way to potentially address both audiences is to co-publish with your participants or key informants in prestigious publications. As well as producing collaborative and more hybrid work, a publication in a top-ranking journal might assist your collaborator or the organisation they work for to gain access to funding, scholarships or promotion. It can be a small but valuable way of giving something back to your collaborators and of enriching your research communities. Collaboration and co-authorship are not in themselves automatically better or more decolonising than singly authored research (for discussion, see Myers, 2010) but are certainly worth considering.

If your participants or collaborators do not speak English, it is also worth trying to publish something in their local language. If you have published something in an English-language journal, you can also find a local journal to publish the same article in translation. You must get permission to reprint from the first journal but if you are publishing the same article later in a different language, permission is usually granted. The disadvantage of this approach is that translation costs are often beyond the budgets of most researchers and even if you are fluent in both languages, you might not have the skills to do your own translation. If a translated journal article is out of the question, you might be able to publish a shorter magazine or newsletter article instead or publish something online and circulate either the URL or hard copies to participants as appropriate. Sometimes it is highly appropriate to share practical aspects of your findings in popular publications (see Box 12.4).

CONCLUSIONS

When writing, it is useful not to lose sight of expanded notions of the field and the impossibility of real closure. Writing will be marked by all kinds of complex ethical, theoretical, representational and emotional issues. As you try to resolve them as best you can, keep in mind that you cannot completely control the power relations in which you, your participants and your various audiences are differentially embedded. You are likely to have on-going personal and professional relationships with research participants and the places in which you conducted fieldwork. You might continue to do fieldwork in that part of the world, you might go back just to visit friends and you might be publishing from your fieldwork material over many years. Even if you don't do any of the above, your thesis will remain in public circulation and you can't fully predict who will read it, how it will be read and with what consequences.

What these dynamics mean is that while deadlines must be met and theses submitted, you should do your best to act responsibly and ethically. Writing the field is a serious responsibility but it is also a wonderful opportunity. It is a transformative process, in which your material, your field site and you as a researcher and a person will undergo substantial transformation. If done well, it will make a valuable contribution to knowledge in development studies, it will establish positive relations of reciprocity and solidarity between you and your research communities, and it will establish and enhance your status as a development researcher.

Summary

- It is important to think carefully about returning to university and writing your thesis.
- You might experience a range of emotions when you return to university to write your thesis. It is useful to have support networks in place.
- Most students return with sufficient material which has already been partially analysed.
- Development researchers have to engage with the ethics and politics of how they choose to represent participants.
- Development researchers find themselves writing for competing audiences, which complicates how and what they write.
- Most development research pays attention to questions of positionality and reflexivity. It is, however, important to connect personal experiences with wider social issues.
- There are many practical things you can do to enhance your capacities as a writer.
- As you complete your thesis, thinking through the complexities of publication and how best to share your work present challenges and opportunities.

Questions for reflection

- How am I going to organise my research materials? Do I need time for transcribing and analysis before writing can commence?
- How frequently am I going to meet with my supervisors and keep them up to date with my progress?
- How am I going to write about my experience and what I learn in ways that are ethical?
- Who are my intended audiences and how do their requirements differ?
- What strategies can I use to avoid undue procrastination and writing paralysis?
- How do I balance my commitments to my research participants with commitments to supervisors, examiners and editors?
- Where does my thesis and publishing from it fit within my future career aspirations?
- What should I include and what should I leave out? How will I write about things that did not work out so well?
- How much personal information should I include? How reflexive should I be?
- Am I going to return to the field, and if I do, will it be as a friend or researcher or both?

RECOMMENDED READINGS

Bailey, C. A. (2007) Evaluation criteria and the final manuscript (pp. 179–195). In *A Guide to Qualitative Field Research* (2nd edn). Thousand Oaks, CA: Pine Forge Press.

This practical, general guide to doing qualitative research includes a chapter on analysis and writing.

Barrett, C. B. and J. W. Cason (2010) Pulling it all together: The post-partum (pp.129–133). In *Overseas Research: A Practical Guide*. Milton Park: Routledge.

This chapter provides useful practical advice to students on how to prepare for the post-fieldwork phase.

Crang, M. and I. Cook (2007). Writing through materials (pp. 150–206). In *Doing Ethnographies*. Los Angeles: Sage.

This chapter provides advice on analysis and writing for those doing ethnographic research.

Fife, W. (2005) Part C. Putting the ethnography together (pp. 119–158.). In *Doing Fieldwork: Ethnographic Methods for Research in Developing Countries and Beyond*. New York: Palgrave Macmillan.

This introduction to ethnographic research methods includes a focus on how to put the ethnography together.

Van Maanen, J. (2011). *Tales of the Field: On Writing Ethnography* (2nd edn). Chicago, IL: University of Chicago Press.

Book discussing three genres of cultural representation in ethnographic writing – realist tales, confessional tales and impressionist tales. It raises issues of authorial voice, style, truth, objectivity and point of view.

13

WAYS FORWARD

REGINA SCHEYVENS

REFLECTIONS ON THE VALUE OF FIELDWORK

As this collection has demonstrated, much can be learned through reading about others' experiences. This is as true for the personal experiences of fieldwork – of ethics, logistics and relationships – as it is for learning about the application of methods. Hopefully the positive relationships and experiences of the authors of this book and the many works of other researchers they have drawn upon have come to the fore, as much as the difficulties and challenges. When well planned and executed, fieldwork can provide a number of benefits for participants as well as being a great learning experience for researchers.

Development fieldwork has a very important function as the primary means by which researchers explore and seek to understand other people's lives and other perspectives on development. However, as noted in various chapters of this book, fieldwork has also been criticised in terms of irrelevance, exoticism and the perpetuation of unbalanced researcher/researched relationships. Thus we cannot be complacent. We need to find ways to move forward and ensure that development fieldwork is more just, ethical and effective in future.

HOW CAN WE AS DEVELOPMENT RESEARCHERS WORK IN A MORE JUST, ETHICAL AND EFFECTIVE MANNER?

My focus here is on identifying factors or approaches that are most likely to lead to a fulfilling and rewarding experience for both the researchers and the researched, while leading to valuable findings which can be used by development planners, policy makers, development agencies and/or communities themselves. In coming to these conclusions, I have drawn upon the findings of all the chapters in this book and thus I am indebted to my fellow authors, those whose work they cite, as well as a number of key authors I cite below.

RECOGNISE THAT THE ARENAS OF DEVELOPMENT FIELDWORK CAN INCLUDE THE NORTH, SOUTH, EAST AND WEST

Poverty and inequality are pervasive problems in almost every country on earth, and there are often similar processes at work which perpetuate these problems. It therefore makes sense to consider doing development research all around the world. This could also aid us in moving beyond criticisms that field research is neocolonial in nature:

> One way to challenge development's colonial roots and the neo-liberal influence is to widen the boundaries of development research to engage with social relations in the North as well as the South. (Smith and Humble, 2007: 22)

Ideally this would see researchers from developing countries regularly coming 'to conduct research of "exotic" and "different" European and North American societies' (Sidaway, 1992: 407). Facilitating linkages between Western and developing country universities is one way of doing this, especially if staff and graduate students take part in exchanges in both directions whereby they conduct research on social phenomena in the 'other' country.

Also, for graduate students in Western universities there are interesting thesis topics that could be 'equally relevant and ethically sound as undertaking research overseas' and that could be based 'at home' (Unwin, 2006: 105). Benefits to locating research 'at home' include keeping costs down, enabling multiple visits, gaining access to sites, and developing a deeper appreciation of development issues in one's home environment (2006: 106).

WORK TO BREAK DOWN THE KNOWLEDGE AND POWER HIERARCHIES BETWEEN RESEARCHERS IN DIFFERENT PARTS OF THE WORLD

Academics in Western universities, in particular, need to work to break down the hierarchies of power and knowledge that situate themselves as outsider in a privileged position. McEwan suggests that 'it is important for Northern academics to de-centre themselves: geographically, linguistically and culturally' (2009: 282). This could involve collaborating more closely, and in more participatory ways, with academics in other parts of the world. For too long, development research has been dominated by foreigners (such as all of the authors of this book, with the exception of Litea Meo-Sewabu), and local researchers have been 'crowded out' of the research space (Sumner and Tribe, 2008a: 42). This has occurred partly because of institutional constraints regarding capacity development and lack of funding for research in developing countries.

Thus breaking down the knowledge and power hierarchies could include providing research mentoring and research workshops, or helping colleagues in other countries to access funding or other resources so they can implement activities identified on their own research agendas.

DEVELOP MORE CONSTRUCTIVE COLLABORATIONS WITH OUR COLLEAGUES IN DEVELOPING COUNTRIES, BE THEY ACADEMICS, STUDENTS, DEVELOPMENT WORKERS, GOVERNMENT OFFICIALS OR COMMUNITY MEMBERS

Given that 'Development problems are no longer the preserve of the South with answers in the North' (Sumner, 2008: 50), we need more genuine research collaboration to constructively address development issues. This could include academics and graduate students as well as development workers, government officials and community members from the North, South, East and West working on the design, implementation, analysis and dissemination of development research. Similarly, we can consider participatory approaches which actively promote opportunities for the less privileged communities we work with to identify issues of concern and undertake research alongside us. Such collaboration, drawing on the skills and knowledge from a wide range of people, is likely to result in more comprehensive research findings that can contribute to effective development outcomes.

Communications technologies certainly could facilitate such collaboration as they enable us to bridge physical distance so much more easily than in the past. Ultimately, however, if we wish for better collaborations, we need to invest more time in relationship-building. This means that those of us coming from the traditionally 'dominant' societies need to practice greater humility, make conscious efforts to share power, and ensure that we show utmost respect for those we are working with. This leads on to my next point.

MOVE BEYOND CRITIQUES OF DEVELOPMENT

There is value in moving beyond the conventional academic focus on the failures of development (McEwan, 2009: 314). For too long, development researchers have focused on the absences, the problems, the gaps in development, without concurrently identifying strengths, assets and successes.

Our research questions, often dreamed up in a nicely furnished office thousands of kilometres away, can seem confronting, inappropriate or annoying to those who we have somewhat arrogantly identified will be our research participants. If we are focused on critiquing everything and everyone in our sights, then rather than building constructive fieldwork relationships we will most likely upset and frustrate many genuinely well-intentioned people who are doing their best to deliver 'development' under trying conditions. This was the case when Fife turned up in a province of Papua New Guinea to research the education system:

> I noticed that the bureaucrats most directly responsible for education were very reluctant to cooperate with my project, even though higher government officials had instructed them to do so ... I finally asked one male official ... why he didn't seem to like the idea of my doing research on primary schools in his province. He took a deep breath and let loose with a stream of angry words, the gist of which was that they, the people directly responsible for education in the province, were sick and tired of outsiders coming in and 'telling us that everything we are doing is wrong'. (2005: 10)

Another thing we can do to move beyond critiques is to consider asset or strengths-based approaches to development, and we can look for 'hopeful' signs of communities determining their own development paths (see, e.g., McKinnon, 2011).

BE PREPARED TO PLACE ONESELF IN A VULNERABLE POSITION

We can also make efforts to reduce power imbalances by placing ourselves in positions in which our informants are comfortable, even if sometimes we are not. This can be part of de-centring ourselves, as noted above. Ng, for example, was very nervous when, as a cosmopolitan woman from Hong Kong, she returned 'home' from a UK university to do research among a minority ethnic group living in a walled village: 'To be honest, I had never felt so vulnerable in my life... Elaine, an acquaintance, commented that I "really have a hairy bladder" (the Chinese saying means I really had a nerve)' (2011: 445).

As long as we are not jeopardising our personal safety, such vulnerability can be a very good thing as it places us in the position of learner, not teacher, and we are required to show humility and invest time in building relationships in order to win the trust of those we wish to work with. Ultimately, it ensures that we do not hold all of the power in research relationships.

REMEMBER WHO IT IS THAT OUR RESEARCH SHOULD BE SERVING

It has been argued in development practice, and particularly under the dominant framing of results-based management (Sumner, 2008: 9), that we need to practise more downward accountability in development research. Many researchers are preoccupied with upward accountability. This includes accountability to those who fund our research: we write reports in a language and format that suits their requirements, rather than disseminating our findings in ways which are truly accessible to those with whom we have conducted research. We are accountable to our institutions – typically, universities – which have their own means for assessing research quality. We need to make an active effort to shift this focus and so ensure more accountability to those with whom we do our research.

As set out in Chapter 1, in this book we posit that 'development fieldwork' should have a strong development component: that is, the issues examined are associated with positive social change and enhanced well-being, particularly for those who are poor, oppressed or marginalised. Thus ideally, most development research should be able to contribute to policy change, improved programmes, or enhanced quality of life for such people. Ultimately when planning for more just, ethical and effective development, it is important that we do not lose site of the people our research should be serving, and their realities.

REFERENCES

Abbott, D. (2006). Disrupting the 'whiteness' of fieldwork in geography. *Singapore Journal of Tropical Geography, 27*(3), 326–341.

Acker, J., Barry, K., and Esseveld, J. (1991). Objectivity and truth: Problems in doing feminist research. In M. Fonow and J. Cook (eds), *Beyond Methodology: Feminist Scholarship as Lived Research* (pp. 133–153). Bloomington, IN: Indiana University Press.

Adams, W. M., and Megaw, C. C. (1997). Researchers and the rural poor: Asking questions in the third world. *Journal of Geography in Higher Education, 21*(2), 215–229.

Alderson, P., and Morrow, V. (2011). *The Ethics of Research with Children and Young People: A Practical Handbook* (2nd edn). London: Sage.

Amadiume, I. (1993). The mouth that spoke a falsehood will later speak the truth: Going home to the field in Eastern Nigeria. In D. Bell, P. Caplan and W. K. Jarim (eds), *Gendered Fields: Women, Men and Ethnography* (pp. 182–198). London: Routledge.

American Anthropological Association (2012). *Statement on Ethics: Principles of Professional Responsibility*. Retrieved 13 May 2013 from www.aaanet.org/profdev/ethics/upload/Statement-on-Ethics-Principles-of-Professional-Responsibility.pdf.

Amit, V. (2000). Introduction: constructing the field. In V. Amit (ed.), *Constructing the Field: Ethnographic Fieldwork in the Contemporary World* (pp. 1–18). London: Routledge.

Anderman, G. M., and Rogers, M. (2003). *Translation Today: Trends and Perspectives*. Buffalo, NY: Multilingual Matters.

Anderson, D. M. (2011). Mau Mau in the High Court and the 'lost' British Empire archives: Colonial conspiracy or bureaucratic bungle? *The Journal of Imperial and Commonwealth History, 39*(5), 699–716.

Angrosino, M. V., and May de Perez, K. A. (2003). Rethinking observation: From method to context. In N. K. Denzin and Y. S. Lincoln (eds), *Collecting and Interpreting Qualitative Materials* (2nd edn, pp. 107–154). London: Sage.

Apentiik, C. R. A., and Parpart, J. L. (2006). Working in different cultures: Issues of race, ethnicity and identity. In V. Desai and R. Potter (eds), *Doing Development Research* (pp. 34–43). London: Sage.

Appadurai, A. (2006). The right to research. *Globalisation, Societies and Education, 4*(2), 167–177.

Arendell, T. (1997). Reflections on the researcher–researched relationship: A woman interviewing men. *Qualitative Sociology, 20*(3), 341–368.

Armbruster, H., and Lærke, A. (eds) (2008). *Taking Sides: Ethics, Politics and Fieldwork in Anthropology*. New York: Berghahn.

Ashley, H., Corbett, J., Jones, D., Garside, B., and Rambaldi, G. (2009). Change at hand: Web 2.0 for development. *Participatory Learning and Action, 59*(1), 8–20.

Association of American Geographers (2009). *Council of the Association of American Geographers: Statement on Professional Ethics*. Retrieved 13 May 2013 from www.aag.org/cs/resolutions/ethics.

Atkinson, P., Delamont, S., Coffey, A., Lofland, J., and Lofland, L. (2007). *Handbook of Ethnography*. London: Sage.

Babbie, E. R. (2010). *The Practice of Social Research* (12th edn). Belmont, CA: Wadsworth Cengage.

Bacchiddu, G. (2004). Stepping between different worlds: Reflections before, during and after fieldwork. *Anthropology Matters*, 6(2).

Back, L. (1993). Gendered participation: Masculinity and fieldwork in a South London adolescent community. In D. Bell, P. Caplan and W. J. Karim (eds), *Gendered Fields: Women, Men and Ethnography* (pp. 199–214). London: Routledge.

Bailey, C. A. (1996). *A Guide to Field Research*. Thousand Oaks, CA: Sage.

Bailey, C. A. (2007). *A Guide to Qualitative Field Research* (2nd edn). Thousand Oaks, CA: Pine Forge Press.

Ballamingie, P., and Johnson, S. (2011). The vulnerable researcher: Some unanticipated challenges of doctoral fieldwork. *The Qualitative Report*, 16(3), 711–729.

Banerjee, A. V., and Duflo, E. (2011). *Poor Economics: A Radical Rethinking of the Way to Fight Global Poverty*. New York: PublicAffairs.

Banks, G. (2000). Social impact assessment monitoring and household surveys. In L. Goldman (ed.), *Social Impact Analysis: An Applied Anthropology Manual* (pp. 297–343). Oxford: Berg.

Barker, D. (2006). Field surveys and inventories. In V. Desai and R. Potter (eds), *Doing Development Research* (pp. 130–143). London: Sage.

Barnes, S., and Lewin, C. (2011). Differences and relationships in quantitative data. In B. Somekh and C. Lewin (eds), *Theory and Methods in Social Research* (2nd edn, pp. 231–255). London: Sage.

Barrett, C. B., and Cason, J. W. (2010). *Overseas Research: A Practical Guide* (2nd edn). Milton Park: Routledge.

Barrett-Gaines, K., and Khadiagala, L. (2000). Finding what you need in Uganda's Archives. *History in Africa*, 27, 455–470.

Barta, B., Brash, C., Burke, F., and Choy, M. (2009). *Lonely Planet: Travel with Children* (5th edn). Footscray, Australia: Lonely Planet.

Battiste, M. (2008). Research ethics for protecting indigenous knowledge and heritage. In N. K. Denzin, Y. S. Lincoln and L. T. Smith (eds), *Handbook of Critical and Indigenous Methodologies* (pp. 497–509). Los Angeles, CA: Sage.

Bauer, M. W., and Gaskell, G. D. (eds) (2000). *Qualitative Research with Text Image and Sound: A Practical Handbook*. London: Sage.

Beban, A. (2008). *Organic agriculture: An empowering development strategy for small-scale farmers? A Cambodian case study*. (Unpublished master's thesis), Massey University, Palmerston North, New Zealand.

Becker, S., Bryman, A., and Sempik, J. (2006). *Defining Quality in Social Policy Research: Views, Perceptions and a Framework for Discussion*. Suffolk: Social Policy Association.

Bennett, K. (2004). Emotionally intelligent research. *Area*, 36(4), 414–422.

Berg, B. L. (2007). *Qualitative Research Methods for the Social Sciences* (6th edn). Boston, MA: Pearson/Allyn and Bacon.

Berg, L., and Mansvelt, J. (2010). Writing in, speaking out: Communicating qualitative research findings. In I. Hay (ed.), *Qualitative Research Methods in Human Geography* (3rd edn, pp. 161–182). Oxford: Oxford University Press.

Bevan, M. (2011). *'The hero stuff' and the 'softer side of things': Exploring masculinities in gendered police reform in Timor-Leste*. (Unpublished master's thesis), Victoria University, Wellington, New Zealand.

Bingo, S. (2011). Of provenance and privacy: Using contextual integrity to define third-party privacy. *The American Archivist*, 74(Fall/Winter), 506–521.

Binns, T. (2006). Doing fieldwork in developing countries: Planning and logistics. In V. Desai and R. Potter (eds), *Doing Development Research* (pp. 13–24). London: Sage.

Bishop, R. (2008). Freeing ourselves from neocolonial domination in research: A kaupapa Māori approach to creating knowledge. In N. K. Denzin and Y. S. Lincoln (eds), *The Landscape of Qualitative Research* (3rd edn, pp. 145–183). Los Angeles, CA: Sage.

Bjerk, P. (2004). African files in Portuguese archives. *History in Africa, 31*, 463–468.

Blackwood, E. (1995). Falling in love with another lesbian: Reflections on identity in fieldwork. In D. Kulick and M. Wilson (eds), *Taboo: Sex, Identity and Erotic Subjectivity in Anthropological Fieldwork* (pp. 51–75). London: Routledge.

Blank, G. (2008). Online research methods and social theory. In N. Fielding, R. M. Lee and G. Blank (eds), *The SAGE Handbook of Online Research Methods* (pp. 537–550). London: Sage.

Blaxter, L., Hughes, C., and Tight, M. (1996). *How to Research*. Milton Keynes: Open University Press.

Blaxter, L., Hughes, C., and Tight, M. (2006). *How to Research* (3rd edn). Maidenhead: Open University Press.

Bleek, W. (1979). Envy and inequality in fieldwork: An example from Ghana. *Human Organisation, 38*(2), 200–205.

Bøås, M., Jennings, K. M., and Shaw, T. M. (2006). Dealing with conflicts and emergency situations. In V. Desai and R. Potter (eds), *Doing Development Research* (pp. 70–78). London: Sage.

Bochaton, A., and Lefebvre, B. (2011). Interviewing elites: Perspectives from the medical tourism sector in India and Thailand. In C. M. Hall (ed.), *Fieldwork in Tourism: Methods, Issues and Reflections* (pp. 70–80). London: Routledge.

Boden, R., Epstein, D., and Latimer, J. (2009). Accounting for ethos or programmes for conduct? The brave new world of research ethics committees. *The Sociological Review, 57*(4), 727–749.

Boesten, J. (2008). A relationship gone wrong? Research ethics, participation, and fieldwork realities. *NGPA Working Papers, 20*.

Bolton, R. (1995). Tricks, friends, and lovers: erotic encounters in the field. In D. Kulick and M. Willson (eds), *Taboo: Sex, Identity, and Erotic Subjectivity in Anthropological Fieldwork* (pp. 140–167). London: Routledge.

Bonnin, C. (2010). Navigating fieldwork politics, practicalities and ethics in the upland borderlands of northern Vietnam. *Asia Pacific Viewpoint, 51*(2), 179–192.

Booth, W. C., Colomb, G. G., and Williams, J. M. (2009). *The Craft of Research* (3rd edn). Chicago, IL: University of Chicago Press.

Bosk, C., and de Vries, R. (2004). Bureaucracies of mass deception: Institutional review boards and the ethics of ethnographic research. *Annals of the American Academy of Political and Social Science, 595*, 249–263.

Bowden, R. (1998). Children, power and participatory research in Uganda. In V. Johnson, E. Ivan-Smith, G. Gordon, P. Pridmore and P. Scott (eds), *Stepping Forward: Children and Young People's Participation in the Development Process* (pp. 281–283). London: Intermediate Technology.

Boyden, J., and Ennew, J. (1997). *Children in Focus: A Manual for Participatory Research with Children*. Stockholm: Radda Barnen, Swedish Save the Children.

Bradburd, D. (1998). *Being There: The Necessity of Fieldwork*. Washington, DC: Smithsonian Institution Press.

Brannen, J. (2005). Mixing methods: The entry of qualitative and quantitative approaches into the research process. *International Journal of Social Research Methodology, 8*(3), 173–184.

Briggs, C. (1986). *Learning How to Ask*. Cambridge: Cambridge University Press.

Briggs, J., and Sharp, J. (2004). Indigenous knowledges and development: A postcolonial caution. *Third World Quarterly, 25*(4), 661–676.

Brockington, D., and Sullivan, S. (2003). Doing qualitative research. In R. Scheyvens and D. Storey (eds), *Development Fieldwork: A Practical Guide* (pp. 57–72). London: Sage.

Brodsky, A. E., and Faryal, T. (2006). No matter how hard you try, your feet still get wet: Insider and outsider perspectives on bridging diversity. [Research Support, Non-U.S. Gov't]. *American Journal of Community Psychology, 37*(3–4), 311–320.

Brohman, J. (1995). Universalism, eurocentrism, and ideological bias in development studies: From modernisation to neoliberalism. *Third World Quarterly, 16*(1), 121–162.

Brown, S. (2009). Dilemmas of self-representation and conduct in the field. In C. L. Sriram, J. C. King, J. A. Mertus, O. Martin-Ortega and J. Herman (eds), *Surviving Field Research: Working in Violent and Difficult Situations* (pp. 213–226). Milton Park: Taylor and Francis.

Brydon, L. (2006). Ethical practices in doing development research. In V. Desai and R. Potter (eds), *Doing Development Research* (pp. 25–33). London: Sage.

Bryman, A. E., and Burgess, R. G. (eds) (1999). *Qualitative Research*. London: Sage.

Bryman, A. E., and Cramer, D. (1995). *Quantitative Data Analysis for Social Scientist*. London: Routledge.

Buchanan, E. A. (2011). Internet research ethics: Past, present and future. In M. Consalvo and C. Ess (eds), *The Handbook of Internet Studies* (pp. 83–108). Chichester: Blackwell.

Bujra, J. (2006). Lost in translation? The use of interpreters in fieldwork. In V. Desai and R. Potter (eds), *Doing Development Research* (pp. 172–179). London: Sage.

Bulmer, M. (1993). General introduction. In M. Bulmer and D. P. Warwick (eds), *Social Research in Developing Countries: Surveys and Censuses in the Third World* (pp. 3–24). London: UCL Press.

Bulmer, M. (2001). The ethics of social research. In N. Gilbert (ed.), *Researching Social Life*. (2nd edn) (pp.45–57). London: Sage.

Burford, J. (2010). *(The) margin(s) speak! A multifaceted examination of practising 'men who have sex with men' development in Bangkok.* (Unpublished master's thesis), Victoria University, Wellington, New Zealand.

Burgess, R. G. (ed.) (1982). *Field Research: A Sourcebook and Field Manual*. London: George Allen and Unwin.

Burrell, J. (2009). The field site as a network: A strategy for locating ethnographic research. *Field Methods, 21*(2), 181–199.

Butler, B., and Michalski Turner, D. (eds). (1987). *Children and Anthropological Research*. New York: Plenum Press.

Butler, R. (2001). From where I write: The place of positionality in qualitative writing. In M. Limb and C. Dwyer (eds), *Qualitative Methodologies for Geographers: Issues and Debates* (pp. 264–278). London: Arnold.

Cameron, E. (2010). *Social development outcomes of participation in the New Zealand recognised seasonal employer (RSE) scheme for ni-Vanuatu seasonal migrant workers.* (Unpublished master's thesis), Massey University, Palmerston North, New Zealand.

Cameron, J., and Gibson, K. (2001). *Shifting Focus: Pathways to Community and Economic Development: A Resource Kit*. Retrieved 15 May 2013 from www.communityeconomics. org/info.html#action.

Cameron, J., and Gibson, K. (2005). Participatory action research in a poststructuralist vein. *Geoforum, 36*(3), 315–331.

Cannon, J. (2002). *Men at work: Expatriation in the international mining industry.* (Unpublished doctoral thesis), Monash University, Melbourne, Australia.

Caputo, V. (2000). At 'home' and 'away': Reconfiguring the field for late twentieth-century anthropology. In V. Amit (ed.), *Constructing the Field: Ethnographic Fieldwork in the Contemporary World* (pp. 19–31). London: Routledge.

Carlson, A., and Duan, H. (2010). Internet resources and the study of Chinese foreign relations: Can cyberspace shed new light on China's approach to the world? In A. Carlson, M. E. Gallagher, K. Lieberthal and M. Manion (eds), *Contemporary Chinese Politics: New Sources, Methods, and Field Strategies* (pp. 88–106). Cambridge: Cambridge University Press.

Carmichael, T. (2006). Bureaucratic literacy, oral testimonies, and the study of twentieth-century Ethiopian history. *Journal of African Cultural Studies, 18*(1), 23–42.

Casey, C. (2001). Ethics committees, institutions and organisations: Subjectivity, consent and risk. In M. Tolich (ed.), *Research Ethics in Aotearoa New Zealand: Concepts, Practice, Critique* (pp. 127–140). Harlow: Longman.

Cassell, J. (ed.) (1987). *Children in the Field: Anthropological Experiences*. Philadelphia, PA: Temple University Press.

Cassell, J. (1988). The relationship of observer to observed when studying up. In R. G. Burgess (ed.), *Studies in Qualitative Methodology* (pp. 89–108). Greenwich, CT: JAI Press.

Caws, P. (1989). The law of quality and quantity, or what numbers can and can't describe. In B. Glassner and J. D. Moreno (eds), *The Qualitative-Quantitative Distinction in the Social Sciences* (pp. 13–28). Dordrecht: Kluwer.

Cernea, M. (1982). Indigenous anthropologists and development-oriented research. In H. Famim (ed.), *Indigenous Anthropology in Non-Western Countries* (pp. 121–137). Durham, NC: Carolina Academic Press.

Chacko, E. (2004). Positionality and praxis: Fieldwork experiences in rural India. *Singapore Journal of Tropical Geography, 25*(1), 51–63.

Chambers, R. (1983). *Rural Development: Putting the Last First*. Harlow: Longman.

Chambers, R. (1994a). The origins and practice of participatory rural appraisal. *World Development, 22*(7), 953–969.

Chambers, R. (1994b). Participatory rural appraisal (PRA): Analysis of experience. *World Development, 22*(9), 1253–1268.

Chambers, R. (1997). *Whose Reality Counts?: Putting the First Last*. London: Intermediate Technology.

Chambers, R. (2008). *Revolutions in Development Inquiry*. London: Earthscan.

Chatterton, P., Fuller, D., and Routledge, P. (2007). Relating action to activism: Theoretical and methodological reflections. In S. L. Kindon, R. Pain and M. Kesby (eds), *Participatory Action Research Approaches and Methods: Connecting People, Participation, and Place* (pp. 216–230). Milton Park: Routledge.

Cheek, J. (2005). The politics and practices of funding qualitative inquiry: Messages about messages about messages ... In N. K. Denzin and Y. S. Lincoln (eds), *The SAGE Handbook of Qualitative Research* (3rd edn, pp. 387–412). Thousand Oaks, CA: Sage.

Cheek, J. (2011). The politics and practices of funding qualitative inquiry: Messages about messages about messages ... In N. K. Denzin and Y. S. Lincoln (eds), *The SAGE Handbook of Qualitative Research* (4th edn, pp. 251–268). Thousand Oaks, CA: Sage.

Chok, S. (2012). The visible/invisible researcher: Ethics and politically sensitive research. In C. M. Hall (ed.), *Fieldwork in Tourism: Methods, Issues and Reflections* (pp. 55–69). London: Routledge.

Chung, M. (1991). *Politics, tradition and structural change: Fijian fertility in the twentieth century*. (Unpublished doctoral thesis), Australian National University, Canberra, Australia.

Clarke, M. (1975). Survival in the field: Implications of personal experience in the field. *Theory and Society, 2*, 95–123.

Clifford, J. (1997). *Routes: Travel and Translation in the Late Twentieth Century*. Cambridge: Harvard University Press.

Clifford, J., and Marcus, G. E. (eds) (2010). *Writing Culture: The Poetics and Politics of Ethnography* (25th anniversary edn). Berkeley, CA: University of California Press.

Cohen-Mitchell, J. B. (2000). Disabled women in El Salvador reframing themselves: An economic development program for women. In C. Truman, D. M. Mertens and B. Humphries (eds), *Research and Inequality* (pp. 143–175). London: UCL Press.

Coleman, S., and Collins, P. (2006). *Locating the Field: Space, Place and Context in Anthropology*. Oxford: Berg.

Conti, J. A., and O'Neil, M. (2007). Studying power: Qualitative methods and the global elite. *Qualitative Research, 7*(1), 63–82.

Cook, I. (2001). You want to be careful you don't end up like Ian. He's all over the place: Autobiography of/in an expanded field. In P. Moss (ed.), *Placing Autobiography in Geography* (pp. 99–120). Syracuse, NY: Syracuse University Press.

Cook, M. (2006). Professional ethics and practice in archives and records management in a human rights context. *Journal of the Society of Archivists, 27*(1), 1–15.

Cooke, B., and Kothari, U. (2001). *Participation: The New Tyranny?* New York: Zed.

Corbridge, S. (1998). Development ethics: Distance, difference, plausibility. *Ethics, Place and Environment, 1*(1), 35–53.

Corbridge, S. (2000). Development geographies. In P. J. Cloke, P. Crang and M. Goodwin (eds), *Introducing Human Geographies* (2nd edn, pp. 67–75). London: Arnold.

Corbridge, S., and Mawdsley, E. (2003). Special issue: Fieldwork in the 'tropics': Power, knowledge and practice. *Singapore Journal of Tropical Geography, 24*(2).

Cormode, L., and Hughes, A. (1999). The economic geographer as situated researcher of elites. *Special issue of Geoforum, 30*, 299–300.

Cornet, C. (2010). Fieldwork among the Dong national minority in Guizhou, China: Practicalities, obstacles and challenges. *Asia Pacific Viewpoint, 51*(2), 135–147.

Cornwall, A. (ed.) (2008). *The Participation Reader*. London: Zed.

Cornwall, A., and Pratt, G. (2011). The use and abuse of participatory rural appraisal: reflections from practice. *Agriculture and Human Values, 82*(2), 263–272.

Cotterill, P. (1992). Interviewing women: Issues of friendship, vulnerability, and power. *Women's Studies International Forum, 10*(5 and 6), 593–606.

Counts, A. M. (1996). *Give Us Credit: How Small Loans Today can Shape our Tomorrow*. New Delhi: Research Press.

Cowen, M., and Shenton, R. (1996). *Doctrines of Development*. London: Routledge.

Cram, F. (2001). Rangahau Māori: Tona tika, tona pono – The validity and integrity of Māori research. In M. Tolich (ed.), *Research Ethics in Aotearoa New Zealand* (pp. 35–52). Auckland: Pearson Education.

Crang, M., and Cook, I. (2007). *Doing Ethnographies*. Los Angeles, CA: Sage.

Creswell, J. W. (1998). *Qualitative Inquiry and Research Design: Choosing Among Five Traditions*. Thousand Oaks, CA: Sage.

Creswell, J. W. (2008). *Research Design: Qualitative, Quantitative, and Mixed Methods Approaches*. London: Sage.

Creswell, J. W. (2011). Controversies in mixed methods research. In N. K. Denzin and Y. S. Lincoln (eds), *The SAGE Handbook of Qualitative Research* (4th edn, pp. 269–283). Thousand Oaks, CA: Sage.

Cross, N., and Barker, R. (eds) (1991). *At the Desert's Edge: Oral Histories from the Sahel*. London: Panos.

Cupples, J. (2002a). *Disrupting discourses and (re)formulating identities: The politics of single motherhood in post-revolutionary Nicaragua*. (Unpublished PhD thesis), Canterbury University, Christchurch, New Zealand.

Cupples, J. (2002b). The field as a landscape of desire: Sex and sexuality in geographical fieldwork. *Area, 34*(4), 382–390.

Cupples, J., and Kindon, S. L. (2003). Far from being 'home alone': The dynamics of accompanied fieldwork. *Singapore Journal of Tropical Geography, 24*(2), 211–228.

Da Corta, L., and Venkateshwarlu, D. (1992). Field methods for economic mobility. In S. Devereux and J. Hoddinott (eds), *Fieldwork in Developing Countries* (pp. 102–123). New York: Harvester Wheatsheaf.

Darwin, J. (1999). Decolonization and the end of empire. In R. W. Winks (ed.), *The Oxford History of the British Empire. Historiography* (Vol. V, pp. 541–557). Oxford: Oxford University Press.

Daviau, S. (2010). Conducting fieldwork with Tarieng communities in southern Laos: Negotiating discursive spaces between neoliberal dogmas and Lao socialist ideology. *Asia Pacific Viewpoint, 51*(2), 193–205.

David, M., and Sutton, C. D. (2011). *Social Research: An Introduction* (2nd edn). London: Sage.

Davies, J. (2010). Disorientation, dissonance and altered perception in the field. In J. Davies and D. Spencer (eds), *Emotions in the Field: The Psychology and Anthropology of Fieldwork Experience* (pp. 79–97). Stanford, CA: Stanford University Press.

de Laine, M. (2000). *Fieldwork, Participation and Practice: Ethics and Dilemmas in Qualitative Research*. Thousand Oaks, CA: Sage.

de Vaus, D. A. (2002). *Surveys in Social Research* (5th edn). St. Leonards: Allen and Unwin.

Dear, M. (1988). The postmodern challenge: Reconstructing human geography. *Transactions of the Institute of British Geographers, 13*(3), 262–274.

DeLyser, D. (2010). Writing qualitative geography. In D. DeLyser, S. Herbert, S. C. Aitken, M. Crang and L. McDowell (eds), *The SAGE Handbook of Qualitative Geography* (pp. 341–358). London: Sage.

Denscombe, M. (2010). *The Good Research Guide: For Small-Scale Social Research Projects* (4th edn). Maidenhead: McGraw-Hill/Open University Press.

Denzin, N. K. (1997). *Interpretive Ethnography: Ethnographic Practices for the 21st Century*. Thousand Oaks, CA: Sage.

Denzin, N. K., and Lincoln, Y. S. (2011). Introduction: The discipline and practice of qualitative research. In N. K. Denzin and Y. S. Lincoln (eds), *The SAGE Handbook of Qualitative Research* (4th edn, pp. 1–19). Thousand Oaks, CA: Sage.

Denzin, N. K., Lincoln, Y. S., and Smith, L. T. (eds) (2008). *Handbook of Critical and Indigenous Methodologies*. London: Sage.

Desai, V., and Potter, R. (eds) (2006). *Doing Development Research*. London: Sage.

Desai, V., Elmhirst, B., Lemanski, C., Mawdsley, E., Meth, P., Oldfield, J., Page, B., Souch, C., Williams, G., and Willis, K. (2008). *Doing Development/Global South Dissertations: A Guide for Undergraduates*. Retrieved 14 July 2013 from www.gg.rhul.ac.uk/DARG/DARG%20dissertation%20booklet.pdf.

Desmond, M. (2004). Methodological challenges posed in studying an elite in the field. *Area, 36*(3), 262–269.

Devereux, S. (1992). 'Observers are worried': Learning the language and counting the people in northeast Ghana. In S. Devereux and J. Hoddinott (eds), *Fieldwork in Developing Countries* (pp. 43–56). New York: Harvester Wheatsheaf.

Devereux, S., and Hoddinott, J. (1992) The context of fieldwork. In S. Devereux and J. Hoddinott (eds), *Fieldwork in Developing Countries* (pp. 3–24). New York: Harvester Wheatsheaf.

Devereux, S., and Hoddinott, J. (eds) (1992). *Fieldwork in Developing Countries*. New York: Harvester Wheatsheaf.

DeVita, P. R. (ed.) (1990). *The Humbled Anthropologist*. Belmont, CA: Wadsworth.

DeVita, P. R. (ed.) (2000). *Stumbling Toward Truth: Anthropologists at Work*. Prospect Heights, IL: Waveland Press.

Diamant, N. J. (2010). Why archives. In A. Carlson, M. E. Gallagher, K. Lieberthal and M. Manion (eds), *Contemporary Chinese Politics: New Sources, Methods, and Field Strategies* (pp. 33–50). Cambridge: Cambridge University Press.

Dockery, G. (2000). Participatory research: Whose roles, whose responsibilities? In C. Truman, D. M. Mertens and B. Humphries (eds), *Research and Inequality* (pp. 95–125). London: UCL Press.

dos Santos, T. (1970). *Dependencia Y Cambio Social*. Santiago: Centro de Estudios Socio Economicos Universidad de Chile.

Doucet, A. and Mauthner, N. (2002). Knowing responsibly: ethics, feminist epistemologies and methodologies. In M. Mauthner, M. Birch, J. Jessop and T. Miller (eds), *Ethics in Qualitative Research* (pp. 123–145). London: Sage.

Dowling, R. (2000). Power, subjectivity and ethics in qualitative research. In I. Hay (ed.), *Qualitative Research Methods in Human Geography* (pp. 22–36). Melbourne: Oxford University Press.

Drybread, K. (2006). Sleeping with one eye open: The perils of fieldwork in a Brazilian juvenile prison. In A. Gardner and D. M. Hoffman (eds), *Dispatches from the Field: Neophyte Ethnographers in a Changing World* (pp. 33–52). Long Grove, IL: Waveland Press.

Duval, D. T. (2011). Managing post-fieldwork interpersonal relationships. In C. M. Hall (ed.), *Fieldwork in Tourism: Methods, Issues and Reflections* (pp. 208–318). London: Routledge.

Dyson, L. (2011). Indigenous people on the Internet. In M. Consalvo and C. Ess (eds), *The Handbook of Internet Studies* (pp. 251–269). Chichester: Blackwell.

Edwards, M. (1989). The irrelevance of Development Studies. *Third World Quarterly, 11*(1), 116–135.

Eklund, L. (2010). Cadres as gatekeepers: The art of opening the right doors? In G. S. Szarycz (ed.), *Research Realities in the Social Sciences: Negotiating Fieldwork Dilemmas* (pp. 129–147). Amherst, NY: Cambria Press.

Ellen, R. F. (1984). *Ethnographic Research: A Guide to General Conduct*. London: Academic Press.

Elwood, S. (2010). Mixed methods: Thinking, doing and asking in multiple ways. In D. DeLyser, S. Herbert, S. C. Aitken, M. Crang and L. McDowell (eds), *The SAGE Handbook of Qualitative Geography* (pp. 94–120). London: Sage.

Emerson, R. M., Fretz, R., and Shaw, L. L. (1995). *Writing Ethnographic Fieldnotes*. Chicago, IL: University of Chicago Press.

England, K. V. L. (1994). Getting personal: Reflexivity, positionality, and feminist research. *The Professional Geographer, 46*(1), 80–89.

Epprecht, M. (2004). Work-study abroad courses in international development studies: Some ethical and pedagogical issues. *Canadian Journal of Development Studies/Revue Canadienne D'études du Développement, 25*(4), 687–706.

Escobar, A. (2012). *Encountering Development: The Making and Unmaking of the Third World*. Princeton, NJ: Princeton University Press.

Esteva, G. (1992). Development. In W. Sachs (ed.), *The Development Dictionary: A Guide to Knowledge as Power* (pp. 6–25). London: Zed.

Evans, M. (2010). *Feeling their way: Four men talk about fatherhood in Valparaiso, Chile.* (Unpublished master's thesis), Victoria University, Wellington, New Zealand.

Evans, R., and Becker, S. (2009). *Children Caring for Parents with HIV and AIDS: Global Issues and Policy Responses*. Bristol: The Policy Press.

Falconer Al-Hindi, K. (2001). Do you get it? Feminism and quantitative geography. *Environment and Planning D: Society and Space, 19*(5), 505–509.

Falconer Al-Hindi, K., and Kawabata, H. (2002). Towards a more fully reflexive feminist geography. In P. Moss (ed.), *Feminist Geography in Practice: Research and Methods* (pp. 103–115). Oxford: Wiley.

Falzone, M. A. (2009). Introduction. In M. A. Falzone (ed.), *Multi-Sited Ethnography: Theory, Praxis and Locality in Contemporary Research* (pp. 1–24). Farnham: Ashgate.

Farrelly, T. (2009). *Business va'avanua: Cultural hybridisation and indigenous entrepreneurship in the Boumā National Heritage Park, Fiji.* (Unpublished doctoral thesis), Massey University, Palmerston North, New Zealand.

Fife, W. (2005). *Doing Fieldwork: Ethnographic Methods for Research in Developing Countries and Beyond.* New York: Palgrave Macmillan.

Findlay, A. M. (2006). The importance of census and other secondary data in development studies. In V. Desai and R. Potter (eds), *Doing Development Research* (pp. 262–272). London: Sage.

Finnegan, R. (2006). Using documents. In R. Sapsford and V. Jupp (eds), *Data Collection and Analysis.* London: Sage.

Fisher, S. (2011). Knock, knock, knocking on closed doors: Exploring the diffuse ideal of the collaborative research relationship. *Area, 43*(4), 456–462.

Fitri, R. (2006). *Informal finance and poverty alleviation: A grassroots study of small farmers' credit in West Sumatra, Indonesia.* (Unpublished master's thesis), Massey University, Palmerston North, New Zealand.

Flicker, S., Haans, D., and Skinner, H. (2004). Ethical dilemmas in research on Internet communities. *Qualitative Health Research, 14*(1), 124–134.

Flinn, A. (2007). Community histories, community archives: Some opportunities and challenges. *Journal of the Society of Archivists, 28*(2), 151–176.

Flinn, J. (1990). Reflections of a shy ethnographer: Foot-in-the-mouth is not fatal. In P. R. DeVita (ed.), *The Humbled Anthropologist* (pp. 46–52). Belmont, CA: Wadsworth.

Flinn, J., Marshall, L., and Armstrong, J. (eds) (1998). *Fieldwork and Families: Constructing New Models for Ethnographic Research.* Honolulu, HI: University of Hawaii Press.

Fontes, L. A. (1998). Ethics in family violence research: Cross-cultural issues. *Family Relations, 47*(1), 53–61.

Fotheringham, A. S. (2006). Quantification, evidence and positivism. In S. C. Aitken and G. Valentine (eds), *Approaches to Human Geography* (pp. 237–249). London: Sage.

Francis, E. (1992). Qualitative research: Collecting life histories. In S. Devereux and J. Hoddinott (eds), *Fieldwork in Developing Countries* (pp. 86–101). Boulder, CO: Lynne Rienner.

Francis, P. (2001). Participatory development at the World Bank: The primary of process. In B. Cooke and U. Kothari (eds), *Participation: The New Tyranny?* (pp. 72–87). New York: Zed.

Frank, A. G. (1967). *Capitalism and Underdevelopment in Latin America: Historical Studies of Chile and Brazil.* New York: Monthy Review Press.

Frankfort-Nachmias, C., and Nachmias, D. (2008). *Research Methods in the Social Sciences.* New York: Worth.

Freeman-Grenville, G. S. P. (1962). *The Medieval History of the Coast of Tangajika, with Special Reference to Recent Archeological Discoveries.* London: Oxford University Press.

Friere, P. (1972). *Pedagogy of the Oppressed* (trans. Myra man). Harmondsworth: Penguin.

Fuimaono, R. S. (2012). *The asset-based community development (ABCD) approach in action: An analysis of the work of two NGOs in Samoa.* (Unpublished master's thesis), Massey University, Palmerston North, New Zealand.

Gaiser, T. J., and Schreiner, A. E. (2009). *A Guide to Conducting Online Research.* London: Sage.

Gallaher, C. (2011). Leaving the field. In V. J. Del Casino, M. E. Thomas and P. J. Cloke (eds), *A Companion to Social Geography* (pp. 181–197). Malden, MA: Wiley.

Gallmeier, C. (1991). Leaving, revisiting and staying in touch: Neglected issues in field research. In W. Shaffir and R. A. Stebbins (eds), *Experiencing Fieldwork: An Inside View of Qualitative Research* (pp. 224–231). Newbury Park, CA: Sage.

Gardner, A., and Hoffman, D. M. (eds). (2006). *Dispatches from the Field: Neophyte Ethnographers in a Changing World*. Long Grove, IL: Waveland Press.

Gaskell, J., and Eichler, M. (2001). White women as burden: On playing the role of feminist 'experts' in China. *Women's Studies International Forum, 24*(6), 637–651.

Gaw, K. F. (2000). Reverse culture shock in students returning from overseas. *International Journal of Intercultural Relations, 24*(1), 83–104.

Gazit, N., and Maoz-Shai, Y. (2010). Studying-up and studying-across: At-home research of governmental violence organizations. *Qualitative Sociology, 33*(3), 275–295.

Gearing, J. (1995). Fear and loving in the West Indies: Research from the heart (as well as the head). In D. Kulick and M. Willson (eds), *Taboo: Sex, Identity, and Erotic Subjectivity in Anthropological Fieldwork* (pp. 168–218). London: Routledge.

Gee, J., and Handford, M. (2011). *The Routledge Handbook of Discourse Analysis*. London: Routledge.

Geertz, C. (1988). *Works and Lives: The Anthropologist as Author*. Cambridge: Polity Press.

Gerber, D. A. (2005). Acts of deceiving and withholding in immigrant letters: Personal identity and self-presentation in personal correspondence. *Journal of Social History, 39*(2), 315–330.

Gibson-Graham, J. K. (2005). Surplus possibilities: Postdevelopment and community economies. *Singapore Journal of Tropical Geography, 26*(1), 4–26.

Giddens, A. (1984). *The Constitution of Society: Outline of the Theory of Structuration*. Cambridge: Polity Press.

Gill, R. (2000). Discourse analysis. In M. W. Bauer and G. D. Gaskell (eds), *Qualitative Research with Text Image and Sound: A Practical Handbook* (pp. 172–190). London: Sage.

Gill, S. (2010). The homecoming: An investigation into the effect that studying overseas had on Chinese postgraduates' life and work on their return to China. *Compare: A Journal of Comparative and International Education, 40*(3), 359–376.

Glaser, B. G., and Strauss, A. L. (2007). *Time for Dying*. Chicago, IL: Aldine Transaction.

Gleisberg, K. (2008). Cultivating fields of knowledge: The problem of knowledge transfer in field research on land use in Burkina Faso. In P. P. Mollinga and C. R. L. Wall (eds), *Fieldwork in Difficult Environments* (pp. 69–82). Zurich: Lit.

Goin, P. (2001). Visual literacy. *Geographical Review, 91*(1–2), 363–369.

Goldade, K. (2006). Pangs of guilt: Transnational ethnography, motherhood and moral dilemmas in Central America. In A. Gardner and D. M. Hoffman (eds), *Dispatches from the Field: Neophyte Ethnographers in a Changing World* (pp. 53–67). Long Grove, IL: Waveland Press.

Goodman, M. J. (1985). Introduction. In M. J. Goodman (ed.), *Women in Asia and the Pacific: Towards an East-West Dialogue* (pp. 1–18). Honolulu, HI: University of Hawaii, Women's Studies Program.

Gordon, G. (1998). Introduction (Part 3). In V. Johnson, E. Ivan-Smith, G. Gordon, P. Pridmore and P. Scott (eds), *Stepping Forward: Children and Young People's Participation in the Development Process* (pp. 66–68). London: Intermediate Technology.

Gottfried, H. (1996). *Feminism and Social Change: Bridging Theory and Practice*. Champaign, IL: University of Illinois Pressgrant.

Goward, N. (1984). Publications on fieldwork experience. In R. F. Ellen (ed.), *Ethnographic Research: A Guide to General Conduct* (pp. 88–100). London: Academic Press.

Graham, E. (2005). Philosophies underlying human geography research. In R. Flowerdew and D. J. Martin (eds), *Methods in Human Geography: A Guide for Students Doing a Research Project* (2nd edn, pp. 8–34). Harlow: Pearson Education.

Grant, L., Ward, K. B., and Rong, X. L. (1987). Is there an association between gender and methods in sociological research? *American Sociological Review, 52*(6), 856–862.

Grodzinsky, F. S., and Tavani, H. T. (2010). Applying the 'contextual integrity' model of privacy to personal blogs in the blogosphere. *International Journal of Internet Research Ethics, 3*(1), 38–47.

Gros, S. (2010). A heuristic blunder: Notes on an ethnographic situation in southwest China. *Asia Pacific Viewpoint, 51*(2), 148–163.

Gula, R. M. (1998). *Reason Informed by Faith*. New York: Paulist Press.

Gupta, A., and Ferguson, J. (1997). Discipline and practice: 'The field' as site, method, and location in anthropology. In A. Gupta and J. Ferguson (eds), *Anthropological Locations: Boundaries and Grounds of a Field Science* (pp. 1–46). Berkeley, CA: University of California Press.

Haanstad, E. J. (2006). The other city of angels: Ethnography with the Bangkok police. In A. Gardner and D. M. Hoffman (eds), *Dispatches from the Field: Neophyte Ethnographers in a Changing World* (pp. 223–235). Long Grove, IL: Waveland Press.

Habermas, J. (1978). *Knowledge and Human Interests*. London: Heinemann.

Hadjor, K. B. (1992). *Dictionary of Third World Terms*. London: Penguin.

Haer, R., and Becher, I. (2012). A methodological note on quantitative field research in conflict zones: Get your hands dirty. *International Journal of Social Research Methodology, 15*(1), 1–13.

Hage, G. (2010). Hating Israel in the field: On ethnography and political emotions. In J. Davies and D. Spencer (eds), *Emotions in the Field: The Psychology and Anthropology of Fieldwork Experience* (pp. 129–154). Stanford, CA: Stanford University Press.

Hales, J. (2008). Negotiating tensions and roles in international development: A workshop for graduate students. *Canadian and International Education/Education canadienne et internationale, 37*(2).

Hall, B. (1992). From margins to center? The development and purpose of participatory research. *The American Sociologist, 23*: 15–28.

Hall, C. M. (2011a). Fieldwork in tourism/touring fields: Where does tourism end and fieldwork begin? In C. M. Hall (ed.), *Fieldwork in Tourism: Methods, Issues and Reflections* (pp. 8–18). London: Routledge.

Hall, C. M. (2011b). In cyberspace can anybody hear you scream?: Issues in the conduct of online fieldwork. In C. M. Hall (ed.), *Fieldwork in Tourism: Methods, Issues and Reflections* (pp. 266–288). London: Routledge.

Hall, S. M. (2009). 'Private life' and 'work life': Difficulties and dilemmas when making and maintaining friendships with ethnographic participants. *Area, 41*(3), 263–272.

Halter, S. (2010). Gaining access to police agencies and records: Trials and tribulations from the field. In G. S. Szarycz (ed.), *Research Realities in the Social Sciences: Negotiating Fieldwork Dilemmas* (pp. 111–128). Amherst, NY: Cambria Press.

Hammersley, M. (2009). Against the ethicists: On the evils of ethical regulation. *International Journal of Social Research Methodology, 12*(3), 211–225.

Hammersley, M., and Atkinson, P. (2007). *Ethnography: Principles in Practice* (3rd edn). London: Routledge.

Hammond, J. (1990). Cultural baggage. In P. R. DeVita (ed.), *The Humbled Anthropologist* (pp. 61–68). Belmont, CA: Wadsworth.

Hannerz, U. (2012). Being there … and there … and there! Reflections on multi-site ethnography. In A. C. G. M. Robben and J. A. Sluka (eds), *Ethnographic Fieldwork: An Anthropological Reader* (pp. 399–408). Malden, MA: Blackwell.

Haque, M. (1998). Understanding with children: Coping with floods in Bangladesh. In V. Johnson, E. Ivan-Smith, G. Gordon, P. Pridmore and P. Scott (eds), *Stepping Forward: Children and Young People's Participation in the Development Process* (pp. 76–78). London: Intermediate Technology.

Harriss, J. (2005). Great promise, hubris and recovery: A participant's history of development studies. In U. Kothari (ed.), *A Radical Distory of Development Studies: Individuals, Institutions and Ideologies* (pp. 17–46). New York: Zed.

Hart, M. A. (2010). Indigenous worldviews, knowledge, and research: The development of an indigenous research paradigm. *Journal of Indigenous Voices in Social Work, 1*(1), 1–16.

Hays-Mitchell, M. (2001). Danger, fulfilment and responsibility in a violence-plagued society. *Geographical Review, 91*(1–2), 311–321.

Heggenhougen, K. I. P. R. D. E. (2000). The inseperability of reason and emotion in the anthropological perspective: Perceptions upon leaving 'the field'. In P. DeVita (ed.), *Stumbling Toward Truth: Anthropologists at Work* (pp. 264–272). Prospect Heights, IL: Waveland Press.

Heller, E., Christensen, J., Long, L., Mackenzie, C. A., Osano, P. M., Ricker, B., Kagan, E., and Turner, S. (2011). Dear diary: Early career geographers collectively reflect on their qualitative field research experiences. *Journal of Geography in Higher Education, 35*(1), 67–83.

Henry, M., Higate, P., and Sanghera, G. (2009). Positionality and power: The politics of peacekeeping research. *International Peacekeeping, 16*(4), 467–482.

Herod, A. (1999). Reflections on interviewing foreign elites: Praxis, positionality, validity and the cult of the insider. *Geoforum, 30*, 313–327.

Hertel, S., Singer, M. M., and Van Cott, D. L. (2009). Field research in developing countries: Hitting the road running. *PS: Political Science and Politics, 42*(02), 305.

Hertz, R., and Imber, J. B. (1993). Fieldwork in elite settings. *Journal of Contemporary Ethnography, Special Edition, 22*, 3–6.

Hesse-Biber, S. N., and Leavy, P. (2010). *The Practice of Qualitative Research*. London: Sage.

Heyer, J. (1992). Contrasts in village-level fieldwork: Kenya and India. In S. Devereux and J. Hoddinott (eds), *Fieldwork in Developing Countries* (pp. 200–216). New York: Harvester Wheatsheaf.

Heywood, A. E., Zhang, M., Macintyre, C. R., and Seale, H. (2012). Travel risk behaviours and uptake of pre-travel health preventions by university students in Australia. *BMC Infectious Diseases, 12*(1), 43.

Hitchcock, P. (1987). 'Our Ulleri child'. In J. Cassell (ed.), *Children in the Field: Anthropological Experiences* (pp. 173–183). Philadelphia, PA: Temple University Press.

Hoepfl, M. (1997). Choosing qualitative research: A primer for technology education researchers. *Journal of Technology Education, 9*(1), 47–63.

Hoffman, D. M. (2006). Swimming through fieldwork: Constructing trust in the Mexican Caribbean. In A. Gardner and D. M. Hoffman (eds), *Dispatches from the Field: Neophyte Ethnographers in a Changing World* (pp. 33–52). Long Grove, IL: Waveland Press.

Holland, J., and Campbell, J. (2005). *Methods in Development Research: Combining Qualitative and Quantitative Approaches*. Cambridge: ITDG.

hooks, b. (1990). *Talking Back: Thinking Feminist, Thinking Black*. Boston, MA: South End.

Hookway, N. (2008). 'Entering the blogosphere': Some strategies for using blogs in social research. *Qualitative Research, 8*(1), 91–113.

Howell, C. (2001). A cupboard of surprises: Working in the archives of the Church of Uganda. *History in Africa, 28*, 411–415.

Howell, N. (1990). *Surviving Fieldwork: A Report of the Advisory Panel on Health and Safety in Fieldwork. A Special Report of American Anthropological Association, Number 26.* Washington, DC: American Anthropological Association.

Howell, N. (2007). *Surviving Fieldwork: A Report of the Advisory Panel on Health and Safety in Fieldwork*. Washington, DC: American Anthropological Association.

Hubbell, L. D. (2010). False starts, suspicious interviewees and nearly impossible tasks: Some reflections on the difficulty of conducting field research abroad. In G. S. Szarycz (ed.), *Research Realities in the Social Sciences: Negotiating Fieldwork Dilemmas* (pp. 325–348). Amherst, NY: Cambria Press.

Huesca, R. (2013). *How Facebook can ruin study abroad*. Retrieved 14 January 2013 from http://chronicle.com/article/How-Facebook-Can-Ruin-Study/136633/.

Hugh-Jones, C. (1987). Children in the Amazon. In J. Cassell (ed.), *Children in the Field: Anthropological Experiences* (pp. 27–63). Philadelphia, PA: Temple University Press.

Huisman, K. (2008). Does this mean you're not going to come visit me anymore?: An inquiry into an ethics of reciprocity and positionality in feminist ethnographic research. *Sociological Inquiry, 78*(3), 372–396.

Humphries, B., Mertens, D. M., and Truman, C. (2000). Arguments for an 'emancipatory' research paradigm. In C. Truman, D. M. Mertens and B. Humphries (eds), *Research and Inequality* (pp. 3–23). London: UCL Press.

Hyndman, J. (2001). The field as here and now, not there and then. *Geographical Review, 91*(1–2), 262–272.

Iarossi, G. (2006). *The Power of Survey Design: A User's Guide for Managing Surveys, Interpreting Results, and Influencing Respondents*. Washington, DC: World Bank.

Ingold, T., and Vergunst, J. L. (2008). *Ways of Walking*. Aldershot: Ashgate.

Irwin, R. (2007). Culture shock: Negotiating feelings in the field. *Anthropology Matters, 9*(1).

Ite, U. (1997). Home, abroad, home: the challenges of postgraduate fieldwork at home. In E. Robson and K. Willis (eds) *Postgraduate Fieldwork in Developing Countries*. Monograph No.9 (pp.75–84). London: Developing Areas Research Group, (RGS-IBG).

Iversen, R. R. (2009). 'Getting out' in ethnography: A seldom-told story. *Qualitative Social Work, 8*(1), 9–26.

Janetzko, D. (2008). Nonreactive data collection on the Internet. In N. Fielding, R. M. Lee and G. Blank (eds), *The SAGE Handbook of Online Research Methods* (pp. 161–174). London: Sage.

Jenkins, K. (2007). Feminist methodologies: Unsettling multiple boundaries in development. In M. Smith (ed.), *Negotiating Boundaries and Borders: Qualitative Methodology and Development Research* (pp. 83–103). Amsterdam: Elsevier.

Jennings, M. (2006). Using archives. In V. Desai and R. Potter (eds), *Doing Development Research* (pp. 241–250). London: Sage.

Johnson, V., Hill, J., and Ivan-Smith, E. (1995). *Listening to Smaller Voices: Children in an Environment of Change*. Johannesburg: ActionAid.

Johnston, R. J., and Sidaway, J. D. (2010). *Geography and Geographers: Anglo-American Human Geography Since 1945* (7th edn). London: Hodder Education.

Jones, E. L. (1983). The courtesy bias in South-east Asian surveys. In M. Bulmer and D. P. Warwick (eds), *Social Research in Developing Countries* (pp. 253–259). London: Wiley.

Kanwat, M., and Kumar, S. (2011). *Participatory Rural Appraisal: Tools and Techniques*. Udaipur: Agrotech Publishing Academy.

Kapoor, I. (2004). Hyper-self-reflexive development? Spivak on representing the third world 'other'. *Third World Quarterly, 25*(4), 627–647.

Karpf, D. (2012). Social science research methods in Internet time. *Information, Communication and Society, 15*(5), 639–661.

Karra, N., and Phillips, N. (2008). Researching 'back home': International management research as autoethnography. *Organizational Research Methods, 11*(3), 541–561.

Katz, C. (1992). All the world is staged: Intellectuals and the projects of ethnography. *Environment and Planning D: Society and Space, 10*(5), 495–510.

Katz, C. (1994). Playing the field: Questions of fieldwork in geography. *Professional Geographer, 46*(1), 65–72.

Keesing, R. (1985). Kwaio women speak: The micropolitics of autobiography in a Solomon Islands society. *American Anthropologist, 87*(1), 27–39.

Keighren, I. M., and Withers, C. W. J. (2011). Questions of inscription and epistemology in British travelers' accounts of early nineteenth-century South America. *Annals of the Association of American Geographers, 101*(6), 1331–1346.

Kellett, M. (2009). *Rethinking Children and Research.* New York: Continuum.

Kendall, K. E., Kendall, J. E., and Kah, M. M. O. (2006). Formulating information and communication technology (ICT) policy through discourse: How Internet discussions shape policies on ICTs for developing countries. *Information Technology for Development, 12*(1), 25–43.

Khan, K., McDonald, H., Baumbusch, J., Kirkham, S., Tan, E., and Anderson, J. (2007). Taking up postcolonial feminism in the field: Working through a method. *Women's Studies International Forum, 30*(3), 228–242.

Kiddle, G. L. (2011). *Informal settlers, perceived security of tenure and housing consolidation: Case studies for Urban Fiji.* (Unpublished doctoral thesis), Victoria University, Wellington, New Zealand.

Killick, A. P. (1995). The penetrating intellect: On being white, straight, and male in Korea. In D. Kulick and M. Willson (eds), *Taboo: Sex, Identity, and Erotic Subjectivity in Anthropological Fieldwork.* London: Routledge.

Kindon, S. L. (2012). 'Thinking-through-complicity' with Te Iwi o Ngati Hauiti: Towards a critical use of participatory video for research. (Unpublished doctoral dissertation), University of Waikato, Hamilton.

Kindon, S. L., Pain, R., and Kesby, M. (eds) (2007). *Participatory Action Research Approaches and Methods: Connecting People, Participation, and Place.* Milton Park: Routledge.

Kishwar, M. (1998). Learning to take people seriously. In M. Thapan (ed.), *Anthropological Journeys: Reflections on Fieldwork* (pp. 293–311). London: Sangam.

Kitchin, R., and Tate, N. J. (2000). *Conducting Research in Human Geography: Theory, Methodology and Practice.* Harlow: Prentice Hall.

Kivits, J. (2005). Online interviewing and the research relationship. In C. Hine (ed.), *Virtual Methods: Issues in Social Research on the Internet* (pp. 35–49). Oxford: .

Kleinman, S. and Copp, M.A. (1993). *Emotions and Fieldwork.* Thousand Oaks, CA: Sage.

Kleinman, S., Copp, M. A., and Henderson, K. A. (1997). Qualitatively different: Teaching fieldwork to graduate students. *Journal of Contemporary Ethnography, 25*(4), 469–499.

Kobayashi, A. (1994). Coloring the field: Gender, 'race', and the politics of fieldwork. *Professional Geographer, 46*(1), 73–80.

Kobayashi, A. (2003). GPC ten years on: Is self-reflexivity enough? *Gender, Place and Culture, 10*(4), 345–349.

Kondo, D. (1990). *Crafting Selves: Power, Gender and Discourse of Identity in a Japanese Workplace.* Chicago, IL: University of Chicago Press.

Kothari, U. (2001). Power, knowledge and social control in participatory development. In B. Cooke and U. Kothari (eds), *Participation: The New Tyranny?* (pp. 139–152). New York: Zed.

Kothari, U., and Hulme, D. (2004). Narratives, stories and tales: Understanding poverty dynamics through life histories. *Working Paper Series, 11 Global Poverty Research Group and Institute for Development Policy and Management.* Manchester: University of Manchester.

Kretzmann, J., and McKnight, J. (1993). *Building Communities from the Inside Out: A Path Toward Finding and Mobilising a Community's Assets*. Evanston, IL: The Asset-Based Community Development Institute.

Krog, A. (2011). In the name of human rights: I say (how) you (should) speak (before I listen). In N. K. Denzin and Y. S. Lincoln (eds), *The SAGE Handbook of Qualitative Research* (4th edn, pp. 381–385). Thousand Oaks, CA: Sage

Krotoski, A. (2010). Introduction to the special issue: Research ethics in online communities. *International Journal of Internet Research Ethics, 3*(1), 1–5.

Kuhn, T. S. (1970). *The Structure of Scientific Revolutions* (2nd edn). Chicago, IL: University of Chicago Press.

Kulick, D., and Willson, M. (eds) (1995). *Taboo: Sex, Identity, and Erotic Subjectivity in Anthropological Fieldwork*. London: Routledge.

Kumar, S. (2002). *Methods for Community Participation: A Complete Guide for Practitioners*. London: ITDG.

Lagisa, L. (1997). *The Impacts of a major development project on women's lives: A case study of mining in Lihir, Papua New Guinea*. (Unpublished master's thesis), Massey University, Palmerston North, New Zealand.

Lakatos, I., and Musgrave, A. (1970). *Criticism and the Growth of Knowledge: Volume 4: Proceedings of the International Colloquium in the Philosophy of Science, London, 1965*. Cambridge: Cambridge University Press.

Lambert, S.J. (2008). *The expansion of sustainability into new economic space: Māori potatoes and cultural resilience*. (Unpublished doctoral dissertation), Lincoln University, Christchurch, New Zealand.

Lammers, E. (2007). Researching refugees: Preoccupations with power and questions of giving. *Refugee Survey Quarterly, 26*(3), 72–81.

Lareau, A. (1996). Common problems in fieldwork: A personal essay. In A. Lareau and J. Shultz (eds), *Journeys through Ethnography* (pp. 196–236). Boulder, CO: Westview.

Lather, P. (1988). Feminist perspectives on empowering research methodologies. *Women's Studies International Forum, 11*(6), 569–581.

Laws, S. (2003). *Research for Development: A Practical Guide*. London: Sage.

Lederman, R. (2006). The perils of working at home: IRB 'mission creep' as context and content for an ethnography of disciplinary knowledges. *American Ethnologist, 33*(4), 482–491.

Lee, R. (1995). *Dangerous Fieldwork*. Thousand Oaks, CA: Sage.

Lee-Treweek, G., and Linkogle, S. (eds) (2000). *Danger in the Field: Risk and Ethics in Social Research*. London: Routledge.

Letkemann, P. (1980). Crime as work: Leaving the field. In W. Shaffir, R. A. Stebbins and A. Turowetz (eds), *Fieldwork Experience: Qualitative Approaches to Social Research* (pp. 292–301). New York: St. Martin's Press.

Lewin, C. (2011). Understanding and describing quantitative data. In B. Somekh and C. Lewin (eds), *Theory and Methods in Social Research* (2nd edn, pp. 220–230). London: Sage.

Lewis, D. J. (1991). The off-stage miracle: Carrying out and writing up field research in Bangladesh. *Journal of Social Studies, Dhaka University, 52*, 44–68.

Lewis, W. A. (1954). Economic development with unlimited supplies of labour. *Manchester School, 22*(2).

Lincoln, Y. S., and Guba, E. G. (1985). *Naturalistic Inquiry*. Newbury Park, CA: Sage.

Lindisfarne, N. (2008). Starting from below: Fieldwork, gender and imperialism now. In H. Armbruster and A. Lærke (eds), *Taking Sides: Ethics, Politics and Fieldwork in Anthropology* (pp. 23–44). New York: Berghahn.

Locatelli, F. (2004). The archives of the municipality and the High Court of Asmara, Eritrea: Discovering the Eritrea 'hidden from history'. *History in Africa, 31*, 469–478.

Locke, L. F., Silverman, S. J., and Spriduso, W. W. (2010). *Reading and Understanding Research* (3rd edn). Thousand Oaks, CA: Sage.

Lockwood, M. (1992). Facts or fictions? Fieldwork relationships and the nature of data. In S. Devereux and J. Hoddinott (eds), *Fieldwork in Developing Countries* (pp. 164–178). New York: Harvester Wheatsheaf.

Louis, R. P. (2007). Can you hear us now? Voices from the margin: Using indigenous methodologies in geographic research. *Geographical Research, 45*(2), 130–139.

Loveridge, D. (2001). *The good governance agenda and urban governance: The case of Dhaka, Bangladesh.* (Unpublished master's thesis), Massey University, Palmerston North, New Zealand.

Maaba, B. B. (2001). The archives of the Pan Africanist Congress and the Black consciousness-orientated movements. *History in Africa, 28*, 417–438.

Mackintosh, H. (2011). *'Another tool in the kete': Māori engaging with the international human rights framework.* (Unpublished master's thesis), Victoria University, Wellington, New Zealand.

Madan, T. N. (1982). Anthropology as the mutual interpretation of cultures: Indian perspectives. In H. Fahim (ed.), *Indigenous Anthropology in Non-Western Countries* (pp. 4–18). Durham, NC: Carolina Academic Press.

Madge, C. (1993). Boundary disputes: Comments on Sidaway (1992). *Area, 25*(3), 294–299.

Madge, C. (1997). The ethics of research in the 'Third World'. In E. Robson and K. Willis (eds), *Postgraduate Fieldwork in Developing Countries* (pp. 113–124). Monograph No. 9, Developing Areas Research Group of the Royal Geographical Society, with the Institute of British Geographers, London.

Mafile'o, T. (2008). Tongan social work practice. In M. Gray, J. Coates and M. Yellow Bird (eds), *Indigenous Social Work around the World* (pp. 117–127). Farnham: Ashgate.

Maines, D., Shaffir, W., and Turowetz, A. (1980). Leaving the field in ethnographic research. Reflections on the entrance-exit hypothesis. In W. Shaffir, R. A. Stebbins and A. Turowetz (eds), *Fieldwork Experience: Qualitative Approaches to Social Research* (pp. 261–281). New York: St. Martin's Press.

Malam, L. (2004). Embodiment and sexuality in cross-cultural research. *Australian Geographer, 35*(2), 177–183.

Malinowski, B. (1967). *A Diary in the Strict Sense of the Word.* New York: Harcourt, Brace and World.

Mandel, J. L. (2003). Negotiating expectations in the field: Gatekeepers, research fatigue and cultural biases. *Singapore Journal of Tropical Geography, 24*(2), 198–210.

Mandiyanike, D. (2009). The dilemma of conducting research back in your own country as a returning student – reflections of research fieldwork in Zimbabwe. *Area, 41*(1), 64–71.

Mann, G. (1999). Dust to dust: A user's guide to local archives in Mali. *History in Africa, 26*, 453–456.

Marchant, J. (2012). *The Equator Principles: CSR in the finance industry. A good beginning, a long way to go.* (Unpublished master's thesis), Massey University, Palmerston North, New Zealand.

Marcus, G. E. (1995). Ethnography in/of the World System: The emergence of multi-sited ethnography. *Annual Review of Anthropology, 24*(95–117).

Markham, A., and Buchanan, E. (2012). *Ethical Decision-Making and Internet Research: Recommendations from the AoIR Ethics Working Committee* (Version 2.0). Retrieved 14 May 2013 from http://aoir.org/reports/ethics2.pdf.

Marshall, C., and Rossman, G. B. (2006). *Designing Qualitative Research* (4th edn). Thousand Oaks, CA: Sage.

Martin, K. L. (2003). Ways of knowing, ways of being and ways of doing: A theoretical framework and methods for Indigenous re-search and Indigenist research. Voicing Dissent, New Talents 21C: Next Generation Australian Studies. *Journal of Australian Studies, 76,* 203–214.

Martin, M. (2000). Critical education for participatory research. In C. Truman, D. M. Mertens and B. Humphries (eds), *Research and Inequality* (pp. 191–204). London: UCL Press.

Mason, J. (2002). *Qualitative Researching*. London: Sage.

Mason, J. (2006). Mixing methods in a qualitatively driven way. *Qualitative Research, 6*(1), 9–25.

Massey University Ethics Committee (2013). *Code of Ethical Conduct for Research, Teaching and Evaluation Involving Human Subjects.* Retrieved 6 June 2013 from www.massey.ac.nz/massey/research/research-ethics/human-ethics/code-ethical-conduct.cfm.

Matthews, H., and Tucker, F. (2000). Consulting children. *Journal of Geography in Higher Education, 24*(2), 299–310.

Mawdsley, E. (2006). Using the World Wide Web for development research. In V. Desai and R. Potter (eds), *Doing Development Research* (pp. 273–281). London: Sage.

May, T. (2011). *Social Research: Issues, Methods and Process* (4th edn). Maidenhead: Open University Press.

Mayoux, L. (2006). Quantitative, qualitative or participatory? Which method, for what and when? In V. Desai and R. Potter (eds), *Doing Development Research* (pp. 159–129). London: Sage.

Mazzei, J., and O'Brien, E. E. (2009). You got it, so when do you flaunt it?: Building rapport, intersectionality, and the strategic deployment of gender in the field. *Journal of Contemporary Ethnography, 38*(3), 358–383.

McClellan, D., and Tanner, K. (2011). Knowledge discovery empowering Australian indigenous communities. *Information Technologies and International Development, 7*(2), 31–46.

McClelland, D. C. (1970). The achievement motive in economic growth. In G. D. Ness (ed.), *The Sociology of Economic Development* (pp. 177–198). New York: Harper and Row.

McConnell, S. C. (2005). Historical research in Eastern Uganda: Local archives. *History in Africa, 32,* 467–478.

McCoyd, J. L. M., and Kerson, T. S. (2006). Conducting intensive interviews using email: A serendipitous comparative opportunity. *Qualitative Social Work, 5*(3), 389–406.

McEwan, C. (2006). Using images, film and photography. In V. Desai and R. Potter (eds), *Doing Development Research* (pp. 231–240). London: Sage.

McEwan, C. (2009). *Postcolonialism and Development*. Abingdon: Routledge.

McEwan, C. (2011). Development and fieldwork. *Geography, 96*(1), 22–26.

McIlwaine, C. (2006). Using indigenous local knowledge and literature. In V. Desai and R. Potter (eds), *Doing Development Research* (pp. 222–230). London: Sage.

McKenzie, B., and Morrissette, V. (2003). Social work practice with Canadians of aboriginal background: Guidelines for respectful social work. *Envision. The Manitoba Journal of Child Welfare, 2,* 13–39.

McKinnon, J. (2010). Ways of seeing environmental change: Participatory research engagement in Yunnan, China, with ethnic minority Hani participants. *Asia Pacific Viewpoint, 51*(2), 164–178.

McKinnon, K. (2011). *Development Professionals in Northern Thailand: Hope, Politics and Practice*. Honolulu, HI: University of Hawaii Press.

McLennan, S. J. (2012). *An alternative model for development?: Promise and politics in the projecthonduras network*. (Unpublished doctoral thesis), Massey University, Palmerston North, New Zealand.

Mellor, M. (2007). Researching for change. In M. Smith (ed.), *Negotiating Boundaries and Borders: Qualitative Methodology and Development Research* (Vol. Studies in Qualitative Methodology, Vol. 8, pp. 177–195). Amsterdam: Elsevier.

Meo-Sewabu, L. (2012). *Ethics and ethnography as an Indigenous researcher: A Fijian perspective.* Paper presented at the Development Studies Seminar Series, Massey University, Palmerston North.

Meo-Sewabu, L. (2014). *Cultural constructs of health and wellbeing amongst indigenous Fijian women in Fiji and New Zealand.* (Unpublished doctoral thesis), Massey University, Palmerston North, New Zealand.

Mies, M. (1983). Towards a methodology for feminist research. In G. Bowles and R. Duelli-Klein (eds), *Theories of Women's Studies,* (pp. 117–139). London and Boston: Routledge and Kegan Paul.

Miles, M., and Crush, J. (1993). Personal narratives as interactive texts: Collecting and interpreting migrant life-histories. *Professional Geographer, 45*(1), 95–129.

Missbach, A. (2011). Ransacking the Field? *Critical Asian Studies, 43*(3), 373–398.

Mizen, P., and Ofosu-Kusi, Y. (2012). Engaging with a world outside of ourselves: Vistas of flatness, children's work and the urban informal economy. *Sociological Research Online, 17*(2).

Mohamed, M. (2012). *Changing reef values: An inquiry into the use, management and governances of reef resources in island communities of the Maldives.* (Unpublished doctoral thesis), Canterbury University, Christchurch, New Zealand.

Mohanty, C. T. (1988). Under Western eyes: Feminist scholarship and colonial discourses. *Feminist Review, 30,* 61–88.

Momsen, J. H. (2006). Women, men and fieldwork: Gender relations and power structures. In V. Desai and R. Potter (eds), *Doing Development Research* (pp. 44–51). London: Sage.

Monchamp, A. (2007). Encountering emotions in the field: An X marks the spot. *Anthropology Matters, 1*(9).

Mookherjee, N. (2008). Friendships and encounters on the political left in Bangladesh. In H. Armbruster and A. Lærke (eds), *Taking Sides: Ethics, Politics and Fieldwork in Anthropology* (pp. 66–87). New York: Berghahn.

Moore, S. F. (2009). Encounter and suspicion in Tanzania. In J. Borneman and A. Hammoudi (eds), *Being There: The Fieldwork Encounter and the Making of Truth* (pp. 151–182). Berkeley, CA: University of California Press.

Moreton-Robinson, A. M., and Walter, M. (2009). Indigenous methodologies in social research. In M. Walter (ed.), *Social Research Methods.* South Melbourne: Oxford University Press.

Morse, J. M., Barrett, M., Mayan, M., Olson, K., and Spiers, J. (2008). Verification strategies for establishing reliability and validity in qualitative research. *International Journal of Qualitative Methods, 1*(2), 13–22.

Morton, H. (1995). My 'chastity belt': Avoiding seduction in Tonga. In D. Kulick and M. Willson (eds), *Taboo: Sex, Identity, and Erotic Subjectivity in Anthropological Fieldwork* (pp. 168–185). London: Routledge.

Mose Brown, T., and de Casanova, E. M. (2009). Mothers in the field: How motherhood shapes fieldwork and researcher-subject relations. *WSQ: Women's Studies Quarterly, 37* (3 and 4), 42–57.

Moser, S. (2008). Personality: A new positionality? *Area, 40*(3), 383–392.

Moses, J. W., and Knutsen, T. L. (2007). *Ways of Knowing: Competing Methodologies and Methods in Social and Political Research.* Basingstoke: Palgrave Macmillan.

Mosse, D. (2005). *Cultivating Development: An Ethnography of Aid Policy and Practice.* London: Pluto Press.

Mosse, D. (2006). Anti-social anthropology? Objectivity, objection, and the ethnography of public policy and professional communities. *Journal of the Royal Anthropological Institute, 12,* 935–956.

Mowforth, M., and Munt, I. (2008). *Tourism and Sustainability: Development, Globalisation and New Tourism in the Third World* (3rd edn). New York: Routledge.

Muir, S. (2004). Not quite at home: Field envy and New Age ethnographic disease. In L. Hume and J. Mulcock (eds), *Anthropologists in the Field: Cases in Participant Observation* (pp. 185–200). New York: Columbia University Press.

Mullings, B. (1999). Insider or outsider, both or neither: Some dilemmas of interviewing in a cross-cultural setting. *Geoforum, 30,* 337–350.

Murray, C. D., and Sixsmith, J. (2002). Qualitative health research via the Internet: Practical and methodological issues. *Health Informatics Journal, 8*(1), 47–53.

Murray, W. E. (1997). *Neo-liberalism, restructuring and non-traditional fruit exports in Chile: Implications of export-orientation for small-scale farmers.* (Unpublished doctoral thesis), University of Birmingham.

Myers, G. (2010). Representing the other: Negotiating the personal and the political. In D. DeLyser, S. Herbert, S. C. Aitken, M. Crang and L. McDowell (eds), *The SAGE Handbook of Qualitative Geography* (pp. 273–387). London: Sage.

Nabobo-Baba, U. (2006). *Knowing Learning: An Indigenous Fijian Approach.* Suva, Fiji: IPS Publications, University of the South Pacific.

Nagar, R. (2002). Footloose researchers, 'traveling' theories, and the politics of transnational feminist praxis. *Gender, Place and Culture, 9*(2), 179–186.

Nagar, R., and Geiger, S. (2007). Reflexivity and positionality in feminist fieldwork revisited. In A. Tickell, E. Sheppard, J. Peck and T. Barnes (eds), *Politics and Practice in Economic Geography* (pp. 267–278). London: Sage.

Narayan, K. (1997). How native is a 'native' anthropologist? In L. Lamphere, H. Ragone and P. Zavella (eds), *Situated Lives: Gender and Culture in Everyday Life.* New York: Routledge.

Narayan, K. (1998). How native is a 'native' anthropologist? In M. Thapan (ed.), *Anthropological Journeys: Reflections on Fieldwork* (pp. 163–187). London: Sangam.

Nash, D. J. (2000a) Doing independent overseas fieldwork 1: Practicalities and pitfalls. *Journal of Geography in Higher Education, 24*(1), 139–149.

Nash, D. J. (2000b). Doing independent overseas fieldwork 2: Getting funding. *Journal of Geography in Higher Education, 24*(3), 425–433.

Nast, H. J. (1994). Opening remarks on 'women in the field'. *Professional Geographer, 46*(1), 54–66.

National Geographic Society (2013). *Enduring Voices Ethics Statement.* Retrieved 24 April 2013 from http://travel.nationalgeographic.com/travel/enduring-voices/ethics-statement/.

Nencel, L. (2001). *Ethnography and Prostitution in Peru.* London: Pluto Press.

Ng, I. (2011). To whom does my voice belong? (Re)Negotiating multiple identities as a female ethnographer in two Hong Kong rural villages. *Gender, Technology and Development, 15*(3), 437–456.

Nichols, P. (1991). *Social Survey Methods: A Guide for Development Workers.* Oxford: Oxfam.

Nissenbaum, H. (2004). Privacy as contextual integrity. *Washington Law Review, 79*(1).

Nowak, B. (1987) *Marriage and Household: Btsisi Response to a Changing World (Malaysia)* (PhD thesis), State University of New York at Buffalo.

O'Connor, H., Madge, C., Shaw, R., and Wellens, J. (2008). Internet-based interviewing. In N. Fielding, R. M. Lee and G. Blank (eds), *The SAGE Handbook of Online Research Methods* (pp. 271–289). London: Sage.

Ó Dochartaigh, N. Ó. (2012). *Internet Research Skills* (3rd edn). London: Sage.

O'Leary, Z. (2010). *The Essential Guide to Doing Research*. London: Sage.

Oakley, A. (1981). Interviewing women: A contradiction in terms. In H. Roberts (ed.), *Doing Feminist Research* (pp. 30–61). London: Routledge and Kegan Paul.

Oberg, K. (1960). Cultural shock: Adjustment to new cultural environments. *Practical Anthropology*, 7, 177–182.

Onwuegbuzie, A. J., and Leech, N. L. (2005). On becoming a pragmatic researcher: The importance of combining quantitative and qualitative research methodologies. *International Journal of Social Research Methodology*, 8(5), 375–387.

Opie, A. (1992). Qualitative research, appropriation of the 'other' and empowerment. *Feminist Review*, 40, 52–69.

Oriola, T., and Haggerty, K. D. (2012). The ambivalent insider/outsider status of academic 'homecomers': Observations on identity and field research in the Nigerian Delta. *Sociology*, 46(3), 540–548.

Ortiz, S. M. (2004). Leaving the private world of wives of professional athletes: A male sociologist's reflections. *Journal of Contemporary Ethnography*, 33(4), 466–487.

Otsuka, S. (2005). *Talanoa research: Culturally appropriate research design in Fiji*. Paper presented at the Proceedings of the Australian Association for Research in Education (AARE) 2005 International Education Research Conference: Creative Dissent-Constructive Solutions [On-Line]. Melbourne, Australia.

Palomino-Schalscha, M. A. (2011). *Indigeneity, autonomy and new cultural spaces: The decolonisation of practices, being and place through tourism in Alto Bío-Bío, Chile.* (Unpublished doctoral thesis), University of Canterbury, Christchurch, New Zealand.

Passaro, J. (1997). You can't take the subway to the Field!: 'Village' epistemologies in the global village. In A. Gupta and J. Ferguson (eds), *Anthropological Locations: Boundaries and Grounds of a Field Science* (pp. 147–162). Berkeley, CA: University of California Press.

Patai, D. (1991). US academics and Third World women: Is ethical research possible? In S. B. Gluck and D. Patai (eds), *Women's Words: The Feminist Practice of Oral History* (pp. 137–154). London: Routledge.

Patton, M. (2002). *Qualitative Research and Evaluation Methods*. London: Sage.

Perks, R., and Thomson, A. (eds) (1988). *The Oral History Reader*. London: Routledge.

Peterson, D. R. (2008). The intellectual lives of Mau Mau detainees. *The Journal of African History*, 49(1), 73–91.

Piggott, M., and McKemmish, S. (2002). *Recordkeeping, Reconciliation and Political Reality*. Paper presented at the Australian Society of Archivists Conference 2002, Sydney, Australia.

Pink, S. (2007). *Doing Visual Ethnography*. London: Sage.

Pollard, A. (2009). Field of screams: Difficulty and ethnographic fieldwork. *Anthropology Matters*, 11(2).

Posner, J. (1980). Urban anthropology: Fieldwork in semifamiliar settings. In W. Shaffir, R. A. Stebbins and A. Turowetz (eds), *Fieldwork Experience: Qualitative Approaches to Social Research* (pp. 203–212). New York: St. Martin's Press.

Potter, R. (1993). Little England and little geography: Reflections on Third World teaching and research. *Area*, 25(3), 291–294.

Pratt, B., and Loizos, P. (1992). *Choosing Research Methods: Data Collection for Development Workers*. Oxford: Oxfam.

Prebisch, R. (1962). The economic development of Latin America: Its principal problems. *Economic Bulletin for Latin America*, 7(1), 1–22.

Prinsen, G. (2011). *Negotiating on a seesaw: The centralisation of education and health services in Uganda and Tanzania from a local perspective and in a historical context.* (Unpublished doctoral thesis), Massey University, Palmerston North, New Zealand.

Prior, L. (2011). Using documents in social research. In D. Silverman (ed.), *Qualitative Research: Theory, Method and Practice* (pp. 93–110). London: Sage.

Punch, M. (1986). *The Politics and Ethics of Fieldwork*. Thousand Oaks, CA: Sage.

Rabinow, P. (2007). *Reflections on Fieldwork in Morocco* (30th Anniversary edn). Berkeley, CA: University of California Press.

Radcliffe, S. (1994). (Representing) post-colonial women: Authority, difference and feminisms. *Area, 26*(1), 25–32.

Raghuram, P., and Madge, C. (2006). Towards a method for postcolonial development geography? Possibilities and challenges. *Singapore Journal of Tropical Geography, 27*(3), 270–288.

Rahnema, M., and Bawtree, V. (1997). *The Post-Development Reader*. London: Zed.

Rashid, S. F. (2007). Accessing married adolescent women: The realities of ethnographic research in an urban slum environment in Dhaka, Bangladesh. *Field Methods, 19*(4), 369–383.

Raybeck, D. (1996). *Mad Dogs, Englishmen, and the Errant Anthropologist: Fieldwork in Malaysia*. Prospect Heights, IL: Waveland Press.

Razavi, S. (1992). Fieldwork in a familiar setting: The role of politics at the national, community and household levels. In S. Devereux and J. Hoddinott (eds), *Fieldwork in Developing Countries* (pp. 152–163). New York: Harvester Wheatsheaf.

Reeves, C. L. (2010). A difficult negotiation: Fieldwork relations with gatekeepers. *Qualitative Research, 10*(3), 315–331.

Richards, P. (1995). Participatory rural appraisal: A quick and dirty critique. In I. Gujit and A. Cornwall (eds), *PLA Notes 24: Critical Reflections from Practice* (pp. 13–16). London: IIEE.

Rigg, J. (2006). Data from international agencies. In V. Desai and R. Potter (eds), *Doing Development Research* (pp. 282–293). London: Sage.

RMIT (2011). *Timor-Leste Research@RMIT*. Retrieved 13 May 2013 from www.timor-leste.org/timor-leste-research/.

Robbins, P. (2006). Research is theft: Environmental inquiry in a postcolonial world. In S. C. Aitken and G. Valentine (eds), *Approaches to Human Geography* (pp. 311–324). London: Sage.

Robinson, G. M. (1998). *Methods and Techniques in Human Geography*. London: Wiley.

Robson, C. (2011). *Real World Research: A Resource for Social Scientists and Practitioner-Researchers* (3rd edn). Chichester: Wiley.

Robson, E. (2001). Interviews worth the tears? Exploring dilemmas of research with young carers in Zimbabwe. *Ethics, Place and Environment, 4*(2), 135–142.

Robson, E., and Willis, K. (eds) (1997). *Postgraduate Fieldwork in Developing Countries*. Monograph No. 9, Developing Areas Research Group of the Royal Geographical Society, with the Institute of British Geographers. London.

Roff, S. (2007). Archives, documents, and hidden history: A course to teach undergraduates the thrill of historical discovery real and virtual. *The History Teacher, 40*(4), 551–558.

Rogers, S. (1978). Women's place: A critical review of anthropological theory. *Comparative Studies in Society and History, 20*, 123–162.

Rosenberg, Å. (2010). Virtual world research ethics and the private/public distinction. *International Journal of Internet Research Ethics 3*(1), 23–37.

Rossman, G. B., and Rallis, S. F. (2012). *Learning in the Field: An Introduction to Qualitative Research* (3rd edn). Thousand Oaks, CA: Sage.

Rostow, W. W. (1960). *The Stages of Economic Growth*. Cambridge: Cambridge University Press.

Roth, R. (2001). A self-reflective exploration into development research. In P. Moss (ed.), *Placing Autobiography in Geography* (pp. 121–137). Syracuse, NY: Syracuse University Press.

Routledge, P. (2010). Major disasters and general panics: Methodologies of activism, affinity and emotion in the clandestine insurgent rebel clown army. In D. DeLyser, S. Herbert, S. C. Aitken, M. Crang and L. McDowell (eds), *The SAGE Handbook of Qualitative Geography* (pp. 388–405). London: Sage.

Rupp, L. J., and Taylor, V. (2011). Going back and giving back: The ethics of staying in the field. *Qualitative Sociology, 34*(3), 483–496.

Salazar, N. B. (2011). Studying local-to-global tourism dynamics through glocal ethnography. In C. M. Hall (ed.), *Fieldwork in Tourism: Methods, Issues and Reflections* (pp. 177–187). London: Routledge.

Sayer, R. A. (1988). *Method in Social Science: A Realist Approach* (2nd edn). London: Routledge.

Scaglion, R. (1990). Ethnocentrism and the Abelam. In P. R. DeVita (ed.), *The Humbled Anthropologist* (pp. 29–34). Belmont, CA: Wadsworth.

Scheper-Hughes, N. (1992). *Death Without Weeping: The Violence of Everyday Life in Northwest Brazil*. Berkeley, CA: University of California Press.

Scheyvens, H. (2001). *Evaluating aid: The developmental impact of Japan's official development assistance*. (Unpublished doctoral thesis), Monash University, Melbourne, Australia.

Scheyvens, R., and Leslie, H. (2000). Gender, ethics and empowerment: dilemmas of development fieldwork. *Women's Studies International Forum, 23*(1), 119–130.

Schneider, L. (2003). The Tanzania National Archives. *History in Africa, 30*, 447–454.

Schrijvers, J. (1993). Motherhood experienced and conceptualised: Changing images in Sri Lanka and the Netherlands. In D. Bell, P. Caplan and W. K. Jarim (eds), *Gendered Fields: Women, Men and Ethnography* (pp. 143–158). London: Routledge.

Schroeder, D. G. (2000). *Staying Healthy in Asia, Africa and Latin America*. Emeryville, CA: Avalon Travel Publishing.

Shaffir, W., and Stebbins, R. A. (1991). *Experiencing Feldwork: An Inside View of Qualitative Research*. Newbury Park, CA: Sage

Shaffir, W., Stebbins, R. A., and Turowetz, A. (1980). *Fieldwork Experience: Qualitative Approaches to Social Research*. New York: St. Martin's Press.

Sharp, J. (2005). Geography and gender: Feminist methodologies in collaboration and in the field. *Progress in Human Geography, 29*(3), 304–309.

Shaw, B. (1995). Contradictions between action and theory: Feminist participatory research in Goa, India. *Antipode, 27*(1), 91–99.

Shenton, A. (2004). Strategies for ensuring trustworthiness in qualitative research projects. *Education for Information, 22*, 63–75.

Shokeid, M. (2007). When the curtain falls on a fieldwork project: The last chapter of a gay synagogue study. *Ethnos, 72*(2), 219–238.

Shope, J. H. (2006). 'You can't cross a river without getting wet': A feminist standpoint on the dilemmas of cross-cultural research. *Qualitative Inquiry, 12*(1), 163–184.

Sidaway, J. D. (1992). In other worlds: On the politics of research by 'first world' geographers in the 'third world'. *Area, 24*(4), 403–408.

Sikabongo, F. M. (2003). *Developing an integrated systems approach to the management of hazardous waste in urban environments: The cases of Oshakati and Windhoek, Namibia*. (Unpublished doctoral thesis), Massey University, Palmerston North, New Zealand.

Silverman, D. (2006). *Interpretative Qualitative Data* (3rd edn). London: Sage.

Simpson, K. (2007). Hearing voices? Negotiating multiple ethical commitments in development research. In M. Smith (ed.), *Negotiating Boundaries and Borders: Qualitative Methodology and Development Research* (Vol. Studies in Qualitative Methodology, Vol. 8, pp. 155–173). Amsterdam: Elsevier.

Sinreich, L. (2009). *Forests for participatory democracy: Emergent patterns in the interaction of actors and space in a community-based sustainable forestry project in San Francisco Libre, Nicaragua.* (Unpublished master's thesis), Victoria University, Wellington, New Zealand.

Sixsmith, J., and Murray, C. D. (2001). Ethical issues in the documentary data analysis of internet posts and archives. *Qualitative Health Research, 11*(3), 423–432.

Slim, H., and Thompson, P. (1993). *Listening for a Change: Oral Testimony and Development.* London: Panos.

Sluka, J. A. (2012a). Danger in fieldwork: Dangerous anthropology in Belfast. In A. C. G. M. Robben and J. A. Sluka (eds), *Ethnographic Fieldwork: An Anthropological Reader* (pp. 283–296). Malden, MA: Wiley-Blackwell.

Sluka, J. A. (2012b). The 'other' talks back. In A. C. G. M. Robben and J. A. Sluka (eds), *Ethnographic Fieldwork: An Anthropological Reader* (pp. 177–182). Malden, MA: Wiley-Blackwell.

Sluka, J. A., and Robben, A. C. G. M. (2012a). Fieldwork in cultural anthropology: An introduction. In A. C. G. M. Robben and J. A. Sluka (eds), *Ethnographic Fieldwork: An Anthropological Reader* (pp. 1–28). Malden, MA: Wiley-Blackwell.

Sluka, J. A., and Robben, A. C. G. M. (eds) (2012b). *Ethnographic Fieldwork: An Anthropological Reader.* Malden, MA: Wiley-Blackwell.

Smith, L. T. (1999). *Decolonizing Methodologies: Research and Indigenous Peoples.* London: Zed.

Smith, L. T. (2008). On tricky ground: Researching the native in the age of uncertainty. In N. K. Denzin and Y. S. Lincoln (eds), *The Landscape of Qualitative Research* (3rd edn, pp. 113–143). Los Angeles, CA: Sage.

Smith, L. T. (2012). *Decolonizing Methodologies: Research and Indigenous Peoples* (2nd edn). London: Zed.

Smith, M., and Humble, D. (2007). What counts as development research? In M. Smith (ed.), *Negotiating Boundaries and Borders: Qualitative Methodology and Development Research* (Vol. Studies in Qualitative Methodology, Vol. 8, pp. 1–34). Amsterdam: Elsevier.

Soja, E. W. (1968). *The Geography of Modernization in Kenya: A Spatial Analysis of Social, Economic, and Political Change.* Syracuse, NY: Syracuse University Press.

Soja, E. W. (1979). The geography of modernization: A radical reappraisal. In R. A. Obudho and D. R. F. Taylor (eds), *The Spatial Structure of Development: A Study of Kenya* (pp. 28–45). Boulder, CO: Westview.

Spivak, G. C. (1988a). Can the subaltern speak? In C. Nelson and L. Gross (eds), *Marxism and Interpretation of Culture* (pp. 271–313). Chicago, IL: University of Illinois Press.

Spivak, G. C. (1988b). *In Other Worlds: Essays in Cultural Politics.* New York: Routledge.

Spivak, G. C. (2004). Righting wrongs. *The South Atlantic Quarterly, 103*(2), 523–581.

Spoonley, P. (2001). Transnational Pacific communities: Transforming the politics of place and identity. In C. McPherson, P. Spoonley and M. Anae (eds), *Tangata o te Moana Nui: The Evolving Identities of Pacific Peoples in Aotearoa/New Zealand.* Palmerston North, New Zealand: Dunmore.

Staeheli, L., and Lawson, V. (1994). A discussion of 'women in the field': The politics of feminist fieldwork. *Professional Geographer, 46*(1), 96–102.

Stebbins, R. A. (1991). Do we ever leave the field? Notes on secondary fieldwork involvements. In W. Shaffir and R. A. Stebbins (eds), *Experiencing Fieldwork: An Inside View of Qualitative Research* (pp. 248–255). Newbury Park, CA: Sage.

Stewart-Withers, R. R. (2007). *Contesting a development category: Female headed households in Samoa.* (Unpublished doctoral thesis), Massey University, Palmerston North, New Zealand.

Storey, D. (1997). 'Hey Joe! What are you doing?: Practicing participatory research in urban poor communities – lessons and experiences from the Philippines. *Working Paper 97/2*: Institute of Development Studies, Massey University, New Zealand.

Stupples, P. (2012). *Breaking the frame: Art in international development.* (Unpublished doctoral thesis), Massey University, Palmerston North, New Zealand.

Subedi, B. (2006). Theorizing a 'halfie' researcher's identity in transnational fieldwork. *International Journal of Qualitative Studies in Education, 19*(5), 573–593.

Sultana, F. (2007). Reflexivity, positionality and participatory ethics: Negotiating fieldwork dilemmas in international research. *ACME: An International E-Journal for Critical Geographies, 6*(3), 374–385.

Sumner, A. (2007). What are the ethics of Development Studies? *IDS Bulletin, 38*(2), 59–68.

Sumner, A. (2008). *Moral ambiguity, quantum leaping and being well: The next 30 years of Development Studies?* Paper presented at the Working Paper, Development Studies Association Conference, UK.

Sumner, A., and Tiwari, M. (2011). Global poverty reduction to 2015 and beyond. *Journal of Global Policy, 2*(2), 138–151.

Sumner, A., and Tribe, M. (2008a). *International Development Studies: Theories and Methods in Research and Practice.* London: Sage.

Sumner, A., and Tribe, M. (2008b). What could Development Studies be? *Development in Practice, 18*(6), 755–766.

Sundberg, J. (2003). Masculinist epistemologies and the politics of fieldwork in Latin Americanist geography. *The Professional Geographer, 55*(2), 180–190.

Swadener, B. B., Kabiru, M., and Njenga, A. (2000). *Does the Village Still Raise the Child? A Collaborative Study of Changing Childrearing and Early Education in Kenya.* New York: State University of New York Press.

Swanson, K. (2008). Witches, children and Kiva-the-research-dog: Striking problems encountered in the field. *Area, 40*(1), 55–64.

Szarycz, G. S. (2010). Challenges and opportunities in elite social science research: Interviewing top executives in tourism-business contexts. In G. S. Szarycz (ed.), *Research Realities in the Social Sciences: Negotiating Fieldwork Dilemmas* (pp. 151–184). Amherst, NY: Cambria Press.

Taddia, I. (1998). The regional archive at Addi Qäyyeh, Eritrea. *History in Africa, 25,* 423–425.

Taggart, J. M., and Sandstrom, A. R. (2011). Introduction to 'long-term fieldwork'. *Anthropology and Humanism, 36*(1), 1–6.

Taylor, P. (1992). Understanding global inequalities. *Geography, 77*(11), 10–21.

Taylor, S. J. (1991). Leaving the field: Research, relationships and responsibilities. In W. Shaffir and R. A. Stebbins (eds), *Experiencing Fieldwork: An Inside View of Qualitative Research* (pp. 238–247). Newbury Park, CA: Sage.

Teaiwa, K. M. (2004). Multi-sited methodologies: 'Homework' in Australia, Fiji and Kiribati. In L. Hume and J. Mulcock (eds), *Anthropologists in the Field: Cases in Participant Observation* (pp. 216–233). New York: Columbia University Press.

Tilley, L., and Woodthorpe, K. (2011). Is it the end for anonymity as we know it? A critical examination of the ethical principle of anonymity in the context of 21st century demands on the qualitative researcher. *Qualitative Research, 11,* 197–212.

Tomm, W. (1989). Introduction. In W. Tomm (ed.), *The Effects of Feminist Approaches on Research and Methodologies* (pp. 1–11). Ontario: Wilfrid Laurier University Press.

Triulzi, A. (2006). When orality turns to writing: Two documents from Wälläga, Ethiopia. *Journal of African Cultural Studies, 18*(1), 43–55.

Trivedy, R. (2007). IDS40: Reflections from Tanzania. *IDS Bulletin, 38*(2), 100–110.

Truman, C., Mertens, D. M., and Humphries, B. (eds) (2000). *Research and Inequality*. London: UCL Press.

Tsai, L. L. (2010). Quantitative research and issues of political sensitivity in rural China. In A. Carlson, M. E. Gallagher, K. Lieberthal and M. Manion (eds), *Contemporary Chinese Politics: New Sources, Methods, and Field Strategies* (pp. 246–265). New York: Cambridge University Press.

Tuck, M. W., and Rowe, J. A. (2005). Phoenix from the ashes: Rediscovery of the lost Lukiiko archives. *History in Africa, 32*, 403–414.

Turner, S. (2010). Research note: The silenced assistant. Reflections of invisible interpreters and research assistants. *Asia Pacific Viewpoint, 51*(2), 206–219.

Unwin, T. (2006). Doing development research at 'home'. In V. Desai and R. Potter (eds), *Doing Development Research* (pp. 104–112). London: Sage.

Vaioleti, T. (2006). Talanoa research methodology: A developing position on Pacific research. *Waikato Journal of Education, University of Waikato, 12*, 23–31.

Valentine, G. (1999). Being seen and heard? The ethical complexities of working with children and young people at home and at school. *Ethics, Place and Environment, 2*, 311–324.

Van Aelst, P., and Walgrave, S. (2002). New media, new movements? The role of the Internet in shaping the 'anti-globalization' movement. *Information, Communication and Society, 5*(4), 465–493.

van Binsbergen, W. (1979). Anthropological fieldwork: 'There and back again'. *Human Organisation, 38*(2), 205–209.

van Blerk, L. (2006). Working with children in development. In V. Desai and R. Potter (eds), *Doing Development Research* (pp. 52–61). London: Sage.

van der Geest, S. (2003). Confidentiality and pseudonyms: A fieldwork dilemma from Ghana. *Anthropology Today, 19*(1), 14–18.

van Donge, J. K. (2006). Ethnography and participant observation. In V. Desai and R. Potter (eds), *Doing Development Research* (pp. 180–188). London: Sage.

Van Maanen, J. (1988) *Tales of the Field: On Writing Ethnography*. Chicago, IL: University of Chicago Press.

Van Maanen, J. (2011). *Tales of the Field: On Writing Ethnography* (2nd edn). Chicago, IL: University of Chicago Press.

Veeck, G. (2001). Talk is cheap: Cultural and linguistic fluency during field research. *The Geographical Review, 1/2*, 34–40.

Veldwisch, G. J. A. (2008). Authoritarianism, validity and security: Researching water distribution in Khorezm, Uzbekistan. In P. P. Mollinga and C. R. L. Wall (eds), *Fieldwork in Difficult Environments* (pp. 161–181). Zurich: Lit.

Waage, H. H. (2008). Postscript to Oslo: The mystery of Norway's missing files. *Journal of Palestine Studies, 38*(1), 54–65.

Walford, G. (2005). Research ethical guidelines and anonymity. *International Journal of Research and Method in Education, 28*(1), 83–93.

Wall, C. R. L. (2008). Working in fields as fieldwork: Khashar, participant observation and the Tamorka as ways to access local knowledge in rural Uzbekistan. In P. P. Mollinga and C. R. L. Wall (eds), *Fieldwork in Difficult Environments* (pp. 137–159). Zurich: Lit.

Walliman, N. (2006). *Social Research Methods*. London: Sage.

Watson, E. E. (2004). 'What a dolt one is': Language learning and fieldwork in geography. *Area, 36*(1), 59–68.

Watts, J. H. (2008). Emotion, empathy and exit: Reflections on doing ethnographic qualitative research on sensitive topics. *Medical Sociology Online, 3*(2), 3–14.

Wax, M. L. (1979). On the presentation of self in fieldwork: The dialectic of mutual deception and disclosure. *Humanity and Society, 3*(4), 248–259.

Wax, R. (1986). *Doing Fieldwork: Warnings and Advice*. Chicago, IL: University of Chicago Press.

Weaver, D. B. (1998). *Ecotourism in the Less Developed World*. Wallingford: CAB International.

Weber-Pillwax, C. (2009). When research becomes a revolution: Participatory action research with indigenous peoples. In D. Kapoor, S. Jordan and C. Cervin (eds), *Education, Participatory Action Research, and Social Change: International Perspectives* (pp. 45–58). New York: Palgrave Macmillan.

Welsh, K., and France, D. (2012). Smartphones and fieldwork. *Geography, 97*(1), 47–51.

Wesche, S., Huynh, N. T., Nelson, E., and Ramachandran, L. (2010). Challenges and opportunities in cross-cultural geographic inquiry. *Journal of Geography in Higher Education, 34*(1), 59–75.

White, H. (2002). Combining quantitative and qualitative approaches in poverty analysis. *World Development, 30*(3), 511–522.

Whiteford, A. H., and Whiteford, M. S. (1987). Reciprocal relations: Family contributions to anthropological field research – and vice versa. In B. Butler and D. Michalski Turner (eds), *Children and Anthropological Research* (pp. 115–136). New York: Plenum.

Wild, K. L. (2007). *Aid, education and adventure: An exploration of the impact of development scholarship schemes on women's lives*. (Unpublished doctoral thesis), Massey University, Palmerston North, New Zealand.

Wiles, R., Prosser, J., Bagnoli, A., Clark, A., Davies, K., Holland, S., and Renold, E. (2008). *Visual Ethics: Ethical Issues in Visual Research*. National Centre for Research Methods. Retrieved 14 July 2012 from http://eprints.ncrm.ac.uk/421/.

Wolcott, H. F. (2005). *The Art of Fieldwork* (2nd edn). Walnut Creek, CA: Altamira Press.

Wolf, D. L. (1996). Situating feminist dilemmas in fieldwork. In D. L. Wolf (ed.), *Feminist Dilemmas in Fieldwork* (pp. 1–55). Boulder, CO: Westview.

Wolf, D. R. (1991). High-risk methodology: Reflections on leaving an outlaw society. In W. Shaffir and R. A. Stebbins (eds), *Experiencing Fieldwork: An Inside View of Qualitative Research* (pp. 211–223). Newbury Park, CA: Sage.

Wolfe, J. M. (1989). Theory, hypothesis, explanation and action. In A. L. Kobayashi and S. Mackenzie (eds), *Remaking Human Geography* (pp. 62–77). London: Unwin Hyman.

Wrighton, N. (2010). *Participation, power and practice in development: A case study of theoretical doctrines and international agency practice in Tuvalu*. (Unpublished master's thesis), Victoria University, Wellington, New Zealand.

Wuelker, G. (1993). Questionnaires in Asia. In M. Bulmer and D. P. Warwick (eds), *Social Research in Developing Countries: Surveys and Censuses in the Third World* (pp. 161–166). London: UCL Press.

Yamagishi, R. (2011). Doing 'risky' and 'sexy' research: Reframing the concept of 'relational' in qualitative research. In C. M. Hall (ed.), *Fieldwork in Tourism: Methods, Issues and Reflections* (pp. 99–111). London: Routledge.

Zapata, C. (2006). Identidad, nación y territorio en la escritura de los intelectuales mapuches. *Revista Mexicana de Sociología, 68*(3), 567–509.

Zeitlyn, D. (2005). The documentary impulse: Archives in the bush. *History in Africa, 32*, 415–434.

INDEX

academic tourism, 5
accommodation, 33, 114–16, 133, 144, 154
    cost of, 114–15
accountability, 62, 209, 256–7
acknowledgement,
    of researcher complicity/influence/bias, 8, 61,
        62, 151–2, 239, 244
    of language limitations, 86
    of participant input to research, 168, 191
action-based research, 7, 15, 25, 67–9,
    academics as activists, 207–8, 210
    see also participatory research
activism, 14, 85, 174, 186, 207–11
advocacy, 14, 23, 27, 85, 174, 177–8, 200,
    207–11
American Anthropological Association, 162,
    168, 170
anonymity, 84, 93, 164, 166, 168–9
    for children, 191
anxiety, 114, 143, 144, 147, 158
    when leaving the field, 222–3, 226, 231
    when writing up, 245
applied research, 25, 38
appropriateness of fieldwork, 4–8, 253
archives/archival research, 14, 44, 64, 81–4,
    86–100, 115, 120, 129, 172
authorship, 8, 91, 233, 250

Bangladesh, 10, 125–6, 128, 129, 147, 176, 194,
    199, 207, 208
behaviour during fieldwork, 73, 78, 109–10, 113,
    127–8, 129, 136, 149–52, 158, 207
    see also ethical issues
benefits of research to country/community, 131,
    161, 165–6, 181, 190, 192, 196–7, 199, 201,
    243, 253
    see also appropriateness of fieldwork;
        reciprocity
blogs, 33, 113, 118, 150, 246–7
    as data, 82, 83, 85, 92–3
bribery, 129
budget, 19, 32–4, 104, 114–5, 155, 250

camera, 88, 113, 119–20, 134
    ethical use, 121–2
    see also electronic devices
charity, 27, 200
children,
    researching, 42, 52, 167, 175, 180, 190–2, 212–3
    taking into the field, 133–4, 136–40
Chile, 34–5, 104, 203, 228–9, 241–2, 245
China, 136
climate, 100, 117–8
clothing, 118–9, 123
codes of ethics, 163–4, 168, 170, 185
collaborative research, 15, 25, 68, 70, 74, 122,
    155, 197–8, 209, 210, 235, 254–5
collaborative writing, 250
communities,
    leaving, 217–35
    living within, 115–6
    over-researched, 131
computers, 13, 43, 46, 47, 59, 69, 76, 84, 97,
    113, 119–20, 134, 150
    laptops, 90, 113, 120, 150
    tablets, 120, 150
    see also electronic devices
confidentiality, 42, 84–5, 95, 96, 134, 151,
    164–6, 168–9, 185, 226, 232, 248, 249
    for children, 190–1
    with photos and film, 121–2, 240
conflicts of interest, 104, 147, 164, 169–71,
    173–4, 181, 185
consent, see informed consent
consent forms, 165, 166–7, 168, 244
contacts, 28, 97, 105–7, 108, 109, 113, 123, 143,
    144, 146, 148, 151, 173, 203–4
    see also networks
conversation analysis, 64
correlation, 30, 49–51, 52–3
Costa Rica, 136, 230
covert research, 25, 122, 181–2
critical science, 23
crisis of legitimacy facing researchers, 6–9, 10,
    15, 174, 205

cross-cultural research, 1–2, 10–13, 138, 150, 152, 159, 160–1, 163, 166, 176, 182–3, 185, 196, 197, 211
cultural mentor/advisor, 33, 152, 154
cultural isolation, 148
cultural sensitivity, 151–2, 173
culture shock, 14, 132, 146–9, 158
    for home-based researchers, 146–7, 158
    when returning to university, 245–6, 247
customs, respect for, 129, 139, 176, 197

danger, 4, 41, 109–10, 112–14, 115, 123, 124, 130, 160
    see also health and safety
data collection,
    qualitative, 63–66
    quantitative, 41–46
data analysis,
    qualitative, 75–6, 79
    quantitative, 41, 46–51, 54, 55, 56
deception, 161, 179–82, 207
depression, 114, 126, 132–3, 147
design of research project, 19–38, 149, 157, 185, 197, 209, 212–3, 219, 255
    and experience of leaving field, 220–1, 222, 234
    see also qualitative research; quantitative research
determination, 64, 126, 130
development research, 2, 5, 20–1, 8–12, 15, 20–1, 253–6
Development Studies, 10, 16, 22–23, 24, 25, 27, 32, 40, 55, 57, 62, 67, 95, 160, 161, 185, 189, 202, 208, 233, 243, 247, 250
diaries, 62, 64, 132, 138, 140, 148–9, 157, 158, 191, 192, 200, 225, 228
    see also fieldwork journal
digital data, 82, 90, 121
digital devices, see electronic devices
disappointment, on leaving, 222–4, 245
discomfort, 3, 6, 126, 132–3, 139, 146, 153, 158, 173

Ecuador, 191
El Salvador, 114, 148, 152, 156, 175, 209
electronic devices, 90, 113, 119–22
elites, researching, 189, 190, 201–7, 212, 213
    access to, 202–4
emails, 104–5, 106, 107, 123, 127, 133, 145, 148, 173, 177, 203
    as research tools, 63, 97–8, 113
    as data, 82, 83, 85, 94, 95–7, 99
emancipatory research, 23, 62, 208, 210–11, 212, 214

emotion, 7, 65, 98, 109, 114, 115, 128, 130–7, 140, 148, 149, 175, 189, 204
    when leaving/returning to university, 218, 221–6, 231, 233–7, 245–6, 250–1
empathy, 11, 128, 139, 151, 180
empirical-analytical perspective, 22–23, 25, 30–1, 38
ethical issues, 1–15, 19, 21, 32, 33, 37, 104, 148, 160–87, 212
    bottom up ethics, 161–2
    in archival and online research, 84–5, 92, 93, 95, 100
    in elite research, 202, 207
    in indigenous research, 73–74, 198–9
    leaving the field, 218, 226, 230–1
    official procedures, 105, 108, 112, 134, 163–72
    of research with children/young people, 190, 192, 213
    when involved in participatory research, 201–11
    when using visual tools, 121–2
ethics boards/committees, 126, 163–4, 166, 167, 171, 172, 154
ethnic minorities, see minority ethnic groups
ethnocentrism, 8, 11, 152
ethnography, 16, 23, 30, 37, 40, 57, 69, 71–2, 80, 124, 140, 159, 164, 181, 183, 202, 205, 220, 227, 235, 238, 239, 240, 244, 252
    auto-ethnography, 171
expatriate populations, contact with, 33, 127
expert, authority of, 5, 61, 68, 74, 143, 206, 226

families, in the field, 73–75, 133–9
feedback, 162, 177, 178–9, 191, 201, 229
field, the, 3–4, 20–1, 207
    arrival in, 143–6
    returning to, 231
    see also leaving the field
fieldwork,
    journal, 62–3, 71, 75, 78, 144, 148–9, 247 see also diaries
    value of, 10–12, 253
    see also site selection
Fiji, 4, 24, 43, 54, 65–6, 73–5, 138–9, 154, 184
findings, feeding back to participants, 178–9, 231, 249–50
first aid, 110–11, 119
first day, 144–5
flexibility, 20, 110
    in ethical decisions, 162–3
    in research design, 32, 34, 36
focus groups, 60, 63, 68, 193

friendships, with participants, 74, 106, 137, 155, 227, 235, 247–8
funding for research, 27–8, 33, 103–5
fundraising, 178, 231

Gambia, 181
gatekeepers, 33, 35, 62, 87–8, 91–2, 99, 172–4, 180, 184–5, 235
Ghana, 192, 249
gift giving, 33, 74–5, 122, 147, 176–8, 226–7, 230–2, 244
giving back, 174–9, 198, 212, 248
    see also reciprocity
good impression, 126–8, 139
grants, 104–5
guilt, 132, 175, 176, 180, 224–5

health, 109–14, 116, 118, 123–4, 148
    and site selection, 32
    of family in the field, 133, 134, 136–8
hierarchy of fieldwork, 4
historical-hermeneutic science, 22–23
home-based researchers, 12, 20–1, 175
    challenges faced, 126–7, 147, 155, 206, 222
    conflicts of interest, 171
    culture shock, 146–7
humanitarian assistance, 199

illness, 109–10, 130, 147–8
immigration clearance, 32–3, 145
immunisations, 110, 111, 118
India, 2, 153, 197, 204
Indigenous research, 195–8
    approaches, 6, 65–6, 72–5
    principles, 198
    see also minority ethnic groups
Indonesia, 5, 40, 67, 117, 128
information sheets, 106, 165–6
informed consent, 43, 84, 93, 134, 164–8, 180, 185–6
    verbal, 167
Internet, 4, 42, 89, 81–100, 120, 150–1, 248–9
    see also online data collection
interpersonal skills, 151
interpreters, 106, 153, 156–7, 159
interviews, 23, 40, 41–3, 63, 65, 71, 75, 107, 119, 120, 127–8, 152, 165–8
    by an outsider, 206
    online, 97–8
    representations/balance of power in, 52, 62
    therapeutic value, 175, 212
    with children, 190–2
    with elites, 203–4
    with women, 193–5

interviews cont.
    see also focus groups
Israel, 130, 206

Jamaica, 206,
Japan, 135, 219–20
journals, see diaries; fieldwork journals
judgements, human element in, 22, 25, 45

Kiribati, 4, 107, 109

language, 5, 7, 20, 33, 35, 64, 71, 106, 153, 156–7, 158, 229, 241–2
    advantage of indigenous researchers, 197
    anglophone bias, 85–6, 89
    for information sheet, 166
    in publications, 249–50, 257
    in questionnaires, 42
    learning vernacular, 9, 107, 136
laptops, see electronic devices
leaving the field, 217–35
    emotions on, 221–6
    ethical concerns, 226–7, 230–1
    exit strategies, 227–30
    practical concerns, 231–2
Lebanon, 130
legitimacy of Western researchers, 5–12, 109, 174–5, 205
letters, to establish contact and approval, 43, 105–9, 118, 203
life histories, 63–4
listening, 9, 35, 129, 237
    in indigenous research, 198
literature review, 33, 76
loans, 105
local knowledge, 7, 68, 69, 156
    of research assistant, 153
logistics, 31–35, 133, 144, 172
    on leaving, 233
loneliness, 3, 130, 134, 148
loss, sense of, 145, 223–4, 225

malaria, prevention of, 32, 111, 118
Maori, 172, 248–9
    control over research, 197
    research principles, 197–8
marginalised groups, 188–214
    principles for researching, 42, 190–1, 198, 239
    working with, 191, 192, 194, 195, 196, 199, 200, 201
marital status, of researchers, 134, 135, 180
mixed methods, 23, 31, 37, 57–8, 66, 68, 78, 79

minority ethnic groups, researching, 72, 188, 195–8, 212, 214, 256
motivations for fieldwork, 6, 27–8, 116, 212, 244

Namibia, 155
Nepal, 136, 192
networks,
    for support when writing up, 245–7
    to support research, 84–5, 107, 144, 203–4
    see also contacts
New Zealand, 107, 164, 197, 214, 248–9
Nicaragua, 136, 137, 138, 177, 184, 227–8
Nigeria, 175
Niue, 131
numbered data, 40

observations, 23, 41, 61, 63–4, 65, 80, 129, 182, 195
online data collection, 82–3, 88, 97–8
    ethics of, 84–5
    see also Internet
open mind, 13, 129, 139, 144
oral histories, 64, 175
oral presentations of findings, 178
outsiders, 9, 11, 15, 35, 62, 128, 131, 146–7, 154, 193, 197–8, 254, 256
    leaving the field, 220
    role of, in participatory research, 68–9
    vis a vis insiders, 3, 7, 37, 115, 147, 198, 205–7

Pacific Islands, 131, 196, 203
packing, 117–22
    for children, 137
    to go home, 231–2
Pakistan, 200
Papua New Guinea, 64, 67, 170, 193, 195, 256
Participant observation, see observation
participatory research, 67–71, 209–114
Participatory Action Research (PAR), 69–71, 209
Participatory Learning and Action (PLA), 7, 69
Participatory Rural Appraisal (PRA), 68–70
partners, in the field, 133–5
patience, 3, 108, 128, 130, 151, 152
permission, 32, 84–5, 89, 107–9, 126, 149, 165, 167, 172–3, 196
personal traits, desirable, 128–32
Philippines, 209
philosophy of research, 19, 21–2, 31
photographs, 64, 120, 192, 232, 240
    ethical, 121–2, 240
    giving back to participants, 177, 228
Polynesia, 13, 172
poor, research on the, 52, 78, 98, 189, 198–201, 208

positionality, 6, 12, 15, 25, 61–2, 140, 189
    of research assistants, 153–4, 158
    in elite research, 205–7
positivism, 22, 25
post-colonial critique, 5, 24
post-fieldwork period, 236–251
    see also leaving the field
power relations, 3, 62, 69, 167, 196, 218
    between researchers and informants, 5, 7, 9–10, 177, 182–3, 221, 250
    breaking down hierarchies, 8, 115, 201, 208, 254–5
practical issues, 103–24
    when leaving the field, 231–2
preliminary visits, 144
pre-testing, 33
proposal, see research proposal
psychological stress, 126, 130, 132–3, 140
    when leaving the field, 221–5
    see also culture shock
public transport, 129, 132, 145
publishing from research, 231, 238, 244, 247, 249–50
    see also shared authorship; writing process
purposeful sample, 45

qualitative research, 31, 59–80, 164, 166, 168, 213
    methods, 63–6
    data analysis, 75–6, 238
    see also mixed methods
quantitative research, 39–58, 77
    data analysis, 46–51
    limitations of, 51–5
    techniques, 41–4
    see also mixed methods
questionnaires, 23, 34–5, 41–3, 46, 54, 57–8, 63, 65, 97, 203
quota sample, 45

racism, 8, 183, 239
readjustment, on return, 135, 147, 135, 239, 245, 247
reciprocity, 14, 74–5, 116, 122, 174–8, 228, 250
reflexivity, 12, 61–2, 71, 78, 132, 186, 244
relationships with participants, 2, 6, 15, 62, 65, 71, 72, 87, 115, 150, 154, 162, 164, 166–8, 188, 191, 205
    post-fieldwork, 218, 247–9
    see also conflict of interest; gatekeepers; reciprocity; sexual relationships in the field
reluctance to leave, 222
representation, 52, 85, 123, 210–11
    the politics of, 5–9, 239–41

representative sample, 44–6
research assistants, 33, 42, 106, 152–5, 192, 195,
    family as, 134
    leaving, 220
research community, *see* communities
research design, *see* design
research findings, feeding back, 178–9, 186, 201,
    211, 220, 231, 246, 248
research proposal, 32–3, 104–5, 107–8
research questions, 28–30, 66
research topic, choice of, 25–8
research, types of, 24–6
researchers, desirable traits, 128–32
responsibilities, 25, 73–4, 138, 169, 189,
    209, 228
    when leaving the field, 226–31
    see also ethical issues
rest periods, 112, 133, 148
returning to university, 236–51
    emotional issues, 245–6
    becoming a writer, 246–7
right of withdrawal, 164–5, 190

safety, 32, 109–10, 112–14, 152, 180, 192,
    194, 256
    of family in the field, 133
    of research participants, 161
    see also health
St Vincent, 184
sampling, 44–6
scattergrams, 49–51, 53
science, types of, 22–3
secondary data, 23, 28, 44, 57,
self-doubt, 130, 143, 148
self-esteem of communities, 175, 193, 212
sensitive research topics/questions, 181, 201,
    204, 211, 221
sexual health, 112
sexual relationships in the field, 182–5
sexual violence, 184
sexuality of researcher, 6, 135, 182–3, 206
shared authorship, 8, 233
    see also publishing from research
Singapore, 182
site selection, 26, 32
slum, research in, 112, 125–7, 194
snowball sample, 45, 61
social media, research using, 81, 83–4, 92–3,
    100, 120
    social use by researcher, 133, 149–51, 218,
        225, 231, 246
social technology, 150–1
statistics, 30, 31, 39, 44, 46–51, 55–6
story-telling, 61, 65–6, 191
stratified sampling, 45

successful/unsuccessful research, 27–8
supervisors, 21, 26, 27, 30, 33, 104, 112, 117,
    127, 148, 150, 171, 211, 222, 235, 238–9,
    241, 246, 251

tablets, *see* electronic devices,
tact, 130, 151
talanoa, see story-telling
Tanzania, 178, 191, 192, 200
textual data, 82–3, 90–3, 98–9
Thailand, 204, 243
theory, 28, 30, 36, 59, 61, 76, 241
Third World, terminology, 16
timetable, 32–4
timing of fieldwork, 19, 117, 123
Timor Leste, 114, 163
transcription, 63, 64, 75–6, 85, 98, 134, 157,
    169, 237, 251
    sharing transcripts with participants, 226, 227,
        229, 234
travel guidebooks, 113, 127
trust, 65–6, 71–2, 98, 115, 121, 126–7, 151–4,
    166, 169–72, 178, 181, 190, 193, 197,
    228–9, 256
truth, 179–82
    of data, 7, 39, 44, 55, 77
Tuvalu, 131

Uganda, 87, 108, 177, 200
Uzbekistan, 115

value of fieldwork, 253
Vanuatu, 107
    regulations regarding research in, 196–7, 214
video cameras, *see* visual research tools
Vietnam, 173, 209, 223–4
virtual data, *see* Internet
    see online data collection
visas, for research, 33, 105–7, 118, 145,
    172, 226
visual research tools, 63–4, 83, 120–2,
    191–2, 240
    see also camera

websites, *see* Internet
women, research with, 42, 193–5
    therapeutic value of interviews, 175
writing process, 239, 243
    becoming a writer, 237–9, 246–7
    see also publishing from research

young people, researching, 52, 54, 177, 190–2
youth, *see* young people

Zimbabwe, 109, 192

CPSIA information can be obtained
at www.ICGtesting.com
Printed in the USA
BVHW092328210821
614413BV00004B/9